Also by Julia Child

Mastering the Art of French Cooking, Volume 1
(with Simone Beck and Louisette Bertholle)

The French Chef Cookbook

Mastering the Art of French Cooking, Volume 2
(with Simone Beck)

From Julia Child's Kitchen

Julia Child & Company

Julia Child & More Company

The Way to Cook

Cooking with Master Chefs

In Julia's Kitchen with Master Chefs

Also by Jacques Pépin

La Technique

La Méthode

Jacques Pépin: A French Chef Cooks at Home

Everyday Cooking with Jacques Pépin

Jacques Pépin's The Art of Cooking, Volume 1

Jacques Pépin's The Art of Cooking, Volume 2

The Short-Cut Cook

Cuisine Economique

Today's Gourmet: Light and Healthy Cooking for the '90s

Good Life Cooking: Light Classics from Today's Gourmet

Happy Cooking: More Light Classics from Today's Gourmet

Jacques Pépin's Simple and Healthy Cooking

Jacques Pépin's Kitchen: Cooking with Claudine

Jacques Pépin's Table: The Complete Today's Gourmet

Jacques Pépin's Kitchen: Encore with Claudine

Sweet Simplicity: Jacques Pépin's Fruit Desserts

JULIA AND JACQUES
cooking at home

JULIA AND JACQUES

cooking at home

BY Julia Child AND Jacques Pépin

WITH David Nussbaum

PHOTOGRAPHS BY Christopher Hirsheimer

ALFRED A. KNOPF | NEW YORK | 1999

This Is a Borzoi Book
Published by Alfred A. Knopf, Inc.

Copyright © 1999 by A La Carte Communications
Photographs copyright © 1999 by Christopher Hirsheimer

www.randomhouse.com

Library of Congress Cataloging-in-Publication Data
Child, Julia.
      [Cooking at home]
    Julia and Jacques cooking at home / by Julia Child and
Jacques Pépin, with David Nussbaum.
        p.   cm.
    ISBN 0-375-40431-7
    1. Cookery, French.   2. Child, Julia.   3. Pépin, Jacques.
I. Pépin, Jacques.   II. Nussbaum, David.   III. Title.
IV. Title: Cooking at home.
TX719.C373   1999
641.5944—dc21   98-32418
                                               CIP

Manufactured in the United States of America
First Edition

Contents

Julia's Introduction

JACQUES AND I HAD A LOT OF FUN DOING THE TELEVISION SERIES THAT WAS THE inspiration for this book, and we have enjoyed doing the book together, but separately—each of us voicing our individual opinions. What has especially interested me in our joint culinary exploits is the tremendous differences between the top-of-the-line professional chef and the serious home cook. The professional, in a wildly busy first-class restaurant, has to do everything as fast and as efficiently as possible yet keep up the strict standards of fine cooking. The home cook is not under those imperatives.

A perfect example is the cutting up of a whole chicken. Jacques can do it in just a few seconds, literally. I have loved seeing Jacques on the same program with Martin Yan, the wonderfully able Chinese TV cook, teacher, and author. Jacques and Martin have a running contest when they are together, vying with each other as to who is the fastest at cutting up a chicken. They go at it with such flashing speed that you, as audience, can barely follow the movements. I, the home cook, on the other hand, go at it with reasonable speed but leisurely. I really love to cut up meat and poultry, and especially chickens. I lift up the knee on one side of the chicken and cut around its skin from vent to small of back. I bend the knee down to the work surface, popping open the ball joint at the back, then I carefully and neatly scrape off the oyster-shaped nuggets of dark meat above and below that joint, and finally I pull the leg-thigh down tailwise and free. That's a nice, reasonably stylish way to go about it, and it takes a good minute. The whole chicken probably takes me five minutes, but I don't have to hurry and I'm having a good time.

However, that would never do in a restaurant. No! Speed is of the essence. As a pro you peel asparagus fast, using the most efficient maneuvers. You aim for the same effectiveness when puréeing garlic or cutting an orange into segments, as well as seeding tomatoes, dicing an onion, and so forth. Home cooks have so many useful techniques to learn from observing the professionals, but we don't have to proceed at their gallop. It's the way to go about things professionally that we want to learn. The more of these good methods we can absorb and put into daily practice, the better and happier we'll be as cooks.

Obviously I learned a great many things working with Jacques, and he learned a thing or two from me! How to remove the leaves from an artichoke bottom without losing any of the meat, for instance! Techniques, however, are not our sole object here. What we both want to show in these programs and in this book is our approach to cooking. Food is not only our business but our greatest pleasure, and we think its preparation should be a joyful occupation. Of course, cooking with two is far more lively than cooking alone, but when you know pretty well what you are doing, the food itself is your companion.

Back to basics—that's how to begin, and it doesn't take too much wit to learn. When you know how to sauté your meat so it browns rather than steams, you're cooking. What's difficult about that? You heat the pan, you dry the meat, you don't crowd it into the pan, and you're browning it. Is that difficult? No! But you do need to absorb the simple facts of how to do it by watching the steps on the screen or reading about them. When you know how to peel, seed, juice, and dice a tomato, you are on the road to making a fast, chic little fresh tomato sauce for this evening's pasta. When you can fearlessly boil up a sugar syrup into caramel, as described here, you're ready to turn that to use in everyone's favorite caramel flan. As soon as we show you how to master the few tricks to the beating of egg whites, the next step can be a chocolate soufflé to celebrate your spouse's birthday. Understanding egg yolks will make you a master of hollandaise sauce, and that along with understanding how to poach an egg will give you Eggs Benedict for Sunday brunch. So it goes, a step or two at a time, and pretty soon they'll call you an accomplished cook.

This is the kind of knowledge we are giving you here—the basics of fine food that looks good, tastes the way it should, and is a total pleasure to eat. We have enjoyed cooking for you, and we wish you

Toujours Bon Appétit!

Julia Child

Jacques's Introduction

FOOD, FOR ME, IS INSEPARABLE FROM SHARING. THERE IS NO GREAT MEAL UNLESS it is shared with family or friends. Likewise in the kitchen. If the process of cooking is to "transform nature into culture," as Lévi-Strauss says, then the greatest satisfaction is to undergo that experience with friends. Sharing recipes, trying out new ideas, tasting together while bantering with one another and enjoying a bottle of wine, always produces the greatest meals.

The cliché of the jealous, secretive cook who conceals his recipes and his techniques from other cooks makes for good talk, but I have never found this to be true. Granted, there may be a few bad apples here and there, but on the whole, most cooks—professional or otherwise—are very sharing and giving. According to George Bernard Shaw, "there is no love sincerer than the love of food," and that love of cooking and of eating is forever present and part of the essence of the true cook. Nothing is more gratifying for a cook than to see people enjoying their food.

At the same time, it is true that if you put two cooks together in the same kitchen, there will be some conflict, dissension, or difference of opinion, because if cooks are among the most giving people in the world, they are also among the most stubborn and inflexible. All this is often for the better, however, because ingredients are relatively limited. A chicken is a chicken is a chicken, but it can be sublime although very different, depending on whether it was prepared by an Indian, French, Italian, Russian, German, or Chinese cook, and that goes to the core of personal interpretation.

I would paraphrase Brillat-Savarin's famous aphorism "You are what you eat" with "You are what you cook." Whether you want to be or not, you are "in" the food you prepare. In the hands of five different cooks, the same recipe for a simple roasted chicken will produce five different results. The bird may be more cooked, less cooked, overly browned, excessively spicy, or too bland—each dish will reflect the character, nature, and mood of the cook.

To learn, to give, and to share with friends in the kitchen is indeed gratifying and joyful. It is in that spirit of friendship that Julia and I decided to meet in her kitchen and to share our experiences with our television audience. We agree about some dishes and disagree about others, but always in a spirit of camaraderie and curiosity. The fascinating part of cooking is that there is invariably another way of doing a particular technique or preparing a recipe that makes it better, or at least different. You are always an apprentice, and the learning is continuous if you keep an open mind.

The shows and this companion book were not created as they usually are. For all of my previous television series, the recipes were completed when we started taping the shows. Whether or not they were followed exactly is debatable, but the basic structure of the shows— which is the recipes—was all set. So the shows evolved in an orderly manner from these recipes within the precise amount of time allotted to me by the producer. But that was not the case when Julia and I did our series together. We had no recipes, just a lot of ideas.

For people like us who love to cook, it is easier, more fun, more exciting, and more rewarding to cook without any recipes. Ingredients were there for Julia and me to transform into dishes, and this is what we set out to do with gusto on these shows. We had nothing written down, no rehearsals, just a thematic division of food, having decided that one show would cover poultry, another fish, another salads, and so on. While it may be a bit more stressful to cook this way, it is more natural to develop ideas and discuss them with the food in front of you—you can let your mood lead you and pull out of the ingredients the taste that you may be craving on that particular day. I may have thought one day that I had a great idea, only to find out that Julia had the same or a better idea, and I learned from this.

The hardest and most frustrating part of this process, in my opinion, was for our writer, David Nussbaum, who had the difficult and confounding job of extrapolating the recipes we created on the spur of the moment during the taping of the shows and organizing them in a form that would make sense to the reader. But, for Julia and me, the taping was great fun. We had our little disagreements—I like kosher salt, she doesn't; I like black pepper, she likes white pepper—but these are relatively superficial differences. On the whole, we agreed as to what is important: taste over appearance, simplicity in recipes, using the proper techniques, using the best-quality ingredients, following the seasons, keeping an open mind to new food preparations, and, of course, sharing both wine and food with family and friends.

We agree that no recipes are written in stone, and as we created dishes *à l'improviste,* or on impulse, we both knew that if we did them again, we would probably make changes. It is in this spirit of flexibility and fun that I would like you to look at the series and use this book. Try to keep an open mind, to take what you need from our recipes and make them your own by adding your own favorite seasonings or creating your own variations.

Especially remember that eating, as well as cooking, should be pleasurable and guiltless. To paraphrase Voltaire, try to imagine how tiresome eating and drinking would be if God had not made them a pleasure as well as a necessity. So, share our recipes with friends and family. If you do, I am sure that you will enjoy them in a deeper way, and we will have achieved what we set out to do with each of our shows: to welcome you to our kitchen and to share and enjoy our food with you.

Jacques Pépin

Preface by David Nussbaum

COOKING AND WRITING ARE ACTIVITIES THAT MOST OF US USUALLY ENGAGE IN alone. Yet, just as the *Julia and Jacques Cooking at Home* programs demonstrate so memorably that cooking with another person can be creative and productive, this book represents a collaborative writing effort. My role has been twofold: to formulate workable recipes for the dishes that Julia and Jacques cooked when they taped the show, and to gather background and explanatory information to accompany the recipes.

For both of these efforts my primary resource was the original uncut videotape of the shows. Though I usually worked by myself, I was never alone. For nearly a year, I have had Julia and Jacques with me on the TV screen next to my computer—live on tape, as the saying goes. When I shopped for recipe test ingredients, I picked out fish or produce with their voices in my head. As I cut up ducks and folded soufflés, mental images of their movements guided my hands. Occasionally, virtual companionship became real company when I met with one of them to discuss the dishes and the recipe drafts.

Each of them thoroughly reviewed and revised the recipes after I had formulated and tested them, rewriting whenever necessary to more accurately reflect their cooking. (In some instances, the procedures were changed from what was done before the cameras.)

This book presents recipes for all the dishes that Julia and Jacques prepared during the taping sessions. As some have been edited from the final TV programs, owing to time constraints, these will be fresh discoveries for those viewing the *Julia and Jacques Cooking at Home* series. The book also includes recipes for the dishes that Julia and Jacques created together for two PBS specials, *Cooking in Concert*. Finally, there are a number of recipes here that were never made before cameras, but have been contributed by Julia and Jacques specifically for the book.

Acknowledgments

WRITING A BOOK CAN BE A FAIRLY SOLITARY ACTIVITY—EVEN A COOKBOOK, where you are literally cooking what seems like endless meals for yourself or one or more indulgent friends. In contrast, hosting a television cooking series involves a collaboration of many, not unlike the running of a great restaurant. As a permanent record of what transpired in our *Cooking at Home* public television series, this companion cookbook brings a seriousness of purpose, depth, and durability to the project that television alone does not seem to carry. Certainly, this was a project of great collaborations, something that neither of us would, or could, ever embark upon without an enthusiastic and strong team.

Therefore, with deep appreciation, we'd like to acknowledge the ongoing creative enthusiasm of Geof Drummond, president of A La Carte Communications, who sowed the seeds of this Julia and Jacques partnership five years ago, and produced the first of our *Cooking in Concert* duets, performed in the Tsai Philharmonic Hall in Boston. Geof has continued to work with us both as a friend and as a producer. On the book side, we want to thank Judith Jones, our editor at Alfred A. Knopf. From the beginning, Judith has been a source of inspiration, an insightful cheerleader, and an unwavering upholder of what sometimes feels like a bygone standard of excellence. David Nussbaum has done a remarkable job of translating what happened spontaneously on camera into workable recipes, as well as collating our notes and comments and ideas for variations that make cooking more challenging and creative. Together, Judith and David have turned our planned improvisations among friends in the kitchen into a unique, original, and, we hope, inspiring book for home cooks.

Supporting them have been Nat Katzman, Geof's partner at A La Carte; Bruce Franchini, our longtime director; Kimberly Nolan, our organized line producer; our good friends Susie Heller and Chris Styler, culinary producers; Herb Sevush, video editor culinaire; Linda Schwartz, recipe tester; and Carole Goodman and Christopher Hirsheimer, this book's visionary designer and glorious photographer, respectively. Would that a CD of the music John Bayless composed and performed for our series were included with each book . . . like a glass of champagne to start off a meal. In spite of often being forced to fly through culinary fogbanks, they have managed to make us look good not only in the kitchen but on screen and in print as well. Our entire crew on the TV series numbered more than twenty-five, and we make a great bow of gratitude to each of these talented professionals.

Projects like this can easily take on a temporal importance and urgency that eclipses the rest of your life. As always, our office and home support teams, Stephanie Hersh in Cambridge and Norma Galehouse and Gloria Pépin in Connecticut, helped maintain our "day jobs" while we pursued this great adventure.

Lastly, no project of this magnitude can happen without the support of friends and sponsors. This is particularly true on public television, where we have been cooking cumulatively for more than fifty years. Cooking on public television has mirrored, and perhaps led to, the growth and appreciation of the culinary arts in America, and we are proud to have been associated with it. Our underwriters, who made this series possible, were Kendall-Jackson Vineyards and Winery, a company exemplifying the remarkable growth of California wines to a level and quality as good as any in the world; Land O'Lakes butter—*"la cuisine au beurre est toujours la meilleure,"* and that's true here in America as well; Eatzi's Markets and Corner Bakery, new ventures in bringing chef-prepared foods and baked goods made from the freshest ingredients to the American table; Farberware Millennium, a longtime supporter of quality cooking shows with products serious cooks can use, and afford to buy; and Oxo, whose kitchen tools utilize great design without forgetting what they—and we, the cooks—are there to do: cook. We'd also like to thank the following friends for supporting our production with great products, produce, and warm wishes: A. Russo & Sons, Banana Republic, Boston Botanicals, Bourgeat, Boyajian, Clear Flour Breads, Cuisinart, D'Elia Kitchens, Flowers by Joanne Yee, KitchenAid, Le Creuset, Lunt Silversmiths, R & M Ostrich, Reynolds Metals, Schreibman Jewelers East, Shreeves, Williams-Sonoma Copley Square, Wüsthof-Trident.

Merci beaucoup, Bon Appétit, and Happy Cooking!
Julia Child & Jacques Pépin

JULIA AND JACQUES
cooking at home

APPETIZERS

WE BEGIN OUR RECIPES—AND OUR CONVERSATION ABOUT FOOD AND COOKING—WITH A few choice morsels. We hope you will do the same. Even a small serving of any of these appetizers will do just what the term implies—get the juices and the talk going, and focus everyone's attention where it belongs, on the pleasures of the table.

In selecting what to serve, there is the practical consideration of timing. You need to get started five days ahead if you choose Julia's traditional salmon gravlax cured with dill and cognac, or Jacques's truffled homemade sausage in brioche, or country pâté with veal and pistachios. Although there is relatively little work involved, they are made in stages and need several days to develop their full flavor.

However, we also have instant versions of gravlax and salmon tartare. Mussels or shrimp in bowls of fragrant broth need only brief cooking. Oysters or clams on the half-shell are easy to prepare once you get the hang of opening them in seconds—we show you how—and are served with sauces that take a minute.

You'll find other ideas in the "Salads and Sandwiches" chapter, such as Celery Root Rémoulade, traditionally served in France as a first course, or a sandwich like Pan Bagnat or Seafood Bread, which, cut in bite-size pieces, make fine hors d'oeuvre.

Julia

The only painless way of opening oysters I know of is to pick out each oyster at the market yourself. Choose only those with just enough of

Holding the oyster curved side down on the counter, insert the beer-can opener into the gap at the hinge end.

a gap at the hinge end so that you can take a beer-can opener, pointed end up, and just be able to force it into the gap. To open the oyster (see photos), you hold it curved side down on your work surface with one hand, force the beer-can opener into the gap with the other hand, bear down hard on the opener's handle, and up pops the hinge end of the top shell. Then take your sharp little knife and scrape down the inside surface of the top shell. Twist it off, and loosen the oyster where it is attached to the bottom shell. Some stylish operators then turn the oyster over in its bottom shell, to make a more handsome appearance.

Press down on the opener to force the shells apart.

(continued on page 6)

Oysters and Clams

For those who love them, there's no finer appetizer than a perfectly fresh raw oyster or clam, right from the shell, with a swallow of its natural briny juices. A platter of them on the half-shell is also one of the simplest appetizers to serve. Follow the photos and explanations in the recipe here, and practice a few times, and your shucking skill should develop rapidly. Be sure to use a pot holder or a thick, folded kitchen towel or napkin to protect your hands against a knife that might slip.

Oysters and clams need little embellishment. Some connoisseurs insist on quaffing them with no interfering flavors whatsoever, but others want lemon wedges for squeezing on a few drops of juice, while still others will go for one or both of the two zesty condiments given here, Mignonnette Sauce and Horseradish Cocktail Sauce. See also the sidebar on cocktail breads on page 6.

Oysters and Clams on the Half-Shell

Yield: 4 first-course servings

A dozen or more fresh, scrubbed, well-
chilled oysters, or 2 dozen fresh little-
neck or other small clams (or a
combination of oysters and clams)
Lemon wedges
Mignonnette Sauce for Oysters (page 7)
Horseradish Cocktail Sauce for Clams
and Shrimp (page 6)
Black bread and butter (see sidebar on
next page)

Special equipment

A sturdy, pointed-tip oyster knife, a towel
or pot holder, and a can opener for
opening oysters; a small, sharp paring
knife for opening clams; oyster forks
(optional) or a spoon (Julia's husband,
Paul, ate his oysters with a spoon); a
serving platter or bowl (it's nice to line
it with seaweed, crushed ice, or rock
salt, to hold the open shells level without spilling their juices, but not necessary if everything is cold)

Hold the oyster in the towel or pot holder firmly in the
palm of one hand, protecting your hand with the towel. Insert
the tip of the knife into the hinge at the pointed end of the oyster, as shown in the photo, then pry the shells apart. Remove
the top shell, and slide the blade underneath the oyster to free it
from the abductor muscle that attaches it to the shell.

Open the clams, following the photos. Serve the oysters
and/or clams right away, with lemon wedges, ramekins of
mignonnette or cocktail sauce, oyster forks if you wish, and
buttered black-bread slices.

Jacques

When opening oysters and
clams, I like to work over a bowl or
plate to catch the juices, should any
spill from the shells. Then, if you are
serving them on the half-shell, you can

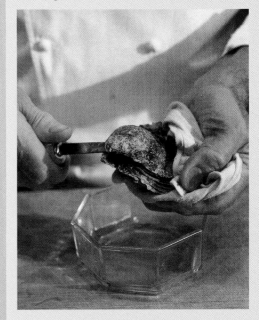

Holding an oyster in a towel over a bowl, insert
the tip of your knife into the hinge at the pointed
end of the oyster and pry it open.

spoon the juices back into the shell.
And if you are shucking them for cooking in chowders or sauce, you can collect the juices in the bowl, strain them,
and add to the dish.

I open oysters with a thick,
sturdy oyster knife, and clams with a
paring knife. Oysters can be very
tightly closed, and you may find that
you can't open them at the hinge. In

(continued on page 7)

Julia (continued from page 4)

This beer-can opener system was uncovered by my producer of the old *French Chef* TV series, Ruth Lockwood, who lived on Cape Cod during the summer. Her Yankee oysterman taught her how, and she, in turn, taught me. It works!

After struggling with oysters yourself, it's always a revelation to watch the pros at an oyster bar, such as at the Plaza in New York City, for instance, or at Grand Central Terminal. It is so effortless. Pick an oyster up in your bare hand and give it a side swipe with your knife, and the oyster is opened in less than a second.

Julia on Cocktail Breads

In the deli section of most markets you can find the perfect breads to go with oysters, clams, smoked salmon, cheeses, and other appetizer titbits. The foot-long loaves I usually find are of remarkably good quality and are neatly presliced into 2¼-inch squares about ¼ inch thick. They come in sourdough rye or pumpernickel, and since they keep well for a week or more I always keep a handy handful in my refrigerator, as well as a whole loaf or two in my freezer. I mix a little Dijon-type mustard and horseradish into my butter or mayonnaise and spread it ever so neatly on the bread. It is a wonderfully convenient "aid to hors d'oeuvre" to have always there ready to use.

Jacques's Horseradish Cocktail Sauce for Clams and Shrimp

This zesty sauce gets its heat from Tabasco and horseradish, and you may add more of both to taste. I prefer fresh horseradish root for its intense flavor. Bottled horseradish is also fine, but you will need to use more. If you can find fresh horseradish in the market, remove the tough outer skin from a small length of the root with a vegetable peeler, and grate (don't shred) the amount you want, on an ordinary box grater. Wrap the remaining root and store in the refrigerator.

This amount of sauce is enough for 3 dozen small clams, or 2 dozen cooked shrimp. Simply multiply the recipe if you need more. You can store it in a jar in the refrigerator for several weeks.

Yield: About ⅔ cup

½ cup ketchup
2 Tbs grated fresh or bottled horseradish, or more to taste
¼ tsp Tabasco sauce, or more to taste
1 tsp Worcestershire sauce (Lea & Perrins)
1 Tbs freshly squeezed lemon juice, or more to taste

Stir together all the ingredients in a mixing bowl. Taste and add more horseradish, Tabasco, or lemon juice, as you like. Serve in ramekins to accompany clams on the half-shell or cooked shrimp. Store in the refrigerator.

Mignonnette Sauce for Oysters

Mignonnette is the culinary term for coarsely crushed pepper-corns (though it also refers to a small medallion of meat). For the best flavor, crush the peppercorns just before mixing—using a saucepan, as we do for Steak au Poivre (see photo, page 312)—so they release all their volatile oils into the vinegar. If your vinegar seems too harsh after you have mixed the sauce, add a tablespoon or two of red wine to soften the flavor. You can make the sauce a few hours ahead of serving to let the fla-vors develop; extra sauce can be refrigerated. It is strong—you'll need only a few drops to sauce each oyster.

Yield: About ½ cup

2 tsp whole black peppercorns
1½ Tbs chopped shallots
⅓ cup red-wine vinegar of the best
   quality
¼ tsp chopped fresh thyme (optional)
A pinch of salt

Crush the peppercorns coarsely with a heavy pan. Scrape the grated pieces into a small bowl or ramekin, add the shallots, vinegar, thyme, and a pinch of salt and stir together. Taste and correct seasonings, if necessary. Serve with oysters on the half-shell.

Jacques (continued from page 5)

that case, insert your oyster knife into the side of a shell to pry it apart, hold-ing the oyster with a pot holder or folded towel. This will always work, but tends to leave shell fragments in the bottom. If you've collected

the juices in a bowl, you can rinse the frag-ments out of the shell, strain the juices, and add a table-spoon back into the shell to serve.

Slide your knife under the top shell to cut the abduc-tor muscle, slide the knife under the oyster to cut the other side of the abductor muscle, then remove the top shell.

Holding the clam in the palm of your hand with the hinge toward you, slide the blade of your knife between the two shells and press, with your fingers behind the blade, so that it slides between the halves and opens the shell. Cut all around to sever any muscles.

Buying Oysters and Clams

In the nineteenth century, when our shorelines were pure and fertile, oysters were plentiful enough to be bought by the barrelful for household use or devoured by the dozens at "oyster saloons" in big cities. Those days are long-gone—oysters today are a relatively expensive treat, most often sold by the pound, or even by the single piece. You will usually get four or five medium-size oysters to the pound—that's the best size for half-shell eating—and you want to serve at least six oysters per person as a first course.

You may find only one or several types of oysters in your market. They develop their distinctive flavor—ranging from mild and sweet to intensely briny—from the beds in which they grow, and are generally identified by their place of origin. Since oysters are harvested wild and farmed in many locales on both coasts, there are myriad varieties in the geographic sense, though only a few scientifically distinct species. Among the most prized, and expensive, if you can find them, are Wellfleet oysters from Cape Cod, Bluepoints from Long Island, Chincoteagues from Virginia, and Olympias from the Northwest. The celebrated flat Belon oyster, originally from the Loire/Brittany region of France, is now being cultivated both in Maine and in the Pacific Northwest.

Clams for half-shell eating are less subtly varied in taste than oysters, but have their own very distinctive flavor—and they're usually easier to open and always less expensive than oysters. Hardshell Atlantic clams are categorized, and named, according to size (though they're all the same species). The smallest clams, called "littlenecks," have sweeter and more tender flesh, the best for eating raw. In some markets, you may find the very smallest ones sold separately as "countnecks"—at a premium price—and slightly larger ones as "topnecks." You can expect to get eight to twelve littlenecks to the pound. The next-larger grouping of clams, medium-size "cherrystones," can also be served on the half-shell. On the Pacific Coast, tender Manila clams and small butter clams are good choices.

Safety. Today's seafood industry has made clams or oysters available in stores almost everywhere, all year round. With active monitoring by health authorities, you can be reasonably confident that any being sold in a reputable market, designated for serving on the half-shell, are safe for raw eating. If you have concerns, ask the store for the certification of inspection. (However, if you gather any kind of shellfish in the wild, on your own, check with local agencies to be sure that they are from unpolluted waters, free of bacteria, and in every respect safe to eat.)

Handling and Storing Oysters and Clams. Hardshell clams and oysters require less cleaning than mussels (page 13), since they usually have little if any sand inside. Give them a good scrubbing under cold water to clean the outside of the shells. If any clams or oysters open, knock them against another and they will close up. If they remain open, or have any trace of an off odor, discard them.

Like all seafood, clams and oysters are best eaten as soon as possible, though both can be stored for several days or a week in a cold part of the refrigerator. Arrange oysters in one layer, resting on their curved bottom shells, so they sit in and retain their liquid; clams can be stored flat in a box or a bowl. Cover both clams and oysters with a damp towel, or seaweed.

Eating Clams or Oysters on the Half-Shell. Take a half-shell with a clam or oyster, and, if you wish, squeeze a few drops of lemon juice or spoon a bit of your chosen sauce on top. Use an oyster fork to lift out the flesh, then sip the juices from the shell—or bring the shell to your lips, tilt it, and slide in the flesh and juices with one slurp.

Opposite: Moules Ravigote

Julia

Moules marinière **is the simplest** way to enjoy these shellfish. The mussels can be eaten as soon as they open, and their natural juices, with the wine and flavorings, create their own fragrant sauce. Don't add salt, though, since there is plenty in the mussel liquid.

The way to eat this dish is to use the shells. I like to find a nice shell still intact at the hinge, and—after I eat the mussel inside—I use it to pluck out the mussels from the other shells. And you can use an empty half-shell as a spoon for broth, too.

Mussels

A plate of oysters may be an expensive indulgence, but mussels can be had by the dozens at relatively little cost. Cultivated mussels are now available most of the year in markets across the country—and as anyone who's walked along the seashore at low tide knows, bushels of wild mussels are often free for the taking. But you *must* be certain that they are safe to eat. Please read all the important information about handling mussels on page 13.

When cooked *à la marinière*—with white wine and aromatic vegetables and herbs—mussels are a snap to prepare and a pleasure to serve and eat. There's no wrestling with shellfish knives or can openers—after a few minutes of steaming, the shells pop right open, revealing the plump yellow-orange flesh, and spilling their juices into a delicious broth. Heap them into soup bowls for everyone at the table—or one enormous bowl, for greater conviviality—ladle the hot broth over them, and serve with lots of fresh French bread for dunking.

If you want to prepare mussels ahead of time—or if you have cooked mussels on hand, left over from making the classic Billi-bi soup (page 62)—dress them with a piquant sauce and serve as *moules ravigote* (page 12), in colorful cups of radicchio leaves for a first course, or on the half-shell as a party hors d'oeuvre.

The recipes that follow call for 3 pounds, or about 50 medium-size mussels, but you can prepare any amount following these basic methods. You may want to steam a few extra pounds of mussels *à la marinière*—eat a few dozen hot with their broth, and dress the rest with ravigote sauce to enjoy the next day.

Moules Marinière

Yield: 4 first-course servings

3 pounds small to medium mussels,
  washed thoroughly, beards removed
  (see page 13)
½ cup finely chopped onions
2 Tbs minced shallots or scallions
1 Tbs butter
2 imported bay leaves
5 or 6 Tbs coarsely chopped fresh parsley
  sprigs
¼ tsp pepper
1½ cups dry white wine or dry white
  French vermouth

Special equipment
  A large stainless-steel saucepan or enam-
    eled (non-reactive) casserole, with a
    cover; large soup bowls

Put the mussels in the pan, along with the onions, shallots, butter, bay leaves, about half of the parsley, and the pepper.
Toss gently to distribute all the flavorings, and pour the white
wine or vermouth over.

Cover the pan and bring to the boil over high heat. Cook
at the boil for about 2 minutes, occasionally shaking and tossing
the pan—holding the cover on tight—to mix the ingredients.
Lift the lid and quickly check to see if all the mussels are open.
If not, cover and cook for another minute or so.

Lift the mussels from the broth with a slotted spoon and
divide among the bowls, discarding any mussels that have not
opened. Ladle portions of hot broth over each serving—take
care not to scoop any sand from the bottom of the pan—
sprinkle on the remaining parsley, and serve immediately, with
fresh French bread on the side.

Jacques

It's much easier to clean cultivated mussels, which are grown on
nets or wires, than wild ones. The cultivated mussels need only a good rinse
or two in cold water and some rubbing
to get the sand off their shells.

Both of these recipes are basic
procedures that you can vary in many
ways. You can flavor the broth for
moules marinière with all kinds of
herbs and vegetables—I sometimes
add sliced celery or fennel, and always
lots of chopped garlic.

I like garlic in my ravigote dressing too (see next page), and plenty of
Tabasco—after all, *ravigoter* means
"to invigorate"—but you should follow your own taste. You do want to
mix the mussels with the sauce while
they are still warm, and let them
absorb the seasonings. As you are taking them out of the shells, you may
also want to pull off the tough loop of
flesh, or mantle, on top of the mussel.
This can be quite chewy, especially on
large mussels, and it's easy to remove.

Moules Ravigote

If you have leftover cooked mussels, here is a fine way to use them. Otherwise, steam fresh ones as described here. The mussels will release over a cup of flavorful juices—which you can strain and freeze, then use in fish sauces, such as *beurre blanc* (page 233), or soups, such as Mediterranean Seafood Stew, page 58. Serve either as a first course or as an hors d'oeuvre.

Yield: 4 to 6 first-course servings

For the ravigote sauce

1½ Tbs minced shallots or scallions

1½ Tbs Dijon-style prepared mustard

2 hard-boiled eggs, finely chopped
  or pushed through a sieve

2 Tbs chopped cornichons or
  small gherkin pickles

1 Tbs capers

1 Tbs chopped parsley

2 Tbs chives

1 Tbs white-wine vinegar

2 tsp freshly squeezed lemon juice

4 Tbs excellent olive oil

⅛ tsp salt

⅛ tsp freshly ground black pepper

⅛ tsp Tabasco (optional)

1 or 2 cloves garlic, minced (optional)

3 pounds small to medium mussels, washed thoroughly, beards removed (see page 13)

½ cup water or dry white wine

For serving

Leaves of radicchio or Boston
  lettuce

Fresh chives, for garnish

Mussel-shell halves, cleaned and
  separated (optional)

Special equipment

A 4-to-5-quart stainless-steel
  saucepan or enameled (non-
  reactive) casserole, with cover

Make the ravigote sauce first, stirring together all the ingredients in a small bowl. Adjust the seasonings to taste.

To steam the mussels, place them in the saucepan with the water or white wine, cover, and set over high heat. Cook for about 5 minutes, shaking the pan occasionally, until all the mussels have opened. Remove from the heat and let the mussels rest in the covered pan for 5 minutes, then lift them from the pan with a slotted spoon onto a tray or a platter to cool slightly. (Strain the pan juices through a fine sieve, being careful not to include any sand from the bottom of the pan, and freeze to use later for fish soup or billi-bi.)

While they are still warm, remove all the mussels from their shells into a medium-size mixing bowl. Fold the dressing into the mussels until all are well coated. Let marinate in the dressing, and cool to room temperature before serving.

To serve as a first course, form a small cup from radicchio or lettuce leaves on individual salad plates, and mound about ⅓ to ½ cup of sauced mussels in the leaves on each plate. Garnish with a spray of chives.

To serve on the half-shell as an hors d'oeuvre: Line a large platter with lettuce leaves. Nestle 1 or 2 sauced mussels each in clean shell halves, and arrange on the platter in a decorative pattern.

Do-ahead notes

The mussels can be dressed and stored covered in the refrigerator, and served the next day. They will keep a couple of days in the refrigerator; bring them back to room temperature.

Selecting, Storing, and Cleaning Mussels

Safety first: Mussels are easily contaminated by pollution and toxins—never prepare or eat mussels gathered in the wild unless absolutely certain that they are safe to eat. Check with local authorities if you have any doubts.

Commercial mussel beds are closely monitored, and almost any store-bought mussel will be safe to eat. (You may ask the store to show you verification of inspection.)

Make sure that the mussel shells are tightly closed and heavy. If a mussel shell is even slightly open, test it by tapping it against another mussel or touching the meat with a knife point. It should close almost at once; if it doesn't, discard it.

Occasionally, closed shells that appear healthy can be filled with sand or mud. Check unusually heavy mussels by twisting the shell halves in opposite directions. They will pivot open if the mussel has died and been replaced by sand—discard.

Mussels are perishable and should be kept refrigerated, covered by a damp towel, or seaweed. Never set them in fresh (unsalted) water or in plastic. They can be kept for a few days or so, but in general it's best to prepare them as soon as possible.

Soaking: Wild mussels may be quite sandy. Soak them in lightly salted water (about a tablespoon of salt per quart) for an hour or two before cooking and they will expel some of the sand. (Some wild mussels are encrusted with barnacles. If you are serving the mussels in their shells, scrape off any barnacles with a sturdy knife.)

Washing and removing the beard: All mussels must be washed thoroughly. Dump them in a large pan of cold, clean water—or under running water—and rub the shells against each other to remove encrusted sand and dirt, or use a stiff brush. Transfer to clean water and repeat the rubbing process. Cultivated mussels may need only one or two washings. Wild or very sandy mussels should be rubbed in several changes of clean water.

Shortly before cooking, remove the beard—the small tuft of fibers sticking out one side of the mussel shell—by grasping it with your fingers and giving a sharp pull downward. If you are storing mussels, don't clean or debeard them until an hour or two before cooking.

Julia

I am fussy about the dark digestive "vein" in the shrimp—it's ugly, and I always remove it. You can—sometimes—pull the whole strand out without slicing open the back. Look for the dark spot at the large end of the shrimp—this is the end of the digestive tract. Grasp it with your fingers or in a paper towel, and draw it out gently. You may not get all of it, but there may not be a lot to remove either. Not all shrimp have a full digestive vein that you can notice.

Shrimp

You can certainly make a shrimp cocktail fast with the already boiled—and often tasteless—shrimp available at supermarket fish counters, but for a superior version cook your shrimp at home. Here we use the classic method of poaching the shrimp in a *court bouillon,* a flavored broth of wine, water, lemon, and aromatics. The shrimp actually boil for only a few moments, then steep in the liquid, cooking through but retaining firm texture, and becoming infused with flavor.

For a classic shrimp cocktail, you will have to remove the shells and clean the shrimp before cooking, and chill them thoroughly, so they curl elegantly and are ready for dipping into Jacques's Horseradish Cocktail Sauce (page 6). But you can also make a casual first course of warm shrimp still in the shell, served family-style in a big bowl of the *court bouillon.* Everyone at the table can retrieve and shell his or her own shrimp, and dunk them into melted butter with lemon and cracked pepper.

Shrimp are sold in sizes based on the average number in a pound. For either of these appetizers, you want large shrimp—designated as "26 to 30 count"—or the jumbo "12 to 16 count" (sometimes referred to as "U16," which means "under 16" per pound). The jumbos are quite expensive, but they make a meaty mouthful, and there are fewer shells to remove.

Shrimp Cocktail and Cooked Shrimp, Family-Style

Yield: 1 pound of shrimp, serving 4 as a first course

1 pound unshelled shrimp, either large
(26 to 30 per pound) or jumbo (12 to
16 per pound)

For the *court bouillon*
1 cup coarsely chopped onions
1 carrot, peeled and sliced into thin
rounds (about ½ cup)
4 sprigs fresh thyme
2 imported bay leaves
¼ large lemon, in thin half-round slices
1 tsp whole black peppercorns
⅛ tsp red-pepper flakes (optional)
1 tsp salt
1 cup dry white wine or dry white
French vermouth
3 cups water

For serving shrimp cocktail
Lemon wedges
Lettuce leaves
Horseradish Cocktail Sauce, page 6

For serving family-style, shell on
Melted butter
Freshly squeezed lemon juice
Coarsely cracked black pepper
Salt

Preparing the shrimp

For shrimp cocktail, peel the shell off each shrimp, leaving the tail and the adjoining small band of shell attached to the body. With a sharp paring knife, slice lengthwise along the middle of the tail—the outside curve—going only about ⅛ inch deep into the flesh, to expose the thin dark strand of digestive tract (it will vary from pale to black in some shrimp, and will be hardly visible in others). Lift the strand with the tip of the knife

Jacques

At home, I usually cook the shrimp in the shell, then serve them warm in a big bowl of broth. It's not only easier—because you don't have to peel the shrimp ahead of time—but it also allows shrimp lovers, like my wife, Gloria, to munch on the shells, which have lots of flavor. We don't bother to remove the digestive tract when we have shrimp this way—you never taste it, and it's perfectly good protein to eat.

Very often I buy whole shrimp with heads on. (You have to buy more to compensate for the weight of the heads.) They are usually less expensive, and the body gives extra flavor to the meat and the stock.

If you do peel your shrimp before cooking, add the shells to the *court bouillon* to give it better flavor, or freeze them to make stock with later. And you should strain and save your *court bouillon*. I love to make consommé or other soups with it.

and discard. Rinse the shrimp and drain. Peel all the shrimp in the same manner and save all the shells for the *court bouillon.*

For family-style shell-on shrimp, simply rinse them before cooking.

Cooking the *court bouillon* and the shrimp

Put all the *court bouillon* ingredients into a large stainless-steel saucepan, including the shrimp peels if you've removed them. Bring to a boil, then cover and cook 10 to 15 minutes, at a gentle boil.

Add the shrimp—peeled or unpeeled—all at once, stir to mix them into the broth, and bring it back to a boil over high heat. Cover the pan and cook for only 10 seconds, then remove from the heat. Let the shrimp cool in the covered pan of broth, either to lukewarm for serving in the broth, or in the refrigerator, until thoroughly chilled.

Serving the shrimp

For shrimp cocktail, chill the shrimp in the *court bouillon,* then remove them and dry on paper towels. Arrange them all on a platter lined with lettuce leaves—along with lemon wedges and cocktail sauce— to serve as an hors d'oeuvre. For individual servings, stand a rolled-up lettuce leaf in a cocktail or wine glass and hang the shrimp on the edge of the glass (6 or more "large" shrimp or 3 or 4 "jumbo" per serving). Cut the lemon wedges in half crosswise and nestle them between the shrimp. Serve with ramekins of cocktail sauce on the side.

To serve unshelled shrimp, family-style, turn both the shrimp and *court bouillon,* while still warm, into a large serving bowl. Into the melted butter stir fresh lemon juice, cracked black pepper, and pinches of salt, to taste. Provide everyone with a bowl for shrimp shells and a nearby ramekin of flavored butter.

Julia's Colossal Barbecued Shrimp

The bigger the shrimp, the more expensive it is, and the official "colossal" grade is next to the top. "Extra colossal" wins the prize, weighing in at 8 to 10 shrimp per pound. Considering its luxurious price, just 1 per person would be acceptable, and 2 or 3 would be generosity itself. These are butterflied, skewered, turned in a marinade, then barbecued or broiled.

To butterfly the shrimp, cut open the shells starting at the outside of the large ends and going down to the tail. Then with a small, very sharp knife cut through the flesh down to but not through the underside of the shells. Remove the intestinal vein lodged along the outside curve of the flesh. Meanwhile soak 2 dozen long, pointed wooden skewers in cold water.

Prepare the marinade for a dozen colossal shrimp: Whisk 2 tablespoons each of excellent olive oil and fresh lemon juice in a small bowl with ½ teaspoon each of dark sesame oil and soy sauce, plus a little puréed fresh garlic and gingerroot and several grinds of fresh pepper.

Open the shrimp flesh side up and push one skewer through the large ends to hold them open, and a second skewer through the tail ends. Paint the shrimp flesh with marinade and reserve any that is left over. Cover and refrigerate for at least half an hour before cooking.

To broil, start flesh side down for a good minute, then turn flesh side up for 1½ to 2 minutes, basting once or twice with leftover marinade or with olive oil. To barbecue, start flesh side down, basting once or twice, and finish flesh side up.

Salmon

Salmon, as you will find in the "Fish" chapter, is one of our favorite fish for cooking. Its distinctive flavor and moderately firm, rich flesh also make it well suited for curing and smoking, and serving as a cold appetizer. You can of course buy exquisite and expensive smoked salmon from Alaska, Canada, Scotland, and Scandinavia, but with fresh, fine, and reasonably priced salmon now available at most supermarkets, you will enjoy the four methods we give here for curing it in your own kitchen.

Three of these are versions of salt-cured, Scandinavian "gravlax." Julia's dilled salmon is made the traditional way: thick slabs of salmon fillet are coated with salt, sugar, and cognac, then stacked with a layer of fresh dill, and set aside to cure for 3 to 5 days. Then it is sliced paper-thin and served as an hors d'oeuvre, a first course, or a garnish for other foods.

If you've not started your cure days ahead of your party—or if you're having just a few guests—our two gravlax variations produce deliciously seasoned cold salmon, all ready to serve in slices, in a fraction of the time. Julia's Quick Gravlax takes just two hours, and Jacques's "instant" gravlax is ready to eat in barely twenty minutes.

A truly instant salmon appetizer is Salmon Tartare, a lemony mixture of chopped raw salmon, shallots, herbs, and seasonings. It's an excellent way to use the trimmings left from filleting a whole salmon, but you can also buy a small piece of salmon just for this purpose. Spread the tartare on black bread or crackers as a canapé, or, if you have gravlax as well, drape a couple of slices over a mound of tartare for a very special first course.

Jacques

Salt is the principal agent for curing the salmon in all gravlax recipes. It draws out moisture, making it difficult for bacteria to survive, and permeates and flavors the flesh. I prefer to use kosher salt for this process, since the pointed larger segments penetrate the meat and cure more effectively.

Curing thin slices of "instant" gravlax with this method takes only 15 to 20 minutes, and you can make as much as you want, as long as you spread the slices directly on the seasonings, without overlapping them. For individual servings, cure just 2 or 3 slices on small plates, 1 for each person at the table. Then cover the slices with plastic wrap, stack the plates on top of each other, and refrigerate until serving time.

Since I cure the slices with only salt, pepper, and a tiny bit of sugar, I like to put a lot of garnishes on my instant gravlax just before serving. You can be very creative at this point. In the recipe here I suggest shallots, lemon zest, radishes, chives, and walnut oil (diluted with peanut oil to temper its strong flavor). And I garnish the salmon with julienne mushrooms, capers, chopped parsley, basil, and olive oil. You can also use chopped red or white onion, black olives, diced

(continued on page 19)

Julia

I use the traditional season-ings of salt, sugar, and dill, as well as cognac, in both my long-cure and quick gravlax. The proportions are the same—1½ teaspoons of salt and ¾ teaspoon of sugar per pound of salmon. I don't like to use a lot of salt to begin with—you can always add more during the cure if needed. The sugar keeps the salmon reasonably soft; otherwise it tends to stiffen. The cognac, while not essential, adds some piz-zazz to the cure.

Following this formula, you can cure any amount of salmon that you want. For a large party, it's as easy to cure two fillets (two halves of a whole salmon) as it is to do one. You'll need only spoon-fuls more sugar, salt, and cognac, a few more dill sprigs, and a larger dish to hold the fish. The cure will still take four to five days. With the quick method, you can cut a whole, skin-on fillet into slices—remov-ing them from the skin—season them on both sides as in the recipe, then reassem-ble the slices on the skin, instead of arranging them on a platter.

Not to worry if you end up with extra gravlax. The long-cured dilled salmon will last for a week—the quick gravlax for several days—and both will freeze nicely. I had never heard of gravlax before I went to Norway in the 1950s, where we lived for two years. At the Grand Hotel in Oslo, we had a memo-rable lunch at which gravlax was served with creamed potatoes and scrambled eggs. I have been making it ever since.

Julia's Traditional Gravlax

Yield: 2 to 2½ pounds, serving 15 to 20 as
  an appetizer

One 2½-to-3-pound salmon fillet, skin
  on, *all* bones removed (as shown on
  page 219)
1½ Tbs salt, plus more if needed
2¼ tsp sugar
4 Tbs cognac, plus more if needed
Fresh dill sprigs, about 1 cup packed

For serving
Fresh dill and parsley
Cucumber Ribbons (page 23)
  (optional)
Breads and other accompaniments, as
  noted below

Special equipment
A glass, enamel, or other non-reactive
  baking dish to hold the salmon (about
  10 inches long); plastic wrap; a plate or
  cutting board, and 5 pounds to weight
  it (such as canned goods)

Curing the fillet

Trim the salmon fillet, cutting away any thin, uneven edges and the thin end of the tail. (You can use the fleshy trimmings for Salmon Tartare, page 24.)

Cut the fillet in half crosswise, so you have 2 pieces of the same length and about the same width, and lay them skin down on the work sur-face.

Stir the salt and sugar together in a small bowl. Sprinkle half the mix

After rubbing the salt and cognac over the fillet, spread sprigs of dill on top.

over each fillet and rub it in with your fingers. Drizzle about 2 tablespoons of cognac over each piece and rub in. Spread the dill sprigs over one fillet, then set it in the baking dish. Lay the other fillet on top, align the sides neatly, and cover with a sheet of plastic wrap (see photos).

Lay a pan or board on top of the fish (be sure it isn't resting on the rim of the dish), weight the top with cans or other heavy objects to compress the fillets, and place in the refrigerator. After one day of curing, remove the weights and top tray, and turn the fish over (so the top fillet is on the bottom), baste with the liquid that has accumulated in the dish, and replace the weights. Turn and baste after the second day, and slice off a sliver of the salmon. Taste, and sprinkle more salt or cognac on the flesh if needed. Cure for another day, turn, and baste once more. After the fourth full day, the cure will be complete and you can serve the gravlax.

Set in a baking dish and lay the other fillet on top, aligning the sides.

Slicing the gravlax

Clean the dill from the flesh of one fillet and wipe dry with paper towels. With a long thin-bladed slicing knife, held at a very flat angle, start slicing a few inches in from the narrow end of the fillet. Cut with a back-and-forth sawing motion, toward the narrow end, to remove a thin slice of fish. Start each succeeding slice a bit farther in from the end of the fillet; always cut at a flat angle, to keep the slices long and as thin as possible. When the blade reaches the skin, shave the slice off—don't

Cover with plastic wrap, lay a pan or board on top, and then weight.

Jacques (continued from page 17)

cucumber tossed with a bit of vinegar—whatever you like and whatever you have available.

I also add many garnishes to the salmon tartare, but in this case there is no actual curing. The fish is essentially raw, although, as in South American seviche, the citric acid in the lemon juice coagulates the protein so the pieces whiten and appear "cooked." For any of these recipes, use very fresh salmon from a reliable fish market.

Julia's Traditional Gravlax (continued)

cut through the skin. You may trim away and discard the dark flesh that was next to the skin. The Norwegians leave it on.

After cutting as many slices as you wish to serve, fold the attached flap of skin over the remaining fish and wrap well in plastic. The gravlax can be stored in the refrigerator for about a week.

With a long, thin-bladed slicing knife held at a flat angle, start slicing with a back-and-forth sawing motion.

Serving suggestions

Serve sliced gravlax as a first course on individual plates, or as an hors d'oeuvre on a serving platter. If the slices are large, you may wish to cut them into smaller, canapé-sized pieces. Garnish individual plates or serving platters with sprigs of dill and parsley, or seasoned Cucumber Ribbons (page 23).

Accompany the salmon with thin slices of dark bread, such as dense European-style rye or pumpernickel, or see sidebar on cocktail breads (page 6). Toasted and buttered slices of brioche, and/or an assortment of crisp rye and wheat crackers, may also be served.

A platter of Julia's Traditional Gravlax

Julia's Quick Gravlax

Yield: 10 to 12 slices, serving 8 or
more as an hors d'oeuvre

1 pound salmon fillet, trimmed
   and boned (pages 218–219)
1½ tsp salt
¾ tsp sugar
1 Tbs cognac, in a small dish, or
   more if needed
1 bunch fresh, clean dill sprigs

For serving
   Cucumber Ribbons (page 23)
      (optional)
   Breads and other accompaniments
      as noted in preceding recipe

Special equipment
   A large serving platter; plastic
      wrap

Slice the salmon as thinly
as possible, as shown in the
photo on page 20. You should
have 10 or more slices, each
about 1½ ounces. Or maybe
you can cajole your fish
man—the way I do—into
slicing the salmon for you.
   Stir together the salt and
sugar in a small bowl. Lay all
the salmon slices flat on a
large cutting board or clean
work surface. Sprinkle each
slice with a pinch or two of
the salt-sugar mix—you should use half the mix, about a
teaspoon in all.
   Then moisten the slices with cognac, dipping your

Sprinkle each slice with a
pinch or two of the salt-
sugar mix.

finger into the dish and rubbing a few drops over the
surface of each. When all the slices are coated, turn them
over and, after drying your fingers, season the second
side evenly with the remaining salt-sugar mix, then rub
with cognac.
   Chop several of the dill sprigs quite fine, to yield a
tablespoon or two. Spread the rest of the sprigs on the
serving platter. One by one, arrange the salmon slices
flat, in an overlapping pattern, covering the dill. Sprinkle
the chopped dill over the slices, cover tightly with plastic
wrap, and refrigerate for 2 hours. (After 1 hour, taste a
small piece of the salmon, and season with more salt,
sugar, or cognac if needed.)
   To serve, simply uncover the platter. Garnish with
cucumber ribbons, if you like, and serve with any of the
breads and other accompaniments suggested for Traditional Gravlax (preceding recipe).

Jacques's Instant Gravlax

Yield: 8 to 10 slices, serving 6 to 8 as
   an hors d'oeuvre, or 4 as a first
   course

12 ounces salmon fillet, trimmed
   and boned (pages 218–219)
1 tsp kosher salt
¼ tsp sugar
½ tsp freshly ground black pepper
For garnishing
   1 tsp lemon peel in fine julienne
      strips or shreds (see page 23)
   1 Tbs chopped fresh chives
   2 radishes, in julienne strips
   4 Tbs thinly sliced shallots (4 large
      shallots)
   1 Tbs walnut oil
   2 Tbs peanut oil

Lay the salmon slices on top of the platter that you have sprinkled with the salt-sugar-pepper mix.

Jacques's Instant Gravlax (continued)

For serving

Lemon wedges
Cucumber Ribbons (page 23) (optional)
Slices of buttered pumpernickel, brioche,
    or crackers

Special equipment

A serving platter; plastic wrap

Curing the salmon

Slice the salmon as thin as possible, as shown on page 20. You should have 8 or more slices, each about 1½ ounces.

Stir together the salt, sugar, and pepper in a small bowl. Sprinkle half of the mixture evenly over the surface of the serving platter. Lay the salmon slices flat, on top of the seasonings, *without overlapping.* Sprinkle the rest of the seasoning mix evenly over the slices.

Cover the slices airtight with plastic wrap—pressing the wrap so it adheres to the salmon—and set it in the refrigerator for at least 20 minutes, to cure. (You may keep it refrigerated for up to 24 hours, tightly covered, before garnishing and serving.)

Garnishing and serving

Uncover the platter. Sprinkle the lemon zest, chives, radish slivers, and sliced shallots all over the slices of salmon. Stir together the walnut and peanut oils, and drizzle them over the slices and garnishes.

Arrange the lemon wedges—and cucumber ribbons, if you like—around the edges of the platter. Serve with slices of buttered bread or brioche toast, or crackers, on the side.

A platter of Jacques's Instant Gravlax

Jacques's Lemon Peel Garnish

The yellow layer of lemon peel, also called the "zest," contains the volatile citrus oils and makes a colorful garnish for cured salmon slices, salmon tartare, and many other dishes. Though you can grate the peel (and sometimes your knuckles) on a regular grater, a better method is to remove the zest in long thin shreds using a special "zesting" tool, which has a row of small, sharp-edged holes. Another technique I use frequently is to shave off 2-inch strips of peel, about ½ inch wide, with a vegetable peeler. Stack these on top of each other, then slice the stack crosswise with a sharp knife, into very fine julienne slivers. This will give you several tablespoons of garnish in just a few seconds.

Jacques's Cucumber Ribbons

These thin strips of lightly dressed cucumber are a fine garnish for all of our salmon appetizers.

With a sharp vegetable peeler, remove the skin from a large, preferably "seedless" (or English) cucumber. Then, still using the vegetable peeler, shave lengthwise strips from one side of the cucumber, until you can see the interior layer of seeds. Rotate the cucumber 90 degrees, shave off more long ribbons until you reach the seeds, then rotate and remove strips twice more. (Now you can discard the rectangular center of the cucumber, with all the seeds.)

You should have about 2 cups of ribbons. Season with ¼ teaspoon each of salt, sugar, and freshly ground black pepper, and about 1 teaspoon of white-wine vinegar. Toss to distribute the seasonings.

For more delicate, spaghettilike ribbons, neatly lay 4 to 6 unseasoned cucumber strips on top of each other, then fold or roll the pile over several times, making a many-layered stack. Cut down through the layers lengthwise, every ⅛ inch or so, creating long thin strips, like spaghetti. Loosen the strands gently and season as above.

You can garnish with the ribbons in many ways: lay them flat in decorative, crisscross patterns on serving plates; form them into small mounds and drape them with slices of gravlax, for individual servings; or spread a loose tangle of ribbons into a ring or nest around a platter of gravlax or salmon tartare.

Jacques's Salmon Tartare

Yield: About 2 cups, serving 4 as a first course or 8 as hors d'oeuvre

12 ounces fresh skinless, boneless salmon (including scrapings and trimmings from filleting)
2 Tbs finely chopped shallots
1½ tsp lemon peel in fine julienne strips or shreds (see page 23)
1½ Tbs freshly squeezed lemon juice
3 Tbs chopped parsley
1 Tbs extra-virgin olive oil
¼ tsp Tabasco sauce, plus more to taste
½ tsp salt, plus more to taste
¼ tsp freshly ground black pepper, plus more to taste

For serving
Thin Cucumber Ribbons (page 23)
1 Tbs chopped fresh chives
Slices of pumpernickel or other black bread, spread with butter or mayonnaise

Cut all the salmon into small (roughly ¼-inch) pieces, and put them in a bowl along with the shallots, lemon peel, lemon juice, parsley, olive oil, Tabasco, salt, and pepper. It is important to cut by hand, because the food processor will purée too fast and make the salmon pasty and mushy. Mix gently and thoroughly. Taste the tartare and adjust the seasonings as you like.

The tartare can be served right away, or refrigerated for an hour or two. (The salmon will whiten, and become opaque, after a few minutes in the marinade.)

To serve as an hors d'oeuvre, pile thin cucumber ribbons on a serving platter, spread them with your fingers into a ring or nest, and mound the tartare in the middle. For first-course plates, make small nests of ribbons and fill each with ½ cup or so of the tartare. Sprinkle the chopped chives over and arrange triangles of black bread, spread with butter or mayonnaise, around the platter.

Sausage in Brioche

Along with its buttery flavor and soft texture, this golden brioche loaf has a treat inside—a homemade sausage, studded with pine nuts and fragrant slivers of truffle. Serve slices of this all-in-one appetizer with cocktails, as a first course, or for a summer lunch.

You can make quick work of both components of the loaf, using a simple technique to shape the sausage by hand and a no-knead, food-processor method for the brioche dough. They can both be conveniently made ahead, with a bit of coordinated planning: the sausage needs to cure for 3 days, or up to a week, in the refrigerator; and the brioche dough will be best if made the night before baking and allowed to rise slowly, also in the refrigerator.

The sausage made here is a variation on the homemade pork sausage, cured and poached, in the "Meats" chapter (page 364). Refer to the more detailed discussion there of meat and seasoning choices, and of shaping the sausage. The black truffles in this recipe add a special (and expensive) fragrant touch to the sausage. If unavailable, you can use pieces of dried cèpes (porcini or king boletus mushrooms), which will also speckle the sausage with black and give it a distinctive flavor.

Jacques

This easily made brioche dough can also be used for encasing other meats, such as pâté. Or you can shape it into a conventional loaf, or even the famous *brioche à tête* shape—with a little "head" on top, made in a fluted mold. But this dough contains less butter, and will not rise as high or be as light as the finest brioche dough, called *brioche mousseline*. Such a dough requires lots of kneading and several periods of long, slow rising at low temperatures, in order to develop the gluten and to absorb a large amount of butter.

Once the dough is wrapped around the sausage, though, it does need a foil collar to maintain the shape during its final rise at room temperature and the first part of baking. Be sure to butter the foil well, so it doesn't stick to the dough, and to remove it after the first 20 minutes of baking, so the sides can brown nicely. The dough will hold its shape at that point without the collar.

Saltpeter, or potassium nitrate, has been used at least since the IMiddle Ages to give meat—from bologna to ham to corned beef to pâté—a beautiful pink color. Salt, in large amounts, will also impart this color, but the end product will be too salty. If no saltpeter is used, the meat will be slightly pink and turn grayish after it's cooked for a while, but the taste will be just as good.

Julia

The combination of meat and bread together makes a very appealing dish, and you can use any kind of homemade sausage.

My food-processor method for brioche dough is a bit different from Jacques's. Though the yeast manufacturers say you can put the dry, rapid-rise type of yeast in with the flour directly, I always "proof" my yeast before adding it to the machine, sprinkling it on warm water with a pinch of sugar to make sure that it gets foamy and is therefore alive.

And while Jacques adds room-temperature butter last, I use cold chunks of butter and cut them into the flour first—before adding liquid—by pulsing with the steel blade. Then I like to let the dough rise at room temperature until doubled, fold it over a few times to deflate, and let it rise again. I find that two rises give the dough more body and flavor.

Jacques's Sausage in Brioche

Yield: 6 to 8 servings as a first course, or 12 or more as an appetizer

For the sausage
$1\frac{1}{2}$ pounds coarsely ground pork, about 25 percent fat (Boston butt is very good)
$2\frac{1}{2}$ tsp salt
$\frac{1}{2}$ tsp sugar
$\frac{3}{4}$ tsp freshly ground black pepper
2 Tbs white wine
2 Tbs pignoli (pine nuts)
2 Tbs black truffle, in julienne slivers (or dried cèpes or porcini, in $\frac{1}{4}$-inch pieces)
$\frac{1}{8}$ tsp potassium nitrate (saltpeter) (optional)

For the brioche loaf
1 large egg
Brioche dough, fully risen, from the following recipe (about 2 pounds)
Flour for rolling
Fresh bread crumbs (from 1 slice of white bread, crusts removed, about 2 to 3 Tbs)

Special equipment
Plastic wrap; aluminum foil; parchment paper; a rolling pin; a pastry brush; a large cookie or baking sheet; kitchen twine

Mixing and forming the sausage several days ahead
Tear off an 18-inch piece of plastic wrap and lay it on the work surface, long side in front of you. Put the pork and all the seasoning ingredients (including the saltpeter, if using) in a large bowl and mix together well with your hands.

Press the meat together into a rough log shape and place it on the plastic wrap. Fold the wrap over and gently squeeze the meat out to form a thin, even sausage, about 12 inches long and 2 inches in diameter; press firmly to eliminate any air pockets in the meat. Now roll the sausage back and forth under the plastic so it is perfectly smooth and cylindrical.

A smooth, even sausage roll about 12 inches long and 2 inches in diameter

At this point, if you don't want to cure in plastic, simply transfer the sausage to parchment paper. Place the sausage on an 18-inch piece of aluminum foil, and roll it up and seal it the same way. Set the sausage in the refrigerator to cure for at least 3 days, or up to a week.

Forming the brioche loaf

Crack the egg into a small bowl, remove half of the egg white, and beat the yolk and remaining white to make the egg wash. This way you have more yolk in the wash, which produces a deeper, more golden color, while the small amount of egg white will give the glaze a shine.

Remove the risen brioche dough from the refrigerator and unwrap. Deflate it gently on a lightly floured work surface, press it flat, and sprinkle a bit of flour over the top. With the rolling pin, roll the dough out to about 14 inches by 10 inches (follow photos). (If the dough has risen at room temperature rather than in the refrigerator, you will need more flour when rolling.)

Roll the dough out to about 14 inches long and 10 inches wide.

Unwrap the cured sausage. Center the sausage roll on the floured area of the dough and brush the top lightly with egg wash before sprinkling on a little flour.

Fold the dough over the sausage.

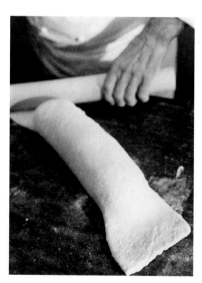

Flatten the flaps with a rolling pin before folding them under.

Score the egg-washed top of the dough with decorative diagonal lines.

Jacques's Sausage in Brioche (continued)

Brush the center of the dough lightly with egg wash, and sprinkle on a little flour. Unwrap the cured sausage and center it on the floured area of dough, then sprinkle a bit of flour on the top and sides of the meat, to help the brioche stick to it during rising and baking.

Fold the dough over the sausage as shown in the photo, brush with egg wash, and fold in the flaps as illustrated.

Line the cookie sheet with parchment paper, turn the loaf over, and place it on the sheet, with the folds and flaps underneath. Brush the top and sides with egg wash. Score the top with decorative diagonal lines, as illustrated. To release steam, make 3 small vent holes.

Cut a 3-foot length of aluminum foil, fold it in thirds lengthwise to form a band, and butter it well on one side. Wrap the foil loosely around the loaf, buttered side in—forming a collar to maintain the shape as the dough rises. Tie a length of kitchen twine around the foil to keep it in place. Let the brioche rise for about an hour, in a warm place (about 72°F).

Baking and serving the sausage

Arrange a rack in the center of the oven and preheat to 375°F.

When the dough feels spongy and soft, brush the top again with egg wash and sprinkle on the bread crumbs. Place the sheet in the oven (with the aluminum-foil band in place) and bake for about 20 minutes. Remove the sheet (be sure to close the oven door) and quickly remove the band, cutting the twine and carefully peeling the foil from around the loaf. Return the loaf to the oven immediately and bake for 25 minutes more, until the loaf is golden and fully baked. Set aside in a warm place and allow it to cool for about 30 minutes before serving.

To serve, slice the sausage in ½-inch-thick slices for appetizer portions—or thicker, if you like—and arrange on individual plates or on a serving platter.

With the point of your knife make 3 vent holes all the way through the dough to allow steam to escape.

Wrap buttered foil loosely around the loaf and tie in place.

Cut slices ½ to ¾ inch thick.

Fast Brioche Dough in the Food Processor

Yield: About 2 pounds of dough

3 cups flour (1 pound exactly)
1 package (2 tsp) dry yeast, quick-rising or "instant"
½ tsp sugar
¾ tsp salt
⅓ cup warm milk
4 large eggs
6 ounces room-temperature butter, in pieces

Special equipment
A food processor

Put the flour, yeast, sugar, and salt in the work bowl of the food processor and pulse briefly to blend. Add the milk and eggs to the work bowl and start processing continuously. Within a few seconds, as the dough forms, drop the butter in piece by piece and continue to process for about 30 or 40 seconds, until the butter is incorporated and the dough is uniformly smooth. It will be soft and slightly sticky. (If it is very sticky, sprinkle on flour by teaspoons only and process briefly.)

Remove the dough from the work bowl and knead it for a moment with your floured hands on a lightly floured surface, to form a ball. Enclose the dough in a clean plastic bag, or put it in a bowl and seal with plastic wrap, and set in the refrigerator to rise slowly overnight. You can use dough after the first rise, or press out the air gently, knead it briefly to redistribute the yeast, and return to the refrigerator (in the bag or bowl) for a second rise. Use the dough as directed in the preceding recipe, straight from the refrigerator.

If you must make the dough for use the same day, remove it from the food processor to a bowl and cover with plastic wrap or a damp towel. Allow it to rise in a warm place for 3 or 4 hours, or until doubled, before rolling.

Julia

There's no reason to be intimi-dated by the idea of making pâté. You can just think of it as meat loaf—a festive type of French meat loaf with wine and various meats.

Nor should you be afraid of eating pâté. This is a rich appetizer, definitely not a diet dish, and you don't want to eat great big pieces. I find that even a half-slice of this pâté makes a nice serving—and such a modest portion shouldn't worry even those who are concerned about fat. There's no reason not to enjoy pâté, or anything else, if you do so in moderation.

Pâté

A small slice of this pâté presents a mosaic of colors and flavors—slivers of veal, country ham, and chicken liver, pistachio nuts, and bits of porcini mushrooms, all bound together in a moist, savory loaf of ground pork and veal. If you've only sampled this classic appetizer at a good French restaurant, or treated yourself to a slice or two from a fancy *charcuterie,* you will be delighted to find how easy and relatively inexpensive it is to make at home. This recipe gives you a good-sized loaf, providing enough generous slices to serve twenty or more at a big party, to enjoy as a first course for several small dinners, or to indulge in whenever you like. It will store perfectly for a week and a half, though it will likely have disappeared much sooner.

Buying and mixing everything on the long ingredient list constitutes most of your work here—after that, it's a simple matter to form and bake the loaf. Because the pâté needs several days to develop its fine flavor both before and after cooking, you can do the initial mixing on the weekend before you want to serve it, set it aside to marinate, then complete the assembling and the baking to suit your schedule.

A well-seasoned base of ground meat, called the forcemeat, is essential for a good pâté. A country pâté is by definition rather coarse-textured, and you can simply use store-ground pork and veal or turkey for the forcemeat, or grind the meat yourself with a meat grinder or an attachment to your electric mixer. Be sure to use—or ask the butcher to grind—pork with about 25-percent fat content, such as the "Boston butt" from the shoulder.

A country pâté is usually formed and baked in the narrow rectangular mold known as a "terrine," pictured here. Made of earthenware or enameled cast iron—and widely available in kitchenware stores—they are used for many kinds of pâtés and similar molded foods which, like the container itself, are often called terrines. If you don't have one, you can use any loaf-shaped pan or other baking dish. It is also traditional but optional to line the mold with pork fat, either the lacy membrane of abdominal fat known as caul, which you can see in the photos, or thin slices of pork fatback or leaf lard. Caul can be found at specialty stores and good Italian butcher shops, or your regular butcher can order it. The saltpeter listed in the recipe is also optional. As with our recipes for homemade sausage, this will give a pink color to the pâté.

You do, however, want to serve the pâté with its traditional accompaniments—the small French pickled gherkins known as cornichons, black olives, good Dijon-style mustard, and country-style bread. All kinds of wine go with pâté. At a summer picnic, enjoy it with a dry white wine; at the table, pour a light Beaujolais, or a more pungent Merlot or cabernet sauvignon.

Jacques

There are three things that contribute to a good pâté. First, it has to be very well seasoned. The proportions of salt and pepper and spices might seem high, but the seasoning mellows as the mixture cures, and is muted when the pâté is eaten cold or at room temperature. Second, the forcemeat has to have sufficient fat to stay moist, but not taste overrich. Here, the pork must provide all the fat, because the veal is entirely lean. The Boston butt, or pork butt, is a common cut from the shoulder with the ideal proportion of fat (because it is so moist, it also makes a great roast). Finally, you have to cook the pâté slowly, in a water bath, as we do here. If you cooked it too fast, all the fat would melt out of the pâté, and it would have a dry texture and too much seasoning.

If you follow these principles, you can make many variations on this pâté. Experiment with the spice mix. Instead of the herbs and spices suggested here, you could add others that you like—cumin, coriander, or cinnamon are some that I use. You can vary the kind of wines and other flavorings, and the garnishes. You could leave some of the pork in small chunks and mix them into the forcemeat, or use different nuts. You might layer different kinds of meat strips—use turkey strips instead of veal—and arrange

(continued on page 33)

Country Pâté

Yield: A 6-cup terrine, making 20 or
more appetizer slices

For the spice mix
1 tsp black peppercorns
24 allspice berries
6 cloves
2 bay leaves
1 tsp dried thyme

For the forcemeat
¾ pound veal shoulder, coarsely
ground★
2¼ pounds pork shoulder (Boston
butt or pork butt), coarsely
ground★
1 tsp minced garlic
⅓ cup chopped shallots
¼ ounce dried porcini mushrooms, chopped dry into ¼-
inch pieces (about 3 Tbs)
⅓ cup pistachio nuts
⅓ cup white wine
2 Tbs cognac
1 Tbs cornstarch
1 Tbs and 2 tsp salt
¼ tsp saltpeter (optional)

For assembling the pâté
½ pound veal shoulder★
4 ounces chicken livers, cleaned
and trimmed of sinews
¼ teaspoon freshly ground black
pepper
1 Tbs cognac

6 to 8 ounces caul fat (optional)
4 ounces cooked country-ham
steak, sliced into long ½-inch-
thick strips
2 large imported bay leaves
¼ tsp fresh thyme

Special equipment
A spice grinder or a very clean
coffee grinder; a meat grinder
or meat-grinding attachment
to an electric mixer; a 5½-cup
rectangular terrine or equiva-
lent-size mold or loaf pan; a
cover for the terrine or aluminum foil; a roasting pan; a
meat thermometer

Mixing the forcemeat and the garnishes for marinating

Using the spice grinder
or coffee grinder, process the
spice-mix ingredients into a
fine powder.

Put the ground meats in
a large mixing bowl. Add the
spice powder, garlic, shallots,
mushroom pieces, pistachio
nuts, white wine, cognac, cornstarch, the 1 tablespoon of salt,
and the saltpeter (if using) and
mix well with your hands.

Slice the piece of veal
into long strips, about ½ inch
thick, put them in a small bowl
with the chicken livers, and
toss with the 2 teaspoons of
salt, pepper, and cognac.

You can now marinate

Drape the caul fat into the
mold to cover the bottom
and sides completely, with
several inches overhanging
the outside all around.

★ You can buy the meats whole and grind them yourself, using
the coarse blade of the grinder. For the veal, buy a 1¼-pound
piece of shoulder and divide it into ¾ pound for grinding and ½
pound for cutting into strips for layering.

both the forcemeat, and the veal strips and livers, in their bowls or other containers. Cover closely with plastic wrap, and let sit in the refrigerator for at least 2 days, or as long as 5 days or a week. Or you can assemble the pâté in the mold before marinating.

Assembling the pâté

Assembling the pâté is the same whether you do it before or after marinating the meat—follow the steps here, or arrange the ingredients as you like, to create an attractive layered pattern when the pâté is sliced.

When the meat is ready to cook, preheat the oven to 325°F.

To line the terrine with optional caul fat, carefully unfurl the lacy sheets—defrost or soften them in tepid water if necessary. Fill the mold, following the photos and captions.

If you did not marinate the component parts of the pâté before assembling it, you should let it marinate now. Cover the assembled pâté tightly with plastic wrap and refrigerate for 3 to 5 days. Before continuing with the recipe, preheat the oven to 325°F and remove the plastic wrap.

Cooking the pâté

Cover the pâté closely with a double or triple thickness of aluminum foil and crimp tightly around the top of the mold to seal. Set the mold in the roasting pan, place it in the oven, and add enough lukewarm water to come halfway up the side of the mold.

Gently press a third of the forcemeat in the bottom of the mold, to make an even layer about an inch thick. On top of the meat, arrange about half of the veal strips end to end, to form 2 evenly spaced rows, running the length of the mold. Press another layer of forcemeat, about ½ inch thick, over the veal, and set the chicken livers in a long row down the middle of the mold, laying some of the ham strips end to end to form 2 rows on either side. Press half the remaining forcemeat over livers and ham.

Make 2 rows of the remaining veal, with a row of the remaining ham in the middle. Press the rest of the forcemeat to cover the meat strips, shaping it to form a smooth loaf, mounded in the middle. Turn the overhanging edges of caul fat to cover the pâté neatly, trimming off any excess.

Jacques (continued from page 31)

them any way you want, to make a design that looks nice when you cut the slices.

We always have pâté at our house around Christmastime. Before the holidays start, I make two terrines just like the one here. Then we have plenty to serve for all the parties and for guests who come by—with the cornichons that Gloria makes every summer. It's fine to serve for 10 days or so. And considering that a slice of pâté like this would cost $15 in a French restaurant—and that there are 20 or 25 slices from each pâté—it's nice to think about the fortune we are saving!

Place the bay leaves on top of the pâté, and sprinkle the thyme over the surface.

Country Pâté (continued)

Bake for about 1¾ hours, making sure that the water never boils, until the internal temperature of the pâté registers 150° to 155°F on a meat thermometer. (The internal temperature will continue to rise by about 5° after the pâté is removed from the oven.) Check the temperature near the end of the cooking time, without removing the mold from the oven—you can poke the thermometer through the aluminum foil, if using. Lift the mold out of the water and remove from the oven when done. Allow the pâté to cool, still covered. Refrigerate at least overnight, but preferably for 2 days, before serving.

Unmolding and serving

Run a knife around the pâté, against the sides of the mold, and invert over a cutting board or platter so the pâté and gelatinized juices drop out. (Dip the mold in hot water for 30 seconds or so, if the loaf seems stuck.) Scrape away the juices (and save them for stock or soup), and dry the pâté with paper towels. Cut off one end piece of the loaf (save it for yourself), and slice the number of pieces you want to serve, ½ to 1 inch thick. (Wrap the remaining pâté well in plastic wrap, and return to the refrigerator. It will keep for 10 days or so.)

To serve, line a platter or individual plates with lettuce leaves, and arrange the slices on top. Overlap the slices if composing a large platter; a single slice is sufficient for first-course servings. Garnish the platter or plates with black olives and cornichons, and serve with Dijon-style mustard, and crusty bread on the side.

Opposite: Country Pâté

SOUPS

HERE'S A REPERTOIRE OF FRESH VEGETABLE, SEAFOOD, AND CHICKEN SOUPS THAT TAKE only an hour or so—start to finish—and in some cases a good deal less. The selection, though small, offers many choices—rustic or fancy, hot or cold, lean or unashamedly rich, clear or creamy. And each recipe is a model method, which you can adapt in almost endless variation.

Creating a quick soup with great taste is not a matter of tricks, but good techniques, fine fresh ingredients, and attention to seasoning. And whenever possible, you want to give your soups the full flavor of homemade stock. With the recipes here, you can make chicken, fish, or veal stock in large quantity, and freeze it to use when the hour for soup making is at hand. But you don't have to forgo the pleasures of real soup, even if you don't have stock. Our basic leek-and-potato soup, and the fragrant broth made with aromatic vegetables and herbs in our Mediterranean fish stew, both serve as fine soup bases you can make from scratch. And good-quality canned broth is an acceptable substitute when stock is called for, but be sure to adjust your seasonings carefully.

Appropriate kitchen tools—can openers aside—are also important aids to fast soup making. A food processor or a blender is essential, and an immersion blender is quite handy for conveniently creaming and puréeing soup right in the pot. And even though it doesn't whirl at incredible speed, a hand-cranked food mill—the sturdy, stainless-steel kind with different disks—is one of the best devices for making soup with fine texture.

Julia

When you want to give extra flavor and depth to braised onions you simmer them in a flavored liquid, usually a chicken stock. Or you are to make a little sauce for your roast chicken—after you have spooned the fat out of your roasting pan, you pour in half a cup of chicken stock and a bit of wine, scrape the brown roasting juices into the liquid, and simmer them together. There! You have just made one of the essential sauces in good cooking, a "deglazing" sauce, or *petit jus*, a chic little sauce to dress up each serving of chicken. Stocks are essential to sauce making, and, whether plain and fast like this one or fancy like a béarnaise, sauces are essential to good cooking. Without them your food is bland, even institutional, while with them you are really cooking.

We could go at great length into the classic brown stocks and the mother white stocks with veal shanks and necks, marrow bones, all kinds of vegetables, and so forth. These you can find fully explained in your Escoffier. We are talking about good home cooking, where you don't have the time or the need to have these grand masterpieces at hand. However, if you are really passionate about good food, take out your Escoffier and make one of them. Just realizing it's there waiting in your freezer for some special occasion will give you a secret pleasure. It is also part of your continuing food mastery to know how good food is supposed to taste.

Poultry and Meat Stocks

In most home kitchens, stock making is a once-in-a-while affair, usually when we have a nice collection of bones and assorted vegetable trimmings, and a few hours (or less for fish stock) to cook, strain, and reduce them. As you cook your way through this book, we hope, your collection will accumulate (though follow Jacques's suggestion in the sidebar on page 41 to keep it from getting out of hand). Use the basic procedures and formulas presented here, to extract all the flavor from whatever bones and stock ingredients you have and to separate and remove fat and impurities.

Some Uses for Specific Stocks

Each of the following stocks will supply you with a sufficient quantity for use in many recipes throughout the book. The master recipe here is for a simple "white" chicken or turkey stock—this is the one you want to use whenever chicken stock is called for in this chapter. Use the white veal stock for such braises as Veal Roast en Cocotte (page 346) and Blanquette de Veau (page 351). You can make dark stock with poultry bones or beef and veal bones—either type can serve as the "flavorful dark stock" called for in our recipes, as a deglazing or braising liquid. (Or use Julia's Quick Dark Stock—see page 41.)

Julia's Simple Chicken or Turkey Stock— Poultry Stock (Fonds Blanc de Volaille)

Yield: 2 to 3 quarts

You get good flavor out of fresh bones and meat, as well as from bones and scraps from a roast chicken or the remains of the Thanksgiving turkey; a mixture of fresh and cooked is fine. For chicken stock, the older the bird the more character—a stewing hen is ideal. But how often will you find that in your usual supermarket? You will sometimes see packages of necks, and backs, and wing tips. If you do, grab them for your freezer. You will usually have more chance of finding what you want in ethnic markets. Save in your freezer any cooked or raw scraps from chicken and turkey, such as necks, gizzards, hearts, bones, and trimmings. For example, if I am making a quantity of stock and expect to freeze some of it, I wait until I have at least 2 quarts of scraps, then I cook up a batch. However, if I'm roasting or broiling a chicken for dinner, I take whatever little collection of bones and scraps it bequeaths me and let them simmer while the chicken cooks; this will give me maybe only ½ cup, but that's enough for my deglazing sauce, my little jus.

Useful equipment suggested

In addition to a soup pot or big saucepan and cover, you will want a colander, a big strainer, a fine-meshed strainer, and a second and smaller pot or a bowl, preferably stainless steel. A fine-screened skimmer is especially useful here, as is a really big long-handled kitchen spoon.

Simmering the stock

The making of a simple, usable, all-purpose white poultry stock is simple indeed. First wash the raw chicken or turkey pieces—I always rinse them rapidly in hot water. Pull off and discard any loose fat, and turn the pieces into a pot with cold water to cover by 1 inch. Bring rapidly to the boil, and immediately reduce to the simmer—if you keep the stock boiling hard, you will cloud it, and it's worthwhile keeping it clear, just in case you need clear stock. Almost at once gray scum will rise to the surface. Skim it off until it ceases to rise—usually in 7 to

Jacques

In classical cooking, several kinds of "white" and "brown" stocks—made with different kinds of bones and by different methods—are kept on hand for use in specific recipes. Often brown veal stock is further reduced to a thick, syrupy liquid called "demi-glace," which is used as a flavorful but bland base for a variety of distinct sauces. You might use it in one instance to deglaze the roasting pan for leg of lamb, along with red wine. Or another time, use it to deglaze the sauté pan for a *steak au poivre*, with some cognac. The sauces in each case will take on the character of the different meats and flavorings, though they have been made with the same demi-glace.

Though it is so versatile, I don't usually make demi-glace at home anymore—unless I am making a classic dish for some special occasion. Instead, as Julia does, my wife, Gloria, and I always save the juices left over from a veal roast or a roast chicken, remove the fat, and keep them in the freezer. These juices are essentially similar to demi-glace; they have enormous flavor concentrated into small volume, with lots of natural gelatin. And we can use them whenever we need to make a sauce in another dish. In fact, my mother, who is a chef and ran a restaurant most of her life, did exactly the same thing. She was never classically trained and didn't make demi-glace, but would always make great sauces from natural leftover juices.

(continued on page 41)

8 minutes. Set a cover askew over the pot—never cover the pot completely or it will boil and cloud the stock. Simmer slowly, skimming off scum and fat occasionally, for about an hour.

Salt

You will note that no salt has been added yet, because you will be reducing the stock and a normal salting now would make it far too salty later. However, I find it difficult to judge the stock quality when it is unsalted, and I always stir in a very small bit, just enough so that I can taste the stock.

Aromatic vegetables and herbs

When I'm doing a stock just to have one on hand, I add nothing else at all except that little bit of salt discussed above. However, when I am making a chicken soup, or a special sauce, along with my 2 quarts of chicken bits, I'll put in

> 1 imported bay leaf
> A handful of fresh parsley stems
> 1 cup chopped onion
> ½ cup peeled and chopped carrot
> ½ cup chopped celery

Straining and degreasing the stock

Drain the stock through a colander into a saucepan or bowl. Wash out the pot and pour the stock through a fine-meshed sieve back into the pot or a smaller saucepan. The fat will rise to the surface in a few minutes.

Chilling. The easiest way to get rid of the fat, if you are not in a hurry, is to let the stock cool, then chill it and peel the solidified fat off the surface.

Fat separator. Or use a Pyrex fat-separator pitcher with its spout on the bottom. You pour in the stock, let the fat rise to the top, and then pour the clear stock out from the spout until the liquid fat appears in it, at which point you stop pouring.

The endless skim. Or just skim, and skim, and skim the fat off the surface with your big kitchen spoon.

Final fat removal. When all possible fat is to be removed, as for making the clarified stock for an aspic or a consommé, bring the degreased stock to a bare simmer and, off heat, drag pieces of a clean white paper towel over the surface to blot up the fat globules.

Strengthening and flavoring the stock

To intensify flavor, boil degreased stock down rapidly by half or more, until it has developed flavor and strength.

Storing stock

Pour the stock into a container and let cool uncovered in the refrigerator. Then cover and chill or freeze. Warning: never cover a warm stock or it will sour.

White Veal Stock (Fonds Blanc)

Yield: 2 to 3 quarts

Veal stock is particularly good in stews and braises, since raw veal bones have their own special flavor. Furthermore, they are naturally gelatinous (especially the knuckles), meaning that they give a certain body to the stock. Have the bones sawed into 1½-to-2-inch pieces. Since they release loads of scum at first, I always advise that you blanch them before beginning. To do so, bring them to the boil in cold water to cover and skim off the scum as it continues to rise for several minutes, drain, rinse off the scum under cold running water, and return the bones to the pot. Proceed exactly as for the preceding chicken-stock recipe, but veal stock will need about 3 hours of simmering. Add water as needed so the ingredients are always submerged.

Brown Chicken or Turkey Stock

To make a brown stock, simply whack the bones and scraps into pieces 2 inches long, and sauté them with a little vegetable oil in a heavy frying pan until nicely browned all over. Or you can roast meat bones in the oven—but not poultry, because poultry bones burn easily and will give an off taste. For a brown stock, you usually include the aromatic vegetables listed previously, and I always have more success browning the vegetables separately. Then proceed as directed in the master recipe, page 39.

Flavorful Dark Stock

Throughout our recipes, we call for "flavorful dark stock" as a braising liquid, or for deglazing pan juices. Either of the dark stocks in this section—Brown Chicken or Turkey Stock (above), or Brown Meat Stock (page 42)—can be used. If you have no time, make Julia's Quick Dark Stock. But the best solution for the home cook is to keep a good supply of frozen small stocks, sauces, and meat juices, as we describe in our comments here—these are the most flavorful dark stocks of all, and the ones we use.

Julia's Quick Dark Stock

An acceptable substitute for a small amount of stock can be made from a can of beef bouillon, the low-sodium variety. Simmer it for half an hour or so with a handful of diced carrots, onion, and celery, perhaps a tomato, and a little dry white wine or vermouth. Strain, season if necessary, and use in your pan sauce.

Jacques (continued from page 39)

Gloria is usually the one who makes our all-purpose stock. It is basically a "white" chicken stock, but she mixes in some Oriental flavors—she blackens shallots and a piece of fresh ginger on the tip of a skewer directly over the gas burner, and adds these to the liquid, along with a piece of star anise. This gives the stock both a darker color and a slightly exotic flavor. We have this all the time in the freezer too.

Saving Up for Stock

Just as Julia and I do throughout this book, many cookbooks (and chefs on television) tell you to save for stock not only bones but stems of parsley, leek leaves, tomato skins, and the like, and to pack them in plastic wrap for the freezer. This works in theory but it's tedious, and after a while you accumulate seemingly hundreds of small packages with crystallized ice around them. So one day you look inside the freezer and throw them all away.

Here's a more practical method: In the freezer, I always have an empty, rinsed-out milk carton. So, when I am working in the kitchen, I keep a bowl in front of me, and I put into it anything that can go in a stock: parsley stems, the seeds and skins of tomatoes, washed leek tops, trimmings from potatoes or carrots, etc. All of this goes into the milk carton. Then, the next time I am making a stock, I simply take the carton out of the freezer, cut off the cardboard, and put the whole frozen block directly into the stockpot. Don't worry about proportions—it doesn't matter.

Julia on Salt and Pepper

I use regular table salt and kosher salt for cooking. I don't go in for fancy salts at all. To me, salt is salt. The prices for some of these "gourmet"-type salts are ridiculous and I don't want to be bothered with three different kinds. There's enough clutter in the kitchen anyway.

Some people say sea salt has more flavor—but if you need more saltiness, I say just add a little more regular salt. I often use coarse kosher salt for soups and stocks, because you can pick it up with your fingers. I do serve it with a boiled dinner, where I want the grains to stand out.

Kosher salt does not dissolve instantly. You might add it to a dish and taste for seasoning, but because it hasn't dissolved yet you think it needs more salt—so you add more and end up with too much.

As for pepper, I use freshly ground white pepper frequently because I do not want black speckles in pale-colored food. As a rule, I use black pepper when it doesn't make any difference—and white pepper when it does.

Brown Meat Stock (Fonds Brun)

Yield: 2 to 3 quarts

For either beef or veal bones, or the 2 combined, the more meat clinging to them the better. Neck and hip are desirable, as well as joints. Raw is best, but cooked bones are usable, too. Arrange them in a roasting pan, in 1 layer if possible, and spread the aromatic vegetables listed on page 40 among and around the bones. You might want to increase the vegetable amounts by half, to accompany 2 to 3 quarts of bones. Roast for an hour or more in the middle third level of a 400°F oven, turning and basting occasionally. You want them well browned but not burned.

Lift the ingredients into your big pot, pour out and discard accumulated fat, and deglaze the roasting pan by pouring in ½ inch of red wine and/or water. Bring to the simmer on top of the stove, scraping up brown bits and coagulated juices from the bottom of the pan with a wooden spoon; pour this into the pot with the browned bones.

Also add the following to the pot (again, assuming you have 2 to 3 quarts of bones):

> 1 medium herb bouquet, tied or untied
> (see page 351), also including 2 large
> cloves of unpeeled smashed garlic
> 1½ cups chopped cored but unpeeled
> ripe red tomatoes (or half fresh and half
> canned Italian plum tomatoes)

Brown Lamb Stock

Make lamb stock exactly the same way as beef stock, but because lamb has its own special character it is always cooked separately.

Fish Stock
(Fumé de Poisson)
and Seafood Stocks

When you are having a fish soup or a special sauce for poached fish, you need a base for it, to give flavor and interest. Ideally this is a fish stock, which is easy indeed to make from the heads, bones, and scraps left over from preparing the fish for market. Use bones and white skin from one kind or a variety of lean fish here, like sole (for an especially high-class stock), halibut, whiting, flounder, cod, hake—no oily fish like mackerel, bluefish, salmon. You might make a good quantity while you are at it, since you can freeze what you don't need.

Yield: 2 to 3 cups

2 to 3 pounds (2 to 3 quarts) lean fresh
   or frozen fish heads, bones, and trimmings
1 to 1½ cups thinly sliced onion (1 or 2
   medium onions)
½ cup or so very thinly sliced celery stalk
½ cup or so thinly sliced white of leek
   (optional)
A handful of fresh parsley stems (no
   leaves, which will color the stock)
About 1 cup dry white wine or ⅔ cup
   dry white French vermouth (optional)
¼ tsp salt (just a little salt at this point)

Jacques on Salt and Pepper

I cook with both kosher salt and regular salt. Because I add salt with my fingers, kosher salt, being easy to grab, is particularly useful. Although it may look like I am picking it up in random pinches, my fingers are differentiating the amount as if I were using a measuring spoon.

In my recipes I specify exactly how much salt I use at each stage, even very small amounts, because it is important to season sufficiently in many situations where you can't "salt to taste"—since the food is still raw and tasting is impossible. I have found that people frequently undersalt at such times. Later on, they know that something is missing but they can't figure out what it is. And then, even if you realize that salt is needed, at this late point in the process—after cooking or at the table—the addition of salt will not have the desired effect of bringing up the other flavors.

All designations here are for conventional salt unless kosher salt is specified. Because the crystals of kosher salt are larger, it has more volume, and a given amount will add less saltiness than the same measure of table salt. So if you want to use kosher salt, you will have to use a bit more. And conversely, if a recipe calls for a certain amount of kosher salt, be sure to use less regular salt—or you will oversalt.

When it comes to pepper, it is always freshly ground black pepper for me. The black speckles in a pale dish don't bother me the way they do Julia. Only the flavor counts, and black pepper, to me, has the best.

Shrimp Stock

Make shrimp stock either in the same way as the chicken stock (page 39)—simmering the shells with onion, celery, leek, and a touch of white wine—or use the lobster system below, first sautéing the vegetables, then adding and sautéing the shells.

Plain Lobster Stock

After a great feast of boiled or steamed lobster, don't throw all those beautiful shells away! Pick them over, discarding any extraneous matter such as the sand-filled stomach sacs from the chests (page 251), and roughly chop them up. Boil them slowly in a big pot of water barely to cover, strain, and there you are. Use some of the stock in the following broth, and save the rest in the freezer for use in fish soups and chowders, and in the Lobster Stew on page 252.

Strew all the above ingredients in a roomy stainless-steel pot and pour in cold water to cover them by ½ inch. Bring to the simmer, skim off the scum which will continue to rise for several minutes, and simmer uncovered for 25 to 30 minutes only—longer cooking does not improve flavor. Strain into a colander set over a stainless-steel saucepan, pressing juices out of ingredients. Rinse out the cooking pot, pour the stock back in, then pour it through a fine-mesh sieve into the saucepan.

Taste very carefully for strength—it will probably need reducing to concentrate flavor. Boil it down uncovered, until it has the flavor you wish.

To store, let the stock cool, uncovered, then cover and refrigerate or freeze.

Variation: Fish Stock Without Fish Frames

Unless you live by the sea, where fish is caught and processed, there is hardly a fish bone to be had in today's markets, except for salmon, trout, and occasionally freshwater fish. Your market buys its fish already boned, filleted, and ready to cook. You can use fish fillets rather than bones if you want to pay the price, or you can use half plain canned low-salt chicken broth and half water, which I have found works very well in giving that little punch of flavor.

Simmer the fish or broth with the other ingredients called for in the basic recipe, and you will have a fine stock if made with fish, a reasonable substitute if made with broth.

A Strong Lobster Shell Broth

So many eaters never touch the little legs and the chests—those treasure chests—with all their good meat. But it's worthwhile sometimes to make a real broth, the way you would prepare the sauce for a lobster *à l'américaine*. Here's a somewhat elaborate method for making a first-class broth to use in lobster dishes, such as a sauté or soufflé.

Yield: 1 cup or so of fine strong broth

1 cup fairly finely chopped onions
½ cup fairly finely chopped carrots
2 Tbs vegetable oil
6 chests from 6 boiled or steamed lobsters (stomach sacs discarded, as on page 251, and the chests halved lengthwise, then roughly chopped)
2 Tbs cognac (optional)
1 small clove garlic, mashed
1 ripe red plum tomato, chopped (or 1 Tbs tomato paste)
½ cup beef broth
1 cup Plain Lobster Stock (see sidebar) or Fish Stock (page 43)
½ cup full-bodied dry white wine or ¼ cup dry white French vermouth (optional)
1 sprig of fresh tarragon or ¼ tsp fragrant dried tarragon
Salt and freshly ground pepper to taste

Sauté the onions and carrots in a small pan with a tablespoon of oil for 5 minutes or so, until tender and beginning to brown. Set aside. Meanwhile, film a 10-inch non-stick sauté pan with oil, set over moderately high heat, and when it is not quite smoking, toss in the lobster chests and pieces. Sauté, tossing, for several minutes, until beginning to brown lightly. Stir in the cooked onions and carrots; then you can pour in the optional cognac and set aflame. Stir in the rest of the ingredients and bring to the simmer. Cover partially and let simmer for 30 minutes. Strain into another saucepan, pressing juices out of ingredients. Taste carefully for seasoning, boiling down to concentrate flavor if necessary. When cool, refrigerate or freeze.

Julia

With all of our soups, a fine strong chicken stock provides the base of flavor. To make sure they are perfectly seasoned, continually taste and adjust your seasonings as you add your ingredients. For my cream soup, only a blender can make the very fine rice purée you want here—a food processor just won't do the complete purée needed to thicken the soup. Some people think they can get along without a blender, but you can't. This is a recipe that proves the point.

Quick Soups with Chicken Stock

Here are several fast versions of homey chicken soups. They will all taste best, of course, with fine homemade chicken stock (page 39).

Julia's creamy chicken soup is made with absolutely no cream—its satisfying, smooth texture comes from a thick purée of cooked rice. With a spoonful or two of sour cream and a sprinkling of chives for garnish—and some good homemade bread—this is hearty enough for a cold-weather lunch.

Jacques's chicken noodle soup has all the taste, texture, and universally curative powers that only this soup can provide. It's teeming with thin angel-hair pasta and lightly flavored with fresh scallions, and once your broth is boiling, it's on the table in less than five minutes.

Julia's Creamy Chicken Soup with Rice

Yield: 6 to 7 cups, serving 4 to 5

6 cups homemade chicken stock, plus
  more if needed
2 cups very tender boiled white rice, plus
  more if needed (page 169)
Salt and freshly ground white pepper
$1\frac{1}{2}$ cups thinly sliced mushroom caps
6 ounces skinless, boneless chicken
  breast, sliced into thin julienne strips
  $1\frac{1}{2}$ inches long (about $1\frac{1}{2}$ cups)
$1\frac{1}{2}$ Tbs minced shallots, sautéed in butter
  until soft

For serving
Sour cream (1 to 2 Tbs per serving)
Chopped fresh chives or parsley

Special equipment
An electric blender; a 3-quart saucepan; a
  medium whisk

Reserve 2½ cups of stock and heat the rest in the saucepan. Put 1½ cups of the reserved stock in the blender with 2 cups of the very tender cooked rice. Purée together on the highest speed for a minute or longer, until you have a very thick and completely smooth purée. Pour this into the hot stock, rinse the jar with a little more stock, and pour into the soup.

Bring to the simmer, whisking. Simmer for several minutes, allowing the soup to thicken. Correct seasoning. Stir in the mushroom slices, strips of chicken breast, and the sautéed shallots. Simmer the soup for several minutes, to cook the mushrooms and chicken. Carefully correct seasoning again.

Ladle the soup into bowls, spoon on a dollop of sour cream, and sprinkle chives or parsley over the top.

Jacques

My chicken noodle on the next page is the kind of soup that my mother made for me, and that we made for my daughter when she was sick. For this very fast version, I like the kind of thin angel-hair pasta that is dried in little bundles or nests. If you can't find them, you can use any small pasta, such as alphabet noodles. You can also make it different with quick-cooking grain products such as oatmeal, couscous, cream of wheat, or cornmeal grits.

Whatever kind of noodle or cereal you use, scallions add wonderful flavor and look very nice; sliced leeks would be fine too. You could add sliced mushrooms, just as in Julia's creamy chicken soup. Mushrooms that are dark, with open caps, are more flavorful than the firm white ones—and they are often cheaper, too.

Julia's New England Chicken Chowder

A chowder base is a fine start for soups that you can make ahead and have in your freezer. You can serve the chowder as is—a potato and onion soup—or you can simmer whatever else you like in it. Add fish and it's a New England fish chowder; add broccoli or spinach or mushrooms, and so forth.

To make a chowder base for 6, start out by sautéing 4 cups of sliced onions in 2 tablespoons of butter. When tender but not browned, blend in 2 tablespoons of flour and cook slowly for 2 minutes; then remove from heat and blend in, by dribbles at first, 4 cups of warm chicken stock. Add 4 cups of sliced "boiling" potatoes and an herb bouquet (page 351), and simmer 15 to 20 minutes, or until the potatoes are tender. Taste, and add salt and pepper as needed.

The base is now ready to become whatever you wish. For this chicken chowder, you will want the equivalent of at least 1 boneless chicken thigh or 1 medium boneless chicken breast half per serving. Cut the meat into slivers about ⅛ inch thick and 1½ inches long. Shortly before serving, bring the chowder base to the simmer, stir in the chicken slivers, and simmer just a minute or so, until cooked through. At this point you may want to blend in half a cup or so of sour cream. Taste again for seasoning and stir in about ¼ cup of chopped fresh parsley and/or chives.

Serve in big soup bowls and accompany with pilot crackers or fresh French bread.

Jacques's Chicken Noodle Soup

Yield: About 5 cups, serving 4

> 4 cups homemade chicken stock or low-sodium canned chicken broth
> ¾ cup or so thinly sliced scallions (4 or 5 whole scallions)
> 4 ounces angel-hair pasta, preferably in bundles or nests
> ¼ tsp freshly ground black pepper
> Salt

Bring the stock to a boil over high heat; add the scallions and the pasta, breaking up the angel-hair "nests" if using, and stir to make sure the noodles separate. Adjust heat to maintain a gentle boil and cook for 4 minutes or more, until the noodles are tender. Add the pepper and the salt to taste (depending on the saltiness of the broth), and serve.

A Richer Variation
Use cornmeal and cream instead of the angel-hair pasta. Put ½ cup of cornmeal in a bowl and pour ½ cup of the hot chicken stock over it, whisking for 4 or 5 seconds until smooth. Now put the moistened cornmeal into the pot of hot broth, add the scallions, and bring to a boil, stirring occasionally. Add ½ cup of cream, salt and pepper to taste, and warm through.

Opposite: Onion Soup Gratinée

Julia

It is important to cook the onions properly and thoroughly. Start them slowly, cooking them covered until tender, then brown them over moderately high heat. Sometimes I add a bit of sugar to deepen the color, but you must always stir frequently so the onions don't burn. For convenience, cook the onions while you are doing something else at the stove. Then you can put them aside—or even freeze them—and finish the soup later.

In Paris, we used to go to the big open market in Les Halles in the old part of the city at four in the morning, when the day began. Around six a.m., everyone in the market would stop in one of the cafés for onion soup and a glass of red wine. They still do at Rungis, the vast new market outside of Paris. It's cold there in the winter and you need a warm-up.

Onion Soup

A few onions, some excellent chicken stock, and three-quarters of an hour are about all you need to make this delicious soup. Its rich taste and deep color come from the first slow sauté of the onions, which concentrates their flavor and allows their natural sugars to caramelize in the pan. You can serve the soup plain or in the popular gratinée version—baked in a crock and sealed with a thick crust of baguette croutons and Gruyère cheese.

Jacques's Onion Soup Gratinée

Yield: 6 cups, enough for 5 or 6 small crocks

2 Tbs oil
1 Tbs butter
1½ pounds onions, peeled and thinly
    sliced (about 5 cups)
1 tsp minced fresh thyme sprigs, or ½ tsp
    dried thyme
½ tsp salt, or more to taste
5 cups hot chicken stock, homemade, or
    low-sodium canned broth
¼ tsp freshly ground black pepper, or
    more to taste
¼ cup red or white wine (optional)
For each crock of onion soup gratinée
3 or 4 slices of baguette, about ¼ inch
    thick cut on the diagonal
2 to 2½ ounces Gruyère or Emmentaler
    cheese, grated (about ¾ cup)

Special equipment

A heavy-bottomed 3- or 4-quart saucepan, with a cover, to make the soup; small (11-ounce) soup crocks or a large crock or heavy casserole for the gratinée version

Set the saucepan over medium-low heat and add the oil and butter. When the butter has melted, add the onions, thyme, and ½ teaspoon of salt and mix together thoroughly. Cover the pan and cook for about 10 minutes, stirring occasionally. When the onions are quite tender, uncover and raise the heat slightly. Cook for another 20 to 25 minutes, stirring frequently, until the onions are dark brown and have caramelized in the pan. (Lower the heat if the onions are in danger of burning.)

Stir in the hot stock, scraping any crystallized juices from the bottom of the pan, and bring the soup to the boil. Taste and adjust the seasonings, adding salt and ¼ teaspoon of black pepper or more to taste, and wine, if you like. (The amount of salt will vary, depending on the broth.) Cover and simmer for about 10 minutes.

The soup may be served plain or gratinéed, as follows.

For onion soup gratinée

To make croutons, toast a dozen or so baguette slices on a baking sheet in a 400°F oven, until crisp and starting to color, about 10 minutes.

When the soup is ready, arrange the individual crocks on the baking sheet. Put the croutons (whole or broken into large pieces) into the bottom of each crock, and sprinkle about 2 tablespoons of cheese on top. Ladle in a cup or more soup, to fill the crock to the inner rim (about ¼ inch from the top). Heap a large mound of grated cheese all over the surface of the soup, using the rest of the cheese for each crock.

Place the baking sheet in the oven and bake for 30 to 40 minutes, until the cheese is dark golden brown and has formed a crust over the soup. Move the hot crocks carefully onto individual plates and serve.

Jacques

It's easy to vary your onion soup. For more flavor, add a bit of white wine—or red wine, as Julia prefers, which adds some color as well. You can serve it plain, just with croutons. If you don't have small crocks for the gratinée, assemble all the croutons and cheese in one large tureen or casserole, and bake it the same way. (I would not use bowls like those in the photograph on page 49, because they don't have rims to contain the melted cheese, but sometimes you have to make do with what you have on hand.)

The *gratinée lyonnaise*, which we used to make in Lyons, where I come from, is baked in a big crock, with lots of croutons and cheese, so it is very thick and crusty. When it came to the table, we broke a hole in the top crust and poured in an egg yolk whipped with sweet port. Then we'd reach into the hole and stir the wine into the soup. You might try that version too.

Julia

Leeks and potatoes have enough flavor to make a wonderful soup, and I like it made with plain water so nothing interferes with the pristine leek-and-potato flavor. You don't need a recipe for making variations—just play it by ear, blending in other vegetables with the base, such as turnips, broccoli, or spinach. The classic—and particularly attractive—combination is leek and potato with watercress, described on page 56.

To keep my basic soup white—which I like, especially for vichyssoise—I use the white parts of the leek and only the pale parts of the green. Save all the other, dark-green leaves for stock. As for potatoes, you can use a good all-purpose variety, such as a Yukon Gold, but I like russets, the baking potatoes, which have lots of starch. They crumble when boiled, but this is no problem if you are mashing or puréeing the soup anyway. Do not wash the potatoes after you have peeled and cut them into pieces, because you want all their starch to thicken the soup. To keep the vegetables from sinking to the bottom of the soup, I often add a sprinkling of flour to the vegetables as I am sautéing them—the flour thickens the liquid and keeps the vegetables in suspension.

Leek Soup

For the home soup maker, the marriage of leeks and potatoes is a heavenly one. Cooked together in broth or water just until tender, with the simplest seasoning, the two unassuming vegetables have an affinity, yielding a thick, satisfying soup of harmonious flavors and hearty textures.

You can serve leek-and-potato soup straight from the pot with the vegetables in coarse chunks, or enjoy its many easy and delicious variations. Without further cooking, you may change the soup's texture and appearance by mashing, straining, or puréeing it, then subtly enhance it with different garnishes and enrichments. Or set some in the refrigerator, to serve chilled, with a bit of cream, as the famed vichyssoise.

Since there's no one formula for a good marriage, here we give you two different ways of making basic leek-and-potato soup: Julia's recipe uses water and a slight thickening of flour and butter; Jacques's uses chicken stock. Each yields 2 quarts of delicious soup in about 30 minutes, ready to serve right away or to vary to your own taste, following our suggestions on page 56.

Julia's Basic Leek and Potato Soup

Yield: 2 quarts

2 Tbs butter

3 cups sliced leeks, white and palest green, trimmed and rinsed as shown on page 54 (from 12 ounces untrimmed leeks)

1½ cups sliced onions (about 6 ounces, or 2 medium onions)

2 Tbs flour

6 cups water

4 cups peeled, diced potatoes, preferably

russets, cut into 2-inch chunks (about
1½ pounds)

1½ tsp salt, or to taste

½ tsp freshly ground white pepper, or to
taste

For serving

Any of the enrichments and garnishes on
page 56

Special equipment

A large, heavy-bottomed 3- or 4-quart
saucepan with cover

Melt the butter in the saucepan over moderate heat. Stir
in the leek and onion pieces to coat with butter, cover the pan,
and reduce the heat. Cook slowly, stirring occasionally, for 10
to 15 minutes, until the vegetables are very soft but not colored.
Uncover, sprinkle on the flour, stir to distribute it well, and
cook for 2 minutes over moderate heat. Remove from heat and
let cool for a moment.

Then, stirring continually, gradually pour in 1½ cups of the
water and bring to the simmer. When the liquid is smooth and
starts to thicken, stir in the rest of the water, then add the potatoes
and season with salt and pepper. Quickly heat the soup to a gentle boil, cover the pan, and lower the heat. Simmer for about 20
minutes, until the potatoes are tender. Correct seasonings.

To serve, mash, blend, or purée the soup to the desired
consistency and adjust the seasonings. Garnish or vary the soup
with additional ingredients as suggested on page 56.

To store the soup, let cool uncovered, then refrigerate or
freeze.

Jacques

There are many ways to vary
the look and texture of the soup. If you
first cut the leeks and potatoes into
small, even pieces, you will have a
potage taillé—a cut soup—that will
cook quickly and won't need any further processing. My favorite form,
though, is a purée of leek-and-potato
soup—*potage parmentier*—which I
make with a hand-cranked food mill.
When pressed through the disk with
the smallest holes, the purée has a fine
texture and any fibers are removed.

The chilled form of this soup,
vichyssoise, became famous here in
America after it was created by Louis
Diat at the Ritz-Carlton in New York
City. But I learned it in France, at
the Plaza-Athénée, from his brother,
Lucien Diat, the chef when I worked
there. They came from a small town
near Vichy, where their mother used to
make the chilled version from leftover
potato-and-leek soup.

Thrust the knife into the leek about 2 inches from the root end and slice down through the trimmed green leaves.

The prepared leeks

Jacques's Method for Preparing Leeks

A member of the aromatic *Allium* family of vegetables—along with onions, garlic, scallions—leeks are considered poor man's asparagus in Europe. Not so here, where they are often expensive and hard to find. But recently leeks have become more readily available at fairly moderate prices.

Almost all of the leek can be used in cooking. Trim the tender white and pale-green parts to use in soups and other dishes, and use the layers of fibrous dark-green leaves in making stock. Leeks are hilled with sand and soil as they grow, so all the layers must be separated and rinsed thoroughly to get rid of the accumulated dirt.

To have enough sliced leeks for our soup recipes here, start with about ¾ pound of whole, untrimmed leeks (1 large or several smaller leeks). If you want to cook only the white parts, as Julia prefers, you may need a bit more.

To trim, clean, and slice a leek

Trim off the root end with its beard and discard. Remove the toughest outer layers of the leek. (Save these for stock, unless spoiled.) To get the most tender parts for soup, don't just cut up the white part of leek. Cut off the leaves of each layer at the point where the dark green begins, then, as shown in the photograph, make 2 or 3 slices lengthwise, starting a couple of inches in from the root end, to expose the interior. (Rinse the leek under running water if you are not slicing it into short lengths.)

Slice the split leek crosswise into pieces of any length— you want ½-inch pieces for soup.

To clean, dump all the pieces into a large amount of lukewarm water and stir to separate the layers and rinse off the dirt. Let the dirt settle, then lift the pieces from the water and drain well. (Do not pour the leeks and rinse water through a strainer.)

Jacques's Basic Leek and Potato Soup

Yield: 2 quarts

2 Tbs olive, canola, or corn oil

4 cups sliced leeks, trimmed and rinsed
as shown (from 12 ounces untrimmed
leeks)

1½ cups sliced onion, 1-inch pieces
(about 6 ounces)

6 cups hot chicken stock, homemade, or
low-sodium canned broth

4 cups peeled, diced potatoes, 2-inch
chunks (about 1½ pounds)

Salt to taste, depending on the saltiness of
broth

½ tsp freshly ground black pepper

For serving

Any of the enrichments and garnishes on
page 56

Special equipment

A large, heavy-bottomed 3- or 4-quart
saucepan with cover

Heat the oil in the saucepan, stir in the leek and onion
pieces, and sauté for about 5 minutes over moderate heat, to
soften.

Add the chicken stock and potato chunks, and season
with salt to taste and the pepper. Bring the soup to a boil over
high heat, cover the pan, and adjust the heat to maintain a gentle boil. Cook for about 20 minutes, until the potatoes are quite
tender.

Mash, blend, or purée it to the desired consistency and
adjust the seasonings. Serve the soup right away, or set aside
until serving time. Garnish or vary the soup with additional
ingredients as suggested on page 56.

Finishes, Garnishes, and Variations for Basic Leek and Potato Soup

Either of our base soups can be varied as follows:

For different textures For the simplest country-style soup, serve as is, with the chunks of soft vegetables floating in it.

For a more uniform, but still somewhat coarse texture, mash the vegetables right in the saucepan with a wide wooden spoon or potato masher, or blend *very briefly* with an immersion blender.

For a smooth purée, pour the hot soup through a food mill, fitted with the fine disk, set over a bowl. Purée the vegetables into the broth, then stir to blend. (You can also purée the vegetables to desired consistency in batches in a food processor or a conventional blender, or right in the pan using an immersion blender.)

Enrichments and garnishes For a rich finish, stir any of the following into mashed or puréed soup base: 2 or more tablespoons of unsalted butter; ½ cup or more heavy cream or sour cream.

To garnish, scatter any of the following over each serving: buttered croutons (page 108); fronds of fresh chervil; chopped fresh chives; chopped fresh parsley. Or add a spoonful of sour cream or crème fraîche, in a swirl or a mound.

Chilled vichyssoise Finely purée the soup base through a food mill or other appliance, then chill thoroughly. Before serving, stir in ½ to 1 cup heavy cream or a mixture of cream and milk, and a tablespoon or two of chopped fresh chives, and adjust the seasonings. Sprinkle more chopped chives over each serving.

Watercress soup While the soup base is cooking, wash 1 or 2 large bunches of watercress and remove the thick stems. Reserve a few whole leaves for garnishing, and finely chop the rest. When the potatoes are tender, mash them in the pot to make a coarse purée, toss in the watercress, and simmer all together for 4 or 5 minutes. Stir in ½ cup of cream or other enrichment and adjust the seasoning. Serve hot or cold; float a few whole watercress leaves on top of each serving. (If you wish, process the soup to a fine purée after simmering the watercress.)

Other vegetable variations Leek-and-potato soup base can be transformed by the addition of many vegetables, just as with watercress. Among the possibilities are spinach, carrots, broccoli, Brussels sprouts, cauliflower, parsnips, turnips, squash, and pumpkin. If using raw vegetables, chop them fine, add to the simmering soup base, and cook until tender. Cooked vegetables can be puréed with the leek and potato pieces and mixed with broth. Be sure to adjust the seasoning as you add ingredients, and finish and garnish as suggested.

Do-ahead soup Purée the soup base and freeze in small containers. Defrost, heat, and garnish or vary the soup with other vegetables as suggested.

Jacques's Lamb Barley Soup

Although this soup can be made with raw lamb bones, my preference is to use the cooked bones (including any leftover juices and pieces of meat) from a roast leg of lamb. This solid, robust soup makes an entire meal when served with crusted bread and a salad.

Yield: About 3 quarts

About 2 pounds of lamb bones, meat trimmings, and juices from a roast leg of lamb

6 ounces (about 1 cup) pearl barley

2 cups diced mushrooms (about 6 ounces)

1½ cups diced celery stalks

1½ cups peeled and diced carrots

1 cup diced onions

3 cups diced leeks (about 2 leeks washed and diced)

1 Tbs salt

1 tsp pepper

3 Tbs chopped parsley

Lea & Perrins Worcestershire sauce (optional)

Place the lamb bones, trimmings, and juices in a large pot with 3 quarts of water and the barley. Bring to a boil, lower the heat, cover, and boil gently for 1 hour. Remove the bones with a skimmer and set aside.

Add the mushrooms, celery, carrots, onions, leeks, salt, and pepper to the pot, bring to a boil, cover, and cook gently for another hour.

Meanwhile, pick the meat off the bones (I had about 2½ cups) and shred it into ½-inch pieces. Add to the soup as it cooks.

At serving time, add the parsley to the soup and serve. Let the guests sprinkle some Worcestershire in their soup, if desired.

Slice through the onion half horizontally, going from stem end to root end at even intervals.

To chop an onion, cut it first in half.

Lay the flat side on a board and cut vertical slices ⅛ to ¼ inch apart.

Bring your knife down sharply and chop through to cut the onion into small pieces.

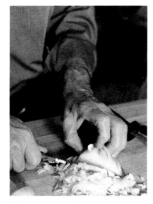
Continue to slice, moving your fingers holding the onion back after each slice, until you reach the root end.

Julia

The soup base is what really counts here, even more than the seafood that you put in it. You want to develop fully the flavors of all the aromatic vegetables and herbs. I like to soften the onion in the olive oil for a good 10 minutes, add the garlic, tomatoes, and seasonings, and then simmer all for at least 45 minutes. With this kind of flavorful base, you can make a Mediterranean-style fish soup wherever you can get a piece of fish, even in Kansas City. In fact, you really don't need fish—you might just add potatoes to the base and you'll have a fine soup.

I love *rouille* in this kind of soup. I often judge the worth of a cookbook by how it does a *rouille*. It's of prime importance that the garlic be thoroughly puréed, because it's the garlic that starts the emulsion. I like to pound mine into a paste with salt, using my big marble mortar and heavy pestle, the way it's traditionally done in France.

A food processor chops the garlic rather than puréeing it, but Jacques's method of processing the garlic along with the bread and cooked potato works for him. Here the bread, potato, and egg yolk all serve as binding agents, thickening the purée and helping to emulsify the olive oil. I slather a big spoonful of *rouille* on several croutons and place them in the empty soup bowl, then ladle the fish and broth over.

Mediterranean Seafood Stew

Here is a hearty main-course soup in the Mediterranean style—a saffron-tinted broth brimming with fish chunks, scallops, clams, and herbs. Serve it with the strong mayonnaiselike garlic sauce known as *rouille*, which gives it such a great swirl of color and burst of garlic flavor that you'll think you're eating a bowl of bouillabaisse in a bistro in Marseilles.

This is so chock-full of seafood that we call it a stew, but the essence of the dish is a versatile soup base. Plain fish stock, or one of its simple substitutes (page 43), is simmered with the aromatic vegetables and herbs. Then, when you are ready to eat, you add the fish and shellfish for only 3 or 4 minutes of poaching.

In general, fish with lean, moderately firm flesh are the most suitable for this kind of dish, since they will cook quickly and hold their shape. Good choices are cod, halibut, haddock, hake, monkfish, sea bass, and snapper. All kinds of shellfish will be good in this soup base—mussels or oysters cooked in soup until the shells open, just the way the clams are done; or add small shrimp at the very end of cooking, since they need only boil for a few moments to cook through.

You can use just one kind of fish if you like, although Mediterranean fish soups typically contain several varieties, and a mix of seafood looks and tastes appealing. For convenience, buy fish fillets and simply cut them into chunks, or buy whole fish if you want the head and bones for fish stock; use skinless fillets, or leave the skin on, making sure that the scales are removed (to scale, skin, or fillet a fish, see pages 218–219). Of course, you can cook a greater amount of fish and shellfish than specified here if you want to have an even more bountiful stew—the soup base will only become more flavorful as you cook more seafood in it.

Jacques's Mediterranean Seafood Stew or Soup

Yield: About 3 quarts, serving 6 to 8

For the soup

  1½ pounds fish fillets, a mixture of 2 or 3
    fish, or all one kind (see recipe intro-
    duction)
  1½ pounds small clams, littlenecks or
    cherrystones
  ½ pound scallops
  3 Tbs olive oil
  1½ cups chopped onions
  5 large scallions, white and green parts,
    thinly sliced (about 1 cup)
  1 Tbs chopped garlic (2 or 3 large cloves)
  2 cups fresh or canned tomatoes cored
    and chopped into ½-inch chunks, with
    skin, juice, and seeds (about 1 pound
    of fresh tomatoes)
  1 cup white wine, like Chardonnay
  4 cups fish stock (page 43)
  1 tsp chopped fresh thyme
  ½ tsp salt, or more if needed (varies with
    saltiness of broth)
  ½ tsp freshly ground black pepper
  1 tsp saffron threads, or less if you wish
  1½ Tbs chopped fresh tarragon leaves

Jacques

Our soup resembles bouilla-baisse—one of the most famous of the Mediterranean fish stews—though it is much simpler to prepare. In Marseilles and other areas, *rouille* (which means "rust," due to its color) is served with bouillabaisse; and saffron is always used in the broth.

Saffron is a flavor that I love. Julia prefers to use just a big pinch in this recipe, but I like to add a greater amount, about 1 teaspoon of saffron threads for this amount of broth. These threads are the dried pistils of the crocus flower, and since it takes about 40,000 crocuses for every pound of saffron, it is easy to understand why this is one of the most expensive spices. Use the finest saffron, from Spain, and add it to the broth for only a few minutes of cooking before you add the fish, to preserve all its flavor.

This soup lends itself to countless variations, in the broth and vegetables as well as in the seafood. As a substitute for fish stock, you can use bottled clam juice, diluted with water; give more flavor to the broth by adding chopped celery, carrots, leeks, mushrooms, or fresh fennel greens, or stir in a small amount of tomato paste. For fish, I sometimes use a lean piece of salmon or a very firm piece of swordfish. The most important thing here is not to overcook the fish. Have everything ready—the croutons, *rouille*, and your guests—before you put the fish in the broth.

For the *rouille*

1 slice firm, home-style white
  bread
6 to 8 large garlic cloves, peeled
⅓ cup cooked potato (1 small
  potato)
¼ cup canned pimiento pieces
¼ cup broth from the soup pot
1 egg yolk
½ tsp salt, plus more to taste
⅛ tsp freshly ground black pepper
⅛ tsp cayenne, or more or less to
  taste
¾ to 1 cup olive oil

For the croutons

24 slices of baguette, about ¼ inch
  thick, cut on the diagonal

Special equipment

A large (4-to-6-quart) heavy-
  bottomed saucepan or soup
  kettle; a food processor

Preliminaries

Skin the fillets if you wish and cut them into even chunks, about an inch thick. (If you want the skin on, make sure it has been scaled.) Scrub the clams and rinse, if necessary. Wash the scallops to remove any sand.

Preheat the oven to 400°F and toast the croutons on a baking sheet until they are crisp and starting to color on both sides, about 10 minutes. Set aside until serving.

Starting the soup base

Heat the oil in the saucepan and stir in the onions, scallions, and garlic. Cook over medium heat until soft, about 5 minutes.

Add the tomatoes, wine, and fish stock, and then stir in the thyme, salt, and pepper. Bring quickly to the boil; meanwhile, taste and adjust seasonings. Cook at a gentle boil for 10 to 15 minutes, partially covered, while you are making the *rouille*.

Making the *rouille*

Tear the bread slice into pieces and put them in the work bowl of the food processor with the garlic cloves. Process until very finely chopped. Add the cooked potato, the canned pimiento, and ¼ cup of broth from the soup pot, and process until completely smooth. Add the egg yolk, salt, black pepper, and cayenne, and process until smooth. With the machine running, pour in the olive oil in a slow, steady stream—taking ½ minute or more—as the emulsion is formed and the sauce becomes completely smooth. Taste and adjust seasonings. Scrape the *rouille* into a bowl.

Finishing the stew/soup and serving

With the soup base at the boil, add all the clams and the saffron and cook for about 2 minutes. Add the fish and the scallops, return to a gentle boil, and cook for 2 to 3 minutes, just until the fish pieces are cooked through and opaque and all of the clams have opened (discard any that remain closed after sitting in the hot broth for several minutes). Stir in the chopped tarragon, taste, and adjust the seasonings for the final time.

Spoon some *rouille* on half of the croutons (or on 2 or 3 per serving). Ladle portions of the seafood and broth into large soup bowls and place some *rouille*-topped croutons alongside each serving—or set them in the broth, if you like. Serve hot, with extra croutons and *rouille* on the side.

Opposite: Mediterranean Seafood Stew

Julia on Soupe aux Moules

Speaking of mussels, their fragrant cooking broth is so very special that I can't resist another recipe—a mussel soup with a julienne of vegetables.

For 6 to 8 servings, prepare Moules Marinière (page 11), remove the meat from the shells, and set aside. Pour the cooking juices (minus any sand) into a quart measure and add fish stock or light chicken broth to measure 4 cups. Put in a 4-quart saucepan 1 cup each of finely julienned carrots, onions, celery, and leeks, fold with 2 tablespoons of warm butter, then add the 4 cups of liquid and simmer until the vegetables are almost tender. Peel, halve, and scoop the seeds out of a large cucumber, cut into fine julienne, and simmer 2 minutes with the vegetables.

Meanwhile make a curry velouté: Melt 2½ tablespoons of butter in a 2-quart saucepan and blend in 2 teaspoons of curry powder and 3 tablespoons of flour. Cook slowly, stirring, for 2 minutes, then remove from heat and let cool briefly. Whisk in 2 cups of hot milk and when well blended bring to the boil over moderate heat, adding salt and white pepper to taste. Pour the velouté into the cooked vegetables and bring to the simmer for 2 minutes, gently blending. Correct seasoning and fold in the mussels.

To serve, heat to warm through, ladle into soup bowls, and top with a spoonful of sour cream and chopped fresh parsley.

Billi-bi

Billi-bi is one of those soups that seduce you the first spoonful you take. It is actually a very simple soup of cream, wine, and the juices of fresh mussels. The shellfish need only a couple of minutes of cooking to release their flavorful essence, and after straining, the soup can be served hot or set aside to chill. Ivory-white and exceedingly rich, billi-bi should be served in small cups or glasses as a luxurious prelude to a special lunch or dinner.

You may recognize this as a variation of the more rustic, brothy appetizer, Moules Marinière (page 11), and you should see the more detailed discussion there about handling and cleaning mussels. As the mussels themselves are not served in billi-bi but remain plump and moist, use them in Moules Ravigote (page 12) as a first course or an hors d'oeuvre.

Jacques's Billi-bi

Yield: About 1 quart, serving 6

3 pounds mussels, washed thoroughly,
  with beards removed (see page 13)
½ cup chopped onions
¼ cup chopped shallots (3 large shallots)
1 Tbs butter
2 bay leaves
5 sprigs parsley
½ tsp thyme, fresh or dried (optional)
¼ tsp pepper
1½ cups dry white wine
2 cups heavy cream
2 Tbs chopped chives, for garnish

Special equipment

A large stainless-steel saucepan or enameled (non-reactive) casserole, with a cover; a colander set over a large bowl for first straining; a fine-mesh sieve set over another bowl or 2-quart measuring cup for second straining

Mix the mussels in the pan with the onions, shallots, butter, herbs, and pepper and pour the white wine over them. Cover and bring to the boil over high heat; steam will emerge. Cook at the boil for about 2 minutes, occasionally shaking and tossing the pan—holding the cover on tight—to mix the ingredients. Open the cover and check to see if all the mussels are open. If not, cover and cook for another minute or two. (This should take 5 to 8 minutes, total cooking time.)

With the wine still at the boil, pour in the cream. Cover, shake the pot to toss the mussels in the cream, and return to a strong, foaming boil. Cook for ½ minute. Remove from the heat and immediately pour all the mussels and the hot soup through the colander into a large bowl. Shake the colander to drain any juices from the open shells; set aside. (When cool, shell the mussels and save for another dish. Discard any that have not opened.)

Let the hot soup sit in the bowl for a couple of minutes, so any sand can settle to the bottom. Then carefully pour it through the fine sieve (except for the sandy liquid at the end).

You may serve the soup warm right away, or chill it thoroughly. Before serving, stir in the chopped chives. Ladle 4 or 5 ounces of soup into a small cup for each portion.

Jacques

At Le Pavillon, where I was a chef when I first came to this country, the billi-bi was always served cold—but you can certainly serve it warm as well. Because it is so rich, you only want to serve a half-cup or so per person.

It is in fact a famous French soup, but named for an American. One story I have heard says that it was invented for a GI who was in Normandy during World War II, but more historical sources say the soup was created at Maxim's in Paris, much earlier in this century. Different individuals are said to be the namesake for the soup, but in any case we know he was a rich American, and his first name was William.

EGGS

WE BOTH LOVE EGGS AND WE EAT THEM ALL THE TIME. DESPITE THE BAD PRESS THEY received in recent years, eggs are very good for you, perfectly safe when handled properly (see below), and, as always, one of the world's most economical, versatile, and satisfying foods.

They are also fundamental to home cooking. With fresh eggs on hand in the refrigerator, you have the basis for countless quick and varied meals. And cooking eggs will provide some of the most instructive and pleasurable of all kitchen experiences. As you shake and flip them into omelets, bake them into golden, puffy soufflés, or whip them into light emulsified sauces, you have to be in control of rapid and remarkable physical transformations. If you do it right, you will enjoy nearly instantaneous and unfailingly delicious results.

Egg cookery is also important as an exercise in combining tastes creatively. Eggs in any form are better with other foods, and there's no end to the tasty things you can place them on, bury them under, or fill them with. In the recipes that follow, we make many suggestions for sauces, fillings, and garnishes. And since eggs invite improvisation, we hope that you will devise egg dishes using your own ideas and the good food you have on hand.

While there is an essential simplicity to all basic egg preparations, each kind requires careful attention and delicate touches, and—as we find when we cook together—there's even more than one way to poach an egg. Through the parallel recipes and illustrated techniques in this chapter, we share the different methods we have learned and developed over the years. We hope you will try them all.

Julia on Egg Safety

Raw eggs can contain harmful bacteria, especially salmonella, but since the salmonella scare some years ago egg producers, distributors, and markets have cleaned up and modernized their egg facilities, and the danger now is minimal if you are careful. Whether or not to eat uncooked eggs is entirely up to you, the consumer. This applies to soft-boiled and scrambled eggs, poached eggs, the coddled egg that goes into Caesar salad, hollandaise sauce, mayonnaise, etc.—some of the most loved foods in the general repertoire of good things to eat.

As for me, I am an enthusiastic egg person, and eat all of the above with greatest pleasure. But I am careful to buy refrigerated eggs at markets that in turn buy their eggs from producers who keep their eggs refrigerated at all times. Bacteria multiply at room temperature, but are quiescent when chilled. Here are some egg safety rules:

Never buy unrefrigerated eggs.

Never buy cracked or dirty eggs.

When you go shopping, never let eggs sit in your warm car; bring along a thermal container and ice pack.

When you come home, refrigerate eggs at once.

Never let raw eggs or uncooked egg mixtures sit about in the kitchen; keep them chilled until you are about to use them.

Scrambled eggs on a buffet—I'm wary of these.

Julia

One of the best reasons for making an omelet is that it is really fun. As you follow the instructions here, don't worry about having an impeccably symmetrical omelet roll onto your plate. It is all right to neaten it up before serving, or cover flaws with a well-placed sprig of parsley.

Successful omelet making—especially for a crowd—depends on your being prepared for the rapidity of the cooking: you want to have everything at hand, including your beaten eggs, already seasoned; butter; your serving plates (warm, not hot); and any fillings (warm as well) or decorative garnishes.

A key to making my omelet successfully is adding the eggs at the right moment. Watch the butter carefully as it melts and foams—you don't want the eggs to go in until the bubbles begin to disappear and before the butter browns. They should sizzle as they go into the pan. But watch, too, that the pan is not so hot it browns the eggs before the omelet is done. Actually, a good omelet is barely browned.

Classic Omelets

Here are, perhaps, the most exciting and satisfying few seconds of cooking that you will find in this book. A classic omelet not only tests your kitchen prowess, but gives you a delicious main course—for breakfast, lunch, or dinner—in a matter of minutes.

In fact, with the two methods we give here, you will have *two* classic omelets in your repertoire. The slight differences in our techniques yield quite distinct omelets—one pale yellow, with a soft, creamy inside, and the other tinged golden brown, with an interior of thick moist curds.

The details of both techniques are illustrated by the accompanying photo sequences. You might want to master Julia's style first, as it is a bit easier, and then move on to Jacques's method, used here for a plain omelet and his Mushroom Omelet, which scrambles sautéed mushroom right into the eggs.

Omelets are useful, not only because you can make them quickly, but because they taste so good with dozens of different garnishes and fillings. See our recommended Fillings for Omelets (pages 70–71), but look first in your fridge for savory leftovers—a small amount of cooked spinach, perhaps, or a slice of ham—to chop up and tuck into your omelet.

A note on pans: Omelet making has become much simpler in recent years, with the availability of high-quality, non-stick frying pans. We both recommend a sturdy ten-inch (top diameter) pan, with a long handle and slanting sides, as illustrated in the following pictures, for making the two- or three-egg omelets in these recipes. While we learned our techniques with traditional French iron or steel pans, they need special curing and treatment. Unless you use and season an iron pan frequently, an omelet can easily stick in it, while the non-stick pan is all ready to use.

Julia's Classic Omelet

Yield: 1 omelet, serving 1

2 or 3 large eggs
A big pinch of salt and 2 or
3 grinds of pepper
1 Tbs unsalted butter

Special equipment
A non-stick frying pan 10
inches top diameter; a
table fork; a rubber spatula; a warm but not hot
serving plate

Wait until the butter foaming subsides before pouring the eggs into the pan.

Pour the eggs in.

Crack the eggs into a bowl, add salt and pepper, and beat just to blend yolks and whites. Set the pan over high heat and add the tablespoon of butter. As the butter melts and begins to foam, swirl to film bottom and sides. Wait until the foaming begins to subside, then pour in the beaten eggs all at once.

Let settle for 4 to 5 seconds, then start shaking and swirling the pan as the eggs sizzle and start to set. Continue for 10 seconds or so, loosening the cooked curds from the pan and swirling the uncooked egg around them, until everything has started to thicken. If you are using a filling, quickly spoon it across the cen-ter of the eggs.

Now give the pan a series of short, sharp jerks—pulling it straight toward you—to shift the eggs to the far edge of the pan. The omelet will start rolling over on itself. (If any eggs

Let the eggs settle a few sec-onds, then shake and swirl the pan.

Jacques

With my technique, you will make the kind of omelet you would be served in a three-star restaurant. It is very tender, with moist small curds, and a perfectly pale-yellow skin. This is the omelet I learned as a young chef in Paris, but in most French homes, omelets are more like Julia's, with a larger, thicker curd and a slightly browned exterior. I like both kinds—I find they actually have a different taste—and I encourage you to enjoy both techniques.

In the classic method, you must move rapidly. First, to avoid any browning, add the eggs to the butter when it is just foaming. Then cook the eggs quickly, over high heat, scram-bling them as fast as you can to break up the curds.

Next, you must tilt the pan so that most of the eggs gather at the lower edge, leaving only a thin skin covering the pan bottom—don't let the eggs set in one thick layer that you roll up like a carpet.

As you practice this method, you will be able to form the pointed ends of the omelet right in the pan, and it will roll out onto the plate in perfect shape. Of course, you can lay a piece of plastic or a clean towel over the finished omelet and press it into better shape—which is what apprentices do before the chef comes to inspect their work.

With a few sharp jerks, pull the pan toward you to shift the eggs to the far side of the pan.

After the omelet rolls over onto itself, use a fork to nudge any stuck bits of egg into the mass at the far end of the pan.

When the omelet has been inverted onto the plate, neaten and garnish with toast (or any other garnish).

are stuck to the middle or side of the pan, push them into the mass of eggs with a fork.)

Make a fist with your free hand and rap sharply on the lower end of the handle to complete the roll.

To flip the omelet out of the pan, switch your grip on the handle, allowing you to tilt the pan all the way up and over—see photo on page 70. With your other hand, hold a warm serving plate against the edge of the pan, right under the omelet. Invert the pan to turn the omelet onto the plate, smooth side up.

Neaten the shape of the omelet, if necessary, using your two hands or a spatula. Garnish as you wish and serve immediately.

Jacques's Classic Omelet

Yield: 1 omelet, serving 1

3 large eggs
⅛ tsp salt
Freshly ground black pepper
1 Tbs unsalted butter

Special equipment
A sturdy, non-stick frying pan, 10 inches
top diameter

Crack the eggs into a bowl, add the salt and several grinds of pepper, and beat well with a fork or whisk, to blend thoroughly the yolks and whites. Set the pan over medium-high heat with the butter, swirling as it melts to coat the pan bottom and sides.

When the butter is foaming, add the beaten eggs all at once. Immediately start shaking the pan with one hand; at the same time, rapidly stir the eggs with a fork held flat in your other hand. Shake and stir continuously for about 15 seconds, quickly scraping any cooked egg off the bottom and sides with the fork and breaking it up into very small curds.

While the eggs are still quite moist, lift the handle and tilt the pan so the loose eggs gather at the lower edge, leaving only a thin cooked sheet of egg over most of the pan bottom.

Loosen the edges of this thin layer with the fork, then flip and fold it over, starting near the handle, so it partially covers the moist mass of eggs—see photo. Quickly spoon any filling across the middle of the folded eggs, and press in gently.

Now with the heel of your free hand rap lightly on the lower end of the handle, which will shift the omelet against the far edge of the pan, so it starts curling over on itself. With the fork, fold this curling edge in toward the center of the omelet, covering any filling, and forming an oval with pointed ends.

Now switch your grip on the handle, allowing you to tilt it all the way up and over—see photo on page 70. Quickly tap the bottom of the pan on the work surface, to loosen the omelet. With your other hand, center a warm serving plate

Rapidly stir the eggs with a fork while shaking the pan with your other hand.

Tilt the pan so the loose eggs gather at the far edge, nudging them with your fork.

Rap lightly on the handle to shift the omelet over onto itself.

With a fork, fold the curling edge in toward the center and press to shape an oval with pointed ends.

Fillings for Omelets

Both of our omelets can be filled while they are cooking in the pan, just before rolling, as shown in the photo sequences. Have your filling warm and ready since you don't want to overcook the eggs. The filling can also be added after the omelet is on the plate: cut a long slit in the top, open the slit to expose the soft center of the omelet, and spoon in the filling.

A classic omelet can be filled with ⅓ to ½ cup of any filling you choose. Try the ones suggested here or create your own.

"Grandmère" filling: Sauté equal amounts of chopped onion, small cubes of potato, and diced country ham (or bacon or pancetta) in butter or oil, with seasonings to taste, until the potatoes are cooked and the mixture is lightly browned.

Crouton garnish: Drop these crisp tiny croutons into a finished omelet after it is on the plate. To make, cut home-style white bread into ¼-inch cubes and toss with butter, or peanut or corn oil (about 1 tablespoon oil per cup of bread cubes). Bake on a sheet pan in a 400°F oven, shaking occasionally, until golden brown all over. For more details, see the discussion of croutons on page 108.

Pipérade filling (page 74): This can be used in rolled as well as flat omelets.

Jacques's Classic Omelet (continued)

under the edge of the pan, then invert the pan to turn out the omelet, smooth side up.

Neaten the shape of the omelet, if necessary, into a narrow, symmetrical oval with tight pointed ends. Garnish as you wish and serve immediately.

Invert the pan to turn the omelet out onto a plate.

Jacques's Classic Mushroom Omelet

Yield: 1 omelet

3 large eggs
Salt and freshly ground
    black pepper
2 medium mushrooms,
    unblemished
2 Tbs or so unsalted butter
Sprigs of parsley

Slice the mushroom dome into thin even pieces.

Beat the eggs well with ⅛ teaspoon of salt and grinds of pepper.

Slice off the cap of each mushroom at the very top of the stem, so it is a solid dome with a flat bottom; then slice both "domes" vertically into thin semicircles. Use only the most uniform center slices—you should have about 10. Finely dice the stems and trimmings of the caps so you have about 2 tablespoons of very small mushroom pieces.

Melt a tablespoon of the butter in the omelet pan over medium-high heat, add the mushrooms, both slices and pieces, and a pinch of salt. Sauté for ½ minute or so, tossing the mushrooms in the butter, just until they start to color and soften. Remove the pan from the heat, pick out the slices,

Chop the stems and trimmings into small pieces.

Sauté the slices on one side of the pan and the pieces on the other.

and lay them, overlapping, on the flat blade of a large knife. They should form a neat row, about 3 inches long.

Return the pan to the stove with the small mushroom pieces. Add the remaining tablespoon of butter and heat the pan again, swirling to coat the sides and bottom. When the butter is foaming, add the eggs and start shaking the pan, at the same time scrambling the mushroom pieces into the eggs with a fork. Follow Jacques's Classic Omelet technique, as shown in the photos, to cook and form the omelet.

Extract about 8 of the mushroom slices from the pan and line them up on the flat blade of a large knife.

As soon as the omelet has been turned out on the plate, lay on top, lengthwise, the knife blade with the mushroom slices. Gently pressing the row of slices with the fingertips of one hand, withdraw the knife blade, leaving the garnish centered on the omelet. Arrange sprigs of parsley at the two ends of the omelet and serve immediately.

Shaking the pan, scramble the mushroom pieces into the eggs with a fork.

After you have turned the omelet out onto the plate, gently press on the row of mushrooms with your fingertips, withdrawing the knife so that the mushrooms slip off and line up neatly on top of the omelet.

Mushroom duxelles: Chopped mushrooms sautéed in butter with shallots and seasoning—plain or simmered with a little cream (page 183).

Cheese: 2 to 3 tablespoons rather coarsely grated Swiss cheese, folded into omelet.

Fines herbes: 1½ tablespoons chopped parsley, chives, tarragon, and chervil, beaten with the eggs to start. Garnish with a sprinkling or small branches. This is the classic fines herbes combination, but if you don't have all of these herbs use at least two of them.

Creamed spinach (page 196) or broccoli (page 191): Cooked, chopped, seasoned, and simmered in a little cream and butter. Either folded in or spooned into slit top.

Chicken livers: Cut into strips and sautéed 1 minute in a little butter. Insert into slit top.

Creamed lobster or crab (page 93).

Elizabeth David's Omelet

England's revered culinary authority Elizabeth David, whose books on Italian and French food revolutionized British cooking in the 1950s, presented another omelet theory. For the tenderest omelet, she advises, don't beat the eggs furiously. In fact, don't beat them at all. Simply stir them with a fork so they are barely blended. It works! Now you have three very different aspects of egg blending, which give three subtly different results.

Presentation of Omelets

Breakfast omelets may be served practically as is, with sprigs of parsley or watercress. Luncheon omelets need more attention. Whatever you choose as a garnish or accompaniment, have it ready at hand so that you can arrange it rapidly on the plate after the omelet has landed. Here are some suggestions in addition to the preceding filling ideas.

Toast points: Freshly toasted rectangles of excellent white bread or brioche, buttered and cut into triangles or the "Lion's Tooth" Croutons (page 337).

Provençal Tomatoes (page 210), or Sautéed Small Tomatoes (page 209).

Hash-brown Potatoes (page 158), or potatoes sautéed with leeks, as for the "Tortilla" omelet, page 74.

Sautéed Mushrooms in Cream (page 205).

A little salad of green leaves, with halved and seasoned cherry tomatoes.

Julia's Tomato Garnishes (page 215).

Two Flat Omelets

In America, we usually think of omelets as rolled and folded into oval shapes, with the filling inside, as in our classic methods. But in many cuisines they are made more like pancakes, the eggs allowed to set in the bottom of the pan, and presented as a large golden disk, usually serving several people.

The two flat omelets here reflect both the cooking of Spain and its influence on southern France. In the first, the colorful sauté of onion and pepper strips—known in France as pipérade—is also typical of the Basque region in Spain. The vegetables are cooked right into the eggs. Slices of unsmoked cured ham, similar to prosciutto, are often added as well.

Our second flat omelet is a large, thick disk called a tortilla in Spain (it has nothing to do with the flour and/or corn tortilla of Mexico) and reminiscent of a frittata, which can easily serve four people. For this, a dozen beaten eggs are poured around sautéed potatoes and leeks in the pan, then allowed to set and brown in the oven. The leeks will float to the top of the eggs, making a nice surface pattern. You may serve it warm, but in Spain this "tortilla" is more commonly cooled to room temperature, and enjoyed as *tapas* in small, appetizer-size slices, with a drizzle of excellent olive oil.

You can serve both omelets with either side up, sliding them out of the pan, or inverting them onto a plate. Just before removing them—or before you try to flip the omelet with pipérade—pour a little oil around the perimeter and shake the pan a bit to make sure the eggs don't stick.

Jacques's Flat Omelet with Pipérade

Yield: 1 flat omelet, serving 2

    4 large eggs
    ¼ tsp salt
    Freshly ground pepper
    1 Tbs or more olive oil
    1 cup Pipérade filling (recipe follows)
    2 pieces thinly sliced prosciutto, 5 or 6
       inches long (optional)
    Sprigs of parsley or other garnish

Special equipment
- A non-stick frying pan, 12 inches top
diameter

Crack the eggs into a bowl, add salt and several grinds of pepper, and beat well to blend.

Set the pan, with about 2 teaspoons of oil, over medium-high heat; add the pipérade, swirl the pan to spread the vegetables and distribute the oil, and heat until sizzling.

Pour the eggs into the pan and begin stirring the eggs and vegetables continuously with a fork, occasionally shaking the pan. Cook for about ½ minute or more, stirring, shaking, and scraping the sides of the pan to draw the cooked eggs into the center.

When all the eggs have started to thicken, clear the eggs from the sides of the pan with the fork, and stop stirring. (If using prosciutto, press a piece flat on each half of the moist eggs.) Cook for another ½ minute or so, until the bottom is fully set. At the same time, drizzle a teaspoon or two of oil around the outer edge of the eggs and then swirl the pan to make sure the omelet can slide easily.

Flip the omelet over with a quick toss of the skillet (or slide it onto a flat plate and invert back into the pan, top side down). Cook the second side for a half-minute or so to set. If flipping is too hard, place the omelet under the broiler for 45 seconds to 1 minute to set the top. Slide the omelet onto the serving plate—or invert so the prosciutto slices are on top. Garnish with parsley sprigs, and serve immediately.

Jacques

In southwestern France, we often made flat omelets like these, using olive oil rather than butter. The pipérade can be used as a conventional omelet filling in a classic-style omelet, but when cooked with the eggs, it's an omelet Basquaise. (It's also quite similar to what we call a Western omelet here in America.) My mother frequently made thick potato omelets like the tortilla, but she would invert it from the pan and serve it hot.

You will find that the sautéed potatoes and leeks for the tortilla are perfectly cooked and quite delicious before you pour in the eggs—and there's nothing to stop you from preparing and serving them on their own.

Pipérade

Yield: About 2 cups, enough for 2
large flat omelets

2 Tbs olive oil
1¼ cups sliced onion (in ¼-inch-
   thick slices)
2½ cups sliced bell peppers of
   different colors (¼-inch-thick
   strips)
½ cup diced tomatoes
1 tsp chopped garlic
¼ tsp salt or more
Freshly ground pepper

Sauté the onion slices in the olive oil for 2 to 3 minutes over medium heat, to soften. Stir in the peppers, tomatoes, garlic, salt, and pepper to taste and sauté 6 to 8 minutes more, tossing occasionally, until the peppers are just tender.

"Tortilla"—Spanish Omelet with Potatoes and Leek

Yield: A 10-inch omelet, for 4
servings

1 medium leek, trimmed of tough
   green parts, split lengthwise and
   well rinsed (see page 54 on
   preparing leeks)
2 medium potatoes (about 10 to
   12 ounces), Yukon Gold or
   other all-purpose variety
1 Tbs unsalted butter
2 to 3 Tbs olive oil
Salt and freshly ground black
   pepper
A dozen large eggs
Drops of Tabasco sauce
4 to 5 Tbs chopped onion
1 tsp minced garlic
Olive oil, extra-virgin, for serving

Special equipment
A non-stick frying pan, 10 inches
   top diameter, or a sauté pan
   with ovenproof handle; a round
   serving plate

Preheat the oven to 350°F.
Slice the leek lengthwise into narrow strips and cut again crosswise into ¼-inch pieces (to make about 1 cup total).
Peel the potatoes and slice crosswise into thin slices, no more than ⅛ inch thick.
Set the skillet over medium heat with the butter and 1 tablespoon of olive oil. When the oil is sizzling, put the potato slices in the pan and spread them out, flipping and turning them to coat evenly with oil. Season with ½ teaspoon salt and ¼ teaspoon pepper and cook

for about 7 minutes, turning occasionally. The slices should be barely soft and still intact; if still firm, cover the pan and cook for 2 to 3 minutes more.

Meanwhile, crack the eggs into a large bowl, season with ½ teaspoon salt, ¼ teaspoon pepper, and drops of Tabasco to taste, and whisk until well blended.

When the potatoes are just tender, scatter the leek, onion, and garlic over the slices and toss to mix. Cook for 2 to 3 minutes, stirring and tossing, to soften all the vegetables.

Pour the beaten eggs all at once over the potato mixture. Allow to set in the pan for about a minute, then stir the eggs and vegetables together gently, and continue to cook over moderate heat, until the eggs have begun to solidify, about 3 minutes. Lower the heat if eggs are cooking rapidly.

Place the pan in the oven and bake 6 to 8 minutes. The eggs will be fully set, slightly puffed, and shrinking from the sides of the skillet. Remove to the stovetop— remember the handle is hot!—and set over medium heat for a minute or two to brown the bottom. While cooking, drizzle a spoonful or so of olive oil all around the outer edge of the omelet, and swirl the pan gently to loosen it.

Slide the cooked omelet out onto the serving plate, to present the top side with the vegetables visible (or invert onto the platter to show the browned bottom).

Serve immediately, or, for a Spanish-style tortilla, cool to room temperature, drizzle extra-virgin olive oil over the top, and cut into wedges.

Julia

Eggs scrambled by my method ought to resemble a soft, broken custard: lumpy, moist, and glossy. You must cook the eggs very slowly, over low heat, always scraping the pan with a spatula, just until they are thickened, but still visibly soft. At this point you have to remember that the eggs are still cooking in the hot pan. You prevent them from stiffening by folding in the little bit of beaten egg you have held back.

Scrambled Eggs Two Ways

It is fascinating that our two versions of scrambled eggs are so different. We use exactly the same ingredients, yet our slight variations in cooking technique produce eggs with distinctive texture, appearance, and even taste. They are both quick to prepare—even the slower-cooked eggs take barely three minutes—so you could easily sample the two side by side.

Both scrambles, you will find, are soft and creamy. For breakfast, accompany the eggs simply with toast or English muffins, or be more elaborate and serve with slices of gravlax (pages 18 and 21), or smoked salmon, bacon, ham, or sausages. For a more substantial lunch dish, serve your scrambled eggs inside a ring of Sautéed Diced Tomatoes (page 78), topped with fresh herbs and a scattering of crunchy croutons (page 108).

The basic recipes that follow are for one serving; double or triple the ingredients for multiple servings, using a larger pan.

Julia's Way

Yield: 1 serving

> 2 or 3 large eggs
> Salt and freshly ground pepper
> 1 Tbs or more unsalted butter
> Heavy cream (optional)

Special equipment
> A non-stick frying pan, 10 inches top
>   diameter; a straight-edged wooden
>   spoon or a rubber spatula

Crack the eggs into a bowl, add big pinches of salt and pepper, and beat with a fork, just to blend. Over low heat, melt a tablespoon of the butter in the frying pan, enough to film the bottom and sides, and then pour in all but 2 tablespoons of the eggs.

Mix the eggs.

Cook the eggs over moderately low heat, stirring rather slowly and scraping the bottom of the pan with the spatula. They will gradually begin to coagulate after a minute or two; keep scraping the bottom clear to draw in the uncooked eggs. When almost entirely thickened into soft, custardy lumps, after 2 minutes or so, remove from the heat and fold in the reserved 2 tablespoons of eggs. Taste and adjust the seasoning. Fold in another teaspoon or two of soft butter, or a dash of cream, if you wish.

Quickly scrape the eggs onto a warm plate (not hot) and serve immediately with a garnish of your choice.

Stir the eggs rather slowly, scraping the eggs from the bottom of the pan with a spatula.

When thickened into soft lumps, pour in the reserved uncooked egg, then fold it into the scrambled eggs.

Jacques

The purpose of scrambling

eggs in a saucepan is to produce the smallest curds possible, and to cook them quickly, before they are toughened by the heat. You need to have a pan with high sides and a small bottom surface, so you can whisk the curds, breaking them up and moving them off the bottom. In a sense this is the opposite of an omelet, where you want a large bottom surface, to form the skin. And though it's not as fast as an omelet, you have to be on the ball. The eggs must still be very soft and loose when you take the pan off the heat.

In France, scrambled eggs like these would be served as a lunch dish, with a garnish like cooked fresh tomatoes, as detailed on page 78. If you want to surround the eggs with such a garnish, the easiest way is first to mound the tomatoes in the center of the plate, then spread them out into a ring, and spoon your eggs in the middle.

Julia on Cooked Fresh Tomatoes for Eggs

Fresh tomatoes can be cooked as a tasty and colorful garnish for soufflés, poached eggs, and omelets as well as these scrambled eggs. While the two preparations are similar, they produce different textures. The Sautéed Diced Tomatoes start with Tomates Concassées, already peeled, seeded, juiced, and chopped into pieces (page 243), and cooks these only briefly to keep the chunky consistency. In contrast, the Tomato Coulis is puréed in a food mill, giving it the thick, somewhat grainy texture characteristic of fruit and vegetable coulis. (Because it is puréed, you don't need to peel or seed the tomatoes.)

Jacques's Way

Yield: 1 serving

2 or 3 large eggs
Salt and freshly ground pepper
1 Tbs or more unsalted butter
1–2 Tbs heavy cream

Special equipment
A 2- or 3-quart heavy saucepan;
a medium wire whisk

When the butter foams, pour in the eggs.

Crack the eggs into a bowl, add ⅛ teaspoon each of salt and pepper, and beat thoroughly with the whisk. Place the saucepan with a tablespoon of butter over medium heat, swirling to film the bottom and sides. When the butter foams, pour all the eggs into hot pan and immediately begin stirring with the whisk, clearing the thickening eggs from the sides and bottom of the pan and breaking up any lumps. Be sure to run the whisk around the bottom corners to dislodge any egg that may stick there.

Cook for a minute or slightly more, steadily whisking, until the eggs are uniformly thickened but still quite soft, with very small and creamy curds.

Remove the pan from the heat, whisk in another spoon of butter and 1 or 2 tablespoons of cream, and quickly spoon the eggs into a soft mound on a warm plate. Serve immediately with a garnish of your choice.

Whisk steadily, clearing the eggs from the bottom and sides of the pan and breaking up any lumps.

Remove from the heat when the eggs have thickened and formed soft, small, creamy curds.

Sautéed Diced Tomatoes

Sauté ¼ cup of chopped onion (with a dash of minced garlic, if you like) in a couple of teaspoons of olive oil until soft. Add one cup of *tomates concassées* (page 243); season with salt and pepper and cook over medium-low heat just until soft and fragrant; add a bit of water if they become dry.

Tomato Coulis

Sauté ¼ cup of chopped onion (with a crushed, unpeeled garlic clove, if you like) in a couple of teaspoons of olive oil until soft. Chop 1 large or 2 small tomatoes into 1-inch pieces—about 2 cups—and add to the onions. Season with salt and pepper and cook for 12 to 15 minutes. Push the thickened tomatoes through the medium plate of a food mill to make the coulis. Serve warm.

Spoon the eggs onto a bed of Sautéed Diced Tomatoes.

Julia

It is good to see that my favorite perforated-metal egg-poaching cups are again available at specialty stores. In recent years, when people seemed so afraid of eating eggs, the cups became hard to find. I strongly recommend using them, as they will hold any egg in a neat shape, even an old one, and you don't need vinegar in the poaching water.

Give the eggs a 10-second boil in the shell before poaching. This slightly firms the outer layer of the egg white, and helps them hold their shape when cracked into the water. (Prick the large end of the eggshell with a pushpin before this brief immersion to allow the air in the shell to escape.)

Like Jacques, I almost always poach my eggs ahead of time and store them in ice water. But don't cover the bowl or a sulfury odor and off flavors can develop.

Eggs Benedict certainly qualifies as an American classic. This delicious combination of poached egg, thin sliced ham, and hollandaise sauce has been popular since it was invented at Delmonico's in New York a century ago. But I prefer rounds of toasted brioche as a base; English-muffin halves too often are tough to saw through. I also recommend warmed slices of black truffle—if you are lucky enough to have one on hand—as a crowning touch.

Poached and Coddled Eggs

Whether simply set on buttered toast, or dressed up with sauces and truffles, a perfectly poached egg is a lovely creation—a shivering oval of just-set white enclosing a soft, runny yolk. Yet, for all its delicacy of taste and appearance, it is also a surprisingly sturdy and versatile item, convenient to cook ahead—even a couple of days ahead—and reheat, and easy to combine with other foods.

Here we each offer our method for poaching eggs—one "free-form" and the other using metal poaching cups. Both will help you meet the major challenge of poaching, which is to keep the eggs together when they've been dropped into simmering water, so they cook into a compact oval. Fresh eggs are essential, as older eggs have thinner whites, which tend to drift away from the yolk, forming strands and irregular shapes. In our comments, we explain the important techniques and touches that will keep your eggs tender and shapely.

We also include a method for the poached eggs' cooked-in-the-shell counterpart—the coddled egg or *oeuf mollet* (*mollet* means "soft" in French). When peeled, a coddled egg retains its perfect shape, but has the same soft-cooked consistency as a poached egg. And it can be chilled, stored, reheated, and served in the same convenient way.

You can use either style of egg in the two dressy dishes that follow, Julia's classic Eggs Benedict and Jacques's colorful presentation of eggs, creamy carrot sauce, and fresh asparagus. You will find more good ways to match soft-cooked eggs with attractive complements in the sidebar on page 82.

Jacques's Poached Eggs

Yield: 4 poached eggs, serving 2 or 4

2 Tbs distilled white vinegar per 2 quarts
water
4 large eggs, the fresher the better

Special equipment
A shallow saucepan or a high-sided
sauté pan, about 8 inches across, non-
stick preferred; a slotted spoon
or a strainer; a clean kitchen towel

Fill the pan with water to a depth of 2 inches or so, add
the vinegar, and bring to a slow boil.

Rapidly crack and open each egg into the water, holding the shell as close to the surface as possible. The eggs will
cool the water; adjust the heat to maintain a slow simmer. After
a few moments, when the whites have just begun to set, drag
the back of the slotted spoon gently across the top of the eggs,
to move them off the pan bottom so they don't stick. Cook the
eggs for about 4 minutes, adjusting the heat as necessary.

To test for doneness, lift 1 egg from the water with the
slotted spoon and press both white and yolk. The whites should
feel fully set but not too firm, and the yolks very soft. Poach
longer for firmer eggs.

When set the way you like them, remove the eggs from the
saucepan with the slotted spoon or strainer and immerse them in
a bowl of warm tap water to wash off the vinegar. Set the spoon
on a clean towel (or folded paper towels) for a moment to remove
excess water, and serve eggs immediately.

Do-ahead notes
To chill and store poached eggs, immediately plunge
the hot eggs into a large bowl of ice water to stop the cooking.
When cool, trim off any uneven strands of egg white with a paring knife. You can keep the eggs submerged in the uncovered

Jacques

While most eggs in the mar-
kets are reasonably fresh, I find that
organic eggs, from free-range chickens,
have a stronger albumen that won't thin
out in the poaching water. But I always
use several techniques to maintain the
shape. The pan must have sufficient
water so that the eggs will be completely submerged at all times and the
water must remain at a gentle simmer, so
that turbulence will not disturb them.
And I use vinegar, since the acid helps to
thicken the whites.

Chilling and storing the eggs in ice
water has many advantages. You can
poach them hours or even days ahead of
time, and then quickly reheat them
before serving. The water also rinses off
any traces of vinegar and keeps the
eggs suspended, so that they do not
break open under their own weight. If
you chill the eggs, you should trim off
any uneven strands of egg white before
serving—and decide which side will
make the best presentation.

Oeufs mollets are a nice alternative to poached eggs, and they are
cooked and used in almost the identical
manner. You don't need vinegar in the
water, but you must make a hole in the
large end of the shell to allow the air
inside to dissipate before it expands and
breaks the shell. To make peeling easier,
I crack them gently as soon as they are
cooked, then immerse them in the ice
water to chill. Holding them under cold
running water will also aid peeling.

Ideas from Julia on Poached Eggs

Just as a pastry chef builds scores of distinct desserts from a few basic cakes, fillings, and icings, you can use poached or coddled eggs as a building block in your kitchen improvisations, setting them on bread and vegetable bases, and topping them with different sauces and garnishes. Here are a few suggestions for combining them with other recipes from this book, and you will think of many more.

With duxelles (page 183): As in the Benedict, spread a brioche round, or a toasted English muffin half, with the *duxelles*, then top with an egg and Hollandaise (page 96).

Try the irresistible luncheon dish with which I lured prospective hosts for my cooking classes (page 182), using Cooked Artichoke Bottoms (page 181) as the base and Béarnaise Sauce (page 99) as the crowning touch.

With creamed spinach (page 196): Use the spinach as a bed for the eggs or as a middle layer on toast.

In a big baked potato (page 148): Pop open the hot potato as usual, butter well, and drop in your poached egg. Sprinkle parsley on top.

As a surprise in a soufflé: Set 3 or 4 chilled, poached eggs in a soufflé mold or gratin dish, and ladle over them Jacques's or my basic soufflé mixture (pages 89, 91). Bake as directed; the eggs will still be soft inside. A bed of creamed spinach in the bottom of the soufflé dish would be nice.

Jacques's Poached Eggs (continued)

bowl of water, refrigerated, for up to 2 days, if you change the water every day.

To reheat

Bring a pan of water to a gentle simmer; with a strainer or a slotted spoon, lower 1 chilled, poached egg at a time into the water and heat for about a minute. Lift out, drain on a clean towel, and serve.

Julia's Poached Eggs

In my method, you crack the egg into an egg poacher—a perforated-metal oval egg-shaped container set in simmering water. The egg takes on the oval poached-egg shape.

Yield: 4 poached eggs, serving 2 or 4

4 large fresh eggs

Special equipment

4 egg poachers; a saucepan at least 3 inches deep and large enough to accommodate the poachers; a strainer

Prick the large end of each egg, going through the shell and into the body of the egg.

Set the egg poachers in the pan and measure in enough water to cover them by ½ inch. Remove the poachers and bring the water to the boil. With a pin, prick the large end of each egg—going through the shell and into the body of the egg—then place in a strainer and lower into the boiling water. Submerge for exactly 10 seconds and lift out. Now set the poachers in and reduce the heat to a simmer.

Scoop the eggs out of the water after their 10-second boil.

Rapidly crack an egg and, holding it as close to the simmering water as possible, drop it into one of the poachers, starting at the pan handle. Rapidly continue with the rest, going clockwise. Poach for 4 minutes per egg. When this time is up, slip the eggs out of the poachers onto a plate or, if you are not planning to use them right away, into a bowl of ice water.

The cracked eggs after being dropped into the poacher

A perfectly poached egg

Julia on Coddled Eggs (Oeufs Mollets): A Substitute for Poached Eggs

A coddled egg is a peeled soft-boiled egg, which sounds easy enough, but peeling a soft-boiled egg is not like peeling a hard-boiled egg because the soft-boiled egg is tender, and tears easily. I think the solution is to boil it a little longer than usual, so that the yolk is still liquid but barely so, and the white is quite solidly set. This is a question of timing, and I suggest you try it out yourself and work out your own system before you serve up a bunch. (Unless forced to do so I would frankly prefer never to coddle at all, but to poach eggs in my oval perforated poachers—no problems!)

To coddle an egg, poke the usual pin hole in the large end of the shell to release the air pocket, and lower it into simmering water. Simmer 6 minutes for large eggs, 7 for extra large, and 7½ to 8 for jumbos. Remove to a bowl of ice water, where I let mine chill for 10 minutes at least, since a real chill seems to help. Then crack very gently all over on the edge of the sink, and peel very carefully indeed under a thin stream of cold water. Some of the eggs may tear, and unless the tear goes down into the yolk, keep them anyway. Handle with care!

Store, reheat, and use coddled eggs just like poached eggs. For serving, in case the eggs have torn open, provide yourself with a sauce or some greenery like parsley or basil to hide your troubles.

Jacques's Coddled Eggs with Carrot Sauce and Asparagus

Yield: 4 servings

For the carrot sauce

2 cups thin rounds of peeled
   carrots
¼ tsp salt, or more to taste
¼ tsp sugar, or more to taste
1 Tbs or more butter
Heavy cream (optional)

For the assembly

4 slices of brioche or home-style
   white bread (or English-muffin
   halves)
4 large eggs
Thin slices of black truffle
   (optional)
Butter
Salt

For the garnish

16 spears asparagus (medium-
   width), peeled and cooked as
   on page 186
1 Tbs unsalted butter

Making the carrot sauce

Put the carrot slices in a skillet or saucepan with the salt and sugar, add water just to cover (about 1½ cups), and heat to a gentle boil. Simmer uncovered until the carrots are very tender, about 15 to 20 minutes.

Pour the carrots and about ½ cup of the hot cooking liquid into the bowl of a blender or food processor. Add a tablespoon or more of butter and, if you like, 2 or 3 tablespoons of cream, and purée until absolutely smooth.

Check the sauce for flavor and consistency: add more salt and sugar to taste and thin if necessary with

spoonfuls of cooking water or cream until it is pourable yet still thick. Blend again. Use immediately, or store in the refrigerator and reheat slowly when needed.

Making the toast rounds

With a round cutter or knife, cut a 4-inch circle of bread from each slice; butter the rounds lightly on both sides and toast on a cookie sheet in a 400°F oven until nicely browned.

Preparing the asparagus garnish

Cut the cooked asparagus spears to a uniform length of about 6 inches. Slit each spear lengthwise in two, from just under the tip through the stem, so they remain joined only at the tip.

Just before assembling the plates, melt the tablespoon of butter in a large sauté pan, lay in the spears, and season with a dash of salt. Heat for a minute or two, rolling the spears in the butter, just until they are warmed through.

Cooking the eggs (and the truffle slices)

Cook the eggs following the previous instructions for coddled or poached eggs, or reheat chilled cooked eggs. (If using truffle slices, heat them at this time in a sauté pan with a bit of melted butter for 10 to 15 seconds.)

To assemble

Spoon about ¼ cup of warm carrot sauce in the center of each serving plate, and smooth out to form a large circular pool. Center a toast round in the middle; place a hot egg on top and nap with another spoonful or two of carrot sauce. (Top with a slice of warm truffle, if using.)

On each plate, arrange 4 warm spears of asparagus with their slit sides spread apart, to create a frame around the circle of sauce, as shown opposite.

Serve immediately.

Opposite: Coddled Eggs with Carrot Sauce and Asparagus

Poached Eggs on Aspic

When you are thinking of what to feed them for an elegant lunch, or what to put on the cold buffet table, think poached eggs. Dressed up in mayonnaise, they can accompany a salad course or a platter of vegetables. Poached eggs molded in aspic are beautiful, but fussy to make. How about eggs *on* rather than *in* aspic? They are much easier to do, and here's how.

Yield: 6 eggs

2 cups best-quality clear consommé
1 package (1 Tbs) plain unflavored
  gelatin
3 Tbs excellent dry port or
  Madeira wine
6 large chilled poached eggs

Serving suggestions
3-inch ovals of boiled ham to hold
  the eggs; chilled plates or a platter lined with finely shredded
  iceberg lettuce or romaine; vegetable decorations such as peppers, black olives, tomato, and
  so forth, all finely diced and
  chilled

Special equipment
  A 9-by-12-inch roasting pan

Pour the consommé into a saucepan and sprinkle the gelatin over. Let soften for several minutes, then set the pan over heat until the gelatin has dissolved completely. Remove from heat, stir in the wine, and correct seasoning. Line a 9-by-12-inch roasting pan with wax paper. Pour a ¼-inch layer of the aspic into it, and chill for an hour or more in the refrigerator until fully set.

Unmold the aspic onto a large tray and peel off the wax paper.

Cut 6 ovals, 3-by-2-inch size, out of the aspic and very carefully lift them onto the ham slices. Set a chilled, dry, well-trimmed poached egg on each.

To decorate the eggs, you might cut 12 quarter-inch strips, 3 inches long, out of the remaining aspic, and crisscross them over the eggs. Using your big knife, chop up handfuls of the remaining aspic and rapidly fold with some of the diced vegetables suggested. Spoon into the empty spaces to make an attractive presentation. Chill until serving time.

Use the remaining aspic as you wish, or heat to liquefy, and keep it in the freezer for another occasion.

Julia's Eggs Benedict

Yield: 4 servings

4 slices of brioche or home-style
  white bread, cut into 4-inch
  rounds, or English-muffin halves
Butter
4 thin slices of boiled ham or prosciutto
Thin slices of black truffle
  (optional)
4 warm poached eggs
1 cup Hollandaise Sauce, page 96

Just before serving, toast the bread circles or muffins lightly, butter both sides, and warm the ham and the optional truffle slices in a frying pan with a tablespoon of butter.

To assemble
Center a toast round on each warm serving plate; cover with a slice of ham and then a poached egg. Spoon hollandaise sauce generously over each egg and top with an optional warm truffle slice. Serve immediately.

Opposite: Scallop Soufflé and Cheese Soufflé

Julia

If you want a soufflé that rises impressively, use a 6-cup mold for the recipe here, with a paper collar attached. But you can also use an 8-cup mold, with or without the collar, which will give you a slightly more stable soufflé with a less dramatic rise.

A plain cheese soufflé is one of my favorites, but it is also nice to find something underneath the soufflé layer, like Jacques's scallops, or his creamed-lobster-or-crab variation, or the good things that you might have on hand, such as cooked broccoli or spinach, mushrooms, or poached fish. You can bury these treasures in either a round mold or a gratin dish.

If you are a real egg-lover, you can mound your soufflé base over several cool poached eggs—a classic combination known as "soufflé Vendôme." If you bake the soufflé to the right point, the egg will still be perfectly soft inside.

Soufflés

If you have never made a soufflé before, you may feel that the dramatic rise of a soufflé is dependent on skills or a magical touch that is beyond you. But you needn't hold your breath worrying about what is happening behind the oven door—remember that *souffler* means "to blow" or "to puff." When you have made your soufflé mixture properly, as we show you in these recipes, it *will* rise, automatically.

Consider that a soufflé is just a thick sauce into which beaten egg whites have been folded, and that, as the air in the whites expands during baking, the entire mixture expands and rises too. The work is done before the dish goes into the oven, when you beat your egg whites to the proper consistency and fold them rapidly into your sauce. And then you take it from the oven when it has set just enough to maintain its airy lightness for a minute or two as you present and serve it. As Jacques says, you must wait for the soufflé, it will not wait for you.

Though a towering soufflé is eye-catching and impressive, we agree that rich flavor and moist, tender consistency are even more important. Jacques's soufflé, made in a shallow oval gratin dish, puffs modestly, but blends the flavors of the soufflé topping with those of the lightly seared scallops underneath. Julia's Gruyère-cheese soufflé, made in a round mold, rises high into its paper collar. Either soufflé makes a first course for six, or a main-course luncheon dish for four. Serve with a salad and a glass of chilled white wine.

Julia's Cheese Soufflé

Yield: A high-rising soufflé, serving 4 to 6

Room-temperature butter, for greasing
 the mold and collar
2 to 3 Tbs grated Parmesan cheese,
 for coating the mold
4 Tbs butter
4½ Tbs flour
1½ cups hot milk
½ tsp salt
⅛ teaspoon freshly ground white pepper
¼ teaspoon paprika
A grating of nutmeg
6 large egg yolks
7 large egg whites
5 ounces Gruyère cheese, coarsely
 grated (about 1½ cups)

Special equipment

A 6- or 8-cup soufflé mold; a 3-quart
 heavy-bottomed stainless saucepan;
 baking parchment or aluminum foil; 2
 straight pins for fastening collar; a wire
 whisk, wooden spoon, and large rubber spatula; egg-white-beating equipment (see page 94)

Preparations

Arrange rack in the bottom third of the oven and preheat to 350°F. Butter the mold, and sprinkle the grated Parmesan cheese all over the bottom and sides. Cut a length of parchment paper or aluminum foil long enough to wrap around the mold with a 2-inch overlap. Fold the sheet in half lengthwise to form a 6-to-8-inch band, and butter it well on one side.

Jacques

It is a good idea to add cheese to the soufflé base, as we both do here, whether you bake it plain or with other ingredients. The cheese not only adds flavor, but also helps to hold the soufflé together. My scallop souf-flé, and the variations with creamed lobster or crab, are all similar to a cele-brated dish, *soufflé de homard Plaza-Athénée*, a lobster soufflé I learned to make as a young chef at the Plaza-Athénée in Paris. In these preparations, the soufflé layer becomes permeated with the flavor of the seafood, as they bake together in the oven.

If using scallops, it is very impor-tant that you sauté them only briefly, in a large pan over high heat—don't crowd them or cook them slowly or they will release their liquid. You want just to sear them, creating a slight crust. Then they will finish cooking in the oven, and will still be tender and moist when the soufflé is done.

When I make a soufflé in a round mold, I never bother to use a collar. The soufflé will rise well anyway and there is no danger of its sticking to the collar. And even if the soufflé happens to fall, you can always unmold it before serving. If you have buttered and coated the mold well with cheese or bread crumbs, you can simply invert the soufflé onto a serving plate. Though deflated, it will still be deli-cious, especially with a nice sauce like the Tomato Coulis (page 79).

Scoop up one-quarter of the egg whites to mix with the soufflé base.

Folding egg whites into the soufflé base

Scrape the soufflé mixture into the bowl.

Julia's Cheese Soufflé (continued)

Making the béchamel

Melt the 4 tablespoons butter in the saucepan over medium heat and stir in the flour with a wooden spoon to make a smooth paste. Cook for about 2 minutes without coloring. This is now a *roux*.

Remove the pan from the heat, let cool a moment, stirring, then pour in all of the hot milk at once, whisking rapidly to blend roux and milk. Bring the sauce to a boil over medium heat, stirring and clearing the sides of the pan with the whisk. Cook for 2 minutes, whisking, as the béchamel bubbles slowly and becomes as thick as a mayonnaise. Remove from the heat and whisk in the salt, pepper, paprika, and nutmeg.

Finishing the soufflé mixture

One at a time, whisk the egg yolks into the hot béchamel.

Beat the egg whites until stiff and shining in a large, perfectly clean bowl, by hand or with an electric mixer, as detailed on page 94.

Scoop one-quarter of the egg whites into the béchamel and whisk into the warm sauce to lighten it. Then scrape about one-third of the lightened sauce *back* over the egg whites in the mixing bowl and sprinkle on a good handful of the grated Gruyère cheese.

Fold in the sauce and cheese by rapidly cutting down to the bottom of the bowl with the rubber spatula, then drawing beaten whites up from the bottom and sides, and turning them over into the sauce to blend. When almost blended, stir in half of the rest of the sauce and cheese, then the remaining sauce and cheese. Work rapidly, and do not overblend and deflate the egg whites.

Filling the mold and fastening the collar

Scrape the soufflé mixture into the mold (if using an 8-cup mold it will be only three-quarters full). Smooth the top, then wrap the parchment band, buttered side in, around the mold to form a tight collar, rising 3 or 4 inches above the top. Fasten at the overlap with 2 straight pins, heads up for fast removal. (The unbaked soufflé can now stand at room temperature for about 30 to 45 minutes, away from drafts, before going into the oven.)

When ready to bake, place the soufflé on a rack in the lower third of the preheated oven.

Baking the soufflé

Bake for 45 minutes or more, until the soufflé has puffed about 2 inches into the collar and the top is nicely browned and slightly firm to the touch. To check if it is done, open the oven quickly and plunge a long skewer into the side of the puff; withdraw it and close the oven. If the skewer has moist bits of soufflé clinging to it, your soufflé will be creamy inside (and may not hold its height); serve now if you like it that way, or bake for a few more minutes. If the skewer is almost clean, the soufflé is more set and will maintain its puffiness better when the collar is removed.

As soon as the soufflé has been removed from the oven, withdraw the pins and unwrap the collar. Immediately bring it to the table.

To serve the soufflé, hold your serving fork and spoon down back-to-back and plunge them into the crust to pull it apart. Spoon out portions that include some of the crusty sides and top, and the soft center.

Wrap a parchment band around the mold to form a collar.

Jacques's Scallop Soufflé

Yield: An 8-cup gratin dish, serving 4 to 6

For the scallops
  1 pound large sea scallops
  3 Tbs butter
  ⅓ cup minced shallots
  ¼ tsp salt
  ¼ tsp freshly ground black pepper
  2 Tbs finely chopped fresh chives

For the soufflé mixture
  3 Tbs butter
  4 Tbs flour
  1½ cups milk
  ¼ tsp salt
  ¼ tsp freshly ground black pepper
  Nutmeg, freshly ground, a large pinch
  6 egg yolks
  6 egg whites
  4 to 5 ounces good aged cheddar cheese
  2 to 3 Tbs finely ground fresh bread crumbs

Special equipment

A very large skillet or sauté pan; a shallow gratin or baking dish, about 8-cup volume; a large, heavy-bottomed saucepan; egg-white-beating equipment; a pastry brush, a wire whisk, and a large rubber spatula; a cookie sheet

Getting ready

Preheat the oven to 350°F. Cut several thin slices of cheddar cheese to use for decorating the gratin and coarsely grate the remainder (about 3 ounces), for a cup or so of grated cheese.

Sautéing the scallops

Pat the scallops dry on paper towels. Melt the butter in the skillet over high heat; stir in the shallots and cook for ½ minute to soften. Add the scallops all at once, toss well with the shallots, and sauté over very high heat for only about a minute, shaking the scallops in the pan. You just want to sear the scallops on all sides as quickly as possible—they will cook through as they bake under the soufflé.

Off the heat, sprinkle ¼ teaspoon each of salt and pepper and the chopped chives over the scallops, toss to mix, then turn them with their liquid into the gratin dish, distributing them evenly. With a pastry brush, coat the sides of the gratin with the buttery juices.

Making the béchamel soufflé base

Melt the butter in the saucepan over high heat, add the flour, and whisk together to form a roux. Cook for only 10 seconds or so, then pour in the milk, whisking and stirring to blend.

Bring the sauce to the boil, whisking continuously and occasionally clearing the sides of the pan. Season with ¼ teaspoon each of salt and pepper, and a few gratings of nutmeg. Reduce the heat and cook for another minute or two, still whisking, as it bubbles and thickens.

Finishing the soufflé mixture

With the béchamel at a gentle boil, add the yolks to the saucepan all at once and whisk vigorously to blend. Stirring continuously, heat the sauce until it just comes back to the boil, then remove from the heat.

Beat the egg whites until stiff and shiny in a large, perfectly clean bowl, by hand or with an electric mixer, as detailed on pages 94 and 95.

Scoop about one-third of the egg whites into the saucepan and whisk thoroughly and quickly into the warm sauce to loosen it. Immediately pour all the sauce over the beaten egg whites in the mixing bowl and begin folding together with the rubber spatula, at the same time sprinkling in the grated cheese. Continue folding until the soufflé mixture is evenly blended.

Completing and decorating the gratin

Pour all of the soufflé over the scallops, smoothing the top with the spatula, filling the gratin dish in an even layer.

Use the long blade of a cake spatula or a knife to mark diagonal lines in a crisscross pattern in the top of the soufflé. Sprinkle the bread crumbs evenly over the top.

Cut the cheddar cheese slices into diamond and triangle shapes, about 1 to 2 inches long, and arrange in decorative designs in the center and around the edge of the soufflé.

Place the gratin dish on a cookie sheet and set in the preheated oven.

Bake for 25 or 30 minutes, until the soufflé is puffy and the top is deeply colored. Remove from the oven. Serve immediately, lifting off a portion of soufflé topping onto each serving plate and spooning out scallops alongside.

Variation with Creamed Lobster or Crab

Cooked lobster or crab meat, heated in a simple cream sauce, is also wonderful as a base for the preceding soufflé or as an omelet filling. The soufflé can be baked in a round soufflé mold or in a gratin dish.

> 1½ cups freshly boiled crab or
>   lobster meat, about 6 to 7
>   ounces
> Lobster tomalley and roe, if any
>   (see page 250)
> 2 Tbs butter, a little more if
>   needed
> 2 Tbs minced shallots or scallions
> Salt and freshly ground white
>   pepper to taste
> ¼ cup dry white French
>   vermouth
> ⅓ cup heavy cream

Pick over the shellfish to remove any bits of shell, and break or cut the meat into roughly uniform size. If you have tomalley and roe, push it through a very fine-meshed sieve with a tablespoon of the butter. Set a 10-inch non-stick frying pan over moderate heat; add the tomalley butter and the rest of the butter. When bubbling, stir in the shallots or scallions and the shellfish meat, season lightly with salt and pepper, and stir with a wooden spoon as the shellfish heats through—about a minute. If you have tomalley, and especially roe, the meat will turn a pale-salmon color. Raise heat to high, pour in the vermouth, and boil rapidly to evaporate liquid. When almost evaporated (in a minute), stir in the heavy cream

and boil rapidly, stirring for several seconds until thickened. Correct seasoning.

To use the lobster or crab in Julia's soufflé recipe, fold 1 cup of the soufflé mixture into the shellfish and spread in the bottom of the soufflé mold. Proceed as in her recipe.

To use in Jacques's soufflé recipe, substitute creamed shellfish for scallops.

Julia on Beating Egg Whites with a Mixer

I like a heavy-duty standing mixer for beating egg whites, because the wire-whisk attachment rotates all around the bowl, keeping the mass of whites in constant motion. This action is terribly important for whipping the whites quickly into stiff shining peaks. You can also do it with a large balloon whip and a large bowl, as Jacques does, but don't try to beat whites with a small narrow whisk—you won't get anywhere.

If you have a hand-held mixer, you can simulate the action of a standing mixer by moving the beaters in a circle around the mixing bowl. But if you are serious about cooking, I encourage you to get a heavy-duty mixer. It is worth the price and will last forever.

Follow these steps for successfully beaten egg whites:

Use an impeccably clean mixing bowl. Any traces of fat or egg yolk in a mixing bowl can prevent the whites from mounting to their full volume. To remove any grease from a stainless-steel mixer bowl, rub the inside with a mixture of one teaspoon of white vinegar and one half teaspoon of salt, then wipe out well.

Never use a plastic bowl, as there are microscopic pockets in the plastic in which fat can collect, and then the whites won't rise.

Separate the eggs one at a time (Jacques's method). Crack one whole egg into a small bowl, then lift out the yolk with your cupped (perfectly clean, of course) fingers, letting the white slide off over your fingers and through them. Pour the egg white into the mixing bowl; put the yolk in a separate container. Separate each egg in turn: if even a speck of broken yolk gets into the white, don't use that one for whipping.

Control the mixer speed. To start beating the egg whites, turn the machine to high for 2 to 3 seconds to break them up—a trick I learned from Jacques. Immediately reduce speed to low and gradually increase to medium, then to fast. Now you have to be careful that you do not overbeat, since these machines are fast and powerful; watch with full attention. When you are familiar with egg whites you can tell their state just by looking at them in the machine; otherwise, stop and check rapidly every four to five seconds, and continue beating until you have upstanding peaks, as in the bottom photo on the opposite page. (If you are to add sugar, beat it in when the eggs make soft peaks, then continue until you have stiff shining peaks.)

Overbeaten egg whites. Within seconds, while the machine is going, your beautifully beaten whites can lose their sheen and will begin to look grainy. You have overbeaten them. You can bring back their glossy texture by beating in another egg white, and they can be used for many purposes but are no longer suitable for cakes or soufflés because they will have lost an important portion of their puffing power. A sad lesson, but one you'll not forget.

Jacques on Beating Egg Whites by Hand

Beating by hand is the fastest method for the small amount of egg white required in most recipes for home cooks, and will give you perfectly risen whites, if you use the correct equipment and the right technique.

The mixing bowl. Use a bowl large enough to allow a big, wide wire whisk to get under the whole mass of egg white and turn it over. Stainless-steel bowls are fine, but, traditionally, unlined copper bowls are used for beating egg whites, because there is a chemical reaction that acidifies the egg whites and improves their stability (just as a few drops of added vinegar or lemon juice or a pinch of cream of tartar does). Unlined copper pans are used for cooking sugar for the same reason.

If you are using a copper bowl, you must first remove all grease and any greenish residue (copper sulfate, which is poisonous) by rubbing the surface with a mixture of white vinegar and salt; rinse well and dry. If you use copper cleaner, just rinse it out and dry.

The whisk. Use a large, flexible, wide wire whisk—preferably the large whisk called a balloon whip—to beat as much air into the whites as possible.

Separating the eggs. The common method of passing the yolk back and forth between the halves of eggshell, if not done properly, can leave about one-third of the white in the shell. I break all the eggs carefully into the mixing bowl, then with my cupped fingers lift out the yolks one at a time, removing all of the clinging white, including the "chalazae," the thick strands that suspend the yolk in the shell.

Here's another common practice that you want to avoid: cracking the eggs on the edge of the bowl can produce tiny shell fragments. Instead, crack the egg on a flat surface, then break the shell open with your fingers.

The temperature of egg whites. If the egg whites are cold, the air bubbles you create in beating are smaller, and you won't get as great a volume as with room-temperature egg whites. But I find that the larger air bubbles from warmer whites break down faster, and then they tend to weep and get grainy more quickly. Therefore, I usually use egg whites right from the refrigerator—the volume may be smaller, but the texture is better. If you need more volume, just use an extra white.

Egg whites broken up and liquefied after being beaten very fast with a balloon whisk for 5 seconds

The correct way to beat the whites. First, whip the whites very fast, for only five seconds or so, to break them up and liquefy.

Then begin to whip slowly and steadily, angling the bowl and the whisk so you can get under all the egg whites, lifting and turning them in a circular motion. You should be able to hear the egg whites falling on themselves. Continue the steady whipping as the egg whites inflate and thicken, changing hands if you get tired.

Egg whites with soft peaks forming

After about a minute, when soft peaks form, the whites are nearly finished. If your recipe calls for sugar you should add it now. Now whip fast for about half a minute, to "tighten" the mass of whites and produce a stiff and glossy—but not dry—texture.

Perfect egg whites—stiff and glossy but not dry

Julia

In these fat-fearing and egg-fearing times, I think we may be forgetting just how good hollandaise is, with its voluptuously silken texture and its lemony-buttery flavor. Nothing coats a poached egg as well, and it is excellent with all kinds of vegetables and fish. I also like its easy variations, like *sauce mousseline*, with a bit of folded-in whipped cream, or *sauce mousseuse*, hollandaise lightened with beaten egg whites.

Don't be afraid of cooking the yolks right on the burner, as we do here. It is much faster than the old-fashioned way of thickening them over hot water. If you see that the yolks are heating up fast, simply move the pan off the heat for a few seconds. But be sure you cook them until you can see the bottom of the pan through the tracks of your whisk. You must also beat in the butter slowly, just droplets at a time, until the emulsion starts, and even then you want to make sure you are incorporating every small addition before adding more.

Hollandaise

Hollandaise sauce is an essential component of Eggs Benedict (page 86), and a lovely adornment for all kinds of egg dishes and vegetable dishes, like warm asparagus and broccoli, and for delicate fish poached in white wine. Like mayonnaise, it is a classic "emulsion" sauce, which depends on the marvelous capacity of an egg yolk to hold in suspension a much greater volume of butter (or oil, in the case of mayonnaise). But in a hollandaise, careful heating and constant whisking bring the butter and yolks together in an even more delicate alliance, with rich flavor and a thick, smooth texture.

Making hollandaise at home, though, is a simple matter. All you need are a good whisk, this recipe, and a few minutes, and you can quickly whip up a cup or more of sauce by hand, a good amount for four poached eggs. For Chateaubriand (page 322) and other grilled meats, or Julia's poached eggs in artichoke bottoms (page 82), you will want to try the famous tarragon variation, Sauce Béarnaise (in the sidebar on page 99), using Jacques's easy method. (And if for some reason your sauce fails to thicken or appears curdled, see the rescue methods on pages 98 and 99.)

Hollandaise Sauce

Yield: About 1 cup

> 3 egg yolks
> 1 Tbs water
> 1 Tbs freshly squeezed lemon juice
>   or more, if needed
> 6 to 8 ounces very soft unsalted butter
> Salt
> Freshly ground white pepper

Special equipment

A 6-to-8-cup heavy-bottomed saucepan (stainless steel or other non-reactive finish); a medium wire whisk; an 8-inch bowl of cold water

Cooking the egg-yolk base

Whisk the yolks, water, and lemon juice in the saucepan for a few moments, until thick and pale (this prepares them for what is to come). Set the pan over moderately low heat and continue to whisk at reasonable speed, reaching all over the bottom and insides of the pan, where the eggs tend to overcook.

To moderate the heat, frequently move the pan off the burner for a few seconds, and then back on. (If, by chance, the eggs seem to be cooking too fast, set the pan in the bowl of cold water to cool the bottom, then continue.) As they cook, the eggs will become frothy and increase in volume, and then thicken. When you can see the pan bottom through the streaks of the whisk and the eggs are thick and smooth, remove from the heat.

Beating in the butter

By spoonfuls, add the soft butter, whisking constantly to incorporate each addition. As the emulsion forms, you may add the butter in slightly larger amounts, always whisking until fully absorbed.

Continue incorporating butter until the sauce has thickened to the consistency you want.

Season lightly with salt and a dash of cayenne pepper, whisking in well. Taste and adjust the seasoning, adding droplets of lemon juice if needed. Serve lukewarm.

Jacques

First, a word of caution about seasoning: don't add too much salt to your hollandaise. Strangely enough, it will take only a very little bit of salt, so give it just a dash to begin with, and taste carefully before adding more.

The form of butter that you use will affect the consistency of your hollandaise. The recipe here calls for very soft butter, which will produce a thinner sauce, fine for napping poached eggs. Classically, however, hollandaise is made with clarified butter, which gives it a thicker consistency, because only the clear melted butter (clarified) is used and the milky residue discarded. It is essential to use when you want to combine the sauce with cream or with fish sauce, for example, to use as a glaze over fish that browns beautifully under the broiler.

It is very important that you cook the yolks sufficiently in the first stage—what we call the sabayon—or they won't be able to absorb the butter. When I was an apprentice in Paris, I was sent to make a hollandaise with 60 egg yolks. I was so afraid that they would turn into scrambled eggs that I didn't give them enough heat. I beat them and beat them with a big whisk and the sabayon foamed up higher and higher, over the bowl. I got kicked in the rear end and then had to do it all over again.

Julia on Preparing Hollandaise Sauce Ahead

You can prepare the sauce ahead and leave it in a faintly warm place, such as over a pilot light on the stove, or in a pan of warm water. If you overheat it you'll scramble the yolks and lose the sauce. However, I wouldn't leave it warm for more than half an hour, since eggs are a prime breeding ground for evil bacteria. Bacteria are slowed down in an acid environment, but does hollandaise contain enough acid? I don't like offering bacteria any opportunities. If I know I am making the sauce ahead, I prefer adding a minimum amount of butter, refrigerating the sauce, and reserving the unused butter. When ready to serve, set a small saucepan in another saucepan of warm water, and stir the sauce by spoonfuls into the small pan, warming it a bit at a time. Heat the remaining butter, and whisk it slowly into the sauce. However, hollandaise is so relatively quick to make, why fuss with doing it in advance unless you want to make a lot and have leftovers?

Julia on Rescuing a Curdled Hollandaise

If your sauce refuses to thicken, or thins out, or curdles, don't throw it out! It probably curdled because you added the butter too fast, or you kept it too warm and the hardening eggs broke the emulsion. In fact it is a good thing for your culinary confidence to let the sauce turn and then bring it back.

The Simple Curdle

Using a blender. Blend all of the turned sauce for several seconds at high speed in the machine, and pour it back into your pan. Scrape down the sides of the blender with a rubber spatula and blend in a tablespoon of fresh lemon juice until creamy and lightly thickened—a minute or so. Blend in a teaspoon of sauce, and when thickened add another and continue until you have a half cup of properly thickened hollandaise. The very small additions at first are the key here, until you have re-created the emulsion. Then you may add the sauce in more generous amounts.

By hand. Vigorously whisk the turned sauce in its pan. Now remove a tablespoon of sauce to a mixing bowl, with a tablespoon of fresh lemon juice. Whisk until smooth and creamy, then whisk in another ½ teaspoon of the sauce, and when creamy whisk in another, repeating the process until you have a good half cup of reconstituted sauce—again it is the small additions and vigorous creaming that do the trick. Then continue with larger additions until all the sauce is reconstituted. Taste and correct seasonings of the reconstituted sauce. Hollandaise sauce may be served tepid, but if it needs rewarming, set a small saucepan in a larger pan of hot water and whisk in two spoonfuls of sauce, whisking in more as the sauce warms.

The Serious Curdle

This is when you have kept the sauce too warm and the yolks have begun to scramble. You can try the preceding methods, but I think you are best giving up, reheating the sauce, and letting the yolks scramble enough so that you can drain off the butter. Start again with fresh egg yolks and the drained-off butter. (Don't discard those scrambled yolks! Use them in a soup, salad, sandwich, or even in a meat loaf.)

Jacques on Rescuing a Curdled Hollandaise

If your sauce doesn't thicken, or curdles or thins out after you have made it, the following procedure may rectify it:

Warm the sauce on top of the stove to break it down even further. Set aside for 10 minutes off the heat. Now spoon off into a bowl as much as you can of the clear butter that will have risen to the top and reserve. Remove to another bowl all but 1 tablespoon of the broken egg at the bottom. Add 1 tablespoon hot water to the tablespoon of egg remaining in the pan and mix vigorously until it comes together. Continue by adding more of the broken egg, mixing between each addition until smooth. At this point start whisking in the remaining soft butter called for in your recipe and as much of the reserved clear butter as you need until your sauce has the texture of a smooth, thick cream sauce.

If you want to make a thicker hollandaise, use clarified butter instead of soft butter in the recipe. If the sauce breaks down as you are making it, follow the same procedure described above, adding only the clear butter that has risen to the top of the bowl and more clarified butter as needed.

I have a simple method to clarify butter, using the microwave. See below.

Jacques's Quick Microwave Method for Clarifying Butter

Cut whatever amount of butter you are using into pieces (if the butter is at room temperature, the process will go more quickly) and put them in a Pyrex cup. Microwave at full power for 1 minute, let rest for 5 minutes, then microwave again for 1 minute. The milky residue should have settled to the bottom, and the butter should be clear. If not, microwave once again for 1 minute.

Jacques's Simplified Sauce Béarnaise

Sauce Béarnaise gets its distinctive flavor from shallots, tarragon stems, vinegar, and cracked pepper. In the classic method, these ingredients are reduced to a small quantity of intensely flavored liquid, which is used to make the sabayon, the first stage of cooked egg yolks. After the butter has been incorporated, the finished sauce is strained through a sieve and chopped tarragon leaves are added.

Here is an easier version, one I often make at home, in which you stir the reduction into finished hollandaise, with no need for straining:

Prepare a cup of Hollandaise Sauce, following the preceding basic recipe.

Cook over medium heat in a small saucepan 2 tablespoons of wine vinegar or tarragon vinegar, 2 tablespoons of dry white wine, ¼ cup very finely chopped shallots, ¼ teaspoon ground black pepper, and ½ tablespoon of finely chopped fresh tarragon until only a tablespoon of the liquid is left. Stir all of this into the hollandaise, along with another ½ tablespoon of chopped fresh tarragon.

SALADS AND SANDWICHES

WITH THE MARVELOUS VARIETY OF SALAD GREENS AND FRESH VEGETABLES IN SO MANY OF our markets today, we can enjoy beautiful salads all year round. When time is short it is convenient to find ready-washed greens in our supermarkets. But when you have the time, do choose, trim, wash, and spin-dry your own greens, and concoct your own special salad. There is no great salad without a fine dressing, and it's so easy to make a dressing from scratch—and cheaper, too.

We also offer in this chapter some ideas for a few out-of-the-ordinary sandwiches. Like the salads, the recipes here are our versions of great-tasting "classics"—with the exception of the seafood bread (a super-sandwich, if there is such a thing), which is wholly Jacques's creation.

Jacques on Salads

When I came to this country 35 years ago, there were only two kinds of lettuce you could buy—iceberg and romaine. But today there are a dozen or more types of salad greens in my local supermarket, along with many other things that you never saw even 5 or 10 years ago, like shallots, fresh herbs, sweet Vidalia onions, and different varieties of wild mushrooms. The change in available produce has been amazing—and today you can make more kinds of salad than ever before.

The same is true of what I can grow in my garden, since it is easy now to buy seeds for literally dozens of lettuces and herbs. My *salade santé* uses a number of different seeds I've scattered in the garden bed.

Julia on Sandwiches

Jacques and I frequently say of our recipes that they're not "written in stone." Certainly this applies to the salad and sandwich ideas we present here—although, if you want to know what the real Caesar salad tastes like, you should follow that recipe closely. But the rest of the recipes are really starting points for you to take off on.

There seems to be more good bread around these days for sandwich making, both homemade types of sandwich bread and the crusty European-style "artisan" breads that you need for Jacques's seafood bread here. Such handmade breads are not standardized, fortunately, so, if you can't find exactly the size or shape or type that's recommended, get something that's close and don't worry about it.

Jacques on Lettuce Core

Don't discard the core of the lettuce.

Whenever I make a salad with head lettuce, such as Boston or romaine, I cut out the core—the center of the stem, where the leaves join—slice it very thin, and add those pieces to the salad. It is one of my favorite parts.

In fact, the cores can be cooked as a tasty vegetable. When I was an apprentice in France, we had to clean cases of lettuce and save all the cores. Then we would prepare them *à la Grecque*—cooked in olive oil and lemon juice with thyme and other herbs—to serve cool as part of the hors d'oeuvre for the customers. Or we'd serve them hot, cooked in a cream sauce or even in a soufflé. The cores only take 4 or 5 minutes to cook and they're delicious—but unfortunately this is something that can be enjoyed only in a restaurant, which would have two or three dozen heads of lettuce on hand.

Basic Green Salad

A plain green salad, made with a single variety of lettuce, can be one of the very best. Our favorite for this salad is Boston lettuce, the soft, loose-headed type, similar to Bibb or butterhead, though Boston heads are larger. The leaves are at once tender and crisp, and good by themselves, with only a simple dressing and perhaps a sprinkling of fresh herbs for embellishment. Follow this basic procedure with any lettuce (or mixture of lettuces) that you like.

Yield: 4 to 6 servings

1 large or several small heads Boston lettuce (about 1 pound)
½ cup or so Julia's Lemon-Oil Dressing or Jacques's Vinaigrette in a Jar (pages 114 and 115)
Salt and freshly ground pepper
Chopped fresh parsley, tarragon, chervil (optional)

Special equipment

A salad spinner; a salad spoon and fork; a serving bowl, large enough for tossing the lettuce

Preparing the lettuce leaves

Fill the sink, or a *very* large bowl, with lots of cold water. Trim the lettuce heads as shown in the photos on the following page, and drop the leaves into the water as you peel them off the head.

Wash the leaves by tumbling them gently in the water. Allow the dirt and sand to settle to the bottom for a few moments, then lift the leaves out in bunches, being careful not to squeeze or bruise them. Lightly shake off excess water and put leaves in the salad spinner. Dry them thoroughly, in batches.

If you are making your salad right away, pile the leaves loosely in the salad bowl; otherwise wrap them in a clean towel and refrigerate, sealed tightly in a plastic bag.

Toss just before serving

When ready to serve, drizzle about ⅓ cup of dressing over the lettuce, and toss the leaves gently with the salad spoon and fork, reaching into the bottom of the bowl, until they are evenly and lightly coated. Taste a piece of lettuce, and if you think the salad needs it, toss with more dressing or season with salt and pepper.

Sprinkle the chopped herbs, if using, over the salad.

Jacques

These days, it seems, you can't go into a restaurant and get a salad with fewer than 15 kinds of greens, but too few cooks know how to make a perfect salad with just one lettuce. You must understand what you're doing. The leaves have to be trimmed properly and washed properly, in lots of cold water. I prefer to use a sink or a large bowl or even the bowl of the salad spinner. The leaves must be lifted and drained, but they can't be squeezed or bruised or they will wilt. And they must be dried very well—only a salad spinner does an adequate job in my opinion. I can remove ¼ cup or more of water from the leaves when I spin them. If that water remains on the leaves, it dilutes the dressing, and the salad is dead!

Finally, the leaves should be cool, but not ice-cold, when you serve them, so take them out of the refrigerator a bit ahead of time, if necessary. And most important, toss your salad just before serving, with the right amount of dressing—not too much, but enough to coat the leaves lightly.

How to Trim a Boston Lettuce

Pull off any large, wilted outer leaves from the lettuce. With a sharp paring knife, cut around the bottom core, and remove it in one piece. Trim and put it in the salad, if you like—see page 102.

With large leaves, tear off any coarse tops.

Using a stainless-steel knife (which won't color the lettuce) slice on either side of the thick central rib to get 2 tender lettuce pieces. Toss these into the water; discard the ribs and tough tops.

With smaller, inner leaves: slice each in half right on the head, cutting down the middle of the rib, and peel the cut pieces directly into the water.

A pile of tender leaves and the heart of the head, which may be used along with the trimmed, sliced core

Jacques's Salade Santé

One of the joys of summer is to pick fresh salad greens and herbs from the garden just before mealtime. I usually go into the garden with a large bowl and a knife, so I can trim and cut the greens and herbs right there, thus eliminating a mess in my kitchen.

In the spring, I mix five or six packages of different salad green seeds in a small bowl and plant them in one area of my garden by tossing out the seeds as one does when seeding a lawn. I use whatever is available at the garden center—greens like red oak, Boston lettuce, romaine, arugula, escarole, and bitter chicory. I also plant many varieties of herbs, some perennials—like tarragon,

thyme, sorrel, and chives—and some annuals—like basil, parsley, and chervil. Purslane grows wild in my garden. Remember that this list of what I plant in my garden is subjective; rely on your own tastes and what is available where you are.

Wash the salad greens and herbs several times, if necessary, changing the water between washings and lifting the greens from the water rather than pouring the water off the greens. Spin-dry the greens and herbs carefully and completely, since water left in them will dilute the dressing.

Yield: 6 servings

Dressing

    1 Tbs sherry vinegar

    1 Tbs red-wine vinegar

    5 Tbs virgin olive oil

    1/3 tsp salt

    1/3 tsp freshly ground black pepper

Mixed herbs (about 5 cups total)

    1 cup sorrel, washed, dried, and cut into
      2-inch pieces

    1 cup purslane, washed, dried, and cut
      into 2-inch pieces

    1/2 cup chives, washed, dried, and cut
      into 2-inch pieces

    3/4 cup parsley leaves, washed, dried, and
      cut into 1-inch pieces

    3/4 cup basil leaves, washed, dried, and cut
      into 1-inch pieces

    1/2 cup chervil leaves, washed, dried, and
      cut into 2-inch pieces

    1/3 cup tarragon leaves, washed and dried

    1 Tbs lemon-thyme leaves, washed and dried

    About 9 cups (3/4 pound) mixed salad
      greens (red oak, romaine, bitter
      chicory, Boston lettuce, curly endive,
      etc.), washed and dried

Mix together the dressing ingredients in a bowl large enough to hold the herbs and greens.

Just before serving, add the herbs and greens to the bowl and toss to coat them with the dressing. Serve immediately.

Jacques on Watercress

I love the assertive flavor of watercress with meat. But you must dress watercress at the very last moment before serving, because it wilts extremely fast.

Mâche, also called field salad, corn salad, or *doucette*, is a delicious mild green, which I grow in my garden. It has the best flavor after the first frost, so I plant it in the garden late in the summer, and then cut it only after it has frozen once. It is very hardy, and some years I can pick it for salads even in December.

Julia

I am probably one of the few people around who saw the real Caesar Cardini making his salad. I was about 9 when my parents took me to his restaurant in Tijuana, just the other side of the border from San Diego. They were so excited when big jolly Caesar himself came to the table to make the salad, which had already been written up and talked about everywhere. And it was dramatic: I remember most clearly the eggs going in, and how he tossed the leaves so it looked like a wave turning over.

This version is quite close to the original, and you can see it is really a very simple salad. Use small, tender whole leaves, real Parmigiano Reggiano —none of the fake stuff—and the 1-minute egg for creaminess (though you can substitute a teaspoon of mayonnaise for the egg). But you don't want herbs and anchovies and things like that—then you have adulterated it.

Caesar Salad

When Caesar first served his famous salad in the early 1920s, he used just the hearts of romaine lettuce, the tender short leaves in the center, and he presented them whole. The salad was tossed and dressed, then arranged on each plate so that you could pick up a leaf by its short end and chew it down bit by bit, then pick up another. However, many customers didn't like to get their fingers covered with egg-and-cheese-and-garlic dressing, and he changed to the conventional torn leaf. Too bad, since the salad lost much of its individuality and drama. You can certainly serve it the original way at home—just provide your guests with plenty of big paper napkins. And plan to be extravagant.

Julia's Caesar Salad

Yield: 2 or 3 servings

18 to 24 crisp, narrow leaves from the hearts of 2 heads romaine lettuce, or a package of romaine hearts (about 1 pound)
1 cup Plain Toasted Croutons (page 108)
1 large clove garlic, peeled
¼ cup or more excellent olive oil
Salt
1 large egg
Freshly ground black pepper
1 whole lemon, halved and seeded
Worcestershire sauce
2 Tbs freshly grated Parmesan cheese, imported Parmigiano Reggiano only

Special equipment
A large mixing bowl; a small frying pan

Preparing the salad components

You will probably need 2 large heads of romaine for 3 people—or use a commercially prepared package of "romaine hearts," if they appear fresh and fine. From a large head remove the outside leaves until you get down to the cone where the leaves are 4 to 7 inches in length (see photo on left)—you'll want 6 to 8 of these leaves per serving. Separate the leaves and wash them carefully to keep them whole, roll them loosely in clean towels, and keep refrigerated until serving time. (Save the remains for other salads—fortunately, romaine keeps reasonably well under refrigeration.)

Separate the leaves.

To flavor the croutons, crush the garlic clove with the flat of a chef's knife, sprinkle on ¼ teaspoon of salt, and mince well. Pour about a tablespoon of olive oil on the garlic and mash again with the knife, rubbing and pressing to make a soft purée.

Scrape the purée into the frying pan, add another tablespoon of oil, and warm over low-medium heat. Add the croutons and toss for a minute or two to infuse them with the garlic oil, then remove from the heat. (For a milder garlic flavor, you can strain the purée through a small sieve into a pan before adding the extra oil and croutons. Discard the bits of garlic.)

Toss to coat the leaves with the egg and dressing.

Jacques

Julia's authentic Caesar salad is excellent, but I love Gloria's almost-Caesar salad, the one my wife makes at home. She mixes all the dressing ingredients together first—oil, lemon juice, Worcestershire, seasonings, chopped garlic, egg, and anchovy fillets in little pieces—and then tosses it with the broken-up romaine leaves. And she tosses in some crumbled blue cheese, either Roquefort or Stilton, as well as Parmesan. She made this for me when we first met, and I have never wanted to change it.

To coddle the egg, bring a small saucepan of water to the simmer. Pierce the large end of the egg with a pushpin to prevent cracking, then simmer it for exactly 1 minute.

Mixing and serving the Caesar

Dress the salad just before serving. Have ready all the dressing ingredients and a salad fork and spoon for tossing.

Drizzle 2 tablespoons of olive oil over the romaine leaves and toss to coat, lifting the leaves from the bottom and turning them toward you, so they tumble over like a wave. Sprinkle with a generous pinch of salt and several grinds of pepper, toss once or twice, then add the lemon juice and several drops of Worcestershire, and toss again. Taste for seasoning, and add more, if needed.

Crack the egg and drop it right on the romaine leaves, then toss to break it up and coat the leaves. Sprinkle on the cheese, toss briefly, then add the croutons (and the garlicky bits in the pan, if you wish) and toss for the last time, just to mix them into the salad.

Arrange 6 or more leaves in a single layer on individual plates, scatter the croutons all around, and serve.

Homemade Croutons

Homemade croutons are essential for our Caesar salad and a fine addition to a basic green salad as well as soups. You can enrich the cubes with melted butter before toasting, if you like, or flavor them after with garlic oil, as in the Caesar recipe. It's easy to make a large batch and freeze any croutons you are not using the same day. Reheat frozen croutons in a low oven until crisp.

Plain Toasted Croutons (makes 4 cups)

Preheat the oven to 350°F. Remove the crusts from 4 or more thick slices of home-style white bread and slice bread into ½-inch strips and then the strips into ½-inch cubes, to make 4 cups. Spread the cubes in a single layer on a cookie sheet and set in the oven for about 10 minutes, turning once or twice, until lightly toasted on all sides. Spread the cubes on a tray to cool before using or freezing.

Butter-Toasted Croutons

Before toasting the bread cubes, toss them in a bowl with ¼ cup of melted butter, then spread them out and bake them.

Two Near-Niçoise Salads

Here are two salads using similar ingredients but put together in quite different styles. Both are inspired by the *salade niçoise*, the appetizer platter of canned tuna, tomatoes, tiny black olives, and other vegetables that is nearly as popular here in America now as it has always been on the Mediterranean coast.

The first is a large composed salad—a colorful arrangement of vegetables, hard-boiled egg halves, and various garnishes, with canned tuna at the center. Serve this as a lunch platter, or as an hors d'oeuvre for a party. There are no rules for "composing" a salad—other than that it please the eye—so use our suggested display of ingredients merely as a starting point for your own design.

The second recipe is a rather contemporary variation on the *niçoise* theme, combining some customary ingredients (tomatoes, olives, potatoes, egg wedges) with sautéed strips of fresh tuna, and mesclun. This mix of small lettuce leaves and other tangy greens also has its culinary origins in Nice and Provence, but has recently become a standard item in the produce section of our markets. Serve the second recipe as a generous main-course salad for one person, or as a first course for two.

Jacques

Even in Nice, *salade niçoise* is put together in different ways and with different ingredients. Conventionally, it will always have canned tuna, tomatoes, and the small olives that are grown in the region. But in some places you will get green beans, potatoes, sliced onion, or anchovy fillets as well. And while it is most typical for the ingredients to be set on the plate in separate bunches, to be eaten like an antipasto, sometimes they are all put in a bowl and tossed.

My mesclun salad (on page 113) with fresh tuna is in the modern style, the kind of thing that young chefs like to do today, combining warm and cool ingredients in a salad. Using vinaigrette as the sauté medium is a special touch, which makes the pan juices very flavorful—you definitely want to use these to dress the salad.

Julia

I strongly suggest that you always use top-quality canned tuna (see below). In my composed salad, and in many versions of *salade niçoise,* the dressing is poured over the various ingredients after they've been set on the plate. Actually, I like to dress most of the vegetables separately—like the green beans here—by tossing them with vinaigrette in a bowl, before arranging them on the platter. Jacques peels his peppers, but I never do.

Canned Tuna

This nation's fear-of-fat phobia has ruined the canned-tuna industry, to my mind. When looking for it on our supermarket shelves, you rarely find anything but tuna canned in "fresh spring water," which has far less taste than tuna packed in oil and, in my experience, eventually tends to disintegrate. I recommend that you look around for solid white chunk tuna packed in olive oil. You might find it in the Italian-foods section, or ask your grocery manager to order it.

A 3-ounce can of tuna in water contains 3 grams of fat, versus 6 grams of fat for the oil-pack. Certainly 3 grams makes a minimal difference nutritionally, but those extra 3 grams in the oil-pack make a notable difference in taste and texture.

Julia's Composed Near-Niçoise Salad

Yield: 1 large platter, serving 4

1 large red onion, peeled, halved, and sliced into thin half rounds

1 large green bell pepper, peeled if you wish (see sidebar), quartered, and sliced into long thin strips

1 cup or more green and black olives

2 to 3 cups small tomatoes, a combination of red-cherry and yellow-pear types recommended

½ pound green beans (about 2 cups), trimmed, blanched, dried, and chilled (page 188)

½ cup or more Jacques's Vinaigrette in a Jar (page 115)

4 hard-boiled eggs, peeled and halved lengthwise

⅓ cup or so mayonnaise

One 2-ounce can of anchovies, packed in olive oil

One 12-ounce can of tuna fish, best-quality, packed in olive oil, or 2 smaller cans

Sprigs of basil, for garnish

Special equipment

A large flat serving platter

Follow these steps for arranging and seasoning the salad on the serving platter, which should be large enough to hold the array of salad components, or create your own composition of colorful piles of the prepared ingredients:

Toss the onion to separate the slices and mound them all loosely in the center of the platter. Then divide the pepper slices into 2 equal portions and arrange on opposite sides of the platter. Similarly, arrange the olives and the tomatoes each in 2 piles, on either side of the onion mound, creating a symmetrical design. Then toss the green beans with a couple of tablespoons of the salad dressing in a bowl to coat evenly, and arrange them in the remaining opposite spaces of the platter.

Nestle each of the 8 egg halves in between the vegetables, or arrange them around the outside of the platter, spaced equally. Top each egg half with a teaspoon of mayonnaise, drape an anchovy fillet over the mayo, and drizzle the anchovy oil on top.

Invert the open can of tuna directly over the onions, and shake to release the fish (with all of its oil) in a round in the center of the salad.

Finally, drizzle ⅓ cup or more of the dressing over the entire salad. Stand a large spray of basil leaves in the center of the tuna and serve.

Pépin Peels a Pepper

I find that bell pepper tastes better (and is more digestible) if you peel it first, especially when served raw in a salad like this *niçoise*. Here is a simple technique:

With a sharp vegetable peeler, strip the peel from the top and bottom of the pepper.

Peel all the skin that your vegetable peeler can reach down the sides.

Slice lengthwise down the middle of each "pleat" and pull apart the lobes of the pepper.

After cutting off the ribs inside and removing any seeds, use your peeler to shave the remaining peel along the edges.

Jacques's Near-Niçoise Salad with Sautéed Fresh Tuna

Yield: 1 large salad, serving 1 or 2

4 ounces fresh tuna, in one
    chunk
¼ tsp salt
⅓ cup or so Jacques's Vinaigrette
    in a Jar (page 115)
2 Tbs chopped scallion
½ cup or so cooked waxy
    potatoes, such as fingerlings
    or small red or white new
    potatoes, in ½-inch chunks
3 Tbs small black Niçoise olives
¼ cup thinly sliced red onion
5 or 6 fresh green basil leaves
1 small ripe tomato, cut into
    wedges
1 hard-boiled egg, quartered
    lengthwise into wedges
⅛ tsp freshly ground black pepper
A large handful mesclun or other
    tender salad greens

Special equipment

A sauté pan; a bowl for mixing

Sautéing the tuna

Cut the raw tuna into ⅓-inch-thick slices (about 4 or 5), and sprinkle with half of the salt. Coat the bottom of the pan with a tablespoon or two of the vinaigrette and set over high heat. When sizzling, quickly lay all the tuna pieces flat in the pan and cook for about 20 seconds, until just opaque on the bottom.

Flip the slices over, cook another 10 seconds, then remove the pan from the heat, allowing the tuna to finish cooking while you assemble the salad.

Mixing the salad

Place the scallions, potato chunks, olives, onion, basil leaves, and the tomato and egg wedges in the mixing bowl. Drizzle on about 2 to 3 tablespoons of the vinaigrette, season with the rest of the salt and the black pepper, and toss briefly to coat. Add the mesclun to the bowl and toss again, gently.

Turn the salad out onto a dinner plate, and arrange the chunky vegetable and egg pieces—if they are hidden by the mesclun leaves—so they are nicely displayed. Lay the tuna slices on top of the mound of greens and drizzle the juices in the pan over the salad. Serve immediately.

Opposite: Near-Niçoise Salad with Sautéed Fresh Tuna

Julia

For dressing a simple lettuce

salad, I prefer the more delicate acidic element of lemon juice, rather than vinegar—and I always mix a fresh dressing, just before tossing it with the greens. A bit of chopped scallions or shallots and a spoon of Dijon mustard are standard for me—the mustard helps emulsify the dressing, making it a bit creamy, as well as adding flavor. For variation, I might add a small garlic clove, mashed and minced with salt, or chopped parsley, tarragon, or chives, or a small amount of lemon zest finely puréed.

Often, though, I don't even mix a dressing for a green salad. I toss the lettuce leaves first with olive oil, just to coat them. Then I whisk together the lemon juice, chopped scallions or shallots, and mustard—and salt and pepper—and spoon this on a bit at a time, tossing and tasting, until there's just enough. That's all there is to it, and the salad is perfectly dressed.

Basic Dressings

Almost all of the salads in this chapter are dressed with a "vinaigrette"—a simple mixture of oil, vinegar or lemon juice, and seasonings—or with the same ingredients added separately. But there's no single vinaigrette formula—throughout the recipes, we vary the proportions of oil and the acidic element of vinegar or lemon juice, and use a variety of seasonings, to give a lively and distinctive flavor to lettuce, lentils, potatoes, avocados, or whatever needs coating.

It is always helpful, though, to have a simple, standard dressing for everyday salads—one with a pleasing balance of oil and acid that you can whip up in a minute. Here are the dressings that we each make and use most frequently for plain green salads, and mixed salads with vegetables, cold meat, or fish. Try them both, and use them interchangeably where they are recommended in our recipes. Most important, adjust and vary them any way you like, to suit your taste and the foods you are dressing.

Julia's Lemon-Oil Dressing

Yield: About ⅔ cup

1 Tbs minced shallots or scallions
2 tsp Dijon-style prepared mustard
2 Tbs freshly squeezed lemon juice
About ¼ tsp salt or more to taste
Freshly ground black pepper, to taste
½ cup excellent olive oil

Put the minced scallions, mustard, lemon juice, salt, and pepper in a small mixing bowl and whisk until well blended.

Pour in the oil slowly, in droplets at first, and then in a thin stream, whisking constantly until the oil has been completely emulsified and the dressing has thickened. Taste and adjust the seasonings. Use immediately; if the dressing separates while standing, whisk to blend.

Jacques's Vinaigrette in a Jar

Yield: About 1½ cups

2 tsp chopped garlic
2 Tbs Dijon-style mustard
½ tsp salt
¼ tsp freshly ground black pepper
¼ cup red- or white-wine vinegar
1 cup extra-virgin olive oil or peanut oil,
   or a mixture of the two

Special equipment

A 12-ounce glass jar with a screwtop lid

Put all the ingredients in the jar, screw on the lid, and shake very well. Taste and adjust the seasonings, adding more oil or vinegar, as you like.

Store in refrigerator up to 2 weeks, and shake to blend before using.

I make dressing in a jar all the time at home, just like the recipe here. In less than a minute, I have enough for several salads. And if I happen to have a jar of mustard that's almost empty it's even faster. I just add the add oil and vinegar, salt and pepper, and shake.

With this method, you can keep the jar in the refrigerator for a couple of weeks at most and use the dressing whenever needed. However, chopped garlic (or shallots, if you use them) will develop an off flavor after a while, so, if you will be storing the dressing longer, add garlic to the vinaigrette only when you dress your salad—don't put it in the jar.

Classically, vinaigrettes are made with a proportion of three parts of oil to one part of vinegar, but for me that is too acidic. I suggest a four-to-one ratio, since the mustard contains vinegar too. But vinaigrettes are a matter of taste: if you like a more acidic dressing, simply add more vinegar or lemon juice; or add more oil if you wish.

Similarly, you can vary the flavor with other kinds of vinegars and oils. Experiment: make a jar of dressing with a good-quality cider vinegar, or use a mild rice vinegar. If you want to try vinegars or oils with dominating tastes, though, add them in small amounts—mix a bit of balsamic vinegar, for instance, with red or white vinegar; or combine a tablespoon of roasted sesame oil, or walnut oil, with a neutral-tasting oil like canola or corn oil. Just try simple combinations and see what you like—there are literally hundreds of vinaigrettes you can make.

Julia on Olive Oil

"Extra-virgin" is the official designation for oil from the first cold-pressing of a batch of olives, with a very low level of acidity, and is presumably the best of that lot. But it is a mistake to assume that an extra-virgin oil will be perfect; there are bad years with olives, and to my taste, extra-virgin oils can sometimes be bitter or have an off flavor. Therefore, I *always* prefer the term "excellent" olive oil, to emphasize that you want to use a fine oil of the best quality—preferably one that you have tasted and truly like.

It is not an easy task to choose among all the fancy extra-virgin olive oils on the market today. There's a good deal of showing off with olive oil, as with other gourmet foods, and some oils are just ridiculously expensive. You might take advice from someone who really knows—a friend with a good palate, or a trusted merchant who's not showing off—but in the end you should rely on your own taste and not be influenced by sales pitches. And I have found that some of the extra-virgin oils sold in the supermarket by such producers as Colavita and Bertolli are in fact "excellent."

My own preference among fancy and pricey oils is for the lighter, fragrant French oils—but, then, I am a Francophile. (And though it is heresy to say in some circles these days, I often find Tuscan oils too bitter for my taste.) In recent years California has produced some fine oils that are worth trying. I save my most beautiful oils just for salad or for special effects. For other uses, like sautéing, I use a modestly priced olive oil, of whatever official grade (extra-virgin, virgin, or pure), so long as it is fresh and has a fine taste.

Mayonnaise

With a jar of mayonnaise in most home refrigerators, and a layer of mayo on almost every fast-food sandwich, it is hardly surprising that few Americans realize that mayonnaise is one of the finest and most important sauces in classic cuisine. The shame is that few of us ever taste the kind of fresh, handmade mayonnaise that deserves such culinary status—and even dedicated home cooks don't realize that making their own is a simple process that takes only minutes and, if you use a food processor, almost no effort at all.

Here we each give you our own personal formulas—the mayonnaise you may want to use for salads and sandwiches in this chapter (Julia's American-style potato salad, celery root rémoulade, our cold lobster roll, and *croque monsieur*) as well as any others that deserve a special touch. It is just the right sauce or garnish for countless cold foods—hard-boiled eggs, cooked vegetables like broccoli or asparagus or fresh tomatoes, poached fish and shellfish, cold chicken, or other meats. And you can vary it with additions as varied as green herbs, curry, puréed garlic, chopped capers and pickles, tomato sauce, horseradish, whipped cream, mushroom purée, the roe or tomalley of lobster, or caviar—you name it.

Whether you use Jacques's hand-whisking technique or Julia's food-processor method, mayonnaise is made by forming an emulsion of oil and vinegar or lemon juice through the medium of egg yolks. The process is essentially the same as making the other classic "emulsion sauces," Hollandaise (page 96) and Béarnaise (page 99), but mayonnaise is simpler and more reliable because the vinegar-and-egg-yolk base needs no cooking. If you follow the rules spelled out here, your mayonnaise will be perfect. Should the emulsion break down for some reason, there are simple methods to "rescue" it (see pages 98 and 99).

A note on safety

Like any raw egg product, mayonnaise requires proper storage and handling to prevent the growth of harmful bacteria. More discussion on egg safety is on page 65 in the "Eggs" chapter. When serving homemade mayonnaise, do not let it sit at room temperature for more than an hour, and always store it in the refrigerator.

If you are wary of using raw eggs, see Julia's Cooked Egg Mayonnaise (page 118).

Julia's Mayonnaise in the Food Processor

Yield: about 2 cups

2 egg yolks
1 whole egg
1 Tbs lemon juice, freshly squeezed,
    plus more if needed
1 tsp Dijon-style prepared mustard
½ tsp salt
Big pinch freshly ground white pepper
Up to 2 cups excellent fresh vegetable oil
    or olive oil (all one or a mixture)

Special equipment

A food processor with the metal blade

Put the egg yolks, egg, lemon juice, mustard, salt, and white pepper in the work bowl of the food processor; process for 10 seconds or more, until creamy.

With the food processor running continuously, pour in the oil very slowly, in driblets at first, to start the emulsion process. When the sauce has definitely thickened, you may add the oil in a thin stream. Do not stop the machine at this point, but cease pouring every few seconds to be sure the oil is being absorbed. Then continue until 1½ cups have been incorporated.

Stop the machine and check the mayonnaise for taste and consistency. Adjust the seasonings and, if the mayonnaise is very thick, process in drops of lemon juice or warm water to thin.

Jacques

When making mayonnaise by hand, pay attention to several factors to avoid breaking the emulsion. Most important, the oil must be at room temperature, never cold. And the first ½ cup or so of oil must be incorporated slowly—after the emulsion forms, you can whisk in the remainder more steadily. Don't stir or whisk chilled mayonnaise that's been stored in the refrigerator; allow it to come to room temperature before stirring.

There are fewer concerns if you are making mayonnaise in the food processor. Unlike Julia, I don't add the oil to the machine slowly—I pour it in a steady stream all in at once, and it never breaks down. The machine rapidly creates a very strongly bonded emulsion, with extremely small particles of oil. The resulting mayonnaise is quite thick and more stable than hand-whisked. Even if chilled, it will not break down when stirred. Because the emulsion is stronger, food-processor mayonnaise has a different taste and mouth feel than handmade. Try both ways and see which you prefer.

The choice of oil for mayonnaise is also a question of personal taste, as is how you are going to use the sauce. If it's to be served with something bland, perhaps a piece of poached chicken, you may want stronger flavor in the oil itself. Then you might use all extra-virgin olive oil—assuming, of course, that you like that taste. On the other hand, if you are using the mayonnaise as a base—say, for a *sauce tartare*, which will have chopped pickles and herbs added—then you can make the emulsion with a neutral (and inexpensive) canola or peanut oil.

Julia

One of the real reasons for making your own mayonnaise is that it is, actually, your own, with your particular vinegar, your special oil, your special seasonings. When you put together your own secret and special signature shrimp salad, for instance, do you want your guests to recognize at once the taste of that familiar bottled supermarket sauce you have used? I have my favorite among them, and although I can try to disguise its taste I still feel it can be recognized. No! For my unique and remarkable salad I'll make my own.

Another good reason to make your own is that it is part of your culinary baggage as an accomplished cook to know the basics, particularly those of the emulsion sauces, which include hollandaise and white butter sauce as well as mayonnaise. Jacques's handmade version here is a fine example of fundamental techniques, and when you know them you also understand what the machine is doing. Besides, if the electricity goes off and you don't know how to hand-whisk the mayo, you'll need a change of menu.

These emulsion sauces are those most dreaded by beginning cooks, because they can obstinately refuse to cooperate. I think this chapter, however, will reassure you, because we go into full detail on the whys and hows and, most important, we offer you our foolproof ways to recuperate.

Julia's Food Processor Mayonnaise (continued)

The mayonnaise may be used at this point, or you can process in some or all of the remaining oil for a thicker sauce.

Transfer the finished mayonnaise to a bowl. If not using right away, cover with plastic wrap and refrigerate. The sauce will keep for a good week.

Note on chilled mayonnaise

Chilled mayonnaise may well break down and thin out if you stir it just out of the refrigerator. I have a small saucepan that I set in a larger pan of slightly warmed water (a little warmer than tepid). I whisk into it a tablespoon of the chilled sauce, and continue whisking as the sauce slowly comes to room temperature before whisking in another tablespoon of chilled sauce. You can't hurry it, but it goes faster as your rewarmed sauce increases in volume. If all fails, see sidebar on next page.

Julia's Cooked Egg Mayonnaise

When you want a homemade mayonnaise that tastes like the real thing yet contains no raw eggs, try this recipe, which uses a simple sauce base containing cooked whole egg and hard-boiled egg yolks. It's not only good for regular use, but is recommended in hot weather: containing cooked rather than raw eggs, it is safer to use and in addition has a longer refrigerator-storage life.

Yield: About 2 cups

2 Tbs flour
½ cup water
1 large egg
2 hard-boiled egg yolks
1 Tbs Dijon-type prepared mustard
½ tsp salt
2½ tsp wine vinegar
2½ tsp fresh lemon juice

1 cup excellent olive oil or other fresh
   vegetable oil
Several grinds of white pepper
More seasonings as needed: salt, vinegar,
   lemon juice, etc.

The cooked-egg sauce base

Measure the flour into a 2-quart stainless-steel saucepan and, whisking constantly, gradually blend in the water to make a lump-free mixture. Whisking slowly and reaching all over the bottom of the pan, bring to the boil on top of the stove. Boil slowly ½ minute, whisking—beat in droplets more water if the sauce is stiff rather than very thick. Remove from heat, break the egg into the center of the sauce, and rapidly whisk it in. Put the sauce over moderate heat again and, whisking slowly, boil for 15 seconds. Scrape the sauce into the bowl of a food processor.

Finishing the sauce

Add the hard-boiled yolks, mustard, salt, vinegar, and lemon juice to the machine. Process 15 seconds—long enough to be sure the egg yolks are well incorporated, so that they will create the emulsion (thickening process). Then, with the machine running, begin adding the oil in droplets, particularly at first, and when the emulsion is established (after about ⅓ cup oil) add the oil in a thin stream of droplets. When as much oil as you wish has gone in and the sauce is thick and glossy, taste analytically for seasoning, adding salt, pepper, etc., as you feel them needed.

Storage

Turn the sauce into a covered container and refrigerate; it will keep for at least a week.

Variation

For 1 quart of sauce: use 4 Tbs flour, 1 cup water, and 2 eggs for the sauce base; to finish the sauce, add 4 hard-boiled yolks, 2 Tbs mustard, ¾ tsp salt, 1 Tbs each of vinegar and lemon juice, and 2 cups of oil.

Julia on Bringing Back the Mayo

When a mayonnaise refuses to thicken, or thins out, or separates so that the egg yolks are massed in blobs with oil between, you have what is officially known as a "turned" sauce. Don't throw it out! You can fix it.

You'll want a whisk and maybe a hand-held electric beater too, and a mixing bowl. Whisk up all of the turned sauce to blend eggs and oil, then take a tablespoon of it and whisk vigorously in a second bowl with ½ tablespoon of prepared Dijon-style mustard. When it is creamed and thickened, in 10 to 15 seconds, with your whisk or electric beater, start beating in more of the turned sauce by the teaspoonful, waiting until each addition has been absorbed and the sauce has creamed and thickened before adding more.

This always works for me—thorough beating and tiny additions are the keys here until you have a good ½ cup of beautiful, creamy reconstituted sauce, and can then add the rest a little faster.

To build your confidence, I actually suggest that you let it happen to you—halfway through the new sauce you are making, add a triple splash of oil, and stir slowly as the sauce thins out. Then go to work reconstituting it, and you will feel a sense of mastery. You will never be afraid of a big bad mayonnaise sauce again.

Jacques on Fixing "Broken" Mayonnaise

If the oil is too cold when you add it to the eggs, you add it too fast, or you add too much, your mayonnaise can break down—that is, the oil and the egg base will separate, and the sauce will be thin and curdled-looking. (This can also happen if you take home-made mayo out of the refrigerator and try to whip it up while it is ice-cold.)

To return it to a smooth emulsion, you can incorporate the broken sauce with another egg yolk or a teaspoon of vinegar, mustard, or hot water. Put one of these in a clean bowl, add 1 tea-spoon of the separated sauce, and whisk together. Continue to add the broken sauce by spoonfuls, whisking until smooth after each. When the fresh emulsion starts to thicken, you can add the broken sauce faster, whisking con-stantly until the mayonnaise is restored.

Alternatively, you can repair the broken sauce right in the mixing bowl (if you've mixed it by hand). Pour the fresh yolk and the vinegar, mustard, or water in one spot on the side of the bowl and, with the tip of the whisk, stir it into the top of the broken sauce. Mix with short rapid strokes, just on the surface, to smooth a small area of the broken sauce. Gradually whisk deeper into the bowl, incorporating more of the sauce into the fresh emulsion, and then whisk in larger circles to smooth and thicken all of the mayonnaise.

Jacques's Hand-Mixed Mayonnaise

Yield: About 2 cups

2 egg yolks
1 Tbs Dijon-style mustard
2 tsp red-wine vinegar, plus more if
  needed
¼ tsp salt, or more to taste
¼ tsp freshly ground black pepper, or
  more to taste
2 cups oil, either peanut oil, extra-virgin
  olive oil, or a mixture of the two

Special equipment
A mixing bowl; a wire whisk

Put the egg yolks, mustard, vinegar, salt, and black pepper in the mixing bowl and whisk for a few seconds to blend.

Pour in the oil slowly, a tablespoon or so at a time at first, whisking rapidly and continuously. As the sauce begins to thicken, add the oil in a steady stream, whisking continuously, until 2 cups have been incorporated.

Adjust the seasonings to taste. If the mayonnaise is very thick, whisk in more vinegar or warm water in small amounts. For greater volume, or a thicker sauce, whisk in more oil.

Potato Salads

Potato salad is perfect picnic fare, but it is a good side dish any time of year, dressed and garnished in various styles to suit the season. Julia's American-style potato salad is garnished with hard-boiled eggs and crisp bacon bits, chopped pickles, onions, and celery, all given a light coating of homemade mayonnaise (pages 117 and 120). Make this at least an hour ahead of time so the flavors have time to ripen, and serve cool or at room temperature. Jacques's salad is particularly nice for winter meals—the hot potatoes are tossed with white wine and oil, sautéed onions, scallions, and garlic. Serve it warm, with slices of hot, homemade sausage (page 364) arranged on top, or with other meats.

The best potatoes for salad are the firm-textured, low-starch "waxy" varieties, which hold their shape well, such as boiling potatoes, small new potatoes, or delicate fingerlings. All-purpose potatoes with waxy flesh, such as the versatile Yukon Gold, are particularly delicious. Whatever kind you use, dress the potatoes while they are still warm so that they best absorb the flavors, and gently fold in all the dressing and seasoning ingredients in one or two additions only, so the potato pieces don't get mashed from overhandling.

Jacques

Fingerlings, also known as ladyfingers, are small oblong potatoes with extremely firm texture and beautiful color, and are terrific for both salads and sautéing. I usually leave the skin on my salad potatoes, but you can, if you like, easily scrape off the thin peel with a paring knife as soon as they are cooked.

Mine, on page 123, is a rustic salad with a very assertive taste from the wine, garlic, mustard, and herbs. The potatoes should be hot, however, when you pour on the wine, so some of the alcohol evaporates, and the sourness and acidity will diminish. For this kind of informal dish, I chop the vegetables and herbs only coarsely and use the dull edge of the knife blade to chop the garlic cloves coarsely. This crushes the garlic and releases its oils for a strong garlic flavor, but keeps the rough texture.

This salad can be served warm or at room temperature, but never cooler. If you make it ahead and store it in the refrigerator, let it return to room temperature or even reheat it a bit in the microwave before serving.

Julia's American-Style Potato Salad

Yield: About 6 cups, serving 4 to 6

2 pounds large Yukon Gold
    potatoes, or other waxy,
    boiling potatoes
2 Tbs cider vinegar
⅓ cup chicken stock or potato-
    cooking water
⅔ cup finely chopped onion
½ cup finely chopped celery
3 or 4 slices crisply cooked bacon,
    chopped or crumbled
2 to 3 Tbs finely chopped pickle,
    sweet or dill
2 hard-boiled eggs, peeled and
    sliced thin
3 Tbs or so finely chopped fresh
    chives or scallions, including a
    bit of their tender green
Salt and freshly ground white
    pepper
1 cup or so mayonnaise, home-
    made if possible (pages 117 and
    120)
Sour cream (optional)

For garnishing
Crisp whole red-leaf or other
    lettuce leaves
Canned red pimiento, diced; sliced
    hard-boiled eggs; tomato quar-
    ters; parsley sprigs (optional)

Peel the potatoes and slice each one lengthwise in half, or in quarters if very large; then cut crosswise into half-round or quarter-round slices, about ½ inch thick.

Put the slices in a saucepan with water just to cover and 1½ teaspoons of salt per quart of water. Heat to a simmer, and cook the potatoes for 5 to 6 minutes, or until just cooked through. It is essential that they be just cooked through. Bite into a slice or two to be very sure. Immediately remove from the heat and drain the potatoes into a colander, but save a cup of the cooking liquid for dressing the potatoes. Transfer the potatoes to a large bowl. Stir the cider vinegar with ⅓ cup of the potato water or chicken stock and drizzle this over the potato pieces, turning them gently to distribute it evenly. Let sit 10 minutes to absorb the liquid.

Add the prepared onion, celery, bacon, pickle, hard-boiled eggs, and chives, and season carefully to taste. Top with ⅔ cup of mayonnaise (or a mix of mayonnaise and a bit of sour cream) and, with a large rubber spatula, gently fold everything together until well blended. Taste the salad and add more salt, pepper, or mayonnaise as needed.

Cover the salad and set aside in the refrigerator for at least an hour or so before serving. If it is refrigerated longer, let it come back to room temperature before serving. Taste and adjust the seasoning again.

To serve, line a bowl or a platter with red-leaf lettuce or other greens, and mound the salad on top. Decorate at the last moment, if you wish, with any or all of the optional garnishes.

Jacques's French Potato Salad

Yield: About 6 cups, serving 4 to 6

2 pounds fingerling potatoes or
other small waxy potatoes

½ cup or so extra-virgin olive oil

½ cup ¼-inch slices of scallion,
green and white parts

½ cup chopped onion

3 cloves garlic, mashed
and coarsely chopped
(1½ tsp)

⅓ cup white wine

1½ Tbs Dijon-style mustard

2 to 3 Tbs chopped chives

2 Tbs or more coarsely chopped
fresh green or purple basil, fresh
tarragon, or parsley

1 tsp kosher salt, plus more if
needed

½ tsp freshly cracked black pepper
(coarse), plus more if needed

For serving and garnishing

Large radicchio leaves, about 6,
from the outside of the head

1 or 2 hard-boiled eggs, coarsely
chopped

Chopped fresh parsley

Scrub the potatoes and put them, whole, in a saucepan with water to cover by ½ inch. Bring the water to a boil, reduce the heat, and cook the potatoes gently until they are just tender and can be pierced with a sharp knife. Drain immediately and let cool slightly. (Scrape the skin from the cooked potatoes, if you want, as soon as they can be handled. For a decorative look with fingerlings, scrape off only a band of skin, about ½ inch thick, all around the long sides of the potato.)

Heat 2 tablespoons of the olive oil in a small sauté pan. When hot, add the scallions and the onion, toss to coat well, and cook for about a minute over medium-high heat. Add the garlic, toss to mix, and cook for just a few moments, then remove the pan from the heat.

Slice the potatoes while still warm, cutting them crosswise into ½-inch sections. Put the pieces in a large mixing bowl, pour the wine and 3 or 4 tablespoons of olive oil over them, and toss gently to distribute. Add the warm vegetables from the pan, mustard, chives, chopped herbs, salt, and pepper, and gently fold all together, mixing well but not crushing the potatoes. Taste the salad and add more seasonings as you like.

Serve the potatoes warm (no colder than room temperature). Arrange the large radicchio leaves, if you have them, in a close circle on the serving platter, with their curved insides up, to form a rough bowl. Spoon the potato salad inside the leaves, sprinkle chopped egg around the edges, and parsley over the top.

Cold Meat Salads

How convenient it is when you find yourself with guests coming to Sunday lunch and you are so fortunate as to have part of a roasted leg of lamb, or a big whole piece of braised beef or veal, and can bring it forth royally. The French served a great number of boiled and braised beef dinners in their earlier classical days, and have bequeathed us their braised beef in aspic, *boeuf en gelée,* as well as their sliced boiled beef elegantly arranged down the length of a platter with bouquets of vegetables *à la Parisienne.* The Italians give us that unusual and addictive dish *vitello tonnato,* veal with tuna mayonnaise. And of course we have our all-American ham, always ready for elegant slicing, chef salads, and just plain garnishing. Here are some suggestions, mostly in sketch form, and mostly using recipes outlined in this book.

A Simple Cold Meat Salad

Yield: 1 large salad, serving 1

About 4 ounces cold roast lamb,
   beef, veal, pork, or ham, thinly
   sliced
3 to 4 cups mixed watercress and
   mâche, loosely tossed, or other
   small-leaved salad green
$\frac{1}{4}$ cup or more Jacques's
   Vinaigrette in a Jar (page 115)
A small wedge of fresh tomato

Arrange the meat slices in a ring just inside the rim of a large dinner plate and drizzle lightly with a little of the vinaigrette. Toss the greens in a mixing bowl with 2 tablespoons of the vinaigrette to coat lightly, then mound in the center of the meat slices.

To garnish, scrape away the inside seeds and pulp of the tomato wedge, press the thick wall of the tomato flat and slice into small diamond shapes. Scatter the diamonds on the mound of greens.

Cold Beef Salad à la Parisienne

You will need a well-trimmed whole piece of braised or boiled beef that you cut into neat thin slices less than $\frac{3}{16}$ inches thick, 3 slices per serving. Note that the meat is well done; otherwise it will not absorb the dressing and pick up its flavor. Choose one of the vinaigrette dressings on pages 114 and 115, 1½ tablespoons per serving. Beat in, if you want, minced shallots or scallions, chopped capers, and a bit of Dijon-type prepared mustard. Spoon a tablespoon or so into the bottom of a baking pan, arrange the slices of meat in it, and baste with more of the sauce. Cover and let marinate at room temperature for an hour.

Meanwhile, prepare all or some of the following:
   Halved or stuffed hard-boiled
     eggs, 2 per serving
   Halved and seasoned cherry toma-
     toes, 3 tomatoes per person
   French Potato Salad, $\frac{1}{3}$ cup per
     serving (page 123)
   Cold green beans, a small handful
     per serving (page 188)
   Small handfuls of washed salad
     greens
   A small bowl of minced parsley,
     chives, and your choice of other
     fresh herbs

When almost time to serve, chop the salad greens, toss them with a little more vinaigrette, and arrange a thin layer over the bottom of a serving platter (preferably oval). Lay the sliced and marinated beef neatly down the center of the oval, surround tastefully with vegetables, sprinkle the herbs over all, and present the salad.

Cold Braised Veal Salad with Tuna Sauce—Vitello Tonnato

If you've never eaten it, this seems an odd combination—veal and tuna, and it is canned tuna at that. However, cold veal is a mild meat and the tuna gives it the flavor lift it needs. The recipe is simple indeed. All you need is a fine big piece of thinly sliced braised veal, and fortunately we have it right here on page 346, and mayonnaise, your own if you have it, as on pages 117 and 120, plus a few capers and miscellaneous condiments. The classic Italian recipe also includes anchovies. Even though some people hate them, anchovies give their subtle punch of flavor, which aficionados will miss if left out. Don't mention them to anti-anchovists, who will never know they are there and will only wonder what gives this dish its especially seductive quality.

I like to serve *vitello tonnato* as the main course of a luncheon, with a simple green salad and toasted brioche bread. My wine consultants agree that a chilled crisp, dry rosé would be a most agreeable choice here.

Since I don't know how much meat you have on hand, here are proportions for the sauce. If you don't use it all now, you will be glad to have some on hand, since it will keep for a week or more and goes well with other foods.

Timing note: Make this dish at least a day before serving so that the veal can absorb the sauce flavors.

The Veal

This is such a delicious dish it is worthwhile to braise a piece just for the occasion. Choose a 2-pound veal roast which will slice nicely, such as the top or bottom round, and follow the recipe for Roast Veal en Cocotte (eliminating the endives) on page 346. Cook it to the well-done stage, 175°F.

The Tuna Mayonnaise

Yield: 2 cups, enough for 6 to 8 servings

2 cans of tuna, 3 ounces each,
   preferably oil-packed solid
   white tuna
2 Tbs fresh lemon juice
2 big pinches of freshly ground
   white peppercorns
6 oil-packed anchovy fillets from a
   freshly opened can
1 Tbs capers
1 Tbs Dijon-type prepared
   mustard
1 cup mayonnaise in a mixing bowl
Salt

Drain the tuna, break it up, and purée in a food processor with the lemon juice, pepper, anchovies, capers, and mustard. Gradually, by spoonfuls, whisk it into the mayonnaise. Taste very carefully, adding salt, more pepper, lemon, etc., if needed.

Arranging the platter

Cut the veal as neatly as possible into very thin slices—about ³⁄₁₆ inch. Spoon a ⅛-inch layer of sauce into the bottom of your serving platter. Arrange the slices of veal close together in overlapping layers over the sauce, painting the surface of each with a little of the sauce as you go. You may make two layers, one arranged and sauced, and the other piled on top in the same way. Spread a thin layer of sauce over all, to make an attractive surface. Cover closely and refrigerate for at least 24 hours. An hour before serving, remove the platter and set at room temperature to take off the chill.

Serving

Just before serving, decorate the platter with parsley sprigs or watercress, little black Italian olives, capers, and wedges of fresh lemon.

Julia

A food processor with a shredding disk is clearly the easiest way to
shred a celery root, but you can use
other kitchen tools, such as a
European-style, hand-cranked shred-
der or a mandoline. A plain old-
fashioned box grater will make decent
shreds too, if it's still sharp. And if
you've no other choice, use your
sharpest knife to slice and julienne the
root as thin as possible.

The thicker your shreds, the
more you want to soften them. You
could blanch them if you like, or, as we
do here, let them sit for an hour after
you've first tossed them with salt and
lemon juice. Then let the shreds marinate in the dressing for a couple of .
hours, if possible, before serving.

Celery Root Rémoulade

Underneath the brown, wrinkled exterior of celery root there
is white flesh with a bright celery flavor and crisp texture that,
when finely shredded, makes a delicious slawlike salad. Dressed
simply with sour cream, mayonnaise, and mustard and heaped
in a lettuce cup, it makes a welcome winter first course or side
dish.

You will need a good shredding device—see Julia's
comments—for this salad. And it is best made a couple of hours
ahead.

Yield: About 4 cups, serving 4 to 6

A 1¼-pound untrimmed celery root
 (about 4 inches in diameter)
½ lemon, for rubbing and for juice
½ tsp salt
1 Tbs Dijon-style mustard
3 Tbs sour cream
2 Tbs mayonnaise, preferably homemade
 (pages 117 and 120)
¼ tsp freshly ground pepper
Optional garnishes
 Boston-lettuce leaves
 Chopped fresh parsley
 Tomato rose (see photos)

Special equipment
 A food processor fitted with a shredding
  disk (preferred), or a food mill with
  shredding disk, a grater, or a mandoline

Peeling, shredding, and marinating the celery root

With a sharp knife, slice off the knobby ends of the celery root and most of the thick brown peel. Trim the bits of brown remaining in the surface cracks (but you don't have to get it all). Slice the peeled root in half, and if you find any spongy area in the middle cut it out. Rub the pieces with the lemon half to prevent discoloring, if necessary, and cut again so that the pieces will fit into the feed tube of the food processor.

Shred in the machine (or by hand) and transfer to a mixing bowl. Toss with the salt and 1 teaspoon of juice squeezed from the lemon half—use your clean fingers or a strainer to catch any pits. Let the shreds marinate and soften for about 30 minutes or up to an hour before dressing.

Dressing and serving

Stir together the mustard, sour cream, mayonnaise, and pepper in a small bowl. Fold the dressing into the celery root and toss to mix well, then taste and add more salt, pepper, or lemon juice as needed. Cover with plastic wrap and refrigerate for an hour or two.

When ready to serve, taste again and adjust the seasonings. If you wish, arrange several large, curving leaves of Boston lettuce on a platter, to form a bowl shape, and mound the salad inside. Garnish with a sprinkle of chopped parsley and a tomato rose (see photos).

Jacques

Shape the first strip into a cup to create the outside of the rose, set on the base.

Most often celery root is prepared as we do it here, in a crisp, mustardy salad. The beige color of the salad is set off beautifully by the bright-red tomato rose placed on top.

However, I particularly love celery root in a purée with potatoes. Just trim and cut the root into chunks, as we do here, then cook them with potatoes and put the mixture through a food mill, just as I do for my mashed potatoes (page 151). Add milk and butter to the purée, and some of the flavorful cooking liquid, too.

Roll the second strip into a tight roll, which will go in the center—see the finished rose in the foreground.

Cut first across the bottom of the tomato to form a flat base, then remove half the peel in one piece, going all around the tomato. Remove the remaining peel in one piece.

Julia

Lentils are not always as easy to cook as people say. Too often in restaurants I find them undercooked and still hard. I like to soak lentils before cooking, until you can bite through them but they still have some crunch— an hour or more. Then I cook them at the slow simmer, tasting them frequently during cooking to make sure they end up cooked through but not mushy or falling apart.

With well-cooked lentils, you hardly need a recipe to make a salad. Add other vegetables as you like, and dress them to taste. It's best to dress the lentils while they are still warm, toss them well but gently, and then let the salad sit for a bit so the flavors can ripen.

Lentil Salad

Lentils cook quite fast, much faster than dried beans. Here they are tossed with a garlicky vinaigrette and small chunks of fresh tomato to make an appealing salad. Serve it with homemade sausage (page 364) or other meats, or as a first course—or bring it to a picnic. We both prefer to use the small *lentilles du Puy* (since they come from Le Puy, in central France), which have a lovely dark-green color and hold their shape especially well. Brown lentils are also fine in this salad, but red and orange lentils, often used in Indian cooking, tend to turn mushy and should not be used here.

Jacques's Lentil Salad

Yield: About 5 cups, serving 6

To cook the lentils

1½ cups French green lentils, rinsed and
   picked over
3½ cups water
1 cup chopped onion (about 4 ounces)
1 or 2 sprigs fresh thyme (optional)
1 bay leaf
½ tsp salt
Pinch of ground cloves (optional)

For the dressing

2 Tbs white-wine vinegar,
   plus more to taste
4 Tbs virgin olive oil, plus more to taste
½ tsp salt, plus more to taste
¼ tsp freshly ground black pepper, plus
   more to taste
1 Tbs Dijon-style mustard,
   or to taste (optional)
Drops of Tabasco, to taste (optional)

1 large ripe tomato, cored and seeded,
   chopped into ½-inch pieces
   (about 1¼ cups)
⅓ cup finely chopped shallots,
   scallions, or onion
2 tsp minced garlic (about 3 cloves)

2 Tbs chopped fresh chives, for garnish

Put the lentils, water, chopped onion, optional thyme, bay leaf, salt, and optional cloves in a medium saucepan. Bring to a boil, cover, and reduce the heat to a simmer. Cook for 25 minutes or longer, until the lentils are cooked through but still hold their shape. Cool to lukewarm; at that point drain off any remaining liquid. Pour the lentils into a mixing bowl and discard the herbs.

To make the dressing, whisk together the vinegar, olive oil, salt, and pepper (and mustard and Tabasco, if using). Stir in the chopped tomato, shallots (or scallions or onion), and garlic. Pour the dressing over the warm lentils and fold in gently, then taste and adjust the seasoning. Sprinkle with chopped chives before serving.

Jacques

In this recipe, the lentils are cooked with herbs and onion to give them flavor, and you could add some chopped garlic to the cooking pot as well. The dressing for lentil salad—as for any other salad—should be mixed to your own taste, and the amounts in our recipe are only a guide. I like to add Dijon mustard, and a dash of Tabasco sauce as well, especially if I am serving the lentils with homemade sausage or other meats. And sometimes I combine cooked lentils and potatoes into one salad, as they are both delicious accompaniments to sausage.

Making a Vinegar Dispenser with a Wine Cork

Here's an easy way to turn a bottle of vinegar into a convenient dispenser: Trim a wine cork to fit securely into the mouth of your vinegar bottle. Cut two small V-shaped grooves on opposite sides of the cork. Fit the cork into the bottle. Whenever you want a little vinegar, just shake to dispense a dash.

Avocado Salad

This colorful, chunky salad is a versatile side dish, as good served with a grilled pork chop as with a grilled-cheese sandwich. Avocados from different growing areas are available in the market all year round. The smaller Hass avocado from California or Mexico, with dark-green rough skin, is generally considered to have superior flavor, though the larger, smooth-skinned Fuerte avocado from Florida can also be used. The avocados must be perfectly ripe, but not soft, for this salad. It's best to buy them still hard and slightly under-ripe, keep them for a day or two, and use them when they just yield to finger pressure.

Jacques's technique, illustrated here, makes quick work of cutting the avocado into even cubes. Toss them gently with the other ingredients so they keep their shape. For an attractive plate garnish, heap each serving of salad into a cuplike Boston-lettuce leaf, or into the empty halves of avocado skin, which you will have neatly cut and hollowed out.

Avocado, Tomato, and Red Onion Salad

Yield: About 5 cups, serving 4 to 6

2 ripe avocados (each about
    7 ounces)
2 ripe tomatoes (each about
    8 ounces)
1 small red onion (about
    5 ounces)
1½ Tbs red-wine vinegar,
    plus more to taste
2 Tbs virgin olive oil, plus
    more to taste
¼ tsp salt, plus more to taste
¼ tsp freshly ground black
    pepper, plus more to taste
Drops of Tabasco sauce to taste
Boston-lettuce leaves, for
    serving (optional)

Halve the avocados, cut the flesh into cubes, and spoon them into a mixing bowl, as shown in the photos.

Core the tomatoes, cut them in half crosswise, and squeeze out the seeds and juice (you can save these for stock). Cut the tomatoes into 1-inch cubes and put in the mixing bowl.

Slice around the avocado through the stem and blossom ends, down to the pit, to divide in half lengthwise. Twist the halves and separate.

Peel the onion, cut it in half lengthwise, then slice each half crosswise into very thin half moons. Toss to separate the slices and add them to the mixing bowl.

Drizzle the vinegar and olive oil over the vegetables (shaking the vinegar from a homemade dispensing cork, as described on page 129). Season with the salt and pepper, and 4 or more dashes of Tabasco. Gently mix the vegetables to dress them and distribute the seasonings. Taste a piece and stir in more vinegar, oil, or seasonings as you wish. Spoon the salad into whole, cup-shaped leaves of Boston lettuce if using, and serve right away.

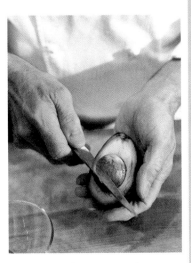

Chop the knife blade into the pit, and lift it out.

With a paring knife, cut through the flesh lengthwise and crosswise to form ½-inch cubes.

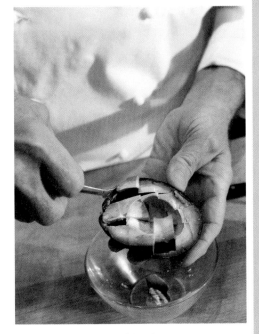

Spoon the cubes out of the skin.

Variation: Avocado and Grapefruit Salad

For a fresh and attractive salad, try the simple but always welcome avocado-and-grapefruit combination. You will need half a peeled avocado and half a pink grapefruit per person, plus a handful of sliced salad greens and a tablespoon or so of vinaigrette—including some of the grapefruit juices. Cut the grapefruit into skinless segments, and the avocado into lengthwise slices to match the grapefruit. Make a shallow bed of dressed salad greens on a salad plate and arrange over it alternating segments of grapefruit and ripe avocado. Spoon on a dribble of the vinaigrette, and accompany with lemon wedges and sprigs of fresh parsley. Serve as a first course, or as a luncheon dish accompanying, for instance, grilled shrimp, cold lobster, crab, or chicken.

Julia

It was in an old edition of *The Joy of Cooking* that I learned to place the pan-toasted sandwich in the oven. You don't want the bread to get much darker as the cheese melts, so keep the temperature around 300°F. If you are in a hurry, you can put the sandwich in a microwave oven for just a few seconds to melt the cheese, but it won't be as crisp. The electric sandwich-cooker, similar to a waffle iron, toasts the bread and melts the cheese perfectly in minutes. It's easy and fun, and many models press the sandwich into a charming shell shape.

You can always play around with these sandwiches. A layer of pipérade (page 74) would be delicious in between the melted-cheese layers, as would a layer of flaked tuna fish, creating your own tuna melt.

Croque Monsieur/ Croque Madame

We don't know why the French, in the early years of the twentieth century, started using the name *croque monsieur* for their famous grilled ham-and-cheese sandwich. The *"croque"* part—which means "crunch" or "crackle"—certainly can apply to the crisply butter-browned outsides of the sandwich. But the trick with a *croque monsieur* (or its sandwich companion *croque madame*, which substitutes sliced chicken for the ham) is to have a perfectly grilled or toasted outside and two layers of nicely melted cheese inside. If the sandwich is just sautéed in a pan, the cheese is unlikely to melt in the short time it takes the bread to brown.

We each have a method which neatly resolves the quandary by melting the cheese in the oven. Julia's *monsieur* is sautéed in the pan just for a minute or two then placed on a baking sheet in a low oven, while Jacques's *madame* is cooked entirely in a hot oven, where it both crisps outside and melts inside. You can use either method for a "mister" with ham or a "missus" with chicken—or the other variations suggested below. Cut them into neat halves on the bias or into bite-size morsels for a hot party appetizer for a crowd.

For variation, use thin slices of any of the following in place of the ham: turkey, corned beef, tongue, bologna or other cooked sausage, crisply cooked bacon, or large thin rounds of mild Maui or Vidalia onion. Instead of the traditional Gruyère, layer the bread with other meltable cheese, like cheddar, Gouda, or mozzarella.

Julia's Croque Monsieur

Yield: 1 sandwich

2 slices fresh, reasonably soft home-style
  white bread, removed from the loaf in
  sequence, for accurate reassembly
1 Tbs mayonnaise, preferably homemade
  (pages 117 and 120)
½ tsp Dijon-style prepared mustard
2 or more slices Swiss cheese (Gruyère or
  Emmentaler), ³⁄₁₆ inch thick and large
  enough to cover each bread slice
1 slice excellent baked or boiled ham,
  ³⁄₁₆ inch thick, trimmed of fat, and
  same size as cheese
2 Tbs clarified butter (see sidebar)

Special equipment
A frying pan that will hold one sandwich
  comfortably (probably about 8 inches),
  or a 12-inch pan for more sandwiches;
  a pancake turner; a baking sheet, if you
  are doing several sandwiches

Forming the sandwich
Lay the bread in front of you and open it up like a book (so that when you close the sandwich the right and left sides will match exactly). Spread an even coating of mayonnaise—about a teaspoon—on the top of each slice, and a smidge of mustard. Lay a slice of cheese on the right slice, followed by a slice of ham, then a slice of cheese. Turn the left slice of bread over on top of the right, and press firmly down on the sandwich with the palm of your hand. Rotate and press several times to hold the sandwich together (that's why you want the bread to be fresh and fairly soft). With a big sharp knife, trim off the crusts all around to form a neat sandwich. (If not to be cooked at once, wrap airtight in plastic—useful when you are doing several.)

Jacques

Croque madame **is a good** way to use cooked, leftover chicken. And I like to give it a bit of heat with a few dashes of Tabasco. These kinds of sandwiches are traditionally made with butter, but you can use oil instead, which gives a nice crust. Spread a thin layer of canola or other oil on the baking sheet and lightly press both sides of the finished sandwiches into it before you bake them.

Simple Clarified Butter

When you melt butter in a saucepan, let it settle for a moment; the clear liquid butter rises to the top and a milky residue sinks to the bottom. It is this residue that burns and creates brown speckles on food when you sauté in regular butter. To avoid that, skim the clear liquid off the residue and you have clarified butter. You might make a quantity while you are at it, since it keeps for weeks when refrigerated in a screwtop jar.

Sautéing

Preheat the oven to 300°F for final baking.

Film the frying pan with a tablespoon of clarified butter and set over moderately high heat. When very hot but not browning, lower heat to moderate and lay the sandwich in the pan, pressing down upon it with your pancake turner, and pressing down several times as the sandwich browns rather slowly on the bottom—2 minutes or so. Add another tablespoon of clarified butter to the pan, then turn and brown on the other side, pressing down upon the sandwich several times until its bottom, too, is lightly browned. (You may sauté 10 to 15 minutes in advance and finish later.)

Final baking

For a single sandwich, set the frying pan in the middle level of the preheated 300°F oven and bake for 7 to 8 minutes, until the cheese is fully melted. If doing several sandwiches, lift them onto the baking sheet to finish in the oven.

Serving

Cut the sandwich or sandwiches in half diagonally and, if you wish, in half again to make small triangles to serve as appetizers. You could decorate the servings very simply with parsley sprigs, watercress, halved and seasoned tomatoes.

Jacques's Croque Madame

Yield: 1 sandwich

2 slices home-style white bread
1 Tbs soft butter, or more if
    needed
2 or more slices Swiss cheese
    (such as Gruyère or
    Emmentaler), about ⅛ inch
    thick (enough to cover both
    bread slices)
Several slices cooked chicken,
    about ⅛ inch thick (enough to
    cover one bread slice)
1 tsp chopped fresh chives
Dashes of Tabasco sauce (optional)

Special equipment

A cookie sheet or shallow-
    rimmed baking sheet,
    large enough to hold all
    the sandwiches at once

Preheat the oven to 400°F.

Spread a thin layer of soft butter on one side only of both bread slices, then cover the buttered sides neatly with a layer of cheese. Arrange a layer of chicken on one bread slice and sprinkle on the chives and a few dashes of Tabasco, if you like. Flip the other piece of bread over on top (cheese inside, of course), press together, and spread more butter on the outsides of the sandwich, coating the slices evenly. Lay the assembled sandwich in the baking dish and prepare others in the same way.

Bake the sandwiches for 10 minutes or so, until the bottom sides are crisp and golden. Flip them over and bake for about 5 minutes more, until the second sides are also well toasted.

Serve hot. For appetizer portions, trim off the crusts and cut each sandwich diagonally into 4 small triangles.

Lobster Rolls

Succulent tail and claw meat from a perfectly steamed fresh lobster (page 249) makes a sandwich fit for a king. But as you might expect from Yankee cooks, the traditional lobster roll has a distinctly common touch—it is always made with a plain hot-dog bun, New England–style only, with flat-cut sides and a slit in the top. Since we are now both New Englanders, and lobster lovers, we offer two kinds of rolls here—a warm one in "drawn" (melted) unsalted butter and a cold roll filled with a traditional mayonnaise-dressed lobster salad. (The rolls themselves are never cold, as they are grilled in butter before being loaded with lobster, just as they would be at a good clam shack along the Maine coast.)

You need about 6 ounces of lobster meat for each recipe, to fill 2 well-stuffed buns. You can reasonably expect to pick this amount of meat from 2 hard-shelled "chicken" lobsters, 1 to 1¼ pounds live weight. Don't expect to get double the amount of meat from a lobster twice this size, though, since a 2½-pound lobster yields only about 4 ounces (see page 248).

Jacques

I worked for Howard Johnson restaurants from 1960 to 1970 as director of research and development. And I remember well the lobster rolls like these with the "split-top" New England hot-dog rolls, the only kind you can toast this way on both sides. In these recipes I add a few ingredients that the Howard Johnson customers didn't get, though, such as tarragon in the butter and shallots in the lobster salad. The rolls are delicious without them, but they add nice flavor. When warming the lobster chunks in butter, it is important to do this very gently and gradually—don't let the butter get hot or the meat will toughen. Use any leftover butter to flavor other seafood dishes, or sprinkle some of it on your lobster roll.

Julia

Up in Maine they don't put as many nice things into a lobster roll as Jacques does—but I prepare my roll with chilled lobster differently. Instead of tossing lobster chunks with all the dressing ingredients like a salad, I cut the tail meat crosswise into slices and season them just with salt, pepper, and lemon juice. Then I spread a small amount of good mayonnaise on each slice and put them back together again inside the roll—which I've lined with a lettuce leaf—so it looks as though it's stuffed with a lobster tail. A crabmeat roll is delicious too, with the same light seasonings and coating of mayo, and chilled cooked shrimp, sliced in half the long way, or flaked-up cold fish—these all make fine seafood rolls too.

If you start with freshly steamed lobster, by the way, you should take the tomalley and roe and mix them into the mayonnaise for your lobster roll. And if you have any left over, just spread it on small croutons—it's absolutely delicious.

Warm Lobster Rolls

Yield: 2 lobster rolls

4 ounces (1 stick) unsalted butter
2 tsp chopped fresh tarragon
1 Tbs or more freshly squeezed
  lemon juice
⅛ tsp salt, plus more to taste
⅛ tsp fresh, coarsely cracked black
  pepper, plus more to taste
6 ounces cooked lobster (about
  1¼ cups), claw meat left whole
  and tail cut into ½-inch chunks
2 hot-dog rolls, split-top
  New England–style
2 large lettuce leaves, red-leaf
  or other loose-leaf type

Melt the butter in a small saucepan, reserving a tablespoon or so to brown the rolls. Heat until warm, then add the tarragon, lemon juice, and salt and coarsely cracked pepper. Stir, taste, and adjust the seasonings. Add the lobster pieces, making sure most are immersed in the butter, and allow them to warm through. Keep in a warm place, but don't allow the pan to get hot, or it will toughen the lobster meat.

Heat the reserved butter in a frying pan until foaming, over medium heat. Lay the hot-dog rolls in the pan with one of the flat sides down, press into the butter, and fry for about a minute, until nicely colored. Flip the rolls over and brown the other side.

Line the inside of the warm rolls with a large lettuce leaf, fill with chunks of lobster, and spoon the seasoned butter generously over them. Serve right away.

Cold Lobster Rolls

Yield: 2 lobster rolls

1 or 2 leaves Boston or other crisp
    lettuce, rinsed and dried
6 ounces cooked lobster (about 1¼ cups),
    cut into ½-inch chunks
2 Tbs mayonnaise
1 Tbs ketchup
1 tsp Dijon-style mustard
2 Tbs finely chopped celery
2 tsp finely chopped shallots or red onion
1 to 2 Tbs freshly squeezed lemon juice
⅛ tsp salt, plus more to taste
⅛ tsp fresh, coarsely cracked black
    pepper, plus more to taste
2 hot-dog rolls, split-top
    New England–style
1 Tbs unsalted butter, for toasting rolls

Slice the lettuce leaves into strips and chop roughly, for about a cup of coarse, crunchy shreds. Toss these in a bowl with the lobster chunks.

In another bowl, stir together the mayonnaise, ketchup, mustard, celery, shallots, 1 tablespoon of lemon juice, and the salt and pepper. Taste and adjust the seasonings, then pour the dressing over the lobster and lettuce pieces and fold together well.

Toast the hot-dog rolls in a hot frying pan with the butter, as for Warm Lobster Rolls (preceding recipe). Open each toasted roll and fill to overflowing with the cold salad. Serve right away.

Julia

This stuffed bread is one of Jacques's wonderful inventions and the kind of dish you can imagine all sorts of good things to put in. I would love to fill a bread with roast turkey or chicken, and flavor it with gravy; beef or ham would be nice too, with cooked onions and other things. This is an idea to play around with.

Seafood Bread

This is a clever creation of Jacques's, fun to make and to serve. Inside a large loaf of country bread, covered by a dome of golden bread crumbs, is a colorful filling of steaming seafood and mushrooms. Cut into wedges or appetizer-size slices and eaten out of hand, it's a great party dish.

The bread loaf, though, is not just a crusty medium for serving the seafood but a highly effective baking vessel. You hollow it out to form a shell, coat the insides with a bright-green herb butter, then fill it with the raw fish chunks and vegetables. Baked for an hour or more, the filling becomes moist, tender, and flavorful.

Since the bread shell also becomes imbued with the savory butter and seafood juices, you need a sturdy country-style loaf, with a hard crust and a firm, uncracked bottom. A hearth-baked, slow-risen loaf will have the best crust and flavor. You may even find such a bread in many supermarkets today, but if you can't find the large, 12-inch bread that this recipe calls for, buy a smaller loaf (or two) and reduce the filling ingredients proportionally. It's also fine to use bread that's a couple of days old and slightly dry.

For convenience, assemble the bread a day ahead, keep it in the refrigerator, and put it in the oven about an hour and a half before you want to serve.

Jacques's Seafood Bread

Yield: 8 large wedges, or 15 to 20 appetizer-
size slices

1 large crusty country bread, about
1½ pounds, 10-to-12-inch round
or oval loaf

For the herb butter
3 or 4 garlic cloves, peeled
⅔ cup fresh dill sprigs, loosely packed
¼ cup slivered almonds

6 ounces (1½ sticks) unsalted butter, at
   room temperature

½ tsp salt

¼ tsp freshly ground black pepper

3 Tbs dry white wine (2 Tbs if
   using liqueur)

1 Tbs Pernod or Ricard (optional)

For the filling

5 ounces tuna, in 1-inch chunks

5 ounces haddock, in 1-inch chunks

5 ounces salmon, in 1-inch chunks

7 ounces squid, sliced in
   1-inch-wide strips

¼ pound mixed wild mushrooms or
   cultivated mushrooms, roughly
   chopped (about 1½ cups)

¾ tsp salt

¼ tsp freshly ground black pepper

¼ cup dry white wine

Special equipment

A food processor; a flat baking
   pan or cookie sheet

Hollowing out the bread

Preheat the oven to 400°F, if you will be baking the bread
right away.

With a serrated bread knife,
slice off the top crust of the bread loaf
and remove it as you would a lid.
(You won't be using the lid, so save it
for another purpose.)

Slice off the top crust.

Jacques

This is a very versatile formula.

You can stuff breads of all sizes and shapes—small individual loaves, skinny baguettes, or large rounds or ovals, as long as they have a sturdy, tight crust that's not broken or cracked. And you can vary the filling any way you like—use a different assortment of seafood, including shrimp and scallops, for instance, or use just one kind of fish or shellfish. You can use different vegetables with the fish too, or even fill a bread with only vegetables.

When you are doing a large loaf with a lot of filling like this one, you want to leave plenty of time for everything to cook. If the loaf is dark to begin with or starts to brown in the oven, you can wrap the sides with aluminum foil. It is also important to season the fish very well, and I put a lot of flavor—herbs, garlic, almonds, and wine—in the herb butter. Here I use dill, but basil, parsley, chives, chervil, and other herbs could be used instead. With seafood, I always like to add a dash of an anise-flavored liqueur like Pernod, but this is a matter of taste.

If you have any leftover herb butter, you can freeze it in a roll—as we do with Beurre Maître d'Hôtel (page 230)—and use a spoonful whenever you want it. It would be delicious with sautéed or grilled fish, with vegetables, or in a seafood soup.

Make a straight wall inside the loaf, slicing down, about ½ inch in from the thick crust, and cutting all the way around the interior (see photo). Don't cut through the bottom of the bread or pierce it.

Remove all the soft bread inside, grabbing small handfuls and twisting to loosen. Clear the bottom and the cut sides to form a neat hollow shell.

Slice down ½ inch in from the crust, going all around the top.

Place about half of the removed bread in a food processor and process to make 2 to 3 cups of medium-fine crumbs. Remove to a bowl.

Making the herb butter

Put the garlic cloves, dill, and almonds in the food processor (no need to clean it after making the bread crumbs); pulse until finely chopped. Add the soft butter, salt and pepper, white wine, and anise liqueur if using (substitute the liqueur for 1 tablespoon of the wine). Process until the herb butter is smooth and uniformly colored.

Filling the loaf

Season all the seafood pieces and the chopped mushrooms well with the salt and pepper and toss together.

Spread half the herb butter inside the bread shell with a rubber spatula, coating the bottom and sides evenly. Distribute half of the fish chunks and squid over the bottom of the bread, sprinkle all the mushroom pieces on top, then the remaining seafood. Spread the remaining herb butter evenly over the filling.

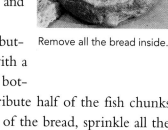

Remove all the bread inside.

Cover the filling with a thick layer of bread crumbs, pressing with your hands so the crumbs hold together and completely hide the butter. Finally, drizzle the ¼ cup of white wine all over the crumbs to moisten.

Baking the seafood bread

Put the loaf on the baking sheet and bake in the preheated oven for about an hour or more, until the bread-crumb topping is deeply colored. Remove from the cookie sheet and let the loaf rest on a cutting board for about 10 minutes before serving.

After spreading herb butter inside, fill the hollowed-out loaf with the seafood and mushrooms.

Use a sharp, sturdy knife to cut the crusty bread, slicing it into wedges, chunks, or slices, depending on the shape of the loaf.

Do-ahead notes

The herb butter can be made in advance, and stored in the refrigerator for a day or two, or rolled in plastic wrap and frozen, like other flavored butters (see pages 229 and 230). Allow chilled butter to soften completely before assembling the loaf. (Extra butter can be used in other seafood or vegetable dishes.)

The bread loaf can be hollowed and filled a day ahead, wrapped well, and refrigerated. Preheat the oven before baking.

Opposite: Seafood Bread

Julia

When I lived in the south of France, you would buy *pan bagnat* at the *charcuterie*, ready-made with small buns, about the size of hamburger rolls. They were a sandwich of *salade niçoise* —tuna, olives, tomatoes, and eggs and that sort of thing—and lots of oil and garlic vinaigrette that just dripped off. The local people would say it isn't any good unless the oil drips down your arm and off your elbow while you're eating it!

You don't need to be fussy about what to use here. If you don't like anchovies, leave them out—try a good olive-oil-packed tuna instead, or a different kind of cheese. Or you can make the kind of individual sandwiches they sell in France, using Kaiser rolls or even hamburger buns, if they're not too squashy.

Pan Bagnat

In the south of France, they make a sandwich with a saladlike assortment of fresh vegetables and other ingredients stuffed into a roll or small loaf of bread. It's so lavishly drenched with olive oil and vinaigrette that the name in the Niçoise dialect, *pan bagnat*—"bathed bread"—is a perfect description.

Our *pan bagnat* is an extra-large version, which would make a good main course for lunch, or a party (or picnic) appetizer, using a round of fresh homemade focaccia. We fill it with lettuce, tomato slices, olives, anchovy fillets, a non-traditional layer of sliced Brie cheese, and plenty of excellent olive oil and fresh vinaigrette. There are no rules for the filling, though, and you can add other vegetables, canned fish such as tuna, or sliced cold meats as you like.

Pan bagnat is best prepared well ahead of time, and pressed under heavy weights for several hours or overnight. This makes the sandwich compact so it holds together—easy to transport to a picnic, and slice and serve in large wedges or small pieces. The rosemary-and-garlic-topped focaccia that we recommend for this is a specialty of our editor, Judith Jones, but you can buy a focaccia or other round bread of similar size, preferably a crusty country-type loaf that's not too high.

A Large Pan Bagnat

Yield: 1 large sandwich, about 8 large
   wedges or 24 hors-d'oeuvre-size pieces

For the vinaigrette
   1 small shallot, minced
   1 Tbs red-wine vinegar
   3 Tbs extra-virgin olive oil
   Salt and freshly ground pepper

   1 round of Garlic and Rosemary
      Focaccia (recipe follows), or other
      round loaf
   Extra-virgin olive oil
   About 6 leaves red-leaf lettuce, washed
      and dried
   8 ounces Brie cheese, in ¼-inch-thick,
      flat slices
   ¾ cup black oil-cured olives, pitted and
      roughly chopped
   1 large fresh tomato, cored, thinly sliced
   2-ounce can anchovies in olive oil

Special equipment
   Plastic wrap; 2 cookie sheets or trays; a
      heavy pan or other weighty items for
      pressing the sandwich

To make the vinaigrette, mix the shallot and vinegar in a
small bowl, and gradually whisk in the oil with a fork. Season
with salt and pepper to taste.

Cut the bread horizontally into even top and bottom
layers. Turn the top over, then drizzle olive oil all over the cut
sides of both layers, using 2 or 3 tablespoons of oil on each.

Make layers of all the filling ingredients. First, completely
cover the sandwich bottom with 5 or 6 lettuce leaves, then
arrange the slices of Brie on top. Scatter the chopped olives and
cover with the tomato slices in a single layer.

Jacques

This sandwich developed out
of the kind of salads that are made in
Provence and other Mediterranean re-
gions, where pieces of leftover bread
are mixed into the salad and soak up
the vegetable juices. That is why I
always weight the sandwich for hours—
to press these juices into the bread and
allow all the flavors to mingle.

Spoon about half the vinaigrette over the tomatoes, then separate the anchovy fillets and distribute evenly. Drizzle the remaining vinaigrette and the oil from the anchovy can all over the filling. Finally, replace the top layer of bread to close the sandwich.

Wrap the sandwich well with several layers of plastic wrap and place on a cookie sheet or pizza pan or tray. Lay another tray on top of the sandwich and center some heavy items to press and flatten the loaf (a heavy pan and a 5-pound bag of sugar, for example).

Place the weighted sandwich in the refrigerator for at least a couple of hours or overnight. Before serving, remove the weight, unwrap the compressed sandwich, and let it come to room temperature. Cut into serving-size wedges or, as an hors d'oeuvre, cut in thin parallel slices, and again into short, bite-size lengths.

Garlic and Rosemary Focaccia

This focaccia can be made in just a couple of hours and is easily mixed in the food processor. It can be shaped in a round or an oval form and should be eaten fresh, still a little warm from the oven.

Yield: A 10-inch round or an oval roughly 8 by 12 inches

1 package (1 scant Tbs)
   active dry yeast
1½ cups warm water
1 tsp salt
3 or slightly more cups
   all-purpose flour
2½ tsp olive oil
Cornmeal

For the topping
½ to ¾ tsp kosher or
   coarse sea salt
2 large garlic cloves, peeled
   and cut into thin slivers
1 large sprig fresh rosemary
   or 1 Tbs dried

Special equipment
A food processor or large standing
   mixer; a dough scraper; a baking
   sheet

Preparing the dough

Put the yeast in a measuring cup and pour ¼ cup of the warm water over it. Let stand a few minutes and stir. Transfer the dissolved yeast to the bowl of the food processor or to the bowl of a standing mixer. Add the remaining water, salt, and 2½ cups of the flour. Process or mix with the paddle for about 2 minutes. Add another ½ cup flour and blend again until the flour is absorbed. The dough will be more moist than the usual bread dough.

Scrape the dough out onto a well-floured work surface and with well-floured hands knead *very* lightly, using a dough scraper to gather it together after each turn. Knead it only about a dozen times this way, just enough to pull it together, then plop it into a large bowl that has been greased with about ½ teaspoon of the olive oil. Cover the bowl with plastic wrap tightly and let the dough rise until doubled—an hour or more, depending on the warmth of your kitchen.

Shaping the dough and baking it

Preheat the oven to 425°F.

Generously sprinkle cornmeal over the center of the baking sheet.

Turn the dough out onto a floured work surface and start patting it into a round or oval shape. It will be sticky and resistant, so when you have partially shaped it distribute the remaining olive oil on top and transfer the dough to the prepared baking sheet. Now continue to stretch and pat the dough with your well-oiled fingers until you have a 10-inch circle or an oval or rectangular shape roughly 8 by 12 inches.

Sprinkle the coarse salt over the surface of the dough (use the lesser amount if you are planning to use the focaccia for a sandwich with a fairly salty filling). Insert slivers of garlic at intervals all over the top of the dough, embedding them deeply and pinching the dough over them so that the garlic is covered. Now top each garlic insertion with several sprigs of the thin leaves of fresh rosemary, or tuck needles of dried rosemary into the insertions.

Let the dough rest and rise slightly for 15 minutes.

Bake the focaccia in the preheated oven for 25 minutes. Remove and serve warm.

POTATOES

AND OTHER ACCOMPANIMENTS

HERE ARE A DOZEN OR SO OF THOSE INDISPENSABLE DISHES THAT MOST COOKS THINK OF as a "starch." They make fine complements to meaty main courses—and are essential as absorbers of sauces—but many could make a satisfying lunch or light dinner on their own.

Our basic cooking methods for potatoes, rice, and beans are simple and straightforward, yet each offers many possibilities for garnishing and variation. As you can see by the roster of recipes, we particularly love potatoes. They can assume a variety of shapes and textures—perhaps only an egg has more guises—and a sack of economical and homely spuds is one of the foundations of home cooking. Fellow potato lovers will also want to see the fine potato salads in the "Salads and Sandwiches" chapter.

Julia

Jacques and I bake potatoes in much the same way, but with one important difference. Before I put them in the oven, I pierce each one deeply with a small, stout knife all over in a dozen places. This allows steam to escape and avoids a "stifled" taste, particularly important when you microwave a potato. But Jacques and I agree on another important question: we do *not* wrap baking potatoes in aluminum foil.

Baked Potatoes

A russet potato, baked in the skin, is one of the simplest and most satisfying of potato preparations. (Idaho potatoes, as baking potatoes are commonly called, are a type of russet. There are others, all high in starch, low in moisture, and excellent for baking.)

A Perfect Baked Potato

Yield: 1 potato

A 10-to-12-ounce baking potato
Salt and freshly ground pepper to taste
½ Tbs or more butter and/or sour cream
  or olive oil
Chopped fresh chives or parsley
  (optional)

Preheat the oven to 425°F, and set rack in lower middle level.

Choose an unblemished, well-shaped specimen and scrub it thoroughly under cold running water. Shave off any doubtful spots.

Place the potato directly on the oven rack and set the timer for 40 minutes. Bake until the potato is soft to the squeeze—pierce deeply with a knife to be sure. As soon as it is done, remove the potato and cut a deep 2-inch lengthwise slash in it. Press the 2 ends toward the center to open it up and let out steam. Fork up the flesh to make room for the salt, pepper, and butter or sour cream or olive oil. Serve as soon as possible, sprinkling in the optional herbs.

For a short wait, season the potato but omit the herbs until serving. Keep the potato warm in the turned-off oven.

Jacques's Variation

After the potato is baked, slice off the top lengthwise. Scoop out the inside and season it with salt, pepper, and chives, mashing lightly with a fork. Spoon the seasoned potato back into the shell, sprinkle 2 tablespoons of grated Gruyère or Parmesan on top, and put it back in the oven until it is brown and crusty.

Julia: Dressing Up the Perfect Baked Potato

A Simple Cheese Topping

Cut a large perfectly baked potato in half horizontally, make 6 to 8 deep crisscross cuts in the flesh, then scumble it up with a fork as you season it lightly with salt, white pepper, and a little soft butter. Lightly press the potato flesh back into place and sprinkle the top with a teaspoon of grated Swiss cheese. Before serving, let brown lightly under the broiler, or reheat and brown for a few minutes in a 500°F oven.

As a Luncheon Dish with a Poached Egg

Follow the previous directions, but after scumbling and flavoring the warm potato half, remove and reserve a spoonful of potato. Make an oval depression in the center of the potato half and set in a poached egg (see page 82). Cover the exposed egg with the reserved potato, and sprinkle liberally with grated Swiss cheese. Slide close under a hot broiler element for a few seconds to brown lightly, then serve immediately.

Jacques

For baked potatoes, it is worth buying excellent-quality large potatoes—weighing at least 10 or 12 ounces each—but be sure to check them for dark spots or soft, bruised areas. You may still be disappointed to find that the insides are dark and spoiled, but, unfortunately, there is no way to know this until you cut them open.

When we are cooking at home, and don't have much time, we occasionally cook baking potatoes in the microwave oven first, for about 5 minutes. Then it takes only ½ hour in the regular oven for a completely baked potato, with a delicious baked skin.

Julia

The drier your potatoes are, the more butter and milk you can add. Therefore, it's a good idea to drain the potatoes as soon as they are done and toss over moderate heat for a few seconds, until the excess moisture evaporates and the potatoes begin to film the bottom of the pan. This is especially important if, instead of russets, you are using a less dry all-purpose potato, such as Yukon Golds.

Like Jacques, I keep my mashed potatoes fresh for 2 or 3 hours, set in a pan of hot water. But I keep mine loosely covered, the lid held ajar with a wooden spoon stuck in the potatoes. You must have air circulating; if the bowl is sealed airtight, I find that the potatoes develop the same disagreeable "stifled" taste that can mar a baked potato.

For mashing, I prefer to use the potato ricer when I have a moderate number, like 6 people. Then I use my big tough German ricer of heavy cast aluminum. But for a mob, like at Thanksgiving, give me my wonderful heavy-duty electric mixer with paddle attachment. It works beautifully, but I operate it very carefully and rather slowly, so as not to overmix and turn the potatoes into glue.

Mashed Potatoes

Mashed potatoes are made with very good russets—Idahos—as well as with boiling potatoes such as Yukon Gold or medium red. They can absorb lots of milk and butter, and will easily whip up smooth and fluffy. You can mash them several hours ahead—a great convenience when you are preparing a dinner for guests. Mash them by hand, or with a ricer, a food mill, or an electric mixer (but not a food processor, lest they turn into glue). Add hot milk and butter to suit your own taste. Or try the garlic mashed potatoes (see sidebar on page 152)—even those who normally don't like garlic will find them delicious, because the garlic is simmered in cream, which gives it a delicate, buttery flavor.

Yield: 6 servings

3 pounds baking potatoes (4 or 5 large),
  or Yukon Gold or medium red potatoes
Salt
½ to 1 cup hot milk, plus more if needed
2 to 4 Tbs unsalted butter, at room
  temperature
Freshly ground pepper (white for Julia;
  black for Jacques)

For garnish
Long fresh chives, a thick bunch

Special equipment

For mashing the potatoes, a heavy-duty electric mixer with paddle attachment (for Julia), or a potato ricer or a food mill; for holding the potatoes, a saucepan and a larger pan or skillet to serve as a double boiler. For Julia: in addition, a cover for the pan, and a wooden spoon; a kettle large enough to hold the potatoes

Cooking the potatoes

Wash and peel the potatoes and cut in quarters, keeping them immersed in a bowl of cold water as you work to prevent discoloration. Put them in a large kettle with salted, cold water to cover (1½ teaspoons of salt for every quart).

Cover the pot and bring to the boil over high heat. Uncover, reduce the heat, and cook at a medium boil for 10 to 15 minutes, or until the potatoes are easily pierced with a sharp knife. Test by eating a few bits here and there to be sure. Drain through a colander.

To dry the potatoes, return them to the empty dry pot. Set over moderate heat and toss the pieces just until the pan begins to film.

Mashing with an electric mixer

Transfer the hot potatoes to the bowl of the electric mixer fitted with the paddle attachment. Mix at low speed to break up the pieces for a few seconds, then whip at medium speed, adding about ⅓ to ½ cup of the hot milk. Still beating, add a tablespoon or two of butter, 1 teaspoon of salt, and several grinds of pepper. Stop and taste the potatoes (scraping down the sides of the bowl and clearing the paddle if necessary). Adjust the seasonings and beat in more milk and butter (or garlic cream) as you wish.

Mashing in a ricer or food mill

Press the hot potatoes through a food mill or a potato ricer into a bowl or large saucepan. With a wooden spatula, beat in butter until potatoes are smooth. Season with ¾ teaspoon

Jacques

I prefer hand tools to an electric mixer for making my mashed potatoes. First I put them through a hand-cranked food mill, one of my favorite kitchen tools. Next I work in my seasonings with a wooden spatula—always the butter first, then the hot milk. Finally, if I want very light potatoes, called *pomme mousseline,* I whip them with a hand whisk.

If I've made them ahead, I keep the mashed potatoes in a double boiler. I cover the top completely with a layer of hot milk or cream—about ⅓ cup—or by putting a tablespoon or so of butter on top to melt and seal the surface. This prevents discoloration and will keep a skin from forming. Just before serving, I beat in the milk (or cream or butter) and the potatoes become fluffy again.

Julia's Garlic Mashed Potatoes

Separate the cloves of 1 large head of garlic and peel them. Put them in a small, high-sided saucepan with ⅔ cup of heavy cream. Bring to the simmer. Turn down the heat to low—barest simmer—and simmer for 25 minutes or longer, until the cloves are very tender; the cream will have reduced and thickened. Strain through a fine-meshed sieve, pressing the garlic through and scraping the purée off the bottom of the sieve. Stir the purée and cream into the hot mashed potatoes immediately before serving.

Mashed Potatoes (continued)

of salt and ¼ teaspoon of pepper, then pour in ⅓ cup or more of the hot milk, stirring slowly until completely incorporated. Adjust the seasonings and stir in more butter or milk (or garlic cream) if you wish. Whip with a wire whisk to lighten.

Serve the potatoes at once or hold as follows.

Holding mashed potatoes for later service

Place the bowl (or pan) of potatoes in a larger skillet with a few inches of hot—not simmering—water. Cover the bowl or pan of potatoes with a pot lid and stick in a wooden spoon to leave an air space open. Stir up vigorously every 10 minutes or so. Alternatively, smooth the top of the potatoes and cover completely with a thin layer of hot milk. Potatoes can be held in the double boiler up to 3 hours. To reheat, bring the surrounding water to a simmer and beat the potatoes with a spoon or spatula to lighten and/or to incorporate the covering layer of milk. Add more butter or milk if desired.

Serving and garnishing

Mound the potatoes on a round flat platter or shallow serving pan.

If you want to have some fun with the presentation, use the flat of a knife to smooth the sides of the mounded potatoes into an even-sloping cone, rotating the platter as you would a cake. Make decorative scalloped indentations—lifting the dull edge of the knife up and down as you twirl the plate—that radiate from the top of the mound out to the side of the plate. Push a cluster of long chives down into the center of the potato mound, so it resembles a volcano erupting.

Pommes de Terre Macaire

Pommes de terre Macaire is a traditional recipe for a flat potato cake cooked in a skillet. It's a type of sophisticated hash-browns. In Jacques's contemporary version, already baked potatoes are removed from their skins, seasoned, and sautéed in one thick layer, then baked again right in the pan. When unmolded onto a serving platter, the crusty bottom becomes the golden top of a beautiful *gâteau*, with the crispiness of fried potatoes and the rich flavor of buttered baked potatoes.

The dish is special enough for a dinner party, particularly when glazed under the broiler with a topping of sour cream and grated cheese. Or enjoy it as a satisfying main course for a vegetarian lunch, matched with a green salad, or on a brunch plate with poached eggs and bacon.

Yield: A large potato *gâteau*, serving 6 to 8

3 pounds russet (Idaho) potatoes (about 5
   large potatoes)
3 Tbs canola oil
2 Tbs unsalted butter
¼ tsp freshly grated or chopped nutmeg
¾ teaspoon salt
¼ teaspoon freshly ground black pepper

Optional topping for Pommes de Terre Byron (recipe follows)
½ cup sour cream
2 ounces Gruyère cheese, grated (about
   ⅔ cup), or ⅓ cup grated Parmesan

Special equipment
A large (10-inch) ovenproof sauté pan,
   preferably non-stick; a round (3-inch)
   cookie cutter or a clean soup can, ends
   removed, for chopping potatoes; a 10-
   inch plate or platter or a baking sheet,
   for turning the potato cake

Jacques

The more luxurious glazed version of potatoes *Macaire* is known as potatoes *Byron*. At the Plaza-Athénée in Paris, when I cooked there, we would cover the top of the potato cake with crème fraîche and Gruyère or Parmesan cheese for glazing. You can use crème fraîche, which is available in some markets in this country, instead of sour cream, or even spread on lightly whipped heavy cream.

The texture of the potatoes is most important here. They must be coarsely chopped up, not mashed, after you peel them. I like to use a clean steel can, like a small soup can, with both ends removed. A round cookie cutter will also work. Then be sure to toss well when you add the potatoes to the sauté pan, so that every bit is flavored with the butter and oil. The touch of nutmeg is important, too: make sure you use freshly grated whole nutmeg. If you don't have a nutmeg grater, just shave off a small amount with a sharp knife and chop it up.

Julia

The basic method for *pommes de terre Macaire* reminds me of something my old chef Max Bugnard would do with baked potatoes. He'd scoop the potato out of the skins and sauté it with butter and seasonings. Then he would stuff it roughly back into the skins, and heat the potatoes again in the oven. They had an appealing rough texture, as this does.

Jacques's technique of breaking up the potatoes with a can is one I first learned about from Jim Beard. He was impressed by some breakfast chefs who used an open-ended can to chop up leftover boiled potatoes, which they fried in bacon fat and butter to make wonderful hash-brown potatoes. Beard's own version of hash-browns, a crusty chunky cake roughly similar to *pommes de terre Macaire*, is the model for my Old-Fashioned Hash-Browns (page 158).

Pommes de Terre Macaire (continued)

Preparing the potatoes

Bake the potatoes until done (see page 148); remove from oven and, if proceeding with recipe immediately, keep oven temperature at 425°F. (Or you can set the potatoes aside at room temperature for 2 or 3 hours before continuing, then preheat the oven to 425°F.)

Cut away all the potato skins and discard. Roughly chop the potatoes with the cookie cutter or the empty can (or a sharp knife), but don't mash or mince them—the potatoes should break apart into ½-to-¾-inch chunks.

Sautéing the *gâteau*

Heat the oil and butter in the pan over medium heat. When hot, spread the potatoes in the pan and sprinkle on the nutmeg, salt, and pepper. Immediately begin turning the potato pieces with a flat wooden spoon or spatula, to thoroughly mix in the seasonings, oil, and butter.

Flatten the potatoes to a smooth, solid layer with a wide, flat spatula, filling the entire pan, then reduce heat to medium-low and cook for 5 to 8 minutes. Near the end of the cooking time, shake and rotate the pan quickly in a clockwise motion—turning it by the handle—to loosen the potato cake from the sides and bottom of the pan. You should be able to see that the sides of the layer are browning nicely.

Place the skillet in the hot oven and bake for 15 minutes or so, until the top is crusty and lightly colored. Remove the hot pan carefully from the oven and let sit 30 seconds or so, then immediately cover it with the serving platter (or a flat baking sheet if that's easier). Invert quickly to unmold the cake (then slide it from the sheet onto your serving platter if necessary).

Serve immediately, whole or cut into wedges, or top the cake as follows.

Variation: Pommes de Terre Byron

Turn on the broiler. With a large spoon or spatula, spread the top of the hot potatoes with the sour cream and sprinkle evenly with the grated cheese. Set the cake about 4 or 5 inches from the heat and broil for 3 to 5 minutes, until the top is golden and bubbling. Remove the very hot platter from the broiler carefully and serve.

Opposite: Pommes de Terre Macaire

Jacques's Pommes de Terre Mont d'Or

Use leftover mashed potatoes to make this golden gratin—crusty on the outside, light and fluffy on the inside. It's almost like a potato soufflé, and whipping in an extra egg will make it rise higher. Serve as an accompaniment to our braised beef dishes, such as Pot Roast (page 328) or Boeuf Bourguignon (page 332).

Yield: 4 servings

4 cups Mashed Potatoes, left over or fresh
3 large eggs
⅔ cup grated Gruyère or Swiss cheese
¼ tsp salt
⅛ tsp freshly ground black pepper

Preheat the oven to 400°F. Butter a shallow baking dish or casserole.

Put the potatoes in the work bowl of a food processor, then add the eggs, about ½ cup of the grated cheese, and salt and pepper. Process briefly, about 10 seconds, to whip all the ingredients together.

Scoop the potatoes into the prepared gratin dish and smooth with a rubber spatula. Scatter the remaining cheese over the top and place on a baking sheet (in case of spills) in the lower part of the oven.

Bake about 30 to 35 minutes, until the top of the gratin is crusty and golden.

Julia's Sweet Potatoes and Yams

Sweet potatoes go wonderfully well with roast turkey, baked ham, roast goose, and duck, as well as with all kinds of pork and sausages. In our markets we generally find the rather dry pale-yellow variety and the more attractive reddish sweet potato with sweet orange flesh, which we often call a yam. However, it isn't a yam, because real yams are tropical tubers of a different sort that don't grow in this country. I shall continue to call it a yam to distinguish it from its pale, dry cousin, which, I have heard, contains more vitamin A, if that is a significant fact in your nutritional considerations. The two are interchangeable, and although I prefer yams, I shall call everything sweet potatoes.

Plain Mashed Sweet Potatoes

Yield: About 4 cups, serving 6

4 to 6 (2 pounds or so) large, fine fresh reddish-skinned sweet potatoes (yams)
1 tsp or more salt
Freshly ground white pepper
2 Tbs or more room-temperature butter, and/or half-and-half, or heavy cream, or milk
A few gratings of fresh ginger, to taste (optional)

Preheat the oven to 425°F. Meanwhile, scrub the potatoes under hot running water, remove any blemishes, and plunge a small sharp knife down about an inch into each potato in 5 or 6 places, to let out baking steam. Line a baking pan with foil (the potatoes will exude juices that will burn, staining your pan), and arrange the potatoes in it, in 1 layer. Bake in the lower middle level of the preheated oven for about an hour, or until they are thoroughly tender when squeezed and a knife pierces through them easily. Cut each potato in half lengthwise and then open up to cool. Scrape the flesh into a heavy-bottomed saucepan, and mash with a mixing fork or potato masher. Or put them in your heavy-duty mixer to break up at slow speed with the paddle attachment—careful not to go too fast and turn them gluey. Blend in salt and pepper, and the butter and/or cream or milk. Taste very carefully and correct seasoning, folding in the optional fresh ginger to taste.

Do-ahead notes

If done in advance, smooth the top and film with a spoonful or so of milk or cream to keep a skin from forming. To reheat, stir over low heat or over a pan of simmering water.

Variation: Orange Flavoring

Rather than stirring in milk or cream, use a little butter and orange juice, and blend in the finely grated rind of a bright fresh orange.

Variation: Marshmallow Topping

This old-fashioned juvenile topping is held in such low esteem that none of the standard American cookbooks I have on hand even mention it. In our family we love it at Thanksgiving with our turkey, particularly when we can find fresh homemade marshmallows. Here is my formula.

Preheat the oven to 425°F. Smear the inside of a 3-inch-deep casserole with softened butter, and scoop in the well-seasoned warm mashed sweet potatoes. Smooth the top surface of the potatoes with a rubber spatula, press a fairly close-packed layer of marshmallows into the surface, and coat with a very light sprinkling of confectioners' sugar. Bake in the upper middle level of the preheated oven until the topping has melted and browned nicely.

May be cooked in advance and kept warm.

Julia's Old-Fashioned Hash-Browns

This is my interpretation of Jim Beard's hash-browns, as he described them in his seminal tome, *American Cookery*. Hash-browns are, in essence, a sauté of boiled potatoes, and you want them barely cooked through before you begin the browning, just soft enough so that you can begin mashing them down roughly as you sauté, gathering and pressing them into a loose brown cake. Fresh-tasting potatoes and good fresh fat are essential here.

As to equipment, I like the omelet-pan shape—10 inches top diameter—with long handle and slanting sides 2 inches high. Well-seasoned cast iron is excellent, or heavy cast-aluminum non-stick. My old cast-iron Griswold skillet is another possibility; its short handle makes tossing more difficult, but it works. I use a sturdy plastic pancake turner for mashing and so forth, and a big plate to act as a cover for the pan as well as to help in unmolding and turning.

Yield: 2 servings

> 2 very big or three medium-big
>   potatoes (preferably Yukon
>   Gold)
> Salt
> 2 Tbs vegetable oil
> 2 Tbs unsalted butter
> Freshly ground pepper

Special equipment

> A 10-inch skillet (see above); a
>   plastic pancake turner; a large
>   plate

Peel the potatoes, then cut them into ½-to-¾-inch cubes—you'll have about 2½ cups. Drop at once into a saucepan of cold water to cover, salt lightly, bring to the boil, and boil slowly, partially covered, for about 5 minutes. Test by eating a cube, which should be almost but not quite done. Drain into a sieve, then toss lightly in a clean towel to remove moisture, and set on a plate. You may do this up to an hour in advance.

Ten minutes or so before you are to serve, set the frying pan over moderately high heat, and when warm swirl in the vegetable oil and 1 tablespoon of the butter. When the butter foam has almost subsided, toss in the potatoes. Let sit undisturbed for 20 seconds or so, then give the potatoes a toss, shaking and jerking the pan toward you by its handle, to let the cubes brown for several seconds on another side.

Continue thus for several minutes, until the cubes are lightly browned all over, adding driblets of oil if they seem to be sticking. Season lightly with salt and fresh pepper, then begin to mash the potatoes down roughly with your pancake turner, breaking some of them up. Lower the heat to moderate, dot the surface with a tablespoon or so of butter, cover the pan, and let steam for a minute or so while a crust forms on the bottom. Check seasoning.

Now you want to turn the cake over and let the potatoes crust on the other side. Either do so with a daring flip, or slide them onto the big plate and reverse into the pan, browned side up—easier said than accomplished, I think. I prefer a slightly messy flip which you can push and shove into place. If you are not quite ready to serve, keep them warm uncovered. To serve, slide them onto a hot platter. Hash-browns make a fine bed for broiled chicken or game hens and, of course, for steaks, chops, and hamburgers.

Scalloped Potatoes

There's nothing better to serve at a family dinner than a pan of sliced potatoes baked in milk or broth until soft and creamy inside, brown and crusty on top. And whether you think of such a dish, as they do in France, as a potato gratin with a specific name and venerable past, or simply call them scalloped potatoes, these dishes are essential to home cooking.

The two we offer here differ mainly in the cooking liquids and seasoning agents—and their traditional names. Julia's potatoes *dauphinoise* are made with milk or cream and a touch of garlic, and Jacques's potatoes *boulangère* with chicken stock, onions, and herbs. Our methods are exactly the same, starting with a brief boil on the stovetop, to thicken the liquid slightly with the starch of the potatoes. (You'll see that the *dauphinoise* potatoes are put directly over heat in a flameproof gratin dish while the *boulangère* potatoes are boiled in a saucepan, then transferred to the baking dish—but you can interchange the techniques, depending on the kitchenware you have, and the results will be identical.)

Boiling potatoes—new potatoes, Yukon Gold, or other moderately waxy, medium-to-low-starch varieties—are best for gratins, since they hold their shape nicely, even when sliced very thin. It's easiest to cut them using the slicing disk of a food processor or a mandoline, or use a good sharp chef's knife. But don't rinse or soak the potatoes in water after slicing them, since this will remove the starch that is so important to the smooth, creamy texture of the gratins.

Serve either variation with roasted or grilled meats and poultry. Both are convenient party dishes, easy to make ahead and then reheat or serve at room temperature. You might well find that they taste even better when they've sat for a while.

Jacques

Potatoes *boulangère* is the traditional garnish for roast leg of lamb. The name means "baker's wife potatoes," so called because the dish was originally prepared in a crock and baked very slowly in the baker's oven. I always use lots of onions, but sometimes I sauté them first, for about 5 minutes, before mixing them with the potatoes. And it tastes better, in my opinion, if it's made several hours ahead and reheated just before serving.

Pommes de terre dauphinoise is a specialty of Grenoble, near the Alps, and is made in many variations throughout eastern France. In the Lyons area, where I come from, we often baked the gratin with cheese on top—but in Grenoble they would regard that as a terrible aberration. The sprinkling of cheese will help to brown the top if you are making the gratin only with milk (just as Julia does with butter). I love gratin *dauphinois* the day after it's made. When we were kids my mother would serve it the next day at room temperature, with a big garlicky escarole salad—that was our whole meal.

Julia

The gratin *dauphinois* can be as rich or as lean as you like, made with all milk, or a mixture of milk and cream or half-and-half, or all cream, if you want to give the potatoes the luxury treatment, as they do in fancy restaurants. If for some reason you want a gratin that's completely fat-free, you can use skim milk, though that's not what I do. In fact, if I've put no cream at all in the gratin, I dot the top with butter, to help it brown and give it the richness it deserves.

Julia's Pommes de Terre Dauphinoise

Yield: A large casserole, serving 6 to 8

1 tsp salt, plus more if needed
1 tsp chopped garlic
3 cups milk, or mixed milk and
    cream, plus more if needed
½ tsp freshly ground white pepper,
    plus more if needed
2 pounds boiling potatoes, peeled
    and covered in water
1 to 2 Tbs butter for topping the
    potatoes (optional)

Special equipment
A food processor with a slicing disk
    (optional); an 8-to-10-cup flameproof
    gratin dish, lightly buttered; a cookie
    sheet

Preheat the oven to 400°F. Slide the rack on the lower third level and set the cookie sheet on it to catch boil-overs.

Sprinkle ½ teaspoon of salt on the chopped garlic and mash together with the blade of a knife, to make a purée. Pour about half the milk (or milk-and-cream mixture) into the gratin dish and add the garlic purée and the rest of the salt and the pepper.

Cut the potatoes crosswise, by hand or in a food processor, into very thin slices (⅛ inch or less)—do not rinse them again. Spread them evenly in the gratin dish and pour in the remaining milk. The liquid should come right to the top layer of potatoes—add more milk or cream if needed.

Place the dish on a burner, bring to a slow boil, and cook for 2 to 3 minutes, until the liquid has thickened slightly. Scrape the bottom gently with a wooden spoon to prevent scorching. Taste the liquid and adjust the seasoning.

Turn off the heat and dot the top of the gratin with a tablespoon or two of butter, if you wish. Place the dish in the oven, on top of the cookie sheet, and bake for 40 to 50 minutes, until the top is nicely browned, most of the liquid has been absorbed, and the potatoes are tender all the way through when pierced with a knife. If not served at once, keep warm in a turned-off oven or set over a pan of simmering water.

Jacques's Pommes de Terre Boulangère

Yield: A large gratin, serving 6 to 8

    2 pounds boiling potatoes, peeled
        and covered in water
    3 cups thinly sliced onions (2
        medium onions, or 12 ounces)
    3 Tbs thinly sliced garlic (about 6
        cloves)
    6 sprigs fresh thyme
    2 bay leaves
    1 tsp salt (less if using canned
        broth)
    ½ tsp black pepper
    3 to 4 cups homemade chicken
        stock, plus more if needed (or
        low-sodium canned broth)
    Chopped parsley, for garnish

Special equipment
    A food processor with a slicing
        disk (optional); a large (12-inch)
        sauté pan or wide saucepan; an
        8-to-10-cup gratin dish; a
        cookie sheet

Preheat the oven to 400°F.

Cut the potatoes crosswise, by hand or in a food processor, into very thin slices (⅛ inch or less) and put them directly in the pan—do not rinse them again. Add the sliced onions and garlic, herbs, and salt and pepper, and mix together with the potato slices. Pour in 3 cups of chicken stock and bring to a boil over high heat. Lower the heat and boil gently for 3 minutes or so, until the stock has just slightly thickened.

Pour the stock and potatoes into the gratin dish. Spread the slices in an even layer just covered by liquid—add more stock if necessary. Place on top of the cookie sheet in the oven, and bake for at least an hour, until most of the liquid has been absorbed and the potatoes are tender all through the gratin and brown and crusted on the top.

Sprinkle the chopped parsley over the gratin and serve.

Jacques's Pommes de Terre Savonnette

Thick, carefully trimmed potato slices are steamed, then crisped in a frying pan in this recipe—a quick process that gives them both a moist interior and a nice brown crust. Serve these miniature "cakes" as a garnish for grilled or pan-fried steaks, like our Steak Diane (page 314).

Yield: 4 servings

4 baking potatoes (narrow,
   evenly shaped ovals are best)
1 Tbs vegetable oil
1 Tbs butter
¼ tsp salt
⅛ tsp freshly ground black
   pepper, or more to taste

Special equipment
A large frying pan (12 inches),
   non-stick preferred, with a
   snug-fitting cover

Cutting the potato rounds
Peel the potatoes and place them in a bowl of cold water. With a sharp paring knife, trim the bulging sides of each to form a smooth cylinder or log, about 2 inches in diameter. Cut off the rounded ends (and save all the potato trimmings for soup or mashed potatoes). Cut the log crosswise into 1¼-inch-thick slices—you should get 3 or 4 from each potato, depending on length—and return them to the cold water. For a nice touch (not essential), shave the sharp corners of each piece—removing only a tiny bit of potato—so that the edges are gently rounded; you can do this with a vegetable peeler or a paring knife.

Cooking the potatoes
Arrange all the potato slices flat in 1 layer in the pan. Set it over moderate heat, and add the oil, butter, and enough water to come almost halfway up the side of each piece. Sprinkle with the salt and pepper. Cover the pan, raise the heat, and let the potatoes boil for about 12 minutes over high heat.

Remove the cover and pierce a potato slice with the tip of a knife. If it is not yet tender, replace the cover and steam for a couple of minutes more. The pieces should be soft all the way through but still firm. Continue cooking uncovered to rapidly evaporate any remaining liquid. Sauté the slices until the bottoms are nicely brown all around the edges. Flip each over with a small spatula and fry until the other side is similarly brown and crisp. Serve immediately.

Pommes de Terre Soufflées

A few cooking procedures are so fascinating, if occasionally frustrating, that every serious cook should try his or her hand at them. Here is one: souffléed potatoes start out as ordinary potato slices, but when sequentially deep-fried in oil at two different temperatures, they suddenly billow into feather-light, hollow ovals with an impossibly thin, crisp, golden shell.

It's a dramatic transformation, tinged with suspense, that requires good preparation, concentration, and practice. Perfectly puffed souffléed potatoes are a satisfying reward, though, for all the effort. And fortunately for potato lovers, the less-than-perfect slices and even the complete failures make exceptionally good potato chips.

The suspense in the process comes from factors that you can't control. Because of age or moisture content, some slices just will not inflate, even when you have done everything right. The three-stage frying method that we have detailed and illustrated here allows you to determine in advance which slices will puff, so that at serving time, when you do the final frying, you will have enough perfect ovals for all at the table.

Good equipment is key to making souffléed potatoes successfully. A mandoline is certainly the best tool to use to slice the potatoes (see photo on page 165). As well, you must have two deep, wide sauté pans or saucepans that can hold a sufficient amount of oil—about one and a half quarts each—to maintain a steady temperature. One of the pans must be light enough for you to slide and shake it on the stovetop for several minutes, and deep enough so that the oil won't splash out. You will also need an accurate and easy-to-read deep frying thermometer, and a wide, flat strainer for transferring, testing, and turning the potatoes.

Good kitchen procedure is also essential. Have the slices completely prepared, both pans of oil hot, and the lined baking trays ready before you start frying—and keep paper towels on hand for drips. *Most important, you must be very careful when handling the pans of hot oil,* especially during the first frying, when you must gently but continuously shake the pan.

Jacques

It is helpful to understand what is happening at each stage of this cooking process. The object of the first frying, during which you keep the potatoes moving in the 300°F oil, is to form a soft skin or crust on the surface of each slice, while the center becomes cooked and mushy like a mashed potato. It is important that the crust not brown or get hard, or it will not be pliable and therefore the potato will not puff—that is why you must carefully control the temperature, and even move the pan off the heat if the slices start to brown.

In the second frying, in the pan of hotter oil, the steam from the moist interior of the slice wants to escape. If the skin has formed properly and is flexible, it will trap the steam and blow up. But if it is already brown and hard, it can't inflate. The brief dip into this hotter oil shows which ones will inflate and which will not. As soon as you take them out of the oil, the good ones—the ones you keep—will deflate, but they'll puff up again when given the third and final frying.

Usually, 80 to 90 percent of the slices should work, but you may have to practice a few times, and you will be happy to see that your percentage of successful slices will improve.

Yield: 4 servings

3 or 4 large, evenly shaped russet
potatoes (about 10 to 12 ounces
each)
3 quarts vegetable oil (corn, cottonseed, or canola oil)
Salt

Special equipment

A mandoline or very sharp chef's
knife; 2 skillets, 10 inches or
more in top diameter, at least 4
inches deep; deep-frying thermometer; a skimmer or large
slotted spoon; a cookie sheet;
paper towels; parchment paper

Preparing the potatoes

Peel, shape, and slice the
potatoes—³⁄₁₆ inch thick—following the photos. Place the
uniform slices—you should get
a dozen or more from each
potato—in a bowl of cold
water as you cut them. (You can
save all the potato trimmings,
also in cold water, to use later in
soups or mashed potatoes.)

Peel the potatoes.

Pour oil into the skillets
to a depth of at least 1½ inches. Heat both skillets on the
stovetop right next to each other, bringing the oil in one
skillet to a steady temperature of 300°F and in the other
to 350° to 375°F. Measure the temperatures frequently
with a deep-frying thermometer.

Frying for the first time to form a skin

Dry all the potato slices well on paper towels; layer
them in towels and keep covered while you fry them in
batches.

Slide about 15 slices into
the first pan of 300°F oil.
Begin shaking the pan, very
lightly, to move the slices
around. Be very careful not to
splatter the hot oil: only small
movement is necessary, and
you should slide the pan in a
steady rhythm that will keep
the potatoes moving but will
not excessively agitate the oil.

Adjust the heat to main-
tain the oil at 300°F and cook
the slices for 5 to 6 minutes,
shaking the pan gently but
continuously, until small blis-
ters begin to form on the surface of the slices (see photo,
page 165).

If the slices are browning,
take the pan off the heat for a
few moments and allow the oil
to cool briefly (but keep shaking). Then return to the heat.

The slices will stay in the
first pan until you remove them,
in batches, for the second frying.

Trim each into a uniform
oblong with flat sides and a
flat bottom.

Starting with the flat bottom,
slice the potatoes lengthwise
along the straight blade of
the mandoline to get uni-
form thin slices like above.

Frying for the second time to test the slices

With the skimmer, scoop
up 4 or 5 slices from the first
pan and allow the oil to drip off
for 6 to 8 seconds so the potato
slices soften slightly. Lower the
skimmer into the hotter oil in
the second skillet, allowing the
slices to puff in the oil for a second or two, then lift them out
immediately.

Or slice by hand, into identi-
cal slices just a bit thicker
than ⅛ inch.

The slices in the first pan starting to blister

The slices after dip into second pan—some puffed, others not

Basketful of finished *pommes de terre soufflées*

Some slices may inflate evenly, some may bubble up a bit, and some not at all. Place the slices that puffed fully (see photo) on a parchment-lined cookie sheet for the final frying. They will deflate right away, but will inflate again in the final frying. (The slices that never did inflate should be set aside to be eaten, whenever you want. You can fry them up again, just to brown, if you like.)

Remove the rest of the slices from the first skillet, 4 or 5 at a time, and fry them as above in the hot oil. Place all the inflatable slices on the cookie sheet, and cover with a towel or plastic wrap. They can be held at room temperature for several hours before final frying and serving.

Repeat the whole procedure with the remaining raw slices of potatoes, frying 15 at a time.

Final frying and serving

When ready to serve, reheat oil in only one of the skillets to 350° to 375°F. Place the reserved slices, 8 or 10 at a time, in the oil. They will inflate again and begin to brown (see photo). Keep turning them over and stirring with the skimmer for about 1 minute, until they are colored evenly and crisp on the outside, then remove them to a tray lined with parchment or paper towels. The finished, puffed potatoes will not deflate, but keep the tray in a warm spot while you fry the remaining slices.

Season the potatoes lightly with salt and serve in a napkin-lined bowl.

Jacques on Frying Oil

For deep-frying potatoes and other foods, I like to use a tasteless vegetable oil, such as corn oil, canola oil, or cottonseed oil, which can withstand high temperatures without smoking or breaking down. Oil should be strained after you have used it for frying, to remove any food particles, and can be reused several times (see next paragraph), though it must be discarded when it deteriorates, gets foamlike, and no longer produces a crisp, dry product.

In restaurants, fresh oil is used first to fry lighter, delicate foods—like apple fritters—then will be used again to fry potatoes or other vegetables. After that, breaded foods such as croquettes can be fried in the same oil, and, finally, fish or other strong-tasting food. You cannot fry a more delicate food in oil that has been used to fry fish.

Cutting Waffle Potatoes on the mandoline

Julia's French Fries

The best French fries are made with the freshest frying medium, solid vegetable shortening or peanut or canola oil. If you have never experienced that freshness you have a treat awaiting you, since it makes all the difference. It makes all the difference, too, when the potatoes are crisp rather than soggy. The potatoes need two fryings. The first cooks them through rather slowly. The second, which mercifully can occur several hours later, browns and crisps them and takes place just before serving them.

Yield: 6 servings

4 or 5 large russet baking potatoes, 10 to 12 ounces each,
about 5 inches long and 2 to 2½
inches across
2½ quarts fresh frying oil
Salt

Special equipment

A 6-quart pot and a frying basket
to fit; a deep-fat frying thermometer; a long-handled wire
scoop; a napkin-lined serving
basket or bowl

Preparing the potatoes

Wash and peel the potatoes, trim into even rectangles, and cut into lengthwise slices ⅜ inch wide. Cut the slices into lengthwise strips ⅜ inches wide, and swish in a basin of cold water to remove surface starch. To prevent discoloration, drain them only just before frying, then dry thoroughly in paper towels.

May be prepared to this point several hours in advance.

The first fry

Provide yourself with a bed of paper towels set on a tray. Heat the oil to 325°F. Take up 2 handfuls of the potato strips (about the equivalent of 1½ potatoes) and scatter them into the frying basket. Lower carefully into the hot fat, averting your face to avoid oil splutters. Fry, turning the potatoes frequently for 4 to 5 minutes, or until the potatoes are soft through but not browned. Lift out the basket, let it drain briefly, then spread the potatoes on the paper towels, and continue with the rest. Let cool for 10 minutes or up to 2 to 3 hours.

Second and final frying

Just before serving, heat the frying oil to 375° to 400°F. Fry the cooked potatoes by handfuls, as described above, turning frequently, only a minute or two, until golden brown. Drain on paper towels, salt lightly, turn the potatoes into your serving basket, and continue. Serve as soon as possible.

Julia on Frying Oil

I don't do much deep-fat frying, because it smells up the house. However, the times I have done it in experiments with fried chicken, French fries, and so forth, I have concluded that solid white vegetable shortening, such as Crisco, is the least smelly and most satisfactory frying medium.

I have found that potatoes "use" the fat. The first batch of fries is delicious, fresh-tasting, a real treat. The second is all right, but by the third the potatoes are beginning to take on that greasy-spoon taste, and I don't want to have anything to do with them.

In other words, I really only like fried foods done in fresh fat, and for that reason I find deep-fat frying an expensive way to cook.

Opposite: French Fries

Rice Pilaf

The term "pilaf" or "pilaff" or "pilaw" comprises a diverse range of dishes—made with different grains by different methods in different cuisines—but here's one of the simplest and best. First, onions, rice, and herbs are sautéed briefly, then cooked in chicken stock. You may serve the rice at that point as a side dish, or toss in a colorful combination such as steamed and sautéed red bell pepper and asparagus pieces and green peas. The rice and vegetables together can be formed into a ring that makes a nice presentation on a plate with almost any kind of grilled meat, poultry, or fish (see photo of Grilled Halibut, page 231), or with our *steak au poivre* or roast chicken.

You can create a variety of pilafs by applying the same methods (although the cooking times will differ) to the many different rices on the market these days, such as basmati, brown rice, and wild rice, and varying the vegetable garnishes according to what's in season.

Jacques's Rice Pilaf with Pepper, Peas, and Asparagus

Yield: 6 to 8 servings

For the rice
1 Tbs butter
1 cup chopped onions
1½ cups long-grain white rice
3 cups chicken stock, preferably
   homemade
¼ tsp fresh or dried thyme
1 bay leaf
Salt to taste (will vary depending
   on stock)
¼ tsp freshly ground pepper

For the vegetable garnish
1 Tbs olive oil
½ cup peeled and diced red bell
   pepper
½ cup fresh asparagus, peeled and
   cut into 1-inch lengths
½ cup shelled fresh green peas
⅛ tsp salt
Freshly ground black pepper

Special equipment
A heavy 3-quart casserole or
   saucepan with a tight-fitting lid;
   a medium sauté pan with lid

Cooking the rice
Melt the butter in the saucepan or casserole over medium heat. When hot, stir in the onions and cook for a few minutes to soften. Add the rice and stir well to coat the grains with butter.

Pour in the chicken stock; add the thyme, bay leaf, salt to taste, and several grinds of pepper; then raise the heat to high and bring to a boil. Cover the pot, reduce the heat to very low, and cook for 15 to 20 minutes, until the rice is tender and all the liquid has been absorbed. (If you want to serve the pilaf plain, you can just fluff the grains with a fork and serve at this point.)

Preparing the vegetable garnish
While the rice is cooking, prepare the vegetable garnish. Set the sauté pan over medium-high heat, add the tablespoon of oil and all of the vegetables, and toss together. Add about 4 tablespoons of water (just enough to come partway up the side of the vegetables), sprinkle on the salt and pepper, and swirl the pan to mix.

Bring the water to the boil, cover the pan, and cook for about 5 minutes. Check the water level once or twice, adding a little more if necessary—and taste the vegetables for doneness.

When the water has evaporated and the vegetables are tender, turn them on top of the rice and toss together with a fork, distributing the vegetables evenly. Serve immediately.

Julia's Plain Boiled Rice

Always easy to do, and always useful to have on hand, 1 cup of regular long-grain Carolina white rice boils up to 3 cups of cooked rice. Measure the raw rice into a 2½-quart heavy-bottomed saucepan and stir in 2 cups of cold water, 1 teaspoon of salt, and, if you wish, 1 to 2 tablespoons of butter or good olive oil.

Bring to the boil over high heat and give it one good stir—and never stir it again until it is done. Reduce heat to the slow simmer, cover the pan, and cook for 12 minutes; this is probably not enough time, but it's wise to be careful. Take a quick peek and a rapid taste. The rice is done when the liquid has been absorbed, when there are little steam holes in the surface going down through the rice, and when the few grains you eat are almost tender—with a faint crunch at the center. If not done, cover and cook a few minutes more, but do not overcook or you will have gummy rice. When it is just done, set it aside, covered, for 5 minutes to finish cooking.

Gently fork up the rice, taste, and correct seasoning, adding a little more butter or oil if you wish.

Do-ahead notes

You may cook the rice 2 to 3 days in advance. Let cool, then cover and refrigerate. To reheat, turn it into a covered bowl and either microwave on low, or steam it, or sauté it slowly in a frying pan with a little oil or butter.

Jacques

It is fine to make pilaf by sautéing the vegetables, such as diced bell pepper and fresh tomato, with the rice and onions and cooking them all together. But sautéing the vegetable garnishes separately, as we do here, will give them more color and texture when they are tossed with the rice.

The best way to make an attractive border of rice—or a similar garnish or sauce—around a piece of fish or meat is first to make a mound in the center of the plate, then push down on the rice with the back of a big spoon, spreading it out from the center. This allows you to form an even ring with a neat, clean edge.

Julia

I think it's best, if you have the time, to start beans well in advance, let them soak, and then cook them very, very slowly.

Too often beans are "crunchily undercooked," and not only are they unpleasant to eat but they produce flatulence, the polite word for plain old gas. I leave my beans soaking until I can bite through one and it has a fresh crunch. I've found that unsoaked beans tend to cook unevenly—and they do need more cooking time and water, especially if they are older than this year's crop. Also, I have always thought that soaking removes some of the complex sugars in the beans, which cause gas.

Of all the ways to cook beans, my favorite is the Crock-Pot or slow cooker. I soak my beans in the afternoon, and at 6 p.m. I dump the beans, water, and seasonings into the Crock-Pot and let it cook on "low" overnight—they are done the next morning. I can adjust the seasoning and consistency as needed, cool them, and refrigerate. They can sit for several days and will be perfect when I want to serve them. If you don't have a Crock-Pot, cook beans in a covered casserole in a 250°F oven. Slower is usually better, I believe, but when I'm in a terrible hurry, I do pressure-cook beans.

White Beans

We call this simple dish a ragout because it has a thick stewlike consistency and a lovely blend of flavors, but it's really just a pot of plain white beans, carefully seasoned and partly puréed to give it a natural creaminess. We use Great Northern or similar pea or navy beans here, but beans of other colors can be prepared by this method—cooked until almost tender, then finished with sautéed onions, garlic, herbs, and other flavoring agents.

The bits of pancetta (unsmoked Italian bacon, really the same as the French *lardons*) which we add in this recipe make these beans especially well suited as an accompaniment to leg of lamb, homemade sausage, and other meats—the beans are good for sopping up the meat juices. But you can serve them as a vegetarian dish, too—just omit the pancetta and add other sautéed aromatic vegetables, such as sweet peppers and celery. And with chunks of cooked vegetables—or leftover meats—this is hearty enough to be a main dish on its own.

Jacques's Ragout of White Beans

Yield: 5 to 6 cups, serving 10 to 12

1 pound (about 2 cups) Great Northern
    or other small white beans, picked
    over, rinsed, soaked or not as you wish
    (see Julia's and Jacques's comments on
    the subject)
1½ tsp salt, plus more to taste
1 Tbs olive oil
3 ounces lean pancetta, diced into ¼-
    inch pieces (about ⅔ cup)
1½ cups chopped onions
3 Tbs peeled and thinly sliced garlic (5
    large cloves)
2 tsp minced fresh thyme, or 1 tsp dried
    thyme, crumbled
¼ tsp freshly ground pepper, plus more
    to taste
2 Tbs or so chopped parsley, for garnish

Special equipment

A large (5- or 6-quart) saucepan or casse-
    role with a cover; a large (10-inch) fry-
    ing pan; a blender, an immersion
    blender, or a food processor

Drain the beans, if you have soaked them, or wash them and put them in the pot with 6 cups of fresh cold water (8 cups if not soaked) and the salt. Bring to a boil and simmer gently, partially covered. After 40 minutes of cooking, taste several beans to check for doneness—you want them all to be tender to the bite but not mushy. Simmer longer if necessary.

While the beans are cooking, heat the olive oil in the frying pan. Add the pancetta pieces, toss to coat with oil, and cook for a couple of minutes over moderate heat. Stir in the onions, garlic slices, thyme, and pepper and cook over moderately low heat for about 10 minutes, stirring and tossing frequently, until the onions and garlic are soft. Set aside.

Jacques

Beans are a perfect canvas, or carrier, for the flavors of whatever you cook with them. At home, we love to put a piece of pork—a pork shoulder or a ham hock—right into the beans to cook, along with a bay leaf and some thyme. You could do the same thing with a pork chop, or just a piece of ham. And beans are delicious when flavored with poultry—cook them with the carcass from a roast chicken or turkey. Or put in some onions and carrots and a package of chicken necks and you have a tasty stew for six people for less than three dollars.

For a dish like this one, I would not soak the beans before cooking. These common small white beans, grown in this country, have usually been harvested and dried just in the preceding year and consequently are not that hard. They will cook relatively fast without soaking, and you can always add more liquid and extend the cooking until they are completely done.

You want to strain out the liquid here so the dish is more like a stew than a soup. If you are making the beans to serve with a roast leg of lamb—which Julia and I did when we cooked together on our show—you could take this reserved bean liquid, which is already slightly syrupy, and use it to deglaze the roasting pan. You'll have a naturally thick and delicious sauce.

When the beans are nearly tender, stir in the sautéed flavorings and return to the simmer. Cook, partially covered, over low heat, stirring occasionally, for about 20 minutes, or until the beans are fully cooked and soft.

Remove from heat. Strain or ladle out any liquid covering the beans (and save it for soup). For a thick and creamy texture, remove a cup of beans and purée them in a blender or food processor. Or, if you have an immersion blender, run it for just a few seconds in one small area of the bean pot to make a small amount of purée. Stir the purée through the rest of the beans. Taste and adjust seasoning.

Just before serving, sprinkle the chopped parsley over the beans.

Do-ahead notes

The bean ragout can be made up to 2 or 3 days ahead; let it cool, then cover and refrigerate. Reheat slowly for serving, using some of the reserved liquid to moisten the ragout, which may thicken on standing.

Julia's Bean Dishes

Beans are on the nutritional lists as being good for one, and that's fine with me, because I just love dried beans. They are also in the "in" group among the fancy restaurants, served elegantly with a salmon dish or a lamb shank. The perfectly cooked bean, discussed on page 170, holds its shape nicely but is fully cooked throughout—no crunchy inner core. Here are a few simple suggestions for serving them.

Beans Simmered with Garlic and Olive Oil

For 1½ cups of cooked beans, serving 4 to 6 people, sauté 2 or 3 large cloves of garlic purée (see page 58) in 2 tablespoons of olive oil for a moment, just to soften. Pour in the beans and a spoonful or two of their cooking juices, and bring to the simmer. Taste carefully, adding seasonings to taste and, if you wish, a few sprigs of fresh thyme, rosemary, or savory. Simmer, covered, for several minutes while the beans absorb the flavorings. Taste again for seasoning, remove the herbs, toss with a good handful of fresh chopped parsley, and they are ready to serve. These will go especially well with pork roasts and chops, roast duck and goose, roast and braised lamb, and sausages.

A Purée of White Beans

Rather than the usual mashed potatoes, how about a purée of beans to go with your turkey or roast lamb or pork? Take the preceding recipe and purée the beans either through a vegetable mill or in a food processor, adding a little more of the bean cooking juices as needed. You may wish to whip in a bit of soft butter or cream before serving. If prepared ahead, keep the beans warm in a double boiler.

White Bean Soup

Simmer the cooked beans with a cup of chopped onions sautéed in butter. Reserve ¾ cup and purée the rest through a vegetable mill or in a food processor, adding 2 to 3 cups of bean cooking liquid and/or chicken stock. Roughly mash the reserved beans with a mixing fork and stir into the soup along with, if you wish, a tablespoon or so of port or sherry. Top each serving with a spoonful of sour cream.

A Few Bean Basics

Buying. There is such a thing as "freshness" even in dried beans. They taste best and will cook more evenly and quickly when used within the year they are harvested. You can't necessarily tell how old a dried bean is by looking at it, so buy them from markets where there is good turnover and cook them before they get drier and harder.

Cleaning. Though beans are cleaned and sorted before packaging, it's always a good idea to spill them onto a platter or pan and check for stones and debris. Then rinse them well in a sieve and turn into a bowl of cold water—discard any "floaters," broken beans, or strange-looking beans. Then the rest can be left in the water for soaking.

Soaking. Though soaking is not necessary (see our comments), beans that have been rehydrated in cold water will cook faster than unsoaked beans. Small beans may need only a couple of hours of soaking, but older and larger ones may need a 6-to-8-hour or overnight soaking. Keep soaking beans in a cool place, since they can begin to ferment if the temperature is warm. Soak beans in 3 to 4 times their volume of water (3 to 4 cups of water for 1 cup of dried beans). Drain after soaking and cook in fresh cold water.

Cooking. Beans can be cooked in a conventional pot, as we do here, or in a pressure cooker, a slow cooker, or an oven casserole. Cooking time varies with each method, the type and age of the beans, and whether or not they have been soaked. If soaked, use 3 cups of cooking water for every cup of dried beans (original volume); use 4 cups if you haven't soaked them. Add water as needed during cooking so beans are always covered, and cook until thoroughly tender. If you have excess liquid, after cooking strain it, freeze, and save for making soup.

VEGETABLES

PROPERLY COOKED VEGETABLES ARE THE MARK OF A FINE MEAL. A HANDFUL OF GREEN beans or a head of cabbage is easy to overlook when you're busy in the kitchen, but these deserve the same respect and attention as the roast they may accompany. And, like different varieties of fish, or cuts of meat, every vegetable needs to be cooked thoroughly, tested for doneness, and seasoned with care.

In this chapter you will see how we cook some of our favorite vegetables to bring out their full flavor and texture. These are, for the most part, everyday vegetables—cauliflower, carrots, onions, tomatoes, and turnips—the ones that are fundamental to home cooking. Most are available year-round in our supermarkets, and with them you can make appetizing first courses, colorful and quick side dishes, and longer-cooking vegetable main courses in every season.

Of course, there's not just one way to trim a beautiful artichoke bottom, or cook a green pea so that it's tender and sweet, and throughout the chapter we present flavorful variations and different cooking methods, with several preparations for the same vegetable. You can adapt these suggestions and techniques to your own taste and cooking style, and use them with other favorite vegetables as well. The ultimate goal is always the same: to cook and season each vegetable with due respect, developing all its natural flavor and distinctive texture.

Julia on Wine and Artichokes, as well as with Asparagus and Eggs

Artichokes contain a property that alters the taste of many foods—makes them taste sweet, among other things. Asparagus does not agree with many wines, nor does the egg. However, I like wine with everything, and the question is: what wine to choose? I posed this problem to Shirley Sarvis from San Francisco, whose profession is the pairing of wines and foods, and to Richard Sanford, wine maker and owner of the Sanford Winery in the Santa Ynez Valley of Santa Barbara County.

Something very dry and fairly strong, they both said. Shirley likes dry white vermouth on the rocks with artichokes, and Richard suggests a rather grassy sauvignon blanc. Both proposed some of the dry rosés, much-neglected wines that have immensely improved in quality. As Shirley says, wine and artichokes are not an ideal combination, and much depends on how the vegetables are served or how they are accompanied. Are the artichokes the main feature or just a part of the dish? She would serve a buttery Chardonnay with asparagus and hollandaise, for instance, and would never refuse brut champagne with a truffled omelet.

I think you show that you are well aware of the challenge, and you do your imaginative best. If your guests are wine buffs you could start a lively conversation on this age-old question.

Julia

Jacques and I give different methods for cooking our whole artichokes here—I prefer to steam them, and he boils them—but each yields a perfectly cooked vegetable in about the same time. Try both techniques and see which you prefer.

I like to serve whole artichokes at room temperature, one per person, and just let them remove the choke and eat their way to the artichoke bottom. On occasion, though, it's nice to strip all the leaves and use the flesh to stuff the artichoke bottom, as detailed in our sidebar recipe for Artichauts Jacques. Jacques and I spontaneously created this delicious stuffing as we cooked together for our television series, but you can vary this formula to your own taste with lemon juice, a bit of mayonnaise, or other herbs.

Artichokes discolor easily, so when trimming them I rub the cut parts frequently and liberally with a lemon half, to prevent them from turning brown. For the same reason, I recommend Jacques's method of trussing the artichokes with a slice of lemon to keep the bottoms white, especially if you'll be storing them for several days. Artichokes will also discolor if cooked in aluminum or iron, so, whether boiling or steaming, use a stainless-steel or other non-reactive pot.

Whole Artichokes

An artichoke offers many pleasurable possibilities to the cook. It has a unique flavor that you can match with a remarkable range of foods. You can trim, cook, and present its unusual leafy body in many delightful forms (see the good ideas for artichoke bottoms, pages 180–185).

But the simplest preparation of all—a large steamed or boiled artichoke, served whole—provides a special pleasure for the eater. You pluck off each leaf to find a morsel of tender flesh at its base, which you scrape off with your teeth. As the leaves get closer to the center they are more succulent, and the pleasure builds until the meaty "bottom" provides a delicious climax to the dish.

There are many possibilities even with these most basic artichokes. You can serve them warm, room-temperature, or cold; as a first course or as the centerpiece of a light meal. You can set them on the table *au naturel*—with the inedible choke still inside—or hollowed out and garnished. Warm artichokes are often served with melted butter or hollandaise; cold artichokes with mayonnaise or vinaigrette. Lemon wedges are appropriate for either.

Cooked Whole Artichokes Two Ways

Yield: 4 servings

    4 medium-size artichokes
    4 round lemon slices, ¼ inch thick (for
       trussing onto the bottom, optional), or
       1 lemon, cut in half (for Julia's
       steaming method)
    Salt
    Sprigs of dill or parsley, for garnish

Accompaniments for cooked artichokes
    Lemon wedges
    Melted butter
    Hollandaise Sauce (page 96)
    Mayonnaise (pages 117 and 120)
    Jacques's Vinaigrette in a Jar or Julia's
       Lemon-Oil Dressing (pages 114 and
       115)

Special equipment
    Knives with stainless-steel blades, cotton
       twine for tying artichokes (optional—
       Jacques's method); a large non-reactive
       saucepan or stockpot; a steamer basket
       and a tight cover, if steaming

Jacques's Method: Boiling Whole Artichokes

Working with one artichoke at a time, break or cut off the stem; trim the base flat so the artichoke can sit on it, upright. Cut off the top 1½ inches of the cone of leaves with a sharp chef's knife. With kitchen scissors, snip off the top third of all the remaining broad leaves, removing the prickly needles.

Jacques

There are different kinds of artichokes in the market these days. You want the traditional Green Globe variety—grown around Castroville, near the California coast. These have a large heart and a meaty bottom, and are the ones to use in our recipes. It is easiest to find them in the market from March to May, when the artichoke harvest peaks, and there is a smaller harvest in the fall too.

You may encounter new varieties that are being grown in desert areas of California and Arizona, but these are heartless! If you cut them open, you see that the leaves join at the stem, and there is virtually no heart or bottom. To tell the difference, press the base of the artichokes—you can feel the heart in the Green Globe artichokes, but the others will be soft throughout.

Serving Whole Artichokes, Boiled or Steamed

Remove the twine and lemon slice, if you've used them, and turn the artichoke upright. For an informal meal, serve the whole artichoke with the inner leaves and choke still inside and let each person remove it.

For a more elegant presentation, remove the choke first: spread the top open slightly, so you can insert your fingers into the center and grasp the central cone of small leaves. Remove in one clump—it resembles a small funnel—and set aside.

With a small spoon, scrape away and discard the hairy fibers of the choke, leaving the bottom clean and smooth. (If the artichoke is overcooked, the choke may pull right out as you remove the inner cone of leaves. If it is undercooked, though, the choke will be hard to remove, and you must scrape carefully to get it all.)

To garnish, invert the small cone of leaves so the pointed end is down, and put it back in the hollow of the artichoke, perched on top of the large leaves. Tuck a sprig of dill or parsley into the inverted cone. Clean and garnish the other artichokes in this manner, and serve on a platter or individual plates.

Jacques's Method: Boiling Whole Artichokes (continued)

To keep the artichoke bottoms white (especially if you plan to store them for several days), center one of the thick lemon slices on the flat base of each. Tie in place with the twine, making two tight loops that cross at the top and the bottom, as when tying a package. Knot securely.

Bring a large amount of salted water to the boil in the pot. Put in the artichokes and place a colander or a plate on top of them (*inside* the pot), to keep them completely submerged during cooking. Return to the boil, and cook uncovered for about 45 minutes. To test, remove one artichoke and pull a leaf: if it comes off easily, they are done.

As soon as the artichokes are cooked, you must refresh them in cold water. Spill out as much of the hot water as you can and place the pot with the artichokes under cold running water, with the colander on top to break up the stream of water, so it does not fall directly on the artichokes.

To serve the artichokes warm or room-temperature, rinse in fresh water only briefly. Lift them from the pot, gently squeeze to press out excess water, then set them to drain, upside down, on a plate for ½ hour or longer.

For chilled artichokes, or for storing, rinse until completely cool; squeeze out excess water and chill in the refrigerator in a baking dish, bottom side up, with the lemon slice still tied in place.

Julia's Method: Steaming Whole Artichokes

Rinse the artichokes under cold water to remove any grit. Working with one at a time, cut off the top inch of the cone of leaves with a sharp chef's knife. Rub the cut surface with the half lemon to prevent discoloring. With kitchen scissors, snip off about ½ inch from the tips of the remaining broad leaves to remove the prickly needles, and rub with lemon. Finally, cut off the stem even with the base, trimming away any small leaves. Rub the flat base with the half lemon.

Pour 2 inches of water into the pot and fit in the steamer basket. Arrange the prepared artichokes in the basket, top side down. Cover tightly and bring to the boil. Reduce the heat to maintain a slow boil and steam for 35 to 45 minutes. The artichokes are done when their bases are easily pierced with a small sharp knife. Remove them from the steamer and rest top side up.

Cooked artichokes can now be served warm, or room-temperature—which I prefer. To store, refrigerate in a covered container—they will keep 2 to 3 days.

Artichauts Jacques

A clever way to present every morsel of a cooked whole artichoke is to remove all the leaves before serving, and use their bits of tender flesh as a stuffing for the hollow artichoke bottom. It takes a bit of time to scrape the leaves of an artichoke clean, so reserve this as a special treat for 2, or at most 4.

For each serving, gently pull off all the broad outer leaves of a cooked, cooled artichoke, keeping the bottom intact. Remove the inner core of small leaves and scrape the hairy choke from the bottom.

With a small spoon, patiently scrape the edible flesh from the reserved leaves (including the inner core). You will have 2 to 3 tablespoons of flesh from each artichoke. Add ¼ teaspoon each of chopped fresh tarragon and minced shallots, and a good drizzle of olive oil. Season with fresh cracked pepper and salt, and mix well with a fork. Pile into the artichoke bottom, and serve surrounded by a leaf of butter lettuce, garnished with a sprig of dill.

Julia

Boiling the bottoms in a flour-thickened *blanc* is a simple method for cooking light-colored vegetables. It keeps them an appetizing pale green and imparts a nice lemony taste. It's also a good storage medium—you can cook the artichoke bottoms several days before you need them, let them cool in the *blanc,* and refrigerate them right in the liquid.

You can use the *blanc* itself as the base for a creamy artichoke soup, since it is already permeated with artichoke flavor and slightly thickened. I add sautéed onions and the flesh from all the leaves that I pulled off the bottoms before cooking. Simmer these leaves briefly, scrape away the flesh, purée it, then finish with a bit of cream. Before serving, I sauté some thin slices of artichoke bottoms for a garnish. Whenever I make a batch of bottoms for stuffing, it's nice to have a couple of extra ones just to slice up and float in this wonderful soup.

Artichoke Bottoms

Artichoke bottoms are a treat by themselves and make delicious and attractive little saucers for savory fillings. Even simply prepared vegetables, eggs, or seafood become quite special when heaped into a shapely and perfectly cooked artichoke bottom—suitable as a first course, as a garnish to a main course, or as the featured dish of a brunch or other light meal.

As chefs know, artichoke bottoms, even though they do take time to prepare, once you have them at hand are a convenient delicacy, ready to be served in a matter of minutes. Here, we cook them in a mix of water, lemon juice, and flour, called a *blanc,* which will preserve their fresh taste and light color for several days. Serve them cold or at room temperature with any of the accompaniments suggested for whole artichokes, page 177, or filled with a chopped vegetable or seafood salad, such as our lobster-roll filling, page 137. They are also delicious simply sautéed, either whole or in wedges, in a bit of butter or olive oil and garlic. And you can stuff and bake them with almost any creamy, savory filling, including the two we give here: the rich concentrate of finely diced mushrooms known as *duxelles,* or a simple sauté of spinach tossed with Parmesan cheese.

We also give you two methods for removing the leaves and trimming the bottoms, (with photos): Julia's patient hand-plucking technique, and Jacques's faster method for those wielding sharp knives (with stainless-steel blades).

Cooked Artichoke Bottoms

Yield: 6 artichoke bottoms

For the cooking liquid, or *blanc*
3 Tbs all-purpose flour
¼ cup freshly squeezed lemon juice
6 cups water
½ tsp salt
6 large artichokes (Green Globe variety)

1 lemon, halved, for
    rubbing on artichokes

Special equipment
A 3-quart stainless-steel or other
    non-reactive saucepan; knives
    and peelers with stainless-
    steel blades

Making the *blanc*
Whisk the flour and lemon juice together in the bottom of the saucepan to make a smooth paste. Still whisking to prevent lumps, add, slowly at first, about 3 cups of the water. Bring to a boil, stirring occasionally. Remove from the heat, stir in the remaining 3 cups of water and the salt, and set aside.

Preparing the artichoke bottoms
Work with one artichoke at a time, frequently rubbing the exposed surfaces with the lemon half to prevent discoloring. Following the photographs, trim the artichokes down to the bottoms.

Cooking the bottoms
Make sure that all the artichoke bottoms (as well as any trimmed stems) are covered by the *blanc;* add more water if necessary. Bring to a boil, and simmer, uncovered, for 20 to 30 minutes, until easily pierced with a sharp knife. Remove from the heat, but leave the bottoms in the liquid.

Starting at the bottom row, bend each leaf back until it snaps, then pull it down and off the artichoke, leaving a bit of the leaf base attached. Don't yank the whole leaf off at the base. Rub with lemon.

Continue snapping and peeling off the leaves (and rubbing with lemon).

Jacques

It is worth a bit of effort to shape a very neat artichoke bottom—we call it *tourner un artichaut.* Julia's method is one of the best. I can remember watching her on TV, many years ago, and learning how to snap the artichoke leaf and pull it down so that the fleshy part stays on the bottom. If you just pull the leaf off at its base, the flesh comes off with it and you lose it. Since then I have always taught apprentices Julia's method. (When I trim the bottoms with a sharp knife, as shown in the photos, I also leave the flesh on the bottom. This requires sharp knives and a bit of practice.)

Artichoke bottoms taste luxurious, but can be quite economical. Since the outer leaves are discarded before cooking, it's fine to use artichokes with yellowing or spotted leaves. You can often buy such older artichokes at a fraction of the regular price, and trim them to make a batch of artichoke bottoms.

Julia on the Allure of the Stuffed Artichoke Bottom

When Paul and I came back from Paris, before my first book was published, I needed to earn a bit of money. So I started to give cooking classes at our house in Cambridge. But with all the shopping and providing the wine—and with half the students not showing up—I'd always seem to lose money.

So I devised a plan to woo others to host the cooking classes. I invited them to lunch, and served them artichoke bottoms—stuffed with mushroom *duxelles*, a poached egg, and béarnaise sauce—and then my Queen of Sheba chocolate cake. It always won them over!

Then I would suggest it would be a good idea to use their own kitchens and their own cookware rather than my professional oven, etc. Then they would be cooking within their own homes, with their own friends, and it would be fun for everyone. That meant that I provided the food and presented them with the bill. They furnished the wine and did the clean-up, and I went back home with $50—the only time I made anything with those cooking classes.

Cooked Artichoke Bottoms (continued)

Serving cooked artichoke bottoms

To serve the cooked artichoke bottoms immediately, lift from the hot *blanc* with a slotted spoon and scrape away all the inedible leaves and fuzzy fibers of the chokes with a teaspoon. Season lightly and serve with any of the accompaniments suggested for whole artichokes (page 177) or stuff them with warm mushroom *duxelles* or sautéed spinach, as in the following recipes.

For cold artichoke bottoms, or to store, allow them to cool completely in the *blanc*. Scrape off the chokes and refrigerate in the *blanc*, in a non-reactive bowl or container, for several days. To warm the bottoms before serving or stuffing, sauté briefly in a small amount of butter, and season with salt and pepper.

When you have exposed the entire artichoke bottom and the interior core of lighter-colored leaves, with a sharp knife cut off this inner core crosswise, just above the fleshy part of the bottom. Trim the cut edge to make it smooth and even. (You will see the inedible choke but don't remove it until after cooking.)

Using a sharp knife or vegetable peeler, trim away the remaining green exterior of the artichoke bottom, exposing the whitish flesh left by the leaves. Cut off the stem.

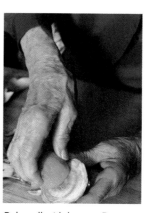

Rub well with lemon. Drop the trimmed artichoke bottom into the *blanc* and prepare the remaining ones. (You can also pare the reserved stems, removing the thick outer layer and discolored ends, and cook these interior sections in the *blanc*.)

Mushroom Duxelles Stuffing
for Artichoke Bottoms

Yield: About ¾ cup, to stuff 6 artichoke
bottoms

For the *duxelles* base
12 ounces common mushrooms (rinsed if
necessary immediately before using)
1 Tbs olive oil
3 Tbs finely minced shallots (see sidebar
on Mincing Shallots)
1 Tbs unsalted butter
Salt and freshly ground pepper to taste

For the enrichment
2 Tbs port or Madeira wine
½ tsp flour
3 to 4 Tbs heavy cream

Special equipment
A food processor; a large frying pan (10
inches top diameter or larger)

Cut each mushroom in half (or in quarters if very large)
and toss into the work bowl of the food processor. Chop, with
short pulses, to a uniform, crumbly texture of very tiny pieces.

Set the pan over medium heat, add the oil and butter, and
when sizzling add the shallots and chopped mushrooms and
sauté for about ½ minute. Cook over moderately high heat,
stirring frequently. The mushrooms will sizzle, then boil as they
release their liquid. Cook for several minutes as the liquid evaporates and the mushroom flavor concentrates.

When the liquid is gone and the mushroom pieces are
dry, they will start to sizzle again. (At this point, the *duxelles* base
has finished cooking. You can season it to taste with salt and
freshly ground pepper and use it for stuffing artichoke bottoms,
or in other recipes, without the following cream enrichment.
The *duxelles* can be frozen at this stage.)

Mincing Shallots

After peeling the shallots completely,
if they are large and rounded cut them
in half lengthwise (from root end to
pointed end) so halves lie flat on work
surface.

With a sharp paring knife,
make 3 sets of slices. First,
slice very thinly with lengthwise vertical cuts (top to
bottom).

Then make 1 or
2 horizontal cuts,
parallel to work
surface, to cut
shallot into
layers.

Finally, slice very thinly crosswise to create a dice of very
small, even pieces (about
⅛th inch square or less).

Jacques's Way of Trimming Artichoke Bottoms to be Served as a Garnish for Meat and Fish Dishes

With a sharp chef's knife, shear off all outer leaves, leaving a cone of inner leaves.

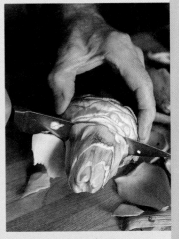

Cut off the cone, leaving only the artichoke bottom with the choke. (Save some of the tender leaves from the cone for cooking in the *blanc*.)

To finish the mushroom stuffing, stir the port or Madeira into the *duxelles* and cook for about a minute, until absorbed. Lower the heat, sprinkle the flour over, and sauté for another minute, stirring. Pour in the heavy cream, blend well, and cook for several minutes more, until soft and thick. Remove from the heat and season with salt and freshly ground pepper to taste. Cool, and store covered in the refrigerator. Use within a couple of days.

Sautéed Spinach Stuffing for Artichoke Bottoms

Yield: About 1 cup, to stuff 6 artichoke bottoms

1 pound fresh spinach leaves, preferably
 young and tender
2 Tbs olive oil
⅛ tsp salt
⅛ tsp freshly ground black pepper
3 Tbs heavy cream (optional)
2 Tbs or so freshly grated Parmesan
 cheese

Wash the spinach leaves well: dump into a sinkful of cold water, swish up and down, and let any dirt and sand settle to the bottom. (Repeat in fresh water if leaves are still gritty.) Remove the stem from each leaf, tearing it away with one hand while holding the folded leaf in the other. Shake off excess water but do not dry.

Heat the oil in a large sauté pan, or wide Dutch oven, over moderate to high heat. Heap all the spinach into the pan with some water still clinging to the leaves. As the bottom leaves start to cook, toss the pile with a wooden spoon, bringing the wilted leaves up so uncooked leaves will start to sauté. If leaves seem to be sticking to the bottom, add a few tablespoons of water to the pan. Season with the salt and black pepper; keep turning the leaves as they release their liquid. You can add the optional cream at this point, for a richer filling, or to soften the taste of older spinach.

Continue to cook, stirring occasionally, for about 6 to 8

minutes—or longer if you have added cream—until the spinach is tender, and almost all of the liquid has evaporated. Remove from the heat, sprinkle the Parmesan cheese over the spinach, and stir to mix. Taste and adjust the seasoning.

Stuffed Artichoke Bottoms

Yield: 6 stuffed artichoke bottoms

6 cooked artichoke bottoms, chokes
   removed
Salt and freshly ground pepper
Mushroom Duxelles Stuffing or Sautéed
   Spinach Stuffing (preceding recipes)
2 to 3 Tbs fresh bread crumbs
2 Tbs freshly grated Parmesan cheese
   (for spinach stuffing)

Special equipment
A lightly buttered baking dish

Preheat the oven to 400°F.

Remove the artichoke bottoms from the *blanc*; drain and dry. Season each with salt and freshly ground pepper to taste and arrange in the baking dish.

Mound 2 to 3 tablespoons of either stuffing into each bottom. Sprinkle plain bread crumbs on top of mushroom *duxelles* stuffing. For spinach stuffing, mix the Parmesan cheese and the bread crumbs and sprinkle over.

Bake for about 15 minutes, until the crumbs are golden brown and the stuffed bottoms are thoroughly heated. Serve the artichokes immediately, either in the baking dish or on individual plates.

(If both the bottoms and the stuffing are freshly cooked and warm, you don't need to heat them in the oven—just put them under the broiler to brown the bread-crumb topping.)

Do-ahead notes
You can stuff the bottoms up to a day before serving, wrap them well, and refrigerate. Bake as directed.

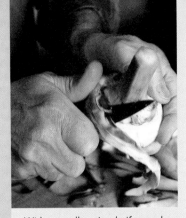

With a small paring knife, peel away the inedible green parts, leaving the flesh at the base of each leaf on the artichoke bottom. Continue to trim the artichoke bottom with a few inches of the stem still attached.

Squeeze on lemon juice.

After cooking in the *blanc*, cut the bottom and stem into long wedges, and remove the choke. Use as a garnish for meat and fish dishes.

Jacques's Asparagus

Asparagus is one of the first vegetables that I harvest from my garden in Connecticut each spring, and I like to serve it many ways—as a first course, a side vegetable for meat, poultry, and fish, in gratins, or as decorative garnish (see Coddled Eggs with Carrot Sauce, page 85).

Fortunately, asparagus is now available in many markets almost all year round. Make sure you choose firm, plump spears with tightly closed tips. To keep them fresh, store them upright in a container, with their bases immersed in an inch or two of water. Before cooking, you should always peel the tough fibrous skin about two-thirds down the asparagus and break off the woody base, as shown in the photos here, so the entire spear will be as tender as the tip after just a few minutes of cooking.

As with green beans, my preferred method is to boil asparagus in a small amount of water until cooked through but still somewhat firm to the bite. It's important to use a large pan in which the spears can fit in one or two layers, so that they will cook evenly and quickly. In this recipe, for the last minute or so of cooking I add butter to the small amount of boiling liquid that is left, to create an emulsion. Warm asparagus is also delicious with Hollandaise Sauce (page 96). I often serve the spears at room temperature, whole or cut into short lengths, with a mustardy vinaigrette (page 115).

Yield: 4 servings (or more as a garnish)

1½ pounds fresh asparagus spears
    (about 2 dozen)
½ cup hot tap water
¼ tsp salt, plus more if needed
⅛ tsp freshly ground black pepper,
    plus more to taste
3 Tbs butter, in small pieces
Chopped fresh parsley for garnish
    (optional)

Special equipment

A large stainless-steel saucepan or sauté pan (12 inches or more top diameter) with a tight-fitting cover

Trimming the spears

Lay each spear on the work surface, holding the base in the fingers of one hand. Rotate the spear as you peel, removing the skin in ribbons. Snap off the bottom as shown.

Cooking the spears

Lay all the spears in the pan in one or two layers, add the hot water, salt, and pepper, cover the pan, and bring to the boil over high heat. Cook the spears at a rapid boil for 4 minutes, or until barely tender. Remove the spears to a plate.

With a sharp vegetable peeler, held flat in your hand, shave off the fibrous skin, starting just under the tip and peeling toward the base.

Add the butter pieces to the pan and boil for a minute or two longer, so that the butter emulsifies in the evaporating liquid. This method of cooking asparagus takes only a couple of minutes at most, so it should be done just before serving time.

Serve the spears moistened with a bit of liquid, and sprinkled with chopped parsley if you wish.

Snap off the tough end of the asparagus with all the peeled skin attached.

Julia on Brussels Sprouts

Choose bright-green Brussels sprouts with firm, compact heads, and no yellowing of the leaves. After washing them, trim the root ends and pierce a cross ¼ inch deep in the end of the roots—to help them cook faster and stay greener.

Brussels sprouts need special treatment to make them tender and tasty. They start out with a blanching or partial cooking before being simmered in butter, or sautéed, or sauced. Following the blanching procedure for green beans on page 188, drop them into a large pot of boiling salted water, cover the pot until steam starts to escape, then uncover and keep at a slow boil.

Partially cooked sprouts (1 quart will serve 4). If they are to have further cooking, boil 6 to 8 minutes; a small knife will pierce them but they have a definite crunch at the center. Fully cooked sprouts need 10 to 12 minutes, and a knife will enter easily; they are tender through but the center still has texture.

If they are not to be finished off shortly after blanching, you can refresh them in ice water, as with the green beans, but they retain their freshest texture when you spread them out in one layer on a double thickness of clean towels. When cool, refrigerate in a covered bowl.

Serving suggestions. The following three ways with Brussels sprouts were favorites of my French colleague Simca, who lived a healthy and vigorous life in Paris and in the south of France almost to the end of her 87 years.

Brussels Sprouts Braised in Butter: For about 1½ quarts of partially cooked sprouts, you will want a 1½-quart covered flameproof casserole. Butter the inside of the casserole and arrange the sprouts in it, heads up, and in one or at the most two layers. Season lightly with salt and pepper, pour on about 2 tablespoons of melted butter, and heat to sizzling on top of the stove. Lay a round of parchment paper on top of the vegetables, cover the casserole, and bake for 20 to 25 minutes in a 350°F oven until the sprouts are tender and buttery.

Creamed Brussels Sprouts: Prepare the vegetables as described above, but use only 2 tablespoons of butter. After they have been in the oven 10 minutes, pour on ½ cup of simmering heavy cream, and continue baking another 10 minutes or so.

Brussels Sprouts Baked with Cheese: Prepare the vegetables as described in the first recipe, and when they have baked 10 minutes turn them into a bowl. Raise oven temperature to 425°F, and have ready 1 cup of grated Swiss and/or Parmesan cheese. Sprinkle ¼ cup of cheese into the casserole to cover the bottom and sides. Return the sprouts to the casserole, sprinkling on cheese as you go. Dribble on about 2 tablespoons of melted butter and place uncovered in the upper third of the oven for 10 to 15 minutes, until the cheese has nicely browned on top.

Julia

I have always followed Escoffier's advice that properly cooked green beans are tender all the way through yet still have texture. This means that you must watch them closely and test them constantly. Often, restaurants seem just to dump them in the water and pull them out right away, so they are nicely green yet still raw.

My old chef Max Bugnard, who worked on the transatlantic steamers as a young man, taught me that the faster you bring the water back to the boil the greener the beans. He used to drop a red-hot stove plaque into the pot as he put in the beans, to bring the water dramatically and instantly back to the boil. I use what I call a buffalo iron—a solid metal poker I heat on a burner until searing and then plunge into the water as I dump in the beans. Of course, the more cooking water you use, the faster it will reach the boil again. Unless he was to serve them at once, Chef Max always refreshed the beans in ice water, to stop the cooking and set the color.

Green Beans

Green beans are very simple to cook—but they must be cooked to just the right point to bring out all their flavor. Raw or undercooked green beans never develop it, and overcooked beans have lost it.

Here are two good and quite different methods, for two varieties of green beans. In Julia's, conventional beans are cooked in a large amount of boiling salted water, removed at exactly the right moment, and then simply seasoned with butter, lemon juice, and salt and pepper.

Jacques's method steams the slender beans known as *haricots verts* in a small amount of water, and then sautées them with shallots. Originally developed in France, *haricots verts* (which just means "green beans") are now grown widely in this country. They are sometimes hard to find, and usually more expensive, but have excellent flavor.

As long as you cook them carefully and thoroughly, you can cook any fresh bean by either method. And, fortunately, most modern bean varieties don't have strings, so you are spared the chore of removing them.

Julia's Blanched and Buttered Green Beans

Yield: About 6 servings

6 to 8 quarts water
3 to 4 Tbs salt (1½ tsp per quart)
1½ pounds very fresh young green beans
1 to 2 Tbs room-temperature butter
Salt and freshly ground pepper, to taste
Freshly squeezed lemon juice, to taste
Lemon wedges or halves, for optional
   garnish

Special equipment

A large 8-to-10-quart kettle or stockpot with cover; a perforated insert or a strainer to remove beans from water; a large bowl of ice water unless serving at once; a frying pan, 12 inches top diameter, for reheating

Bring the water and salt to a boil in the pot over high heat (with the insert in place if you are using one). Meanwhile, wash and drain the beans; snap off the stems and tails, and remove strings, if any, by pulling the stem down the sides.

When the water is boiling vigorously, dump in the beans all at once. Clap on the cover and remove it the instant the water is again at the boil. If you have a buffalo iron or iron poker, it should be burning hot and ready to insert into the water the moment the beans go in.

Cook at a boil for several minutes, then check frequently; they are done when they are cooked through but still have texture; they bend slightly when held horizontally by one end. Take a bite to be sure. As soon as they test done, remove them by lifting out the insert, or scooping the beans out with the strainer.

Unless you are serving now, transfer them to the bowl of ice water to stop the cooking and set the color. When chilled, in 5 minutes or so, scoop them out onto a clean towel.

To serve cold

Dry them in the towel and refrigerate, where they will keep nicely until dinnertime. If stored longer, they may lose their fresh taste.

To serve hot

Melt the butter in the large frying pan, toss in the beans, and continue tossing frequently over moderate heat until the beans are well warmed through. Season to taste with salt, pepper, and drops of lemon juice. Serve on hot plates or in a bowl and garnish, if you wish, with wedges of lemon.

Jacques

More than most vegetables, green beans need adequate cooking. If they are undercooked, they have a distinctly different flavor, which I don't like.

My method breaks many conventional rules. Instead of a big pot of water, I use a little liquid, so it almost all evaporates by the time the beans are cooked through. I don't add any salt to the water, and I cook the beans covered—which of course you are not supposed to do. Still, the beans develop a deep-green color, and full flavor. Finally, they are carefully seasoned during the brief sauté with shallots.

This method is good for small quantities—four to six servings maximum. For larger quantities it is much better to cook the beans in a big pot of boiling water.

Jacques's Sautéed Haricots Verts

Yield: 4 to 6 servings

1 pound *haricots verts* or very thin string
   beans
1¼ cups water
2 tsp olive oil
2 tsp unsalted butter
3 Tbs thinly sliced shallots
¼ tsp salt
¼ tsp freshly ground black pepper

Special equipment
   A medium or large sauté pan (10 inches
      top diameter) with close-fitting cover

Trim the ends of the beans by snapping them between your thumb and forefinger; rinse and drain.

Heat the water in the pan until boiling rapidly, add the beans, and cover. Cook over high heat for 5 to 6 minutes, until the beans are tender but still firm to the bite and the water has nearly evaporated. (Thicker beans might need more steaming; add a bit more water if necessary.)

Immediately transfer the beans to a bowl. Discard any water remaining in the hot pan, add the olive oil and butter, and heat. Add the sliced shallots, sauté for ½ minute, then return the beans to the pan and season with the salt and pepper. Toss the beans and shallots together and sauté for another minute or two, tossing occasionally, until the beans are thoroughly cooked and the shallots are light golden.

Transfer to a warm bowl or platter and serve.

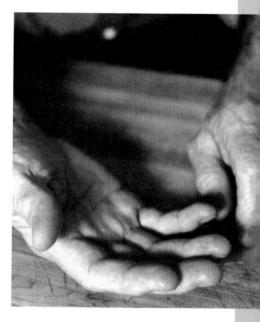

Julia on Broccoli and Cauliflower

Peeling broccoli and cauliflower. Both broccoli and cauliflower cook faster and are more tender when the stems are peeled. To do so, cut the floret clusters from the central stem. The stem will need deep peeling down to the tender core, which you cut into ½-inch bias strips. Larger stems of the floret clusters want peeling also—start at the cut ends, grabbing a piece of the skin with a little knife and your thumb, tearing it loose toward the bud end; continue around rapidly. This takes a little time, but it is just such careful attention to details that distinguishes fine cooking from the humdrum.

Blanching broccoli. Steaming works well, especially for small quantities, but I think blanching produces the freshest-tasting and greenest broccoli. It needs your full attention, however, since it is too easy to overcook. I put my prepared broccoli in an old-fashioned wire salad basket, which goes into and comes out of the pot easily. If I don't have that handy I use a perforated inset basket, or fish out the broccoli with my great Italian scoop, or a Chinese wire-mesh retriever. You will want a big pot but it need not be as large as that used for green beans—4 to 5 quarts of boiling water with 1½ teaspoons salt per quart.

Ahead-of-time note. If the broccoli is to be served simply, with melted butter or a sauce, it cooks so quickly I don't think anything is gained by doing it ahead. I prefer to get everything ready to go, and then cook the broccoli at the last minute. Another problem with broccoli is that, once cooked, it cools off quickly. You can cover it with folded towels, but too long a wait and it begins to lose its bright-green color.

When you are ready to blanch the broccoli, have it prepared and arranged in a salad basket or bowl and have the salted water at a rolling boil. Plunge the basket or the loose broccoli into the boiling water. Clap on the cover, and the moment the steam starts to escape, remove the cover. Start testing the broccoli after 2 minutes. It is done when a small knife pierces a stem quite easily and if you hold up a piece horizontally it bends a little but is not limp. Remove it at once and arrange on hot plates or a platter, season lightly with salt and pepper, spoon melted butter or a sauce over it, and serve right away.

Serving suggestions for broccoli. Use the same suggestions as those for asparagus, page 186, and here are other ideas:

Toasted bread crumbs: For 4 servings, heat 1½ tablespoons of unsalted butter in an 8-inch frying pan. When the butter foam begins to subside, toss in ½ cup of fresh bread crumbs (page 212). Season lightly with salt and pepper and continue tossing until lightly browned. Set aside, and reheat briefly before serving. Sprinkle the crumbs over the hot, seasoned, and lightly buttered broccoli as you bring it to the table.

Chopped broccoli: This makes an attractive green-vegetable accompaniment to almost anything from poached eggs to fish and fowl, and when you need a filling for stuffed or mounded crêpes or a rolled soufflé, chopped broccoli, carefully seasoned, is often just what you want. After blanching the broccoli, chop it into pieces of ¼ to ⅜ inch on a cutting board with your big chef's knife. For 1½ cups, serving 4, heat 1 tablespoon of unsalted butter in a 10-inch frying pan; when the butter is bubbling, turn the chopped broccoli into it. Fold in ⅓ cup or so of heavy cream or Jacques's béchamel sauce (page 193). When well blended, taste and carefully correct seasoning. Serve hot, as a vegetable, or set aside as a filling or stuffing (film top with a spoonful of milk or cream to prevent a skin from forming).

Cooking cauliflower. Since we needn't worry about color, steaming is the easiest way to cook cauliflower, particularly when you have separated it into florets and have peeled the stems as described at the beginning of this section. Arrange the prepared cauliflower in a steaming basket set over 1½ inches of salted water, cover airtight, and bring to the boil. Lower heat to a slow boil, and let steam for several minutes, or until a small knife pierces the stems fairly easily—the fresher the cauliflower the faster it cooks. Eat a little piece to check: the stems should be just cooked through but not soft; they should still have texture.

Cauliflower florets cook so quickly it is hardly worthwhile to cook in advance unless you have special reasons or are doing a baked dish. In that case, you want to stop the cooking as soon as it is done, thus retaining the fresh taste. Have ready a large basin of cold or iced water and when the cauliflower tests done turn it into the cold water. Then drain and set aside in one layer on folded towels. When thoroughly cold, refrigerate in a covered bowl.

Serving suggestions for cauliflower

Melted butter: Season the freshly steamed cauliflower with a sprinkling of salt and pepper; spoon on melted butter and, if you wish, a sprinkling of chopped fresh parsley.

A broccoli finish: When you are doing a filling of cooked chopped broccoli, for instance, save out a branch or two and cut off the bud ends. Season and warm the little buds in butter, and sprinkle over the cooked cauliflower as you serve it—an unusual but logical cousinly garnish.

Jacques's Cauliflower au Gratin

In these fat-conscious times, we home cooks don't drown our everyday vegetables in white sauces—full of butter, milk, cream, or cheese—as we used to. But for an occasional reminder of how good the combination can be, try this exemplary gratin of tender cauliflower florets, coated with well-seasoned béchamel sauce and crusted in the oven with excellent Swiss cheese.

This is an especially practical vegetable dish for a large dinner party, a perfect accompaniment to a lean roast, such as our Leg of Lamb (page 368) or Roast Chicken. It's large enough for six to eight, and rich and hearty enough to take the place of potatoes or other starch. You can prepare the entire gratin hours ahead and finish it in the oven in forty minutes or so. A nice touch is to arrange and bake the sauced florets in individual gratin dishes (set them on a cookie sheet to facilitate handling and catch spills).

You will need a very big fresh cauliflower, three pounds or more untrimmed, if you want to serve the larger number (or have second helpings). Choose a firm, snowy-white head, with tightly compacted florets, and with the central stem and thick leaves still attached to the base (usually a sign of freshness). You can trim these easily and quickly, following this technique, so a brief steaming will evenly cook the entire head.

Yield: A large gratin dish, serving 6 to 8

1 large head of cauliflower (2½ to 3 pounds)
¼ tsp salt
2 cups milk, plus more if needed
½ cup cream
4 Tbs unsalted butter (plus butter for the baking dish)
⅓ cup flour

Salt and freshly ground white pepper
Freshly grated nutmeg, a pinch or two
¾ cup coarsely grated Gruyère or other
    Swiss cheese (about 3 ounces)

Special equipment
A heavy pot or Dutch oven with a tight-fitting lid, just large enough for the whole cauliflower; a 3-quart saucepan for the sauce; an 8-to-10-cup gratin or baking dish, lightly buttered; a cookie sheet

Trimming and cooking the whole cauliflower

If you are planning to complete the gratin right away, preheat the oven to 400°F.

Turn the cauliflower upside down and cut all around the big central stem with a sharp knife, slicing off the tough leafy stems that are attached to it. Then pick off any leaf pieces still clinging to the base and cut out the big stem, exposing the central core, where the florets are joined—but be careful not to cut through the floret stems or separate them.

Put the cauliflower, cored end down, into the large pot with an inch of water (about 1½ cups) and ¼ teaspoon salt. Cover tightly and bring the water to a rapid boil. Cook for 8 minutes or so, just until you can pierce a floret with a sharp knife. Using a spatula or tongs, lift the cauliflower out of the pot right away and place it in the gratin dish to cool briefly.

Turn the cauliflower upside down and slice all around the cooked core, through all the floret stems, so the head falls apart. Arrange the florets in one layer in the dish—turn them round side up—then chop up the cooked core and scatter the pieces in the dish. Pour off the cooking water remaining in the pot and reserve for the sauce.

Making the white sauce, or béchamel

Pour 2 cups milk, and ½ cup each of the warm cooking liquid and cream, into a small saucepan and heat slowly; don't boil.

Jacques

The small amount of cooking liquid left after steaming the cauliflower has a lot of the vegetable flavor. You can use a cup or so of this in place of milk or cream in the béchamel sauce, and you'll have more cauliflower flavor in the whole dish. Remember that this liquid is salted, so you have to adjust the seasoning in your sauce accordingly.

Many people think "au gratin" means "coated with cheese," but it means "crusted": you can also make cauliflower au gratin with a nice crust of fine, fresh bread crumbs. Sauté the crumbs in butter until golden—or just toast them, dry, in the oven—and then sprinkle over the hot cauliflower florets in the gratin dish.

Julia

Vegetables like cauliflower or broccoli are delicious in a béchamel sauce—or a Mornay sauce, if you mix grated cheese right into the sauce—but these dishes have a bad reputation. That's probably because they were made with a floury sauce, or because they were served after sitting too long on a steam table. The key to a good béchamel, without a pasty taste, is to cook the flour and butter together for a couple of minutes before adding the milk or cream. It's also important not to overcook the cauliflower in the gratin—if the steamed florets and sauce are both warm when you put them together, you don't need to bake the dish for a long time. Just set it under the broiler long enough to melt the cheese.

Melt the butter in the large saucepan, and whisk in the flour to make a loose paste. Cook the roux over moderate heat for 2 minutes or so, stirring constantly, until the paste is frothing and foaming; don't let it color more than a light beige.

Remove the roux from the heat. Pour in the hot liquid and whisk vigorously to blend. Return the saucepan to the heat and bring to a gentle boil, stirring constantly. Whisk in ½ teaspoon of salt, ⅛ teaspoon of white pepper, and a large pinch or two of nutmeg; taste and add more seasonings if needed. Simmer for 2 to 3 minutes, stirring all around the bottom and sides of the pan with a wooden spoon. The cooked sauce should be thick yet still pourable. Thin it, if necessary, with splashes of milk or cooking liquid, stirring to blend well, and adjust the seasonings once again.

Finishing the gratin, right away or hours later

Season the cauliflower florets with ⅛ teaspoon each of salt and pepper and scatter ¼ cup of the grated cheese on top. Set the gratin on the cookie sheet, then ladle or pour the sauce over the vegetables, coating the tops of the florets. Sprinkle on the rest of the cheese.

Place the sheet in the middle rack of the oven and bake until the sauce is bubbling and the cheese is nicely browned, about 25 minutes.

Do-ahead notes

The assembled gratin can be made several hours ahead, and stored, well wrapped, in the refrigerator. Preheat the oven to 375°F and allow 30 to 40 minutes for heating the gratin and browning the cheese.

Julia on Spinach

When spinach is carefully prepared for cooking and then carefully cooked, I love it. But when it's a bit long in the tooth and slightly bitter to the tongue, include me out. Very young tender spinach has leaves that are relatively small and lighter in color than mature spinach. It can simply be well washed, quickly drained, and then thrown into the pot to simmer in a little butter. But large-leafed dark-green mature spinach wants the full treatment, which, to me, means that you stem it to get rid of the useless parts, blanch it to eliminate its bitterness, and then get into the butter part. This is work! But, again, these are the touches that make for fine cooking.

Amounts to buy. To serve 2 people, buy 1 bunch or 1 package (10 ounces) of fresh spinach; 1 bunch of fresh spinach makes a good ½ cup of cooked chopped spinach.

To stem spinach. Fold a leaf in half lengthwise with the underside up. Hold it firmly in your left hand, its stem end to the right. With your right hand grab the stem; lift it up and to your left, pulling the stem out of the leaf. When you get the rhythm this will go reasonably fast. Pump the leaves up and down in a basin of cold water to loosen any dirt, then let them sit for a moment so dirt will sink to the bottom. If there's lots of dirt and sand, repeat the process. (If the leaves are a little wilted, let them stay for an hour in the water and they will freshen quite remarkably well.) Lift the spinach leaves out of the basin with your hands, leaving any sand and dirt behind. (May be done a day or two in advance; refrigerate in a plastic bag lined with paper towels.)

Preliminary cooking: blanching. Provide yourself with the equipment suggested for blanching green beans, page 188). Drop the stemmed spinach leaves into a big pot containing 4 to 5 quarts of rapidly boiling salted water (1½ teaspoons salt per quart of water). Cover the pot only until steam begins to escape; then uncover at once. Let boil just a minute or two, until the spinach is wilted and only partially tender. Remove to a large basin of ice water (put the ice in a sieve for easy removal) to stop the cooking and set the color. When spinach is chilled, remove by big handfuls and squeeze out as much water as you can between your two hands. (May be done a day in advance; refrigerate in a plastic bag.)

Serving suggestions. Carefully cooked spinach goes with almost anything, like broiled or poached fish, baked or broiled ham, chicken breasts, steaks and chops, eggs, and so forth.

Plain Buttered Spinach: For 4 servings, you will want 2 bunches or packages of blanched spinach leaves, squeezed only lightly so that you can separate them. Shortly before serving, melt 2 tablespoons of butter in a stainless-steel saucepan—iron or aluminum can give spinach a metallic taste. Fold in the spinach, seasoning to taste with salt and pepper and, if you wish, a small pinch of powdered clove. Let simmer slowly, folding gently for several minutes, until the spinach is tender and buttery. Correct seasoning and, if you wish, fold in droplets of lemon juice. Serve soon, to keep the color green.

Cooked Chopped Spinach: This is the spinach you use for fillings, crêpes, etc.; it's really the same as the preceding recipe for buttered spinach, but after its blanch and squeeze, you set it on your chopping board and chop it fine with your big stainless-steel knife. Always use stainless-steel knives with spinach, as well as stainless-steel pots, so as not to get that metallic taste; also, use a knife rather than a machine so you will not turn it into a purée. Proceed exactly as for the buttered spinach above, but you may want to sauté a medium-size shallot, quite finely minced, with the butter.

Spinach Sautéed in Olive Oil with 20 Cloves of Garlic: A fantasy title, recalling James Beard's famous dish of chicken with 40 cloves of garlic. Here the garlic is so slowly simmered with the spinach that you may hardly know it's there, and it's not really 20—just a head of garlic, with the cloves quartered lengthwise. You can certainly put in Beard's 40 if you wish, but then you might want more spinach! Serve with steaks, chops, hamburgers.

For 4 servings, you will need a head of large peeled garlic cloves, page 212, halved or quartered lengthwise. Simmer them slowly with 2 tablespoons of olive oil in a small saucepan for 4 to 6 minutes, or until almost tender—they are not to brown at all. Then turn them into a stainless-steel 10-inch frying pan and mix gently with the blanched chopped spinach (page 195). Season to taste with salt and pepper, adding a tablespoon or so more of oil if you think it needed. Simmer, folding gently, for several minutes until the spinach is tender.

Creamed Spinach: This goes beautifully with sautéed brains, sweetbreads, chicken breasts, fish fillets, veal chops, and the like. For 4 servings, briefly sauté the previously described cooked chopped spinach slowly in a 10-inch stainless-steel frying pan with a tablespoon of butter, to evaporate its moisture. Stir in 1 tablespoon of flour and continue the slow sauté for about 2 minutes to cook the flour. Remove from heat and blend in ¼ cup of heavy cream. Bring to the simmer again for 2 minutes or so, blending in driblets more cream if spinach seems too thick. Season carefully with salt and pepper, and blend in a tablespoon or so of butter if you think it is needed.

Variation: Use beef or chicken broth rather than cream—if you are serving the spinach with a rich or creamy dish.

Julia on Small Onions

Small Glazed Onions: Small onions, 1 to 1¼ inches in diameter, are often called for as a garnish with chicken sautés, beef stews, and the like. Cook them almost the same way as you would the carrots and turnips on page 198, but first peel them as follows. Drop them whole into a saucepan of rapidly boiling water, and let cook for exactly 1 minute. Slip off the skins, and shave the roots to even them. Then, to help prevent the onions from bursting, pierce a cross ¼ inch deep in the root ends.

Cook them as directed for Jacques's glazed vegetables but treat them gently—no rough turning or shaking and no boiling—only a slow, covered simmering so they will keep their shape. They are done when a small knife will pierce them through easily. If you want them to stay white, keep a little liquid in the pan and maintain a low heat; to brown, roll them gently in the pan over higher heat.

Creamed Onions: Simmer onions as above but only until almost tender, then pour in either heavy cream or béchamel sauce (page 193) to come halfway up. Boil slowly, uncovered, until the liquid has thickened enough to coat the onions. Carefully correct seasoning. May be cooked several hours in advance, but if so, and you are using béchamel, film the top of the sauce with stock or milk to prevent a skin from forming.

Julia on Shredding Cabbage in the Food Processor

Shredding cabbage by hand is remarkably quick when done by Jacques but slow and uneven when attempted by me. Carl Sontheimer, the engineer who introduced the Cuisinart to America some years ago, invented this system, which goes even faster than Jacques does. Slice off the top and the bottom of the cabbage, leaving yourself with a thick cylinder. Core out the central stem with a stout, sharp knife, and cut the cylinder into wedges of a size to fit into your machine. Shred wedge by wedge.

Braised Red Cabbage

Cooking thin shreds of cabbage in a small amount of liquid is a simple and traditional way to prepare this earthy vegetable. Braised red cabbage makes an especially colorful side dish, with wonderful flavor and a pleasing crunchy texture. It is a good foil for pork—try it with our Roast Pork Loin (page 356) or Pork Chops (page 360)—or with our homemade sausages, or roast turkey, or duck.

Here, chicken stock is the braising liquid, and currants, onions, sugar, and cider vinegar contribute a pleasing contrast of sweet and sour flavors. But you can vary this dish easily to suit your taste or the ingredients you have: use regular or Savoy cabbage; add minced garlic, apple slices, or caraway seeds; or use part red wine or apple cider in the braising liquid.

Yield: 4 to 5 cups, serving 6 to 8

1 head of red cabbage, 2 to 2¼
   pounds
2 cups or so thinly sliced onion
   (from a large, 8-ounce onion)
½ cup currants
3 Tbs cider vinegar
2 Tbs sugar
1 tsp salt
¼ tsp freshly ground black pepper
1 Tbs vegetable oil
½ cup chicken stock, plus more if
   necessary

Special equipment
   A large non-stick or stainless-steel sauté pan (12 inches top diameter) with a tight-fitting cover

Cut out the core of the cabbage and discard any tough or discolored outside leaves. Slice the cabbage in half or quarters, then slice lengthwise into ⅛-inch shreds. You should have about 12 cups.

Toss the cabbage and the onion slices in the pan and add the rest of the ingredients. Bring the stock to a boil over high heat and cover. Reduce the heat to medium, and braise for about 45 minutes, stirring occasionally, until there is only a small amount of liquid left and the cabbage is moist and just slightly crunchy. (If the pan starts to dry before the cabbage is done, add a little more chicken stock and continue cooking.)

Adjust the seasonings and serve.

Jacques's Glazed Carrots and Turnips

Carrots and turnips are natural companions—tended together in the garden, stored in the root cellar, and tossed into the same hearty soups, stews, braises, and boiled dinners. Here, the two humble vegetables are featured in an elegant dish which displays their colors and complementary flavors—the mild bitter tang of the turnips and the sweetness of the carrots.

In the classic paring technique known as *tourner,* chunks of the vegetables are literally "turned" into uniform, shapely ovals. They are cooked together (following Jacques's customary method), first boiled until tender, then sautéed to glaze on all their neatly cut sides. The caramelization accents the natural flavors, and tinges the white and orange nuggets with brown and gold. This is a vegetable dish for a dinner party—full of flavor on its own, and a beautiful garnish for roast meat, poultry, or game.

The "turning" techniques (illustrated in the accompanying photos) can be used to make many other vegetable garnishes, such as the cucumbers served with poached fish (page 243). Zucchini can be shaped in the same manner. Small round potatoes can be cut into wedges and turned just like the turnips, then cooked by the same method (boiling and sautéing) to make a handsome accompaniment to Chateaubriand (page 322) or other grilled meats.

Yield: 4 servings

4 or 5 carrots, 7 to 8 inches long and 1 inch thick (about 1 pound)

3 fresh purple-top turnips, 3 inches or so in diameter (about 1¼ pounds)

1 or 2 tsp sugar

1 Tbs unsalted butter

Salt

Chopped fresh chives, for garnish

Special equipment

A frying pan or sauté pan large enough to hold all the vegetable pieces in one layer, with a tight-fitting lid

Turning the vegetables

Peel the carrots, remove the ends, and cut crosswise into 2-inch lengths. Following the photos, trim the pieces into uniform barrel shapes.

Trim off the tough tops of the turnips, cut them in

half through the top to the root end, then slice each half into 3 or 4 equal wedges. Following the photos, "turn" the wedges into uniform oblongs, with rounded edges, about the same size as the carrots.

Peel and trim the ends of the carrots, then cut them into equal (approximately 2-inch) lengths. Cut thick pieces lengthwise in half, thirds, or quarters, so the pieces are all about the same width.

With a sharp paring knife, trim the long side of each piece in a curving motion, tapering both ends. Turn the piece slightly after each cut and repeat all around, forming uniform barrel-like or football shapes.

Cooking and glazing the vegetables

Cut off the tops and with a sharp knife trim off the peel. Cut the turnips in half from the top through the root end. Slice each half into 3 or 4 equal wedges.

Put the carrots in the pan in one layer and pour in enough water to come about halfway up the sides of the carrots. Add a teaspoon or more of sugar (depending on your taste), the tablespoon of butter, and ¼ teaspoon of salt. Bring the water to a boil, cover the pan, and cook the carrots over medium-high heat for 3 to 4 minutes. Toss the turnip pieces into the pan (the carrots and turnips should still be in one layer) and cook, covered, at a steady boil for another 5 to 6 minutes, shaking the pan occasionally, until both the carrots and turnips can be pierced with the tip of a knife.

Uncover and continue to cook at a rapid boil to evaporate the cooking liquid. When the liquid is gone, shake the pan frequently, rolling the pieces around, as they begin to glaze and color in the butter and sugar. Lower the heat, and continue to roll and glaze the vegetables until nicely tinged with brown on all sides and tender all the way through.

Turn the vegetables into a serving dish, sprinkle on the chopped chives, and serve.

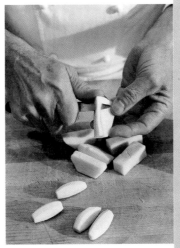

With a sharp paring knife, shave off strips to round all the sharp points and edges, so the pieces can roll in the pan.

Jacques

The purpose of "turning" vegetables is more than just aesthetic. This technique produces pieces of a uniform size which can cook evenly, and allows them to be tossed and rolled easily in the sauté pan, so that they will glaze and color on all sides.

Because you want to end up with pieces of equal size, it is easiest to start with carrots and turnips of consistent dimensions. Try to find carrots of uniform thickness, and firm, fresh turnips about 3 inches in diameter. The small turnips with white-sided purple tops usually have a mild flavor; the larger, all-white turnips can be bitter. Older turnips are sometimes spongy inside, too, and you must discard those parts. Do not discard the good trimmings from the turned pieces, though. You can use these in soups or cook them up and mash them—I love to mix puréed turnips with mashed potatoes.

Julia

This dish is a simple version of ratatouille, in which the different vegetables (including onions and peppers) are sautéed separately in olive oil before they are cooked together. Here, only the eggplant slices need to be cooked separately, so the eggplant can finish baking in the same time as the other vegetables, and will also lose some of its bitter moisture. (Baking the slices to soften them is a far better method than sautéing, since it uses much less oil.)

However, I suggest that you also let the zucchini slices stand for about 15 minutes, after you have salted them well, before layering them in the gratin. This rids them of some of their juices, which could make the dish soupy, and will help them cook faster too. As with most dishes, you can vary this gratin to your taste: add a bit of minced garlic to the bread crumbs if you like, or layer sautéed onion and/or bell-pepper slices in with the other vegetables.

Gratin of Eggplant, Tomato, and Zucchini

Around the Mediterranean basin, you can find many dishes that combine eggplant, tomatoes, zucchini, and other summer vegetables, from the classic ratatouille of Provence and the tangy caponata of Sicily, to the vegetable salads and stews of Middle Eastern and North African cooking. The forms and cooking methods vary widely—sometimes the vegetables are cooked all together, sometimes they are sautéed separately, or grilled, and then mixed together.

Here we combine the three vegetables in a gratin, in the style of southern France. Thin slices of eggplant, tomato, and zucchini are seasoned and arranged in a colorful pattern of alternating rows, filling a large, shallow gratin dish. In the oven, the vegetable flavors mingle with those of olive oil and *herbes de Provence,* and a topping of bread crumbs and Parmesan cheese forms a golden crust.

Serve this as a vegetarian main course, or as an accompaniment to leg of lamb or other roasts or grilled meats. It will have the finest flavor, certainly, at the end of summer, when ripe locally grown eggplant, tomatoes, and zucchini are abundant and absolutely fresh. But this can be a midwinter casserole too, as all three vegetables are generally available year-round in markets. Fine and generous seasoning can compensate for a lack of perfection in the vegetables. Select eggplants and zucchini with firm flesh and unblemished, shiny skin, and the ripest tomatoes available. If you have a choice, buy narrow rather than fat eggplants, as it will be easier to arrange the slices in even rows.

Eggplant and Zucchini Gratin

Yield: A large gratin dish, serving 6 to 8

½ cup or so olive oil, excellent-quality
1 large or 2 medium eggplants, about 1¼
    pounds
1 Tbs *herbes de Provence*
1 tsp salt
2 medium zucchini, about 1 pound total
3 or 4 ripe tomatoes, about 1 pound total
½ tsp freshly ground pepper

For the bread-crumb topping
½ cup or so fresh bread crumbs, not too
    finely ground (see page 212)
⅓ cup or so freshly grated Parmesan
    cheese

Special equipment
A large shallow-rimmed jelly-roll pan or
    cookie sheet; a gratin or shallow baking
    dish, 8-cup volume

Preparing the vegetables

Arrange the rack on the lower-middle level of the oven and preheat to 400°F. Smear the baking sheet generously with ⅓ cup of the olive oil.

Trim off the ends of the eggplant and slice it on the diagonal into ovals ½ inch thick. One at a time, lay the slices on the sheet, press to coat lightly with oil and turn them over. Arrange the slices, oiled side up, in a single layer and sprinkle on ½ teaspoon each of salt and *herbes de Provence.*

Bake for about 15 minutes, until the eggplant slices are soft and somewhat shriveled; allow to cool briefly. Leave the oven on if you will be baking the gratin right away.

Meanwhile, trim the ends off the zucchini and cut lengthwise into slices no more than ¼ inch thick. Core the tomatoes and cut into slices ¼ inch thick. Spread out the slices and sprinkle them lightly with ½ teaspoon of salt and ¼ teaspoon of freshly ground pepper.

Jacques

We use the term "gratin" to refer both to a kind of preparation—like this Provençal-style casserole of vegetables—and to the shallow, oval baking pan in which they are usually cooked. In French, *gratin* literally means "crust." (Just as we call the higher echelons of society "the upper crust" in English, in France they are called *le gratin.*)

A top crust is characteristic of most gratins, consisting of a bread-crumb crust in this recipe, the crispy glaze of cheese in our cauliflower au gratin, or the thick topping of bread and cheese that covers a crock of onion soup gratinée. But sometimes we make a gratin that just gets slightly brown on top when baked in a shallow dish, as in our gratin *dauphinois* and *pommes boulangère.*

With a gratin like this one, you have a balance between properly cooking the vegetables and nicely crusting the top. If you find that the topping is getting dark but the vegetables are not finished, cover the gratin loosely with a sheet of foil. On the other hand, if the crumb topping isn't as brown as you like when the vegetables are done and ready to come out of the oven, simply put the gratin under the broiler for a few moments to give it more color.

Assembling the gratin

Film the gratin or baking dish well with 1 teaspoon olive oil and sprinkle a teaspoon of the dried herbs all over the bottom.

Lay one or two eggplant slices, lengthwise, against a narrow side of the dish. Arrange a long slice or two of zucchini in front of the eggplant, then place 2 or 3 tomato slices in front of the zucchini. Repeat the procedure to fill the pan with alternating rows of eggplant, zucchini, and tomatoes. Arrange each new row of slices so the colorful top edges of the previous row are still visible.

Topping and baking the gratin

Mix together the bread crumbs, Parmesan cheese, and a teaspoon of the *herbes de Provence.* Add a tablespoon of olive oil, then toss and rub it in with your fingers to coat the crumbs but keep them loose. Sprinkle the crumbs evenly over the vegetables and drizzle the rest of the oil over all.

Place the dish in the center of the oven and bake for 40 minutes, until the vegetables are soft, the juices are bubbling, and the top is a deep golden brown. (If the crumbs need more browning, you can stick them under the broiler for a few moments.)

Serve hot, directly from the baking dish.

Do-ahead notes

After the vegetables are assembled and topped with crumbs, the gratin can be covered lightly and stored in the refrigerator for several hours. Preheat the oven and drizzle on the last olive oil just before baking.

Opposite: Eggplant and Zucchini Gratin

Julia

Wild mushrooms have their distinctive flavors, and when I have a special kind, like chanterelles or porcini (also known as cèpes), I prefer to cook them separately, rather than mixed with other varieties. All they need is a brief sautéing in a bit of butter and careful seasoning.

With more ordinary mushrooms, the cream finish that we give in this recipe brings special flavor and texture to the mushrooms. You can omit the cream and just finish them with dry Madeira or port (which you should always have on hand). When the juices have evaporated and the mushrooms are beginning to turn brown, add 2 or 3 tablespoons of wine to the pan, and cook for another minute or so, until it's reduced to a syrupy consistency. Adjust the seasonings, sprinkle in some chopped parsley, and serve with a sizzling steak.

Sautéed Mushrooms

As a glance at the produce display in almost any market will tell you, wild mushrooms are not so wild and rare anymore. Alongside common white mushrooms of various sizes, you may see bins, baskets, and even plastic cartons of once wild and exotic varieties that are now being cultivated or commercially foraged—among them chanterelles, morels, hedgehog, oyster, porcini, straw, and shiitake mushrooms. Most supermarkets won't have all of these, of course, but you are likely to find a few, and certainly cremini and portobello mushrooms. These may seem unusual, but are in fact the once-common "brown" mushroom (the same species as cultivated whites), now being sold at different stages of maturity and with clever new marketing names.

For all the newly available mushroom varieties—and the still quite tasty old ones as well—a simple sauté is a good and reliable cooking method. Here we present a standard procedure that can be used with a single variety of mushrooms or any mixture of fungi of different shapes, colors, and flavors. Whether you sauté the mushrooms covered or uncovered, rapidly over high heat or quite slowly, the fundamental process is the same—you must allow the mushrooms to release all their liquid, and cook them further to evaporate the liquid and concentrate the flavor.

In this sauté, we add a rich finish of cream and Madeira to the mushrooms, creating a slightly thick sauce. Serve on toast, or as a garnish for our Steak au Poivre (page 310) or other grilled or sautéed meats.

Sautéed Mushrooms in Cream

Yield: About 2 cups, serving 4

12 ounces mixed wild and/or cultivated
   mushrooms (6 to 8 cups)
3 Tbs unsalted butter
3 Tbs minced shallots or scallions
Salt
1 tsp flour
½ cup or more heavy cream
2 to 3 Tbs dry port or Madeira
Freshly ground white pepper

Special equipment
A non-stick skillet or sauté pan, 10
   inches top diameter or larger, with a
   cover

Break up or cut the wild mushrooms into 1-inch pieces, and halve or quarter the common mushrooms to roughly the same size.

Set the pan over high heat with 2 tablespoons of the butter, swirling to film the bottom and sides. When the butter foams and begins to subside, add the mushroom pieces and the minced shallots. Toss and stir for a minute or two to coat with butter, then cover the pan, lower the heat, and cook for 3 or 4 minutes as the mushrooms exude their juices. Uncover, season with ⅛ teaspoon of salt, and sauté over medium-high heat until the juices are absorbed and the mushrooms start to brown, about 3 to 4 minutes.

Add the remaining tablespoon of butter and toss with the mushrooms. Sprinkle the flour over all, stirring well and shaking the pan for a few moments to incorporate the flour.

Pour in ½ cup of cream, stirring as it heats and thickens; then stir in the port. Bring to a boil and cook for another 2 minutes or so. Taste the sauce and season with salt and white pepper; if too thick, add more cream. Serve hot.

Jacques

Finding wild mushrooms has always been a part of my life. As a child in France, I used to go out to the fallow fields where cows had grazed and pick meadow mushrooms, which my mother prepared with the same cream sauce as in this recipe. Today, I can pick these meadow mushrooms (*Agaricus campestris*) on my lawn in Connecticut. I also forage for wild mushrooms in the woods near my home—each year I gather over 100 pounds of 30 or more varieties. It is great fun, and genuine wild mushrooms have the finest flavor, but you have to know what you are doing. Before you even pick up a strange mushroom, contact your local mycological society or the extension service of the university and learn from an expert.

It's a mistake to think that mushrooms have to cook only a short time. I always cook wild mushrooms for at least 20 minutes—sometimes I roast them in the oven for an hour or even more, as the long cooking improves the texture and concentrates the flavor. I also like to sauté domestic white mushrooms slowly, keeping them covered the whole time, as the liquid evaporates and the mushrooms turn brown very gradually. In fact, the common white mushroom is really one of the best to cook—I especially like to use the older ones, with open caps and gills that have started to turn brown. These have excellent taste and are often a really good deal at the market, too.

Julia

The important part of my technique, learned from my old chef Max Bugnard, is to work a small amount of salt and sugar—and as much butter as you like—into the skins of the peas. I like to use my bare hands for this "bruising": you do want to crush the peas a bit so as to coat them really well.

Then it is important to check the peas while cooking, to see how they are coming along and how the seasoning is when you taste them. You will be amazed at what a really fine flavor they have. They taste like fresh green peas!

Green Peas

If you are fortunate enough to harvest small green peas right from your own garden, you need barely heat them through to make them tender and bring out their natural sweetness. Store-bought peas, however, may be large and green but hard and lacking in flavor. For these, you will want to use Julia's method: literally bruising the peas by rubbing them with the seasonings and then boil-steaming them. It works remarkably well, turning a punky pea into a pleasantly edible object.

In Jacques's recipe, peas, pearl onions, and bits of ham combine in a hearty country-style dish. The vegetables and meat cook rapidly in a small amount of water until it evaporates, and then take on a flavorful glaze from the butter and sugar in the pan. It is delicious with young and tender peas, whether fresh or frozen.

Julia's Green Peas

Yield: 6 servings

3 cups shelled green peas (about 3
    pounds in the pod)
2 Tbs room-temperature butter, plus
    more if needed
½ tsp sugar, plus more if needed
½ tsp salt, plus more if needed

Put all the ingredients in a 3-quart saucepan and mix briefly. Begin to "bruise" them with your bare hands by rubbing them vigorously between your palms and fingers, working the butter and seasonings against the peas until all have been well coated.

Add just enough cold water to reach the top of the peas. Cover tightly, bring to the boil, and boil slowly. Check for doneness after 6 minutes, and check frequently to be sure the water has not boiled off before the peas are tender. Taste, adding pinches more sugar if needed, but be very careful that the peas don't taste even slightly sugary.

Add a little more water if needed, and if the peas are tender before the water has boiled off, uncover, and boil until it has evaporated and the peas are simmering in their butter. (If you have more than a teaspoon of water remaining, drain it off into another saucepan and boil it down, then pour it over the peas.) Taste carefully for seasoning. Set aside uncovered, and toss over moderate heat to warm through before serving.

Jacques's Country-Style Green Peas

Yield: 6 servings

1½ cups peeled pearl onions (about 24
    tiny or 12 small onions) (see page 196)
4 ounces fully cooked ham steak, 1 inch
    thick, trimmed of all fat
2½ cups shelled green peas (2 to 2½
    pounds in the pod)
1 Tbs canola or corn oil
1 Tbs unsalted butter
½ tsp sugar, plus more if needed
½ tsp salt, plus more if needed
¼ tsp freshly ground black pepper,
    plus more if needed

If you have tiny onions (½-inch diameter or less), leave them whole; cut larger onions in half or quarters. Cut the ham into ½-inch pieces.

Put the peas, onions, ham, oil, butter, sugar, salt, and pepper in a medium saucepan. Pour in ½ cup cold water, then cover the pan, bring to a boil, and cook rapidly over medium-high heat.

For smaller peas, taste for doneness after 6 minutes or so. When the peas are tender, remove cover and cook rapidly to evaporate the remaining liquid. (Larger peas may need to cook covered for 8 to 10 minutes, even longer for very old, starchy peas. Add spoonfuls more water if needed.)

When the liquid is gone and the vegetables begin to take on a shine, stir to glaze them evenly and remove from the heat. Taste and adjust the seasonings. Pour the peas into a warm bowl and serve.

Jacques

Green peas are delicious in combination with other foods. One of my favorite summer dishes is peas and fresh lettuce leaves from my garden, cooked together with pearl onions—a classic French combination. The recipe here is the kind of thing my mother cooked when I was a kid. In addition to onions and peas, and some kind of leftover meat—like the ham here—she might put in carrots and potatoes. This would be our main dish for supper.

When fresh peas are not available, I often cook with frozen small peas. Of all frozen vegetables, they are my favorite. Commercially grown peas are separated by immersion in salted water: the ones high in starch sink to the bottom; those high in sugar float to the top, and are sold as tender or tiny peas. Those are the ones you want in this recipe. Be sure to get plain peas—nothing that has been sauced or seasoned. When using frozen tiny peas in this recipe, place the onion, ham, oil, butter, salt, and pepper in a medium saucepan with ½ cup water. Bring to a boil, cover, and cook rapidly for 5 minutes. Add the frozen peas (I usually rinse them, still frozen, in a sieve under tap water, just to break them up), bring to a boil, and cook for 2 to 3 minutes, then serve.

Julia

These are useful recipes. A quick sauté is the only cooking I ever give snow peas. I find that boiling or steaming makes them mushy and they're never right after that. Make sure, however, that you trim the strings off the snow peas before cooking. The brief cooking of small tomatoes can improve their taste at those times of the year when they are not perfectly juicy and sweet—though they always seem to have more taste off season than larger tomatoes. If you can find both colors, sautéing red and yellow tomatoes together makes a colorful dish.

Sautéing—and the Jerk-Toss

Tossing rather than stirring food when sautéing in a frying pan is a useful technique everyone should master. It is not only fast and efficient, it makes cooking more lively, and the cook looks more professional. I use a "jerk-toss" constantly for omelets as well as vegetables, chicken livers, and other smallish bits. Hold the frying pan with both hands, thumbs up; extend your arms, then jerk the pan hard toward you. This forces the food to hit the far side of the pan and turn over. Try it several times: JERK. JERK. JERK. Don't tilt the pan at all—it's a straight, hard jerk toward you, difficult at first because you want to flip the pan. Jacques's dried-bean practice is good for this technique. Then try it with some mushrooms, and your next omelet.

Two Simply Sautéed Vegetables— Snow Peas and Small Tomatoes

Small whole vegetables, such as snow peas or cherry and pear tomatoes, can be sautéed to make a side dish in just a few minutes, without previous blanching or steaming. Chopped shallots, scallions, or onions, or sliced or minced garlic, will add flavor to either sauté (add garlic only for the final minute or two, so it doesn't burn). The brief cooking gives a nice color and sheen to the vegetables too, and together these make an attractive garnish for a platter of whole roasted fish (see page 232) or Chateaubriand (see page 322).

For quick sautés like these, you want to use a large, 12-inch frying pan with curved sides, constructed with copper or aluminum for good heat distribution and a durable stainless-steel or non-stick interior. A frying pan with curved sides makes it easy to toss the vegetables, so they cook rapidly and evenly.

Sautéed Snow Peas

Yield: 4 servings

> 1 Tbs butter or olive oil (or a combination)
> 3 Tbs finely chopped onions, shallots, or
>   scallions
> ½ pound snow peas, strings removed
> Salt and freshly ground black pepper

Heat the butter and/or oil in a frying pan, 12 inches top diameter, until the butter foam is subsiding. Add the onions or shallots and cook for about ½ minute to soften, then add the peas and toss several minutes, until bright green. Sprinkle with a big pinch of salt and several grinds of pepper and sauté for a few seconds more, tossing and tasting, until the peas are cooked through but still slightly crunchy to the bite.

Serve immediately.

Sautéed Small Tomatoes

Yield: About 2 cups, 4 servings

1 Tbs butter or olive oil (or a
   combination)
About 2 cups cherry or small pear
   tomatoes (red and yellow tomatoes
   if available)
2 large cloves garlic, thinly sliced
   crosswise
Salt and freshly ground black pepper

Heat the butter and/or oil in a frying pan, 10 inches top diameter, over medium-high heat. When the butter foam is subsiding, turn in the tomatoes, toss and roll them in the butter, and sauté for about a minute. Then add the garlic slices, season with a big pinch of salt and several grinds of pepper, and cook for 2 to 3 minutes, tossing occasionally, until the tomatoes are warmed through and soft but still holding their shape. Serve at once.

Jacques

I cook snow peas differently

from Julia, preferring to give them a couple of minutes of cooking before sautéing. You can blanch them ahead of time in a pot of water, then sauté them for just a minute or two. Or, as I do with green beans, carrots, turnips, and other vegetables in this chapter, you can set them over high heat in a covered frying pan with a very small amount of water, which will blanch the snow peas and evaporate. Uncover the pan after a couple of minutes, when practically no water is left, then add the oil, butter, and seasonings. Sauté a few seconds, and serve.

Sautéing

Tossing small pieces of food while sautéing is a skill that cooks must use all the time. If you are not confident about your ability, practice the motion by using dried beans in a cold pan. For a frying pan with curving sides, move the pan in a circular or an elliptical motion, so the food is thrown against the far edge and comes back on itself. If you are using a pan with straight sides, called a *sautoir*, the food will just bounce back when it hits the far side, so you have to use a different motion, tossing the pan upward so the food flips over and keeps turning.

Julia

In summer, I like tomatoes just as they are, with only a bit of salt and pepper, and little droplets of olive oil and vinegar. Or a plain tomato sandwich—a little mayonnaise on fresh white bread, with sliced tomatoes on top—what could be nicer?

But with unripe tomatoes a bit of help is in order. Merely heating them, with salt and pepper and a little oil, will certainly improve them. If you want to use them raw, often a tiny sprinkling of sugar helps develop a nice flavor—just give it 10 minutes or so to bring out the juices.

I don't agree with people who huffily declare that you should never use sugar this way on a fresh vegetable. To me it's a fine flavor-enhancer—in the same way a tiny amount of sugar will bring out a lot of flavor in cucumbers. But use a light hand: if people notice the sugar, you have put in too much. Another booster is a few drops of balsamic vinegar—but, again, no one must be aware of it.

When you are stuffing tomatoes in this recipe, some of the bread crumbs will inevitably fall into the baking dish and darken in the oven. Some people like these brown bits—Jacques, for one—but if you wish to avoid this, stuff your tomatoes on a small wire rack before you put them in the dish. Or bake the tomatoes on a rack set in the dish, and then lift them out and serve without any crumbs clinging to them.

Provençal Tomatoes

It is easy to love tomatoes in summer. A real tomato—freshly picked, perfectly ripe, preferably from one's own garden—is one of those great foods best enjoyed with an absolute minimum of preparation.

But what can we do in wintertime? Supermarkets now stock very nice-looking tomatoes almost all year long. And although they will never have the sweet juiciness of home-grown tomatoes, many have decent flavor that can be enhanced with good cooking.

Here we present two recipes for tomatoes in Provençal style, both of which will taste good even in the depths of winter (and wonderful in summer, of course). In Julia's, they are emptied of seeds and juice, then filled and baked with a stuffing of bread crumbs, Parmesan cheese, and *herbes de Provence*. In Jacques's, tomato halves are sautéed, then softened in the oven and topped with *persillade*.

Provençal tomatoes are a traditional accompaniment to a leg of lamb and grilled meats, and either of these preparations would be a fine garnish for the omelets and other egg dishes in the "Eggs" chapter.

Julia's Stuffed Tomatoes Provençal

Yield: 6 tomato halves

3 large firm ripe tomatoes
Salt and freshly ground pepper

For the stuffing

1 to 1½ cups fresh bread crumbs (see page 212)
2 Tbs minced shallots
1 tsp dried *herbes de Provence*
3 Tbs freshly grated Parmesan cheese
2 to 3 Tbs chopped parsley
3 to 4 Tbs olive oil

Special equipment

A shallow baking dish, lightly brushed
with olive oil

Preparing the tomatoes

Set a rack on the upper-middle level and preheat the oven
to 400°F.

Core the tomatoes and cut them in half crosswise. Over a
plate or bowl, squeeze each half gently to force out the seeds
and juice (reserve for stock). With your fingers, clean the cavities of any clinging seeds. Arrange in the baking dish cut side
up. If any halves are wobbly or tilted, trim a bit off the bottom
so that they sit flat in the pan. Season with a sprinkling of salt
and freshly ground pepper to taste.

Stuffing and baking the tomatoes

Stir together the bread crumbs, shallots, dried herbs, grated
cheese, and chopped parsley in a small bowl. Add 2 or 3 tablespoons of the olive oil, tossing well to moisten the crumbs evenly.

Spoon the stuffing into the tomato halves, pushing it
down into the cavities and mounding on top. Drizzle a scant
teaspoon of oil over the top of each half.

Bake for approximately 20 minutes, or until the topping has
browned and the tomatoes are hot but still keep their shape. Serve
hot in the baking dish, or move them carefully to a clean platter.

Do-ahead notes

The tomato halves can be stuffed several hours in advance
and refrigerated before baking.

Jacques's Tomatoes Provençal

Yield: 6 tomato halves

3 large firm ripe tomatoes
1 Tbs or so olive oil
¼ tsp salt
¼ tsp freshly ground black pepper

Jacques

As you sear the tomato halves

in a hot pan, in my recipe, you caramelize the cut surfaces and juices of the
vegetable, just like browning a steak or a
roast. With meat, you want this crystallization to crust the pan, so you can
deglaze it for a sauce. But here, with a
non-stick pan, these browned parts stick
to the tomato and give them a delicious
sharp-sweet taste and a beautiful look.
And don't shove a spatula under the
tomatoes to lift from the frying pan since
it ruins the browned edges—pick them
up instead with tongs, or a knife stuck
into their round side.

When the tomatoes come out of
the oven, I finish them with a *persillade*,
the mixture of garlic and parsley which is
so typical of French home cooking. In
the photos on page 214, I show how I
peel, crush, and chop garlic. With these
techniques, you can prepare your garlic
for the *persillade* in just a few moments.
Some people discard the "germ" of the
garlic, the small sprout in the center of
the clove. In fact, I think it is the most
tender part and always use it. In China, I
discovered, they grow the germs and
sell them in the market to be cooked like
scallions.

Julia on Bread Crumbs

I always use freshly made bread crumbs—never the packaged dry kind, which can be stale and have an off taste. Start with homemade-style white bread, crusts removed, either genuinely home-baked or a commercial variety like Pepperidge Farm that has some texture and chew. If the bread is a day or two old, so much the better, since it is easier to make crumbs from bread that is slightly dry. The simplest method is to tear the bread into small chunks, then pulse them, about 2 cups at a time, in a food processor until the crumbs have the texture you want. You can also use an electric blender, but work in smaller batches.

Julia's Way of Peeling Garlic

When you have a whole head of garlic to peel, buy one with large cloves. Slice off the top just where the ends of the cloves begin, and set the head upright. Place the flat of your big knife or cleaver on top and smash down on the knife with your fist to break open the head. Drop the cloves into a 2-quart pan of boiling water and boil exactly 10 seconds. This loosens the skin, and you can peel with ease.

Jacques's Tomatoes Provençal (continued)

For the *persillade*
> 4 cloves garlic, peeled
> Handful of flat-leaf parsley (about ½ cup packed), large stems removed
> 1 Tbs olive oil
> 1 Tbs butter

Special equipment
> A large non-stick frying pan or sauté pan; a shallow baking dish large enough to hold all tomato halves

Cooking the tomatoes

Preheat the oven to 400°F. Remove the cores from the tomatoes and cut the tomatoes in half crosswise.

Set the pan over medium-high heat, add the olive oil, and swirl to coat the bottom. When hot, lay in the tomatoes cut side down. Sauté for 3 to 5 minutes without moving the halves, until they are well seared, brown (but not burnt) on the cut sides and edges. To check the tomatoes, and to remove them from the frying pan, lift them with tongs or a paring knife stuck in the side.

Arrange the halves in the baking dish seared side up and season with the salt and pepper. Set the dish in the oven and bake 10 minutes or more, until the tomatoes are soft and hot but still holding their shape.

Preparing the *persillade*

While the tomatoes are baking, smash the garlic cloves and chop roughly with a large knife (see sidebar). Pile the parsley on top of the garlic and chop together until finely minced. You should have ⅓ to ½ cup of *persillade*.

When the tomatoes come out of the oven, heat the oil and butter in a medium sauté pan. Add the *persillade* and sauté over medium heat for half a minute, shaking the pan and stirring, until hot and fragrant.

Top each tomato half with a tablespoon or more of the *persillade* and serve.

Opposite: Stuffed Artichoke Bottoms, Stuffed Tomatoes, and Provençal Tomatoes

Jacques's Techniques for Peeling and Chopping Garlic

To peel individual cloves, first cut off the stem end, then loosen the skin by hitting the clove sharply with the side of a chef's knife. The skin should pop free and peel away easily.

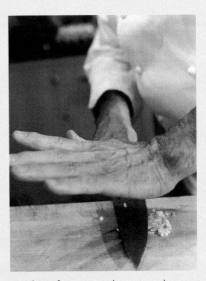

To break apart the cloves of a whole garlic bulb quickly, place the bulb on its base and forcefully rap the pointy top with the heel of your hand (or a flat, hard object such as a pan).

To chop, first cut any large round cloves in half so they lie flat. Smash each clove forcefully with the side of the knife; then drag the flat of the blade against the work surface, really crushing the garlic beneath it.

Now mince the garlic as fine as you want.

A knifeful of very finely minced garlic

Peeling, Seeding, and Chopping Tomatoes Julia's Way

Drop the tomatoes into rapidly boiling water and boil for exactly 10 seconds. Remove with a slotted spoon or strainer.

Cut out the core and peel the skin down from the hole left by the core.

Halve the tomato crosswise and squeeze each half over a bowl to extract the juice and seeds.

If you are using canned tomatoes, open them up and scrape out the seeds with a knife.

With a large knife chop both the fresh and the canned tomatoes together into small dice.

Julia's Diced Tomato Garnishes

A simple and always welcome accompaniment. When tomatoes are out of season, I combine canned Italian plum tomatoes with fresh tomatoes and briefly cook them; even though the fresh may not have much flavor, they add texture and give the illusion of freshness.

Fresh Diced Tomato Garnish: Ripe red tomatoes peeled, seeded, cut into ½-inch dice, and placed in a bowl. Season to taste with salt and pepper, adding drops of vinegar and of olive oil; toss with a little finely minced parsley or shallot. Let macerate for 10 minutes or longer, folding several times. Just before using, correct seasoning, fold in chopped fresh parsley if you wish, and drain.

Cooked Diced Tomato Garnish: Out of season, use half fresh tomatoes and half drained, seeded, and diced canned plum tomatoes. Season with salt and pepper, add minced shallot or scallion, and cook uncovered at a fast simmer for several minutes to evaporate juices and concentrate flavor. Finish as above.

FISH

IF YOUR BUSY LIFE AFFORDS LITTLE TIME IN THE KITCHEN, YET YOU WANT TO SERVE A home-cooked dinner of which you can be proud, the repertoire of fast fish dishes in this chapter will prove invaluable. In less than ten minutes, you can poach a fillet of red snapper in white wine, while enjoying a glass yourself. Or you can lay a salmon fillet in a hot pan, cook it covered while you set the table, and serve it just a little later, with delectably crisp skin covering perfectly moist flesh. And even if you have only an hour to make a stylish dinner for eight, you can put a whole Arctic char into the oven, stuffed with thyme sprigs, and set it on the table within forty minutes—time enough to make a light and lemony *beurre blanc* and a colorful platter of sautéed vegetables.

The prerequisite for all this simple cooking, though, is impeccably fresh fish. If the fish isn't fresh, it's not worth even a small amount of your time. We both prefer to buy fish from a knowledgeable fish-monger, but these days most supermarkets are improving their seafood counters and display their fish on ice, so you can inspect it yourself. Look for a bright eye and a bright-red gill in whole fish; open the inside cavity to see that the flesh is firm and nicely colored. Most important of all, use your nose to tell you if it's fresh. It shouldn't have a stale or fishy odor, but a clean, oceany smell. There's no substitute for sniffing. If you have to shop in a market where the fish is wrapped in plastic, be bold and do what we do: open the package and smell it.

You don't have to give up on dinner, though, if the kind of fish specified in a recipe is not acceptably fresh, or is unavailable. Numerous varieties of fish are suitable for every cooking method, and the recipes always suggest good alternatives. We hope, indeed, that you will approach these recipes as models of basic fish-cooking methods—poaching, sautéing, roasting whole, grilling, broiling, and cooking in parchment (*en papillote*). With an understanding of how to cook one fish properly by any technique, you can easily do it with other varieties. And as emphasized in our comments and parallel recipes, there's great latitude for variation and improvisation even within a single method.

In the first section of the chapter, we focus on salmon as an example of this versatility and as a model for handling a whole fish, with illustrated instructions for scaling, filleting, trimming, deboning, and skin-ning. Although a good fishmonger can always do the work for you, mastering these techniques will give you flexibility and confidence as a cook. And you will be prepared when a market special, fisherman's luck, or an angler friend presents you with a whole salmon, red snapper, pike, bass, or any other finfish treasure.

We close this chapter with a comprehensive look at lobster, the great shellfish of our New England waters. A fresh lobster is as fast and easy to cook as a piece of fish. Getting to the meat is a bit trickier, but with the proper guidance you will learn how to liberate every morsel.

Salmon

Salmon is perhaps the most popular and widely used fish in this country, for good reason. It is available year-round, reliably fresh, and is relatively low-priced—all thanks to the highly developed salmon-raising industry, which supplies the U.S. from farms in Canada, Chile, and Norway.

As home cooks, though, we appreciate above all the good flavor and versatility of salmon. In this section you'll find recipes for salmon fillets baked in parchment (*en papillote*) and sautéed "on the skin." But you can also cook it using the other methods in this chapter: as a baked whole fish, poached, broiled, or grilled. And of course you can cure salmon to be savored as a cold delicacy—for which you'll find four different methods in our "Appetizers" chapter.

In the following photos, Jacques demonstrates how to cut up and dress a whole salmon. Although you can readily purchase salmon all prepared, when you do it yourself, you'll get the exact pieces you want, and save money too. And a large whole salmon will provide you with lots of good things to cook: fillets and steaks; a slab or slices for gravlax (see more photos and recipes, pages 18–22); trimmings for Salmon Tartare (page 24); head and bones for fish stock (page 43); and even the salmon skin to bake into cracklings (see below).

Salmon-Skin Cracklings Don't throw away the salmon skin when you are trimming a fillet (but be sure the salmon has been scaled)—bake it into cracklings. Rub it with a bit of oil, sprinkle with salt, and bake in a 375°F oven on a cookie sheet. Check in 25 minutes; the skin should still be pliable but lightly browned. If necessary, bake another 5 minutes. Then slice it into thin shreds and use as a garnish for sautéed salmon or in salads.

To remove the scales, put the salmon in a large plastic bag (so the scales won't fly all over the kitchen) and with a spoon (or a clamshell or a specially designed implement) scrape vigorously against the skin all over the salmon until you can no longer feel any scales. Remove from the bag and rinse thoroughly.

Slice under the gill, toward the head. (Later, when you turn the fish and repeat this step on the other side, you will be removing both gills and the head.)

Slice along the rib cage the length of the salmon to remove one whole side.

After you have taken off the top fillet, scrape with a spoon along the hollows of the carcass to extract loose bits of salmon and save them for Salmon Tartare (page 24).

Feel for the fine line of bones that are embedded in the flesh, and, using pliers, pull them out one by one (you will get about 30). Turn the fish over and repeat all of these steps on the other side. When the head has been removed, scrape off any bits of flesh around the gills and in the head and save them for Salmon Tartare. The head, minus the gills, and the carcass can be used for stock.

Cut the side of salmon into fillets of whatever size you want.

Trim away the fine bones at the side of the fillet and, again, save any flesh for the tartare.

To skin the salmon, hold on to the tail end with one hand and, with your knife at about a 45-degree angle, using a seesawing motion, cut away the flesh from the skin.

Julia

With a handsome package such as Jacques's, you can neatly cut the top open at the table with a pair of scissors, the way a maître d'hôtel would do in a swank restaurant, then eat your fish right from it. But for informal occasions, I just fold the paper up tightly and use pins to keep it shut. After cooking, slice or tear the paper open and slide the fish and its juices onto the plate. Cooking *en papillote* does not have to be fancy—it's a fine method for everyday cooking.

The different garnishes described show how to vary the flavors of a dish. Yet, as always, you can adapt these recipes to what you have on hand. If you don't have shallots, use scallions. If your tomatoes are hard or tasteless, mix the pieces with moister pieces of canned tomato. And you can use other kinds of herbs, if you have them, rather than parsley.

Salmon en Papillote

A classic way to cook a fish fillet is to seal it inside a tightly folded package of parchment paper and bake it briefly in a hot oven. Known as *en papillote,* this gentle method cooks the enclosed fish in its own moisture and creates its own sauce of natural juices. Cooking *en papillote* is also fun—assembling and wrapping the fish and seasonings in paper—and it is thrilling to open the package at the table, revealing a beautifully cooked dish and releasing all the pent-up aromas in one heady burst.

Our recipes give you two salmon fillets with different vegetable garnishes, and our two quite different ways of making the paper case—Jacques's carefully shaped and dramatically inflated enclosure, and Julia's easier fold-and-pin package. You can use either for your own fish creation—both produce fine results—and you can substitute any fish fillet or steak: red snapper, halibut, cod, and swordfish, among many others. *En papillote* is also an excellent method for cooking various cuts of meat as well as poultry and vegetables.

Julia's Salmon Fillet en Papillote with Shallots and Tomato

Yield: 1 fillet, serving 1

1 Tbs unsalted butter, soft
1 skinless salmon fillet, 6 to
    8 ounces
Salt and freshly ground
    white pepper
1 Tbs very finely minced
    shallots (or scallions)
½ cup diced fresh tomato
    garnish (see page 215)
Whole leaves of flat-leaf
    parsley, about a dozen

Arrange the dressed salmon on the buttered center of the paper.

Lift up the sides of the parchment.

Special equipment
A sheet of parchment paper, about 20 inches by 15 inches; a cookie sheet

Preheat the oven to 425°F.

Smear the butter in the center of the parchment paper.

Season each side of the salmon with a big pinch of salt and several grinds of pepper, and lay the salmon, its most attractive side up, on the buttered area of the paper.

Mix the minced shallots and tomato together and spread on top of the salmon fillet. Scatter the parsley leaves over and around the fish.

Lift the shorter (15-inch) sides of the parchment so the edges meet right above the salmon, like a tent. Fold over several times, then fold the sides together. Crimp the folds tightly with your fingers, or use several pins at the end to seal the package completely.

After folding up the long sides of the paper, fold the short ends.

Set the package on the cookie sheet and bake 8 minutes for a fillet less than an inch thick, or 10 minutes for a thick fillet 1 to 1¼ inches thick.

To serve, carefully transfer the package to a dinner plate, remove the pins if you have used them, and simply unfold or cut the parchment open. If you'd rather remove the package before eating, cut or tear the paper alongside the fillet, and slide the fish right onto the plate.

Insert several pins to secure the folds.

Jacques

The reason for folding a large case and inflating it as I do is not just to make a beautiful presentation. The principle of *en papillote* cooking is to create a kind of hothouse atmosphere. You need to inflate the case—before it goes in the oven—so there is enough air space between the food and the dome of the package. Then the hot, very moist air can circulate all around, as in a pressure cooker, cooking everything very quickly but keeping it moist. If you crimp your paper tightly, it's easy to blow it up like a balloon—in restaurants I used a bicycle pump, but at home I just blow into a straw.

Even if you are using a quick method like Julia's, without inflating, it's a good idea to leave some air space on top of the fish. One of the simplest ways to cook *en papillote* is to use an ordinary brown paper bag—just put your fish in the bottom and fold the top over. You can also use aluminum foil for your package—which I do when I cook fish *en papillote* on an outdoor grill.

Jacques's Salmon Fillet en Papillote with Zucchini, Carrot, and Shiitake Mushroom

Yield: 1 fillet, serving 1

1 skinless salmon fillet, 6 to 8 ounces
¼ tsp salt
¼ tsp freshly ground black pepper
¼ cup fine julienne of zucchini, about 3 inches long
¼ cup fine julienne of carrot, about 3 inches long
¼ cup very thin slices of fresh shiitake mushroom (about 1 medium cap, stem removed)
Whole leaves of flat-leaf parsley, about 10
1 Tbs or so unsalted butter

Special equipment

A rectangular sheet of parchment paper, 24 inches by 16 inches; a cookie sheet

Preheat the oven to 425°F.

Fold the paper in half. Season both sides of the fillet with half the salt and pepper and place it in the center of one half of the parchment sheet. Scatter the slivered vegetables and the parsley leaves over and around the fillet, dot the top with butter, and season with the remaining salt and pepper.

Fold and inflate the parchment casing, following the photos.

Set the package on the cookie sheet and bake 8 minutes for a thin fillet (less than an inch) or 10 minutes for a thick fillet (1 inch or more).

To serve, carefully transfer the package to a dinner plate and simply unfold or cut the parchment open. If you'd rather remove the package before eating, cut or tear the paper alongside the fillet, and slide it right onto the plate.

After arranging the salmon and vegetables in the center of one half of the parchment paper, fold the other half over.

Start at one end to fold and pleat the paper along the edge.

Continue folding and pleating the edge, making a half circle.

To secure the folds, press down firmly with the edge of a small ramekin or cup, rubbing it back and forth over the pleats.

Twist closed after last fold.

After removing the straw and twisting the opening closed, paint the surface of the parchment lightly all over with vegetable oil.

Now open the twist just enough to insert a straw into it.

Blow through the straw until the package is fully inflated.

Jacques's Way to Julienne Vegetables

For my salmon fillet *en papillote*, the pieces of carrot, mushroom, and zucchini must be very thin, so they soften in the short cooking time and release their flavor, aroma, and juices. These very thin sticklike slices are called a "julienne." A fast way to make them is to stack wide strips of the vegetable and slice them into julienne strips. For other dishes, you can cut the sticks thicker, the width of matchsticks, a garnish called *bâtonnets*.

Jacques's Salmon Fillet Sautéed on Its Skin

Unilatéral is the French term for this kind of sauté, and it has the same meaning as in English: one-sided. Put the salmon fillet in a hot pan; cover and cook for five minutes—no turning, until you flip it onto your serving plate. You'll marvel at the contrasting textures of the fillet, with its crackling cap of seared skin and pink, tender flesh beneath.

For this easy method to work, you must use a non-stick pan and be certain that the skin of the fillet has been scaled. You add no fat—the skin contracts immediately when it hits the pan and crisps on the hot bottom, while the flesh releases its fat and cooks in the moist atmosphere of the covered pan.

You can also use this method with other skin-on fillets, such as cod, red snapper, or sea bass. Finish the fillet with the zesty sautéed garnish of capers, onion, and lemon juice that we give here, or serve simply topped with a pat of herb or plain butter.

Yield: 1 fillet, serving 1

One 6-to-8-ounce salmon fillet,
  skin on, scaled
⅛ tsp salt or more
2 tsp unsalted butter
¼ cup (loosely packed) very thin
  slivers of onion, about an inch
  long
1 to 2 tsp capers, drained
2 tsp lemon juice
1 tsp coarsely chopped flat-leaf
  parsley, for garnish

Special equipment
  An 8- or 9-inch non-stick frying
    pan or sauté pan with a tight-
    fitting cover

Set the pan over high heat for a minute, until quite hot. Season both sides of the fillet with the salt and lay it skin side down in the dry pan. The skin will shrink on contact with the heat.

Cover the pan and cook for 5 to 7 minutes at medium-high heat, depending on the thickness of the fillet. Test for doneness by piercing the top with a sharp knife: the outside will flake but the center should still be rare and slightly translucent; the skin will be very crisp. Cook longer for a better-done fillet.

With a long spatula, lift the fillet and flip it onto a dinner plate, with the cooked skin on top. Wipe out the pan with paper towels to remove the fat released by the salmon, and add the butter. As it melts, sauté the onion slivers for ½ minute or so. Add the capers and sauté briefly, tossing them with the onions, then swirl in the lemon juice, heating it for just a few seconds. Pour the sizzling garnish over the fillet, sprinkle on the chopped parsley, and serve immediately.

Salmon in Potato Case

This is really a variation of a simple salmon sauté. Here a piece of fish is wrapped in a blanket of potatoes, which becomes brown and crisp when sautéed, while the salmon inside remains moist and tender. The fillet has to be butterflied so it is thin enough to cook through quickly.

The best equipment for cutting the uniformly thin slices of potato that you need is the expensive French mandoline. But there is an American version at a fraction of the cost that does the job well (just watch out for your fingers). And if you have neither, use an ordinary vegetable peeler. With the mandoline you can also cut perfect straw potatoes to encase the salmon. Or you can use the coarse holes of a grater to the same effect; work quickly, though, before the potatoes discolor.

Make the Tomato Coulis first so that it is ready to receive the potato-encrusted fish straight from the pan.

Yield: 1 fillet, serving 1

One 2-inch-wide salmon fillet—
    center cut (about 5 ounces)
⅛ tsp salt
Freshly ground pepper
1 large russet potato
2 tsp chopped dill
2 tsp butter
2 tsp vegetable oil
Tomato Coulis (page 79)
1 or 2 sprigs fresh dill, as garnish

Special equipment
A mandoline, vegetable peeler, or grater;
    a large, long spatula; an 8- or 9-inch
    non-stick frying pan

Jacques

I like salmon slightly under-cooked—just a bit on the rare side, so it remains moist. We used to serve salmon well cooked, which many people found dry and pasty, but these days many chefs have gone to the other extreme, cooking fish very rare.

With this method, it is easy to control the degree of doneness. I sauté the fillet so that it flakes on the outside, but is just hot in the center. You can cook the fillet shorter or longer, depending on the thickness, until it is cooked to taste. But whose taste? That is the question anytime you cook meat or fish. Some people like flesh well done, some prefer rare or very rare, but generally you don't know. Unless you have a direct indication from your family or guests, the proper way is to prepare it the way you like it. Your cooking is best when it reflects your own taste.

To butterfly, slice lengthwise through the 2-inch-wide salmon fillet, stopping just short of the opposite end, then open the fillet up like a book.

Cover the salmon with thin slices of potato, slightly over-lapping.

Lower the potato-lined salmon into the hot fat.

Top the salmon fillet with overlapping slices of potato to cover it completely.

Salmon in Potato Case (continued)

Butterflying the salmon fillet

Starting at one of the long sides, with a large, sharp knife slice through the salmon fillet, stopping just short of the opposite end. Now open the two sides up like a book and flatten the piece out. This butterflied piece should be about ½ inch thick. Season both sides of the fish with salt and a few grinds of the pepper mill.

Peel the potato and, using a mandoline or a vegetable peeler or a sharp knife, cut very thin lengthwise slices. Lay about 5 or 6 pieces, slightly overlapping, on your work surface and set the salmon on top (see photo); you should use just enough potato slices to make a bottom covering for the fish. Heat the butter and oil in the non-stick frying pan, and when it is sizzling, pick up the potato-lined piece of salmon and slip it into the pan. Sprinkle the dill on top and cover the fish with 5 or 6 more slices of potato.

If you have a long spatula, you can arrange directly on the spatula the bottom layer of potato slices, the salmon and dill, and the top layer of potatoes, and then slide everything neatly into the pan.

Alternatively, you may cut straw potatoes with your mandoline or grate the potato through the coarse holes of a grater. Spread half of the straw or grated potatoes on the spatula, put the salmon on top, then the dill, and finish with the the rest of the potato, making sure that the top and bottom of the potato blanket meet to enclose the fish.

Heat the butter and oil in the non-stick frying pan and, when sizzling, slide the potato-covered salmon into the pan. Cook over moderate heat for 4 to 5 minutes, then check to see if the bottom has browned. When well crusted, turn the fish over carefully and cook the other side about 4 to 5 minutes, or until the potatoes are browned.

Spoon several tablespoons of the coulis onto a serving plate; then, with the back of the spoon, clear a place in the center. Carefully pick up the potato-encrusted salmon with your spatula and arrange it in the center of the plate with the coulis surrounding it. Garnish with sprigs of dill.

Opposite: Salmon in Potato Case

Julia

This grill-and-low-oven method is a good one for thick fish fillets. I like to rub a bit of butter over the grilled pieces *before* they go into the oven, to give a bit more flavor and moisture. With lean fish, like halibut or cod, you can also braise steaks and fillets in a moderate, 350°F oven, with some wine and fish stock in the baking pan. Don't cover the dish as you do when poaching, but occasionally baste the fish pieces with the pan juices.

Flavored butters like the two given here are very useful to have on hand. They take only moments to make in a food processor, and you can keep them for months in the freezer, cutting off a slice or two whenever a dish needs a flavorful finish. For anchovy butter, be sure to open a fresh can of anchovy fillets, and use excellent olive oil, rather than the sometimes inferior oil from the can. Too often, people use anchovies from a half-empty can in their refrigerator, after the flavor has gone off. Use all your anchovies while they are fresh—perhaps in a salad or sandwich, such as my Composed Near-Niçoise Salad (page 110) or a Pan Bagnat (page 142).

Grilled Halibut with Flavored Butters

Halibut is one of our favorite fish, and Americans are fortunate that excellent varieties are caught in both Atlantic and Pacific waters. They are also successfully raised on farms. Halibut is a large flatfish, with pure-white flesh that can be poached, baked, sautéed, broiled, or grilled, as we do in this recipe. The fish is most often cut into steaks, but you want wide skinless halibut fillets for this recipe, so you may have to ask your fishmonger to cut them specially for you. The firm flesh grills beautifully and you don't have to contend with the large central bone and membrane found in a halibut steak.

Since halibut fillets can be quite thick, use the same grill-and-oven method as for a thick beefsteak, like Chateaubriand. The top and bottom of the fillets are seared for a couple of minutes each, just long enough for them to be distinctly marked and flavored by the grill. Then they are placed in a very low oven to cook through to the center, with no danger of drying or burning the outer surfaces on the grill.

For a touch of extra richness and flavor, top the fillets with either of the flavored butters suggested here. Both the anchovy butter and the classic herb butter, *beurre maître d'hôtel*, go nicely with mild-flavored halibut, and other grilled fish and meat.

For a colorful presentation, make a bed of Rice Pilaf with Pepper, Peas, and Asparagus (page 168) on each plate and set a grilled fillet in the middle.

Yield: 2 fillets, serving 2

> Two 8-to-10-ounce skinless halibut fillets
> ½ tsp or so vegetable oil, such as canola
>   or corn oil
> ¼ tsp salt
> Several grinds of pepper
> 2 Tbs or so Anchovy Butter or Beurre
>   Maître d'Hôtel (recipes follow), or plain
>   unsalted butter, soft, for garnishing

Special equipment

A ridged stovetop grill (flat grill or grill pan); a shallow baking dish, lightly buttered or oiled

Preheat the oven to 200°F. Set the grill over high heat for several minutes while preparing the fish. It must be very hot and completely clean to prevent sticking.

Brush the top and bottom of the fillets lightly with oil and season both sides with the salt and pepper. Lay the pieces on the hot grill, skinless side down.

Sear on the first side for about $1^{1}/_{2}$ minutes; then turn the fillets and grill the second side for $1^{1}/_{2}$ minutes or longer, until well marked.

Transfer the fillets to the baking dish, turning them over so the side you are presenting is up. Set in the oven for 5 to 10 minutes to finish cooking. When done, the flesh will be firm but still moist on the exterior, and opaque and warm all the way through. If you need to keep it in the oven longer, reduce the heat to 160°F—you can hold it up to an hour. Remove from the oven, and top each warm fillet with a tablespoon of soft butter—either flavored or plain—and serve.

Anchovy Butter

Yield: About 1 cup

1 stick (4 ounces) unsalted butter, at
    room temperature
$^{1}/_{2}$ tsp Dijon-style mustard, or more to
    taste
A pinch of black pepper, or more to taste
$^{1}/_{2}$ lemon (for about 2 Tbs juice)
6 to 8 anchovy fillets packed in olive oil,
    from a freshly opened can
$^{1}/_{2}$ teaspoon excellent olive oil

Put the butter, mustard, and pepper into the work bowl of a food processor. Squeeze in the lemon juice, and add the anchovy fillets and olive oil. Process until smooth. Taste and adjust the seasonings.

Jacques

Whenever you grill fish, indoors or out, your grill has to be extremely hot and very clean, or the fish may stick. If you are using a large stovetop grill, which extends over two burners, there can be hotter and cooler spots. Place your fillets only where the flame really heats the grill. Only a thick piece of fillet is good on the grill—thin ones will stick and become too dry. In my opinion most outdoor grills are never really hot enough to grill successfully. If a grill is not available, use a cast-iron pan. Heat the pan for 6 to 8 minutes so it's *very* hot. Sear each oiled fillet $1^{1}/_{2}$ minutes on each side and proceed with the recipe.

It is good to mark the fish on both sides on a very hot grill, then finish it in a 200°F oven where it will relax and become more tender and remain juicy.

Be sure to lay the side of a fillet that has been skinned on the grill first. The fibers on this side contract and cause the fillet to curl in their direction. After this side has been marked, you can turn the fillet onto the fleshy, inner side—the more attractive side that you want to present—and finish grilling. This way, the fillet will not curl out of shape.

Jacques on Flavored Butters

I think of flavored butters as a modern convenience form of hollandaise or béarnaise sauce, just cutting a frozen slice to use on grilled food instead of whipping up yolks and butter. I especially love the butters on grilled lamb kidneys, one of my favorite dishes. *Beurre maître d'hôtel* is classic, but the anchovy butter is excellent, too. My seafood butter (page 138), with almonds and wine, would also be nice with the halibut or any grilled fish.

Anchovy Butter (continued)

Alternatively, beat the butter with a wooden spoon in a mixing bowl until very soft. Chop the anchovies into a purée and beat in the rest of the ingredients one at a time until smooth, adjusting the seasonings to taste.

To store, mound the butter on a sheet of plastic wrap. Fold the wrap over the mound, then roll the butter back and forth under your palms to form a log shape. Roll up the log in the plastic wrap and twist the ends to tighten and seal. Refrigerate the butter for up to a week, or freeze for a month or more.

Beurre Maître d'Hôtel

Yield: About ½ cup

1 stick (4 ounces) unsalted butter, at
    room temperature
3 Tbs finely chopped fresh parsley
1 Tbs lemon juice, or more to taste
½ tsp salt, or more to taste
½ tsp freshly ground black pepper, or
    more to taste

Purée all the ingredients in a food processor until smooth. Add more seasonings as needed.

Alternatively, beat the butter in a mixing bowl with a wooden spoon. When fluffy, beat in the rest of the ingredients one at a time until smooth, adjusting the seasonings to taste.

Wrap and store as for Anchovy Butter (see preceding recipe).

Opposite: Grilled Halibut

Julia

Not having fingers as tough as Jacques's, I use my sharp-pointed little lobster shears to remove the gills, snipping them loose from their attachments. Then it's easy to pull them out. For an illustration of gills, see page 234.

You must make sure that your roast fish is done before serving it. A good indication is when you can smell roasting fish, which means the juices have started to come out. Use both tests given in the recipe—tugging on the back fin and checking the belly cavity for any red juices. You will also know if your fish is done when you lift up the bones at serving time. If they don't pull up easily, the fish isn't done—but it's a bit late to make that discovery.

You will find a layer of dark flesh on the top of the fish when you remove the cooked skin. The fish looks prettier when this is removed, so I always scrape it away before I present the fish and begin serving. Norwegians like this dark fatty flesh and Jacques tells me that the Japanese do too. But I don't.

Roast Char and Beurre Blanc

A whole roasted fish, served on a large oval platter still steaming from the oven, surrounded with colorful sautéed vegetables, is a dramatic centerpiece for a dinner party. From the cook's perspective, though, it's hard to imagine an easier or quicker way to delight a table of guests. There's almost no work to getting the fish in the oven, and none at all in the forty minutes or so that it takes to roast to moist tenderness.

In this recipe, we call for Arctic char, an excellent freshwater fish related both to salmon and to trout. Wild char is taken from cold lakes in the Northern United States, Canada, and many other parts of the world, including the high Alps of France, where it's called *omble chevalier*. In recent years, successful farming has made this once rare and pricey creature widely available and more moderately priced, and farm-raised char have the striking pink-spotted skin and delicately flavored pale-pink flesh that chefs have long appreciated. In most good fish markets, it's easy to find (or to order) a three-to-four-pound char, enough to feed six people amply. Other good choices for roasting are salmon, trout, and striped bass.

Finishing and presenting the roast fish will be the cook's only busy time. It's simplest to roast and serve the fish on the same ovenproof platter if you have one—otherwise you'll need to slide it from the baking sheet to a serving platter. After removing the crisp skin, you can surround the fish with Sautéed Small Tomatoes (page 209) and Sautéed Snow Peas (page 208), or simply garnish the platter with lots of lemon wedges and clusters of fresh parsley.

For an elegant touch, you can fillet and reassemble the fish in the kitchen, as Jacques demonstrates in the photos on pages 234–235, allowing you to serve boneless portions of fish. But you can also serve right at the table, first cutting portions from the top of the fish, then removing the central bone, and continuing with portions from the bottom.

To sauce your roast fish, whisk together the rapid *sauce beurre blanc* given here as soon as the fish comes out of the oven. Have your pan and whisk at the ready, your lemon juice squeezed, and the butter in pieces, and it will only take a minute.

Yield: 6 to 8 servings

1 whole Arctic char or scaled salmon,
    3 to 4 pounds, gutted
Salt and freshly ground pepper
2 to 3 Tbs chopped shallots
Fresh thyme sprigs, a good handful
Olive oil

For the *sauce beurre blanc*
1½ sticks (6 ounces) room-temperature
    unsalted butter, in tablespoon-sized
    pieces
2 Tbs or so minced shallots
3 Tbs freshly squeezed lemon juice
5 Tbs water
Salt and freshly ground white pepper

For garnish
Parsley sprigs, in large bunches
Lemon wedges

Special equipment
An ovenproof platter for both baking and
    serving, or a large, shallow-rimmed
    baking sheet and separate serving plat-
    ter—large enough to hold a fish 20 or
    more inches long; a medium frying pan
    or sauté pan and a small wire whisk for
    making the sauce

Jacques

It is important to work care-fully when handling the roast fish at serving time. To keep the top fillets intact so you can put the fish back together, split them in half lengthwise with your knife and open them like a flower, lifting them to the sides as shown in the photo on page 235. Then the central bone is revealed, which has many tiny bones attached, especially in the rib-cage area. Whether you're doing it in the kitchen or at the table, try to remove all of these together. But you should advise your guests that there might still be bones in the fish and they should look out for them.

In the rapid method for *sauce beurre blanc,* which produces a thinner *beurre blanc,* you want to keep the liquid boiling, so that the butter and liquid bind together. Here the proportion of butter and liquid should be nearly equal, whereas the classic *beurre blanc* has at least two to three times as much butter as liquid. Because of that, if the sauce gets too hot—near the boil—it will break down. Should you see this happening, whisk in a few drops of water to hold the suspension.

Remove the gills using your fingers. You can snip them first with lobster shears to loosen them, as Julia does.

To remove the crisp skin on top of the fish, loosen the edge along the cavity and peel the skin off in one piece. Scrape away the dark flesh, if you like.

Roast Whole Arctic Char (continued)

Preparing and baking the fish

Preheat the oven to 400°F.

Pull out the gills through the gill opening and discard (see photo at left). Rinse and dry the fish.

Season the belly cavity with salt and pepper and spread the shallots and thyme sprigs inside. Rub a spoonful or two of olive oil over the entire outside of the fish; oil the roasting tray or pan well. Lay the fish on its side in the tray—on the diagonal if necessary—and set in the oven.

Bake for 30 to 40 minutes, depending on size; remove from the oven and check for doneness. Tug lightly on the dorsal fin, in the center of the back, to see if it comes off easily. You can also pry open the cavity gently, push aside the herbs, and look for bloody redness near the backbone. If there are red juices, or if the dorsal fin does not slip out, return the fish to the oven for a few more minutes.

Making the sauce

As soon as you take the fish out of the oven, set the frying pan over moderate heat. Heat 1 teaspoon of butter and the minced shallots until sizzling. Pour in the lemon juice and water, add a good pinch of salt, and swirl to mix. Heat rapidly to a boil.

Pick up one tablespoon-sized lump of butter with the tip of the whisk and rapidly whip it into the hot liquid. As soon as the butter is nearly absorbed, whisk in another piece. Adjust the heat to maintain a slow boil and add the remaining butter, whisking each piece until almost completely absorbed before adding the next. Whisk in salt and white pepper and more lemon juice, to taste. Remove from the heat.

Presenting and serving the fish

Peel the crisp skin from the fish, as in the photo at left. If you like, gently scrape off the dark flesh with a paring knife. (Then, if necessary, transfer the fish from the baking pan to a

separate serving platter.) Surround the fish with sautéed vegetables (see page 232), if using, and garnish with clusters of
parsley sprigs and lemon wedges.

To serve the fish, remove portions of the top fillet first,
then pull up the central bone carefully and remove to another
plate before serving the bottom fillets, as shown in the photos.
To fillet the fish before serving, set aside the top fillets, remove
the central bones, then reassemble the fish, as shown in the
photos.

Nap each serving with a spoonful or two of *beurre blanc.*

Reassemble the fish after
flipping the top fillets back in
place.

Split the top fillet in half lengthwise, cutting down only to the
central bone.

Lift out the central bone,
carefully pulling out all the
tiny bones attached to the
bottom fillets.

Julia

There's lots of room for choice and improvisation in these poaching recipes, as in most of our cooking. Jacques likes to use fillets with the skin on, but I prefer the skin off, and I score the skinned or "milky" side to keep them from curling. Use whatever aromatic or seasonings you like or have available. If you don't have shallots, use scallions. If you like garlic, add some.

The more classical oven-poaching has you arrange the seasoned fillets in a buttered flameproof baking dish with their sprinkling of shallots and their poaching liquid. You bring them just to the simmer on top of the stove, cover them with buttered wax or parchment paper to protect and to help steam as well as bake them. You slip them into your preheated 350°F oven and they usually need 7 to 10 minutes.

When are they done? Whichever way you poach your fish fillets—oven or stovetop—they are done when the color has changed from translucent (not solid white) to opaque (milky white). The flesh is no longer squashy and raw; it has taken on texture, and is lightly springy to the touch. When just done the juices have swelled in the flesh and are ready to escape; you can begin to smell cooking fish. That is the moment you are waiting for. A little longer and the juices will have left the flesh; you have overcooked your fish, it will have stiffened, and the flesh will flake.

Poached Snapper

French chefs have long understood the simplicity and creative possibilities of poaching fish. In *La Répertoire de la Cuisine,* the authoritative but surprisingly slim compendium of classical French dishes, you can find over 250 different preparations for poached fish fillets in white wine. (All 7,500 condensed recipes are in the English edition of this invaluable guide, for which Jacques wrote the introduction.)

Here we only give you two such recipes, but they show why poaching in wine is an essential method for American home cooks as well as French chefs: it is quick, nearly foolproof, and marvelously adaptable to different tastes and occasions. With our basic techniques, you can take almost any fresh fillet that catches your eye at the fish counter and cook it perfectly in just a few minutes, preserving its distinctive flavor. And you can use the wine you like and the seasonings and vegetables you have on hand, and finish the dish as simply or as fancifully as your time allows.

Both our recipes call for fillets of red snapper, a tasty fish with moderately firm flesh that's well suited for poaching. There are different types of red snapper in various parts of the country. The one we use, with its distinctive pink tint and round profile, comes from Florida and is widely available, but many other fish varieties are marketed under the same name, not all of which have the same flavor and texture. Check with your fishmonger to be sure of what you're getting. If he's selling whole fish, you can have them filleted, or do it yourself, using the exact procedure as shown for whole salmon (pages 218–219). Make sure that the fillets are scaled, if you are poaching them with the skin, and save the head and bones for a fine fish stock. Snapper fillets will vary in thickness, and you have to adjust your cooking time accordingly. Use the amount of liquid given in the recipes, and only allow it to bubble slowly while the fillets are poaching.

Any of the flatfish fillets that we recommend for sautéing (page 224) are also excellent poached, as well as the imported varieties such as Dover sole or turbot or the more commonly available gray sole, petrale sole, and flounder. Thick fillets of white fish like cod, scrod, and haddock are fine for poaching too.

One of the rewards of poaching is the cooking liquid, which unites the flavor of the fillets, the wine, and the seasonings. In the recipes here, we turn the poaching liquid into different sauces—Jacques's becomes a classic velouté and Julia's a rich *beurre blanc*. These procedures are interchangeable and you can use them with any similar recipe. For the simplest finish, you can also just reduce the poaching juices (sidebar, page 242). Jacques's Cucumbers Tournés (page 243), a traditional "turned" garnish for fish, makes a colorful presentation as well as a pleasing textural contrast to either of our poached fillets.

A fragrant, spicy white wine, such as a sauvignon blanc, is essential in these dishes, both for the poaching liquid (though Julia prefers vermouth) and to accompany the fish. A California Chardonnay is always appropriate.

Jacques

The quickness of poaching is

a great advantage to the cook, but it means that you must have all of your garnishes, your sauce ingredients, and everything else ready to serve as soon as the fillets are done—you don't want them to sit around. If you must prepare your fish ahead, you can cook them in the poaching liquid very briefly, so they are still basically just raw in the center. Then you can set the pan in a low oven, about 180°F, covered with parchment (page 242), and let the fillets finish cooking for 15 minutes or so.

People worry about what kind of wine to cook with. While you don't need an extraordinary wine for the poaching liquid, you can't cook a good dish with a bad wine either. A useful principle is to make your poaching liquid with a wine that you would be happy to drink.

Julia on Cooking with Wine, Especially with White Wine

Finding a white wine suitable for cooking is more of a problem, I think, than finding a red. What you want in a red wine is a frank, healthy wine you'd be as happy to drink as you would be to cook with—a French Mâcon is ideal, as is an Italian Chianti, or a California zinfandel. In whites you are looking for a full-bodied dry wine that will not sour your sauce. Again the French Mâcon is my choice, but where do I find a reasonably priced bottle here? That is why I have always turned to dry white French vermouth, which gives the flavor and body of white wine but none of the acid. I use about two-thirds cup of vermouth for every cup of white wine called for. An added plus is that you can always have a previously opened bottle of vermouth in your refrigerator, but not an opened bottle of white wine.

Julia on Sauce Beurre Blanc (White Butter Sauce)—The Classic Method

It looks like a hollandaise sauce when you spoon it over your beautifully poached fish, but it is only warm flavored butter—butter emulsified, held in suspension by its strongly acid flavor base. You'll not find this sauce in your Escoffier since it is a regional not a classical recipe. Some regional sauces didn't get recognition until the 1920s and 1930s, when they became popular with the French themselves as they toured the country in their new-

Julia's Stove-top Poached Fillets of Red Snapper with Mushrooms and Fast White Butter Sauce

Fillets of fish poached in white wine with mushrooms, always an attractive dish, especially when served in a white butter sauce. I had never done a fast one until I saw Jacques make it some years ago on one of his TV shows. I love the old-fashioned version, described on page 240, but I like this, my version of Jacques's, too—and it is fast!

Yield: 1 or 2 fillets, serving 2

2 tsp butter
2 Tbs minced shallots
Approximately 10 ounces skinless
    red snapper fillets
A big pinch of salt
Several grindings of white pepper
⅔ cup dry white French vermouth, plus
    ⅓ cup Fish Stock (page 43) or water
1 cup thinly sliced mushrooms
For the *sauce beurre blanc*
    2 tsp lemon juice
    4 or 5 Tbs room-temperature butter, in
        tablespoon-sized pieces
    Salt and pepper
    Drops of lemon juice
For garnish
    Chopped parsley
    Cucumbers Tournés (page 243)
        (optional)

Special equipment
    A stainless-steel frying pan, 10 inches top
        diameter, with tight-fitting lid; a but-
        tered paper cover (see page 242); a
        6-cup stainless-steel saucepan and a
        medium whisk, for the sauce

Set the pan over moderate heat, swirl in the butter, sprinkle in the shallots, and cook slowly for a moment to soften without coloring. Remove from heat.

Season the fillets on both sides with the salt and pepper and lay them in the pan, skin side down. Pour in the liquids, adding more if needed to come halfway up the fish. Scatter the sliced mushrooms over the fish and fit the paper into the pan, buttered side down.

Put on the lid and bring the liquid just to the simmer. Adjust the heat to maintain very slow bubbling and poach about 5 minutes for thin fillets (½ inch or less), or more for thicker fillets. Pierce the center of a fillet with a sharp knife to make sure that the flesh is opaque, or cooked, throughout (see page 236).

Making the sauce

Then, holding the cover askew, drain all of the poaching liquid into the small saucepan. Keep the fillets warm in the covered poaching pan while you make the sauce.

Set the saucepan over high heat, add the lemon juice, and rapidly boil the poaching juices until there is only a tablespoon of syrupy liquid remaining. Lower the heat to a gentle boil, pick up a tablespoon-sized lump of butter with the tip of the whisk, and rapidly whip it into the hot liquid. As soon as the butter is nearly absorbed, whisk in 3 more lumps of butter, one at a time, incorporating each completely before adding the next and keeping the liquid at a gentle boil.

When the butter has all been incorporated, taste the sauce and season with salt and pepper and lemon juice to taste. Remove from the heat.

Pour any juices that have accumulated around the fillets into another small pan; boil down rapidly to a syrup and whisk into the sauce.

Serving

Remove the fillets to warm plates or a platter. Spoon the sauce over them and sprinkle with chopped parsley. Serve immediately, with warm Cucumbers Tournés alongside, if you have prepared them.

fangled automobiles, and, of course, with foreign tourists.

White butter sauce was a specialty of Nantes, on the Loire River, where the local culinary specialty was *brochet au beurre blanc. Brochet,* or pike, is a fine large white-fleshed fish with splendid taste and texture but full of big and little bones seemingly running in every direction—much like a shad. It has taken something like this divine sauce to make it a desirable fish. The sauce emerged from obscurity in the 1930s, but began to be known in the 1950s, about the time Paul and I came to Paris. It then became immensely popular during the era of nouvelle cuisine, and is now in limbo because, however marvelous its flavor, it is a *butter* sauce.

In those 1950 days of ours my colleague Louisette Bertholle, who had a good nose for culinary gossip, had heard that an authentic *beurre blanc* was to be had at a small Paris restaurant, Chez La Mère Michel, in the sixth arrondissement. Obviously we had to go at once and the six of us—Louisette, Simca (my other colleague), and our husbands foregathered for lunch at the restaurant on the rue Rennequin.

It was indeed a small and modest restaurant with six to eight tables and an open kitchen at the side. Madame Michel was a small white-haired woman probably in her sixties, who had a modest air and quiet vigor. Her husband was her helper, meeter, greeter, waiter, and factotum. The two of them ran it alone, it seemed.

"No *brochet* today," Madame announced to us and the two other occupied tables. It was not the season. She was giving us all some fine fresh turbot.

As we sipped our cool white wine, a Muscadet from the Loire, and gossiped amiably with the other guests, we learned that this was the meal she always served. It was what her faithful clients came for: carefully poached fish of excellent quality, her famous sauce, good French bread, small boiled potatoes, and a little parsley or watercress for garnish. For dessert she offered an excellent fruit tart made in the neighborhood, and coffee.

We asked her to come sit with us, during a lull, and as we talked she invited us to come with her to the kitchen during her next order—exactly what we had hoped she would do. Soon, after four new customers arrived, she beckoned to Louisette, and the three of us joined her in the tiny kitchen adjacent to the dining room. As I remember, it was just a little room, with counters on either side of an old household-type stove.

As we crowded around her she poured a good dollop of white wine and of white-wine vinegar into a very French-looking enameled saucepan, brown on the outside, with a marbled gray interior (I bought one just like it after lunch and still have it). She started boiling her liquids, rapidly adding a generous spoonful of minced shallot and several grinds of white pepper. "Look," she said, while boiling the liquid down to a syrupy glaze, "very important, this base." She explained that it was the strong acid base that would force the butter to cream and remain in suspension.

Sauce Beurre Blanc (White Butter Sauce)

Proportions for 1¼ to 1½ cups of sauce

¼ cup white-wine vinegar
¼ cup dry white wine or dry white
   vermouth
1 Tbs finely minced shallots or scallions
Salt and freshly ground white pepper
8 to 12 ounces chilled best-quality
   unsalted butter, cut into 16 or 24 pieces

Making the sauce. Follow Madame Michel's procedure as described by Julia in the columns to the left and right.

Holding a butter sauce. Careful here! White butter sauce is much more delicate than hollandaise. Too much heat and the emulsion breaks down and you'll have melted butter. Keep just barely warm to prevent it from congealing.

Leftover sauce. It will congeal. Use like flavored butter, or heat it a little bit at a time, as for the Hollandaise on page 96.

Jacques's Poached Red Snapper Provençal

Yield: 1 or 2 fillets, serving 2

4 Tbs finely chopped onion
Approximately 10 ounces red snapper
   fillets, skin on
¼ tsp salt
⅛ tsp freshly ground black pepper
1 cup dry white wine, such as
   Chardonnay, plus more if needed
½ cup Tomates Concassées (peeled,
   seeded, juiced, and cut into ½-inch
   pieces; see sidebar, page 243)
1 tsp fresh thyme leaves

For the sauce
    2 tsp unsalted butter, soft
    2 tsp flour
    ¼ cup cream
    Salt and freshly ground pepper
    Drops of freshly squeezed lemon juice
      (optional)

For garnish
    Cucumbers Tournés (page 243)
      (optional)
    Chopped parsley

Special equipment
    A 10-inch stainless-steel sauté pan with
      tight-fitting lid; a gratin dish to hold
      the fillets; a small wire whisk

Scatter the onion in the bottom of the pan and lay the fillets on top, skin up. Sprinkle the salt and pepper on the fish and pour the wine over them. Scatter the tomato pieces and thyme over the fillets. (If you wish, fit a paper cover into the pan, buttered side down.)

Cover the pan, and bring the liquid to a steady, very gentle boil; poach 3 to 4 minutes for thin fillets or more for thicker fillets. Pierce the center of a fillet with a sharp knife to make sure that the flesh is opaque, or cooked, throughout.

Making the sauce

Transfer the fillets with a slotted spoon or spatula to a gratin or baking dish, skin up, and spoon the tomato pieces over them. Place the dish in a warm spot on the stove or in a very low oven, with the paper cover on top if you have one.

Mix the butter and flour together in a small bowl to make a smooth paste (*beurre manié*). Bring the liquid in the poaching pan to the boil, then scoop up the paste with the tip of the whisk and rapidly stir it into the liquid until completely incorporated. Pour in the cream, whisk to blend, and boil for a minute to thicken. Add any fish juices that have accumulated around the fillets and cook a few moments more, until the sauce is thick enough to coat a spoon. Correct the seasoning, adding

Then she pointed to her butter. It was cold, and cut into tablespoon-sized lumps. She removed her pan from the heat and vigorously whipped in two lumps of the cold butter, which creamed, then two more that creamed. She then set her pan over very low heat, tossed in a new lump of butter, and continued to toss in a new lump as soon as the last had been absorbed. "*Alors,*" she said finally, as the last lump disappeared into the sauce. "*Goutez!*" We tasted, and found it good, but she shook her head and beat in a little more salt. She tasted again; it was thick like a mayonnaise, ivory yellow, smooth. "*Bien!*" She nodded in satisfaction as she dipped and drained her pieces of poached turbot onto warm plates and crowned each with a generous serving of sauce; then she handed them to her husband for garnishing and serving.

"Now you go home and make it yourselves," she beamed at us, shaking our hands cordially as we thanked her a "thousand times"—*mille fois.*

And we did go home and make it, me with my new brown-enameled pan. I made sure that my base was strongly acid, and the sauce was beautiful. I did note that if your base is really acid the sauce itself can be a bit too acid. In that case, simply add more butter to dilute it.

Poached Fish with Pan Juices au Naturel

You can serve the poached fillets from either of our recipes with just the reduced poaching liquid. Remove the fillets to a serving dish or individual plates, and, using a slotted spoon, scoop up the mushroom or tomato pieces and scatter them over the top. Bring the liquid in the pan to the boil over high heat and reduce for a couple of minutes, until syrupy. Off the heat, swirl in a tablespoon or two of butter, if you wish. Taste and adjust the seasoning, and spoon the thickened juices over the fillets. Garnish and serve.

Fold a 1-foot square of parchment paper (or wax paper) into quarters.

Fold on the diagonal, to make a triangle. Fold in half 2 or 3 times more to make a very narrow triangle.

Jacques's Poached Red Snapper Provençal (continued)

drops of lemon juice if the sauce seems to lack acidity.

Serving the fillets

When the sauce is ready, arrange six warm Cucumbers Tournés (if you have prepared them) to form rings on individual dinner plates. Place one fillet, topped with tomato pieces, in the center of the ring, and coat generously with sauce. Sprinkle with chopped parsley and serve.

A Paper Cover for Poached Fish

When I use wet cooking methods like poaching, braising, or steaming, I often cover the food with a piece of parchment that fits snugly in the pan. As with the paper cases, or *papillotes,* for baking salmon fillets (pages 222–223), this system creates a kind of hothouse, in which the steam hits the paper and drips back down, maintaining a moist environment. It's a good technique for cooking rice, too. With this method, you can quickly make a cover to fit a pan of any size.

Place the point of the triangle over the exact center of the pan and measure its radius; trim the triangle at that length.

Open the paper, butter half of the circle, then fold and press the paper together to spread butter on other half. Fit the open circle into the pan.

Cucumbers Tournés

**Yield: 12 or more pieces, to garnish 2 or
3 servings**

1 large cucumber, about 8 inches long
Salt
½ Tbs butter

Remove the rounded ends of the cucumber, then slice it crosswise into 3 equal sections, each about 2 inches long. Cut each of the sections lengthwise into quarters, so you have 12 wedge-shaped pieces.

With a sharp paring knife, "turn" each wedge: first cut away the seeds on one side, then remove the skin in smooth curving peels. Make sure not to remove too much of the flesh; if you do not feel proficient enough with a knife, use a vegetable peeler. Now shape each piece, as demonstrated in the photos on page 198, so it has slightly rounded sides and tapered ends.

In a saucepan just large enough to hold the cucumber pieces in one layer, bring to the boil ¼ cup of water with ⅛ teaspoon of salt. Add all the cucumbers, cover the pan, and cook for 2 to 3 minutes.

Pour off any water remaining in the pan, add the butter and a large pinch of salt, cover again, and melt the butter over very low heat. Shake the pan so the cucumbers are well coated with butter and turn off the heat. Leave them in the covered pan until needed, and briefly reheat before serving if necessary.

Jacques's Method for Tomates Concassées

Diced fresh tomato adds flavor and color to my poached red snapper as well as to many other dishes in this book. It is customary to use only the flesh of the tomato—referred to as *tomate concassée* —first removing the skin, seeds, and juice. A large ripe tomato, 7 or 8 ounces in weight, will yield a cup or so of diced flesh. I always freeze the skin, juice, and seeds to use for stock.

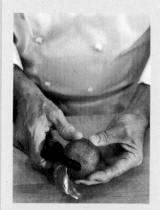

Use a sharp vegetable peeler or paring knife. Slice out the core and start peeling from the cut edges, turning the tomato as you peel.

Cut the peeled tomato in half crosswise, and squeeze out the seeds and juice.

Cut into diced pieces.

Julia

I often wish they were farm-ing Dover sole, as they do salmon and other popular fish. I understand that attempts at raising them are being made—let us hope these are success-ful, and that this unique fish will be more available and moderately priced in years to come. Meanwhile, it is nice to make an authentic *sole meunière* every once in a while, despite the expense.

I prefer to remove the white skin as well as the dark. You peel it off the same way. And, considering the cost, I suggest that you trim only the outer edges of the fins—leave the bony strip next to the fleshy fillets. When sau-téed, these crinkly little bones have nice bits of tasty flesh around them that you don't want to miss. I was always impressed when M. F. K. Fisher, who adored sole, wouldn't let the maître d'hôtel cut away these crinkly bones, as they do in fancy restaurants, because she wanted to enjoy every last bit of the fish.

Sole Meunière

Here is a famous recipe for a prized fish, as simple as it is deli-cious. Dredge a whole Dover sole in flour—something the miller's wife, *la meunière,* always had on hand—and sauté it in butter, on each side, until the coating is crisp and golden and the firm flesh is tender. Sprinkle on chopped parsley, pour over a few spoons of sizzling nut-brown butter, *beurre noisette,* and it's done.

The only challenging part may be finding the authentic fish for the dish, the true Dover sole, the flatfish that comes only from the English Channel and other faraway waters. No domes-tic sole has flesh with such delicate flavor and satisfying texture; moreover, it stays intact in the sauté pan. While imported Dover sole can be found at fine specialty fish stores, it's frequently unavailable and always expensive. For a special-occasion meal, though, it's absolutely worth the cost, certainly cheaper than a flight to London or Paris for a *sole meunière* dinner at a fine restaurant. (See the opposite page for other, more readily avail-able fish to fry *à la meunière.*)

Preparing the dish at home also offers unique pleasures to both cook and guests. As shown in the photos on pages 246–247, skinning and trimming a real Dover sole is a fascinat-ing procedure, and quite easy. Serving the fish can be elegant or casual, as you please. In fine restaurants, the maître d'hôtel will lift off the top fillets, remove the central bones, and reassemble the sole, before saucing it and serving. You can do this in the kitchen and bring each guest a perfectly boneless fish. Or let guests have the enjoyment of doing it themselves, eating their way from top to bottom, and removing the bones when they get to them. Provide guests with a plate to which they can remove the bones and scraps—and offer tips on technique for those who need it. The photos on page 235 show how to fillet and reassemble a whole cooked fish. Use the same techniques for your sautéed Dover sole, but don't remove the crisp skin—it's delicious.

Fish Fillets for Sautéing à la Meunière

Numerous kinds of flatfish and round-fish fillets can be lightly floured and sautéed for a quick and tasty dish, even if they don't have the exceptional qualities of imported Dover sole. Flatfish fillets labeled simply as flounder or "fillets of sole" are always suitable. If the fish varieties are identified, particularly good choices are gray sole, lemon sole, winter flounder, and yellowtail flounder on the East Coast; and petrale sole, rex sole, and rock sole on the West Coast. Do *not* choose the inferior Pacific flounder marketed in the West as "Dover sole"; it's nothing like the real thing. In fact, all of the flatfish caught in American waters and called "sole" are actually species of flounder, including the desirable varieties just named.

You can also sauté fillets of round fish like salmon, snapper, and bluefish. Small whole trout are another possibility.

To sauté

Whatever the variety, use small fillets, of 4 to 6 ounces. As in the master recipe, film your frying pan with butter and oil, and lay in as many floured fillets as will fit easily. Sauté only a minute or two on each side, until the skin is crisped and the flesh is just springy rather than squashy. Turn the fillets carefully, as soft-fleshed varieties can break apart. Finish with *beurre noisette* (page 247).

Jacques

For sautéing, whole gray sole is a particularly good alternative to Dover sole. The top gray skin will not peel off, but you can slice it off with a sharp knife, using the technique for skinning a fish fillet (see page 219). Turn the fish top skin down, loosen a flap of skin near the tail so you can grab it, then cut the skin away using a jigsaw motion. Trim off any pieces of skin that stick to the flesh, and then continue to trim the fish as with Dover sole.

Another method for Dover sole is grilling. It's the *only* sole, in my opinion, that grills well—it is delicious. The flesh is so firm, you can pick it up and turn it over like a steak and it won't fall apart. Leave on the white skin, previously seasoned, for grilling, as it helps hold the fish together and is quite tender. I also prefer to use real wood or charcoal rather than briquettes in the grill. Charcoal makes a very hot fire and its good flavor permeates the fish.

My wife and I both love the roe that's hidden in the belly side of sole. To get it out in one piece, cut into that side carefully and remove it, rather than pushing it out as you see in the photo on page 247. Sauté the roe briefly in butter for a real treat.

With a spoon, scrape the scales off the white skin, then rinse the fish under water. (If you are going to peel off the white skin, as Julia does, then scaling is unnecessary.)

Trim the tail and loosen enough of the dark skin so you can get hold of it.

Grasping the skin in one hand, pull it off in one piece while holding the fish steady with your other hand. The skin will peel off easily. (Peel off the white skin in the same way, if you wish.)

Sole Meunière

Yield: 2 whole fish, serving 2

    2 Dover sole, each approximately
       1 pound
    ⅛ tsp salt
    ⅛ tsp freshly ground pepper
    ⅓ cup or so flour, in a large flat platter
       or on wax paper, for dredging
    2 Tbs vegetable oil
    2 Tbs unsalted butter

For the *beurre noisette*

    2 Tbs chopped fresh parsley
    2 to 3 Tbs unsalted butter
    1 Tbs capers, drained
    1 Tbs freshly squeezed lemon juice

Special equipment

    One very large (more than 12 inches top
       diameter) non-stick or heavy frying
       pan, or 2 large pans; 2 spatulas for
       turning the fish; a medium pan for the
       beurre noisette; a warm serving platter,
       or warm dinner plates

Sautéing the sole

Prepare the fish, as detailed in the photographs here, removing the scales, black skin, head, roe, and fins.

Set the frying pan or pans over medium-high heat. Season both sides of the fish with the salt and pepper. Just before cooking, holding the fish by the tail, dredge first one side, then the other in the flour. Press lightly to coat, then shake off the excess. Swirl the oil and butter in the pan and, when the butter foam subsides, lay in the fish, white skin side down. Repeat with the second fish.

Sauté for 4 to 5 minutes, until nicely browned on the first side. Turn the fish over carefully with the spatulas and sauté for 4 to 5 minutes or more, until crispy and golden brown. To check for doneness, stick a sharp knife into the top fillet, along the center line, and push gently to one side; the flesh should separate easily from the center bone and no pinkness should be visible.

As soon as the fish are done, remove to the warm platter, skin side up, or to individual plates. (At this point, you can fillet the fish before making the sauce. Follow the procedure shown on page 235, to lift off the top fillets, remove the central bones, and reassemble.)

Slice off the head with a diagonal cut of the knife.

Finishing with *beurre noisette*

Sprinkle half the chopped parsley on each fish. Place the clean medium-sized pan over high heat with the fresh butter. Watch the butter carefully as it melts, bubbles, and starts to brown. Remove the pan from the heat, and, as the butter darkens to a hazelnut color, toss in the capers and the lemon juice and swirl together. Pour the sizzling butter over the 2 fish, crisping the parsley, and serve immediately.

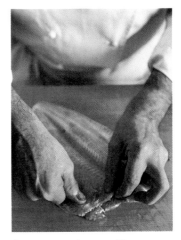

Squeeze out the roe with your thumb or with the handle of a knife (or, if you want to have the roe whole to eat, cut it out with a sharp knife).

With scissors, trim off the side bones. Note that all the skin and trimmings can be saved for stock.

Julia on Lobsters

Buying and storing live lobsters. Live lobsters bought out of a holding tank must be very lively. When picked up, they should be waving their claws and flapping their tails up against their chests. Buy them the day you are going to cook them and at the last minute before coming home so they will not be sitting in a warm closed car. Keep them cool—from 40° to 60°F. I like to store them in a big brown paper shopping bag in which I have pierced some holes for air circulation, and I keep them in the fridge.

What size to buy? When you are serving one whole lobster per person, the 1¼-pound so-called chicken lobster is the most popular choice; it is easy enough to handle, it cooks in 13 minutes, and can give anyone determined to pick out all the meat 3¼ ounces. Larger sizes require bigger pots, of course, but I have not found the meat of larger lobsters any tougher than that of the smaller ones. In full winter, the shells are certainly harder.

Tough lobsters. "Why are lobsters sometimes tough?" I have been disappointed, particularly in restaurants and on buffet tables. So we posed this query to all our sources, and the unanimous response was "overcooking." However, I still wonder if this is the only reason. So far we have no answer.

Notes on the cooking of live lobsters. It would be wonderful to have an immense cauldron of boiling seawater to cook your lobsters in. It's so easy to drop them in, the water stays at the boil, you set your timer, and that's it—the perfect boiled lobster every time. Unless you have that ideal situation, steaming rather than boiling seems the best solution for the home cook. It is of absolute importance in either case that you use a big enough pot. Equally important for steaming is a really tight cover; otherwise you must improvise (I think of the rented summer houses I have cooked lobsters in!). Find a pizza pan or a baking sheet, for instance, and make it a tight cover by weighting it down with a rock (not too heavy a one, though, since you don't want to convert the pot into a pressure cooker!)—you want the steam to escape only by its own pressure. If you do not have a tight fit you cannot time correctly, and the lobsters will be overcooked, which does toughen them, or undercooked and inedible.

Pot sizes. A 5-gallon pot holds 6 lobsters, 1¼ pounds each; 4 lobsters, 1½ pounds each; and 2 lobsters, 3 pounds each. It is recommended that the lobsters have a rack to sit on (or you could use small stones). These requirements make steaming easier, but often you don't have the equipment away from home. I have had disastrous results when piling several layers of lobsters atop one another; now I will only do a little bit of overcrowding if forced, but I prefer to cook them in 2 or 3 batches.

Amounts of meat per lobster. A hard-shell 1-pound lobster produces about 3½ ounces of meat, while a jumbo of 2½ pounds gives some 4½ ounces, or only an ounce more! Lobsters give a little less in the summer when shedding and a little more in the winter when fully hard-shelled.

Steaming timetable. I have checked with various official and unofficial sources in the New England area, and the following timings are generally agreed upon:

WEIGHT	MINUTES
1-pound "chicken"	10
1¼-pound "chicken"	12–13
1½-pound "select"	14–15
2-pound "select"	18
2½-pound "select"	20
4–5-pound "jumbo"	21–25
5 pounds	40–45

Sources

Maine Lobster Promotion Council, 382 Harlow Street, Bangor, ME 04401

Lobster Institute, 22 Coburn Hall, University of Maine, Orono, ME 04469

Lobster at Home, by Jasper White (Scribner, 1998). Jasper White is one of Boston's leading chefs and is famous as a specialist on the lobster.

Purveyors

Legal Seafoods Inc., 33 Everett Street, Allston, MA 02134

James Hook Lobster Co., 15 Northern Avenue, Boston, MA 02210

Steamed Lobsters

This recipe is for six or more lobsters, but the general system applies equally well for two or three. I am assuming you are having an informal lobster feast, each to his own with finger bowls and piles of paper napkins, on a big dining table covered with newspapers. In my house we don't serve much else but pilot crackers, a big bowl of cole slaw, and our favorite white wine for lobsters—a chilled Alsatian gewürztraminer.

Ingredients for 6

Fresh seawater, or tap water with 1½ tsp salt per quart

6 live lobsters, 1¼ pounds each (all the same weight, if possible)

Fresh lemon quarters, little pots or dishes of melted butter and/or olive oil, as suggested accompaniments

Special equipment

A 5-gallon pot with steamer rack insert (or stones), a tight-fitting pot cover, and a weight of some sort to hold in both the steam and the lobsters

Lobster shears (see photos, pages 250–251) and/or a nutcracker; a cleaver or heavy knife; tongs for lifting

A small stout knife for testing

A big bowl on the table, for the shells to come

Pour seawater or salted water into the pot to a depth of 2 inches. Insert the rack, cover the pot, and bring to the rapid boil over highest heat until the steam is pushing its way out. Uncover and rapidly add the lobsters head first. Cover the pot at once, and weight it down to make a tight seal (but not a pressure cooker!).

As soon as the water is steaming again, time the lobsters for exactly 13 minutes. When time is up, uncover the pot, remove a lobster, and rapidly test for doneness. The long antennas at the head should pull out easily—a useful indication but not foolproof. To be sure, turn the lobster on its back and plunge your stout knife into the lengthwise center of the chest; twist the chest open enough so that you can see the contents. If all black, the lobster needs several minutes' more cooking. When you see softly set, pale-green tomalley and, if you have a female, salmon-red roe, the lobsters are done.

Drain the lobster before serving

Hold it, head and claws up, vertically, to drain any water down into the body. Then make an opening at the front of the head shell. Now hold up the lobster vertically the other way, by its tail, and drain any water out through the head. The lobster is now ready to serve.

Julia on How to Eat a Boiled or Steamed Lobster

Remove the tail section. Grip the chest section in your left hand and the tail section in your right hand. Firmly twist the tail section clockwise to break tail from chest. (Note that if the lobster is not quite done, the tomalley—the matter inside the chest—will be black rather than a just-coagulated light green. See page 249 to avoid this problem.)

Push out the tail meat. Break or snip off the flippers at the end of the tail and push out the meat with your index and third fingers.

Remove the intestinal vein. With your sharp little knife, slit open the tail meat at the middle of its outside curve to reveal the intestinal vein, which may be black, brown, or translucent. Lift it up and pull it away from its attachment at the end of the flesh; discard it.

Remove the tomalley (the green matter) and the red roe (the eggs, if a female). Spoon this out of the chest into a small bowl, adding the rest when you open the whole chest, later. Reserve. Note that some people are either afraid of it or have no idea that this is a creamy lobster treasure, a most desirable part of the

In the female lobster (left), the two tiny swimmerets underneath the tail where it joins the chest are fringed with hair. The male swimmerets are clean and pointed.

The body meat is twisted away from the tail section.

beast. It gives color and flavor to lobster bisque, lobster mayonnaise, and lobster sauces. The roe, which is much prized, gives, for instance, a beautiful rosy color to my Lobster Stew on page 252.

The claws. Twist off the claw joints with claws attached. Twist claws from joints. If you don't have the lobster shears shown here, whack or crack open the claw shells and pick out the meat as best you can. With shears, starting at the open end, cut open the claw shells as shown, going up to the shell opening at the small pincer claw. Hoping to remove all of the claw and pincer meat in one piece, bend the pincer claw back and forth (not up and down) to break its attachment to the main claw shell. With slow and careful movements plus luck, you will now be able to remove the entire claw and pincer meat in one piece, leaving the flat piece of claw cartilage behind. (This is not a necessary maneuver, but it clearly identifies the claw and is a nice little show-off accomplishment.)

The joints. Crack or cut open the claw joints to remove some of the tenderest meat of the lobster.

Note that the tomalley here is still black, which means that the lobster has not been cooked long enough.

Snip off the flippers at the end of the tail so you can push out the meat with your finger.

Twist off the claws from the claw joints.

The little legs. Break the little legs from the chest. Either serve them as is, or cut them off above the joints and squish out the small lengths of meat under a rolling pin. Again, it is some of the tenderest of the lobster meat. If you don't want the bother, chop them up and add to your lobster-stock collection.

The chest. There is tender meat also in the chest, if you want to go all the way. If you don't, do save the chest for your stockpot. In either case, open the chest with your fingers and reach into the head, to pull out and discard the stomach sac—a half-inch membrane-covered object filled with a sandy substance. To get at the meat, cut the chest in half lengthwise and you will find a maze of little cartilaginous pockets enclosing tiny nuggets of the best and finest lobster meat. Lobster fanatics will pick out every bit, and are happy to take their time about it. Even when these scavengers are through, save the remains of the chests for your stockpot.

Try to remove the claw and pincer meat in one piece, using shears if necessary. See perfect extraction.

With scissors, cut through the shell of the joint and remove the meat in one piece.

Using a rolling pin, push out the meat from the little legs.

Push out the body meat with your fingers.

After removing the stomach sac, scrape out the nuggets of meat from the chest.

Julia's Lobster Stew—An Almost Bisque

When you are steaming lobsters, do a couple extra (preferably females, since they have the roe) and save them for lobster stew. We have a fine, rich example here, but not quite the sinfully rich bisque version that is made almost entirely with cream.

Yield: 4 to 6 servings

1½ cups lobster meat, removed
   from shell as illustrated on pages
   250–251, plus tomalley and roe
   (if any), from 2 lobsters, 1¼–1½
   pounds each
6 Tbs unsalted butter, at room
   temperature
4 cups Plain Lobster Stock (page
   44), or part Lobster Stock and
   some fish or chicken stock
1 medium shallot or 2 large
   scallions
Salt and freshly ground white
   pepper
1 large sprig fresh tarragon or
   a big pinch fragrant dried
   tarragon
1 to 2 tsp tomato paste, if needed
2 Tbs cornstarch blended with
   ¼ cup dry white French
   vermouth
½ cup heavy cream (optional)
⅓ cup heavy sour cream
   (optional)
Sprigs of fresh parsley, if needed

Preparing the lobster meat

Remove the meat, keeping the claw meat intact if possible. Carefully cut claw meat in half horizontally and reserve with 4 or 5 thin slices of tail; cut the rest of the meat into dice no more than ⅜-inch-sized. Refrigerate all of this in a covered dish.

The lobster-stew base

Push the tomalley and roe (if any), with an equal amount of soft butter, through a fine-meshed sieve into a small bowl and refrigerate, along with the tomalley-covered sieve. Bring the broth to a simmer, and swish the tomalley-covered sieve in it, to collect all that special flavor. You want to end up with about 3 cups of broth, so do not reduce it too much.

Flavoring the lobster meat

Heat the reserved tomalley butter in an 8-inch stainless-steel saucepan or frying pan. As it comes to the bubble it will turn a beige color—pinky-beige if it contains roe. Fold in the diced lobster meat along with finely minced shallot or scallions and 2 tablespoons of unsalted butter. Season with a little salt and freshly ground white pepper plus a sprig or big pinch of tarragon. If you lack the roe with its good color, fold in a teaspoon or so of tomato paste. Let bubble slowly for 5 minutes, as the lobster picks up a rosy color.

Adding the broth and finishing the stew

Blend ½ cup of the lobster broth into the vermouth-cornstarch mixture, and pour it into the lobster meat along with 3 cups of lobster broth and, if you wish, ½ cup of heavy cream. Simmer another 5 minutes. Meanwhile, warm the reserved lobster claws and tail slices in a small pan with a little butter. Taste very carefully and correct seasoning.

Serving

Serve in soup cups or bowls, topping each with a dollop of sour cream, if you like, upon which you set a warm piece of lobster and a nice leaf of tarragon or sprig of parsley. Accompany with toast points, pastry fleurons, or toasted pita triangles. I would serve with a chilled bottle of Alsatian gewürztraminer.

Another Lobster Idea

We have the background now to do almost anything anyone can think of to do with lobsters. We know how to cook them, how to open them and get all the meat out of the shells. We can also make a lobster stock using those shells, and we can make an especially fine rich sauce out of that stock. We can make a splendid soup. In that soup we learned the secrets of lobster butter made with the tomalley and roe, and in that special brew we warmed our lobster meat to a lovely salmon pink. Now it's time to put some of that acquired talent to work in a dish that is considered by some to be the epitome of lobster cookery.

Lobster à l'Américaine

Yield: 4 to 6 servings

This, simply told, is fresh lobster meat sautéed in butter, simmered in a rich lobster sauce, and enriched in tomalley butter. It would take a lot of space to outline all the steps involved, but since we have them all in this chapter, we need just an order of battle to produce the dish. Why is it called *"à l'Américaine"*? Nobody seems to know. It is certainly not an American recipe. Did some Parisian chef serve it to a famous or wealthy American client, and it became famous? Or was it conceived in Paris at what was once known, apparently, as the Café Americain? Whatever its history, Lobster *à l'Américaine* is one grand dish to present as a first course for six people or a luncheon dish for four, with a fine buttery white wine, such as your best Chardonnay.

> About 2 cups sliced or diced
>   cooked lobster meat, from 3
>   female "chicken" lobsters, $1^{1}/_{4}$
>   pounds each (pages 250–251)
> 1 shallot, minced

> 2 Tbs butter
> A dollop of white wine or ver-
>   mouth
> Salt and freshly ground white
>   pepper
> About $^{1}/_{2}$ cup heavy cream
> $^{2}/_{3}$ to 1 cup Strong Lobster Shell
>   Broth (page 45)
> Tomalley butter (see page 252)
>   (optional)
> A handful fresh parsley or tar-
>   ragon, for garnish

Sauté the lobster meat and shallot for several minutes in the butter, stirring and tossing to heat the lobster nicely. Add the wine and seasonings and simmer a moment, then add the cream and a good $^{2}/_{3}$ cup of the lobster broth. Simmer several minutes while you taste carefully and correct seasoning.

All of this you can do in advance while you decide whether to spoon this fragrant ragout over steamed rice or toast points, or into a pastry shell. When nicely reheated but not boiling, and just before serving, fold in the tomalley butter, if you have some, letting it poach (warm slowly but not simmer or boil) in the sauce for a minute or so, so it gently thickens. Taste again just to check on seasonings, top with a small decoration of herbs, and serve at once.

Nutritional note

You can, of course, leave out some or even every trace of the butter and cream. Simmer the lobster in the broth rather than sautéing it in butter, omit the cream, and omit the final enrichment of butter mixed in with the tomalley. Every deletion, of course, diminishes the whole. However, there is so much natural flavor here that you will still have a good dish that guests will enjoy; and though it may lack a certain fullness, they will never suspect the more sumptuous experience that could have been theirs.

POULTRY

WE HAVE A SMALL AND MIXED FLOCK OF POULTRY RECIPES HERE—SEVEN CHICKENS, three ducks (if you include the giblets), and two turkeys. You don't need many, though. Just one good roast chicken in your cooking repertoire assures you of a fine dinner at least once a week—and here you will find two.

But, more important than the quantity of recipes, our focus in this chapter is on a few excellent cooking methods that will deepen your understanding and enjoyment of cooking birds of all kinds. Proper cutting-up is an important part of every dish here, so you'll find instructions and photos for many practical techniques—trimming, trussing, and carving chicken, dividing ducks and turkeys, boning and stuffing.

Since all birds are built basically the same way, you will become more familiar with these techniques as you cook your way through the chapter. Even if you've never removed the wishbone from a roasting chicken, with attention to the photos you'll have no trouble, and that includes skinning and dividing a duck into nice lean pieces, or taking out every single bone from a turkey to make a splendid galantine.

Of course, those bones—and duck fat—are not to be discarded. Throughout the chapter you'll find ways to use the many bonuses—bones and trimmings for stock; giblets for gravy and salads; pan drippings for sauce; poultry fat for sautéing and vinaigrettes; skin for cracklings. The stock that you make from duck bones in one recipe can be used to deglaze the turkey-roasting pan in another. The satisfying kitchen cycle that starts every time you cook a bird is one of the fundamentals of good home cooking.

Safe Handling of Raw Poultry

You must assume that raw poultry may contain harmful bacteria (including salmonella and campylobacter), but with proper handling and sufficient cooking (see page 261) there is no danger. Discard immediately all the wrappings from the bird and any paper towels used to dry it. Wash, in hot soapy water, all surfaces and utensils—including your hands—that come in contact with the raw poultry. If you touch anything else with unwashed hands, such as a salt shaker or scissors, wash them too.

Julia

A cooking process such as roasting a chicken is inexact—there is no one way that is the right way. Just start with a good chicken and pay attention to how you cook it.

Not everything that I do with my roast chicken is necessarily scientific. Many aspects of my method are based on my feeling and experience. For instance, I *always* give my bird a generous butter massage before I put it in the oven. Why? Because I think the chicken likes it—and, more important, *I* like to give it. I learned the butter massage when I started cooking for the first time in France and would never give it up.

Another aspect of roasting that is very important to me—also a lesson from my early years in France—is making the deglazing sauce from the drippings and brown bits in the roasting pan. These brown bits are the precious, caramelized natural juices, their flavor intensified and concentrated by the process of roasting and basting. When you turn these bits into a "deglazing" sauce, as shown on page 263, you are preserving an essence of pure, delicious chicken. There is nothing better to serve with your roast.

Jacques and I have different techniques in regard to chickens, and that is just as well, since it illustrates our individual approaches in this book—that there are many ways to cook the same thing, be it a roast chicken or a serving

(continued on page 258)

Roast Chicken

A well-roasted chicken is the mark of a fine cook. Even among professionals, it is a source of pride to present a shapely chicken, with beautifully colored skin and perfectly done meat, juicy and tender. There is nothing technically difficult about roasting a chicken, but there are many approaches to take.

In the comments and the several sidebars in this section, we discuss and demonstrate many aspects of roasting—including trimming, stuffing, and trussing a chicken before it goes in the oven and carving it with style at the table. For serving either of our chickens, we suggest a delicious pan sauce (page 263).

Julia's Roast Chicken with Lemon and Herbs

Yield: 4 servings

1 fine, fresh 3½-pound chicken

Salt and pepper

6 fresh sage leaves (or 4 sprigs of fresh tarragon, or ½ tsp dried *herbes de Provence*)

1 large lemon, cut in ¼-inch slices

2 Tbs unsalted butter at room temperature

⅔ cup mixed roughly chopped carrots and onions

For the deglazing sauce

1 Tbs minced shallot or scallion

⅓ cup dry vermouth or dry white wine

⅔ cup chicken stock

1 Tbs or so unsalted butter (optional)

Special equipment

A roasting pan 2 inches deep; a V-shaped roasting rack; a pastry brush for basting; a board or platter for resting and carving; cotton kitchen twine

Preparing the chicken

Set the rack on the lower middle level and preheat the oven to 425°F.

Rinse the chicken thoroughly, inside and out, under hot water, then dry it with paper towels. Remove any lumps of fat from inside the cavity near the tail opening.

To make carving easier, remove the wishbone, as shown in the photo on page 259. Lift the flap of neck skin and insert a thin, sharp knife into each end of the breast; then slice diagonally along both sides of the wishbone. Use your finger and thumb to loosen the bone, pry it out at the top, and pull it down. If it breaks, carefully wiggle out the pieces.

Trim the small bony protrusions, or "nubbins," from the wing-tip joint. Then fold the wings up against the breast, where they will be held in place by the V-rack.

Salt and pepper the cavity and stuff it with the sage leaves and 3 or 4 thick slices of lemon; give the slices a squeeze as you put them in. Massage the butter over the entire chicken skin, including undersides, then salt generously.

Tie the ends of the drumsticks together with twine. Arrange the chicken breast up on the rack in the roasting pan and tuck the flap of neck skin underneath. Finally, squeeze the juice of the remaining lemon pieces all over the top of the chicken.

Roasting the chicken

Set the roasting pan in the oven. After 15 minutes, lower heat to 350°F. When the chicken is beginning to brown rapidly, baste the chicken with accumulated pan juices. Roast for an hour, adding the onions and carrots after 30 minutes and basting several times. Very carefully test for doneness (as described on page 261), checking for easy movement in the leg joint and clear color in the juices. Return it to the oven if there is any

Jacques

Roast chicken is family food—

we have it every week at my house. My favorite part, in fact, is the carcass, after I have carved off all the meaty pieces. I love the bones, with so much juicy meat still on them, along with a lettuce salad dressed with the chicken fat and pan juices.

When I want to serve a chicken that is more elegant, I will make it as I do on the next page, with a stuffing under the breast skin. This gives the roast a distinctive look, but the primary purpose is to bring flavor to the meat—more directly than if you just put herbs or other aromatic ingredients in the cavity. Here I use sautéed shallots and fresh savory, but you can use many kinds of flavoring agents—sautéed or not—such as onions, garlic, other herbs or spices, or chopped mushrooms. A classic French way is to slip slices of truffle under the breast skin, and because the chicken then appears both white and black, it's called *en demi-deuille*—"half in mourning."

To me it is very important to place the chicken on its sides for all but 10 minutes of roasting. The meat around the joint of the thigh and drumstick needs the most cooking, and on its side, this part of the leg is in direct contact with the heat. The skin on the sides also becomes golden and crisp. For this technique, it is essential to use a heavy-bottomed roasting pan with good heat

(continued on page 259)

of spinach. For instance, I like to roast my chicken on a V-shaped rack in a shallow roasting pan 2 inches deep and just large enough to hold the rack and chicken, where the oven heat can circulate around the bird for even browning. The V-shape of the rack also holds the chicken in shape, so I needn't truss it, except for tying the drumstick ends together. There are some knowledgeable cooks who maintain that trussing is unnecessary, and they leave the legs splayed. But this, I believe, can lead to overcooked drumsticks—and it gives the chicken a rather wanton look.

Although I used to make a great to-do about turning the chicken from one side to the other, roasting it upside down, and so forth, I have not found that all the fuss makes for a better small roasted chicken. Now when I have a nice chicken up to about 3½ pounds, I roast it breast up for its entire time in the oven. It is so easy to do, and so good to eat.

I do believe in basting with the accumulated juices in the pan, and I start after 15 minutes of roasting. The chicken goes in at 425°F for its 15-minute preliminary browning, and at that point it gets its first rapid basting, brushed on with the accumulated juices in the pan. Then the roasting continues at 350°F throughout, with a rapid basting every 15 to 20 minutes. After 30 minutes, I like to strew a small handful of chopped carrots and onions into the pan to flavor the juices for my sauce.

sign of pinkness. (A small chicken will roast in about 1¼ hours; a larger one may take 1½ hours or more.)

When done, remove the chicken from the rack and set it on a board to rest for 15 minutes before carving. This allows the juices to retreat back into the flesh.

Final steps

While the chicken is resting, make the deglazing sauce in the roasting pan (see page 263).

To carve the chicken, see the simple method detailed in the photos on page 264. Drizzle about half the pan sauce over the carved pieces and serve, passing the rest of the sauce.

Jacques's Savory-Stuffed Roast Chicken

Yield: 4 or 5 servings

For the stuffing

 1 Tbs unsalted butter
 1 tsp virgin olive oil
 ½ cup minced shallots (4 or more large
  shallots)
 4 Tbs chopped fresh parsley
 1 Tbs finely chopped fresh savory
 ⅛ tsp salt
 ⅛ tsp freshly ground pepper
 1 chicken, 3½ to 4 pounds

 ¼ tsp salt for sprinkling on the chicken
 Butter or vegetable oil for the roasting
  pan

For the deglazing sauce

 1 Tbs minced shallot
 ⅓ cup dry vermouth or dry white wine
 ⅔ cup chicken stock

Special equipment

A small frying pan; a shallow-sided heavy aluminum or copper roasting pan or heavy cast-iron skillet, just large enough to hold the trussed chicken; a 1-quart glass measuring cup or deep bowl; cotton kitchen twine; a basting brush; a board or platter for resting and carving

Preparing the herb stuffing

Preheat oven to 425°F.

Heat the butter and olive oil in the frying pan over medium heat. When hot, add the shallots, parsley, savory, salt, and pepper, stirring well and tossing in the pan. Cook for about a minute, just until the shallots begin to soften. Scrape the mixture onto a plate to cool.

Preparing the chicken

Remove any lumps of fat from inside the cavity near the tail.

To make carving easier, remove the wishbone, as shown here. Lift the flap of neck skin and insert a thin, sharp knife into each end of the breast; then slice diagonally along both sides of the wishbone. Use your finger and thumb to loosen the bone, pry it out at the top, and pull it down. Try to remove it whole—if it breaks, carefully wiggle out the pieces.

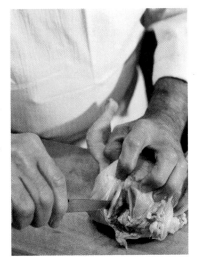

Lift the flap of neck skin to expose the wishbone. Using a knife, loosen the bone from the flesh around it, then pry it out with your thumb and fingers.

Jacques (continued from page 257)

diffusion, so the chicken browns and the juices crystallize but nothing burns on the bottom. Heavy aluminum or copper pans have the best heat transfer, although you can also roast a small chicken in an ovenproof non-stick skillet or a heavy cast-iron skillet. If you are worried that the skin will stick to the pan, put a lightly greased piece of parchment in the bottom.

I also believe in roasting a chicken at a high temperature to get a beautifully brown, crisp skin without overcooking the meat.

I recommend a 425°F oven for the chicken in this recipe—the smaller the chicken, the higher the temperature—and if you need to baste, do it very quickly, or temporarily remove the pan from the oven, shut the door quickly, baste, and then return the chicken to the oven. Otherwise, much heat may be dissipated, and the chicken ends up having to cook too long, or it never gets brown. My solution is to baste only a couple of times, during the last 15 to 20 minutes, when the chicken is roasting on its back and is already nicely browning. Constant basting isn't really necessary if the chicken is cooked mostly on its side; gravity brings the juices down into the breast.

Julia on Getting a Good Chicken

I don't think it is easy to buy a good chicken unless one has access to special sources. I want a fine, fresh, top-quality chicken that has never been frozen and thawed and frozen and thawed and/or kept at almost freezing so long that its flesh shreds and is mushy. I don't care what it says about itself, such as "organic," "naturally grown," or "free-range"; I want a chicken with great flavor and fresh texture, and I will go to great pains to find that chicken. Furthermore, I am ready to pay for it. How can you tell the quality of a fresh chicken by looking at it? If it has freezer burn or some such obvious blemish you won't buy it, but otherwise even the experts can't tell, which means, as usual, that you must find a reputable market and a butcher whose word you can believe.

Jacques's Savory-Stuffed Roast Chicken (continued)

Cut the wings at the "elbow" joint (see photo). Use the trimmed parts in stock (or form them into "lollipops"; see page 266).

Place the chicken on its back. To loosen the breast skin, lift the neck flap and work your fingers between the skin and the flesh, taking care not to puncture the skin. Slide your fingers down the breast and to either side along the legs, especially the thighs.

Stand the chicken on its tail end in the measuring cup or bowl; hook the wing sections over the rim, to keep the bird upright. Hold the neck flap away from the breast and stuff the cooled herb mixture down between the skin and the flesh, pushing it gently with your fingers, including the sides. Lay the chicken on its back, tuck the neck skin underneath, and smooth the surface, to distribute the stuffing evenly over the entire breast.

Truss the chicken as shown in the photos on page 262.

Cut the wings off at the joints, leaving only the meaty section attached to the shoulder.

Roasting the chicken

Sprinkle ¼ teaspoon salt all over the chicken. Grease the center of the roasting pan with a small amount of butter or a dash of oil to prevent sticking (or place a small piece of oiled parchment paper in the pan bottom). Set the chicken on its side in the greased pan and place in the oven.

With the chicken on its back, slide your fingers between the skin and the flesh and push stuffing in all around.

Roast for 25 minutes for a 3½-pound chicken (3 or 4 minutes longer for a 4-pound bird), then turn the chicken onto its other side, grasping it with kitchen tongs or towels. The first side on which it rested will be deeply colored; be careful not to tear the skin when turning. Lower the heat to 400°F and roast for another 25 to 28 minutes, depending on size, then turn the chicken breast side up; baste with the pan juices. Roast for 15 to 20 minutes and baste once again during this final cooking.

Julia on Getting Good Chicken

I don't think it is easy to buy a good chicken unless one has access to special sources. I want a fine, fresh, top-quality chicken that has never been frozen and thawed and frozen and thawed and/or kept at almost freezing so long that its flesh shreds and is mushy. I don't care what it says about itself, such as "organic," "naturally grown," or "free-range"; I want a chicken with great flavor and fresh texture, and I will go to great pains to find that chicken. Furthermore, I am ready to pay for it. How can you tell the quality of a fresh chicken by looking at it? If it has freezer burn or some such obvious blemish you won't buy it, but otherwise even the experts can't tell, which means, as usual, that you must find a reputable market and a butcher whose word you can believe.

Jacques's Savory-Stuffed Roast Chicken (continued)

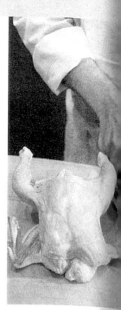

Cut the wings at the "elbow" joint (see photo). Use the trimmed parts in stock (or form them into "lollipops"; see page 266).

Place the chicken on its back. To loosen the breast skin, lift the neck flap and work your fingers between the skin and the flesh, taking care not to puncture the skin. Slide your fingers down the breast and to either side along the legs, especially the thighs.

Cut the wings off at the joints, leaving only the meaty section attached to the shoulder.

Stand the chicken on its tail end in the measuring cup or bowl; hook the wing sections over the rim, to keep the bird upright. Hold the neck flap away from the breast and stuff the cooled herb mixture down between the skin and the flesh, pushing it gently with your fingers, including the sides. Lay the chicken on its back, tuck the neck skin underneath, and smooth the surface, to distribute the stuffing evenly over the entire breast.

Truss the chicken as shown in the photos on page 262.

Roasting the chicken

Sprinkle ¼ teaspoon salt all over the chicken. Grease the center of the roasting pan with a small amount of butter or a dash of oil to prevent sticking (or place a small piece of

With the chicken on its back, slide your fingers between the skin and the flesh and push stuffing in all around.

oiled parchment paper in the pan bottom). Set the chicken on its side in the greased pan and place in the oven.

Roast for 25 minutes for a 3½-pound chicken (3 or 4 minutes longer for a 4-pound bird), then turn the chicken onto its other side, grasping it with kitchen tongs or towels. The first side on which it rested will be deeply colored; be careful not to tear the skin when turning. Lower the heat to 400°F and roast for another 25 to 28 minutes, depending on size, then turn the chicken breast side up; baste with the pan juices. Roast for 15 to 20 minutes and baste once again during this final cooking.

Jacques's Method for Trussing a Roasting Chicken

Trussing a roasting chicken is mainly for appearance, to form a compact and plump bird, but it also makes it easier to set the bird on its side, to turn it, and to hold in any loose stuffing. This simple truss is especially useful in my recipe, as it does not disturb the stuffing under the breast skin.

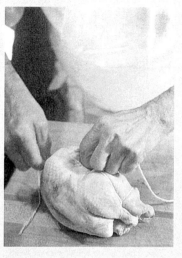

Draw the twine along both sides of the chicken, over the wing stubs and around the neck end. The twine should go over the neck bone, to anchor the truss and prevent it from slipping under the bird.

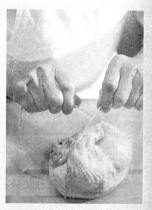

Tie the ends of the twine together with several hitches, near the neck or on the side—turn the chicken on its side, as shown. Tighten the twine/hitches, drawing the chicken into a plump shape, and secure with a top knot.

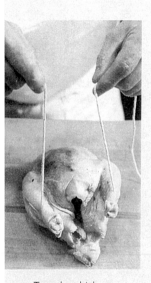

Turn the chicken so the neck end is nearest to you. Slide the twine under the tail and draw it up around the drumstick tips.

Cross the twine above the chicken. Loop down and slide the twine under the drumsticks. Pull tight, bringing the tail and leg ends together, closing the cavity.

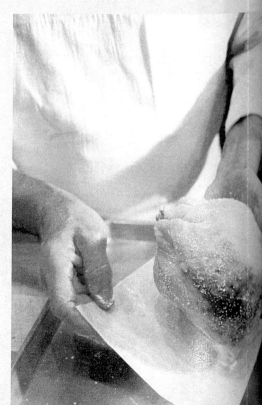

The trussed chicken

Jacques on Getting a Good Chicken

When I am shopping, I always try to get real organic, free-range chickens. I find that they have more flavor—a result, I believe, of more natural diet and growing conditions. The environment for mass-produced chickens, where the noise levels are horrible and the birds don't have any space, leads to stress that affects their growth. I can taste the difference in both the eggs and the meat from free-range chickens (more so in the eggs than in the meat). I also will often buy chickens from kosher butchers, since the selection and slaughtering of the birds tend to make them of better quality.

But even regular supermarket chickens in the United States are on the whole excellent buys for the price, and although people often say that chickens don't taste as good as they used to, I believe ordinary supermarket chickens are better today. Thanks to improvements from cross-breeding, the meat is more moist and tender than it has ever been. When I was a teenage apprentice, the chicken had to be constantly basted and rested upside down after roasting, in order to keep the breast moist, but today it is almost impossible to dry out the breast. I still turn the chicken over for resting—old habits don't change easily—but I hardly ever baste.

The famous chickens of Bresse, the region where I come from, have blue legs, white plumage, and a very thin skin. They can be excellent but very expensive.

I had an interesting experience a couple of years ago when I was visiting my friend Jean Claude in upstate New York. A farmer had given him a dozen free-range chickens, which we slaughtered and plucked and eviscerated, putting most of them away in the freezer. But when we cooked a few of them, the aroma was so distinctive I thought I was nine years old again—for me the taste was fantastic. However, when my friend's daughters tasted them, they found the flesh tough and the flavor too strong. So I am not so sure that most people would be happy if chickens were really the way they used to be.

A Natural Sauce from the Roasting Pan

The juices from any roast—poultry or meat—caramelize in the pan, leaving a residue of brown glaze with intense flavor. In the process called "deglazing," we melt these brown bits in hot liquid (wine, stock, and/or water), to create a quick sauce of concentrated natural essences. Make this pan sauce for either of our roast chickens, or the split roasted chicken on page 268.

Yield: About 1 cup

1 to 2 Tbs minced shallots
⅓ cup dry white French vermouth
   or dry white wine
⅔ cup or more chicken stock
Salt and freshly ground pepper
1 to 2 Tbs unsalted butter (optional)

Remove the chicken to rest; have ready a strainer set over a small saucepan. Tilt the roasting pan so the remaining fat and juices accumulate in one corner. Carefully spoon off most of the fat (reserve for vinaigrette or other uses).

Place the roasting pan on a stove burner over medium heat; add the shallots and stir for a moment, until sizzling. Pour in the wine or vermouth and the stock and heat rapidly to a simmer, scraping up all the glazed bits in the pan. Cook briefly until the glaze is melted. Strain into the saucepan, pressing the strained bits to release their juice. (If you like the bits, don't strain.)

Taste the sauce and adjust seasoning; you may add more wine or stock, and boil it down a bit to thicken. Whisk in the butter just before serving, if you wish, for a richer finish.

If you find it difficult to deglaze a large roasting pan over a burner, first scrape the defatted juices and as much of the glazed bits as you can into the saucepan. Pour a small amount of boiling water into the roasting pan and scrape to melt the remaining glaze. Add to the saucepan with the shallots, wine, and stock; bring to the boil and cook until thickened. Strain, and whisk in optional butter.

Test the chicken for doneness (see sidebar); return to the oven for a few minutes if necessary.

Remove the chicken to a cutting board, place it on one side or breast down, so the juices flow into the breast meat, and let rest for 15 minutes.

Final steps

Make the deglazing sauce in the roasting pan (see page 263). Tip the pan to one side and skim as much fat as possible off the top of the juice. Stir in the minced shallot and then the vermouth and chicken stock. Add the juices accumulated on the carving board and bring to a boil.

To carve the chicken, see the simple method detailed in the photos on page 264. Drizzle about half the pan sauce over the carved pieces and serve, passing the rest of the sauce.

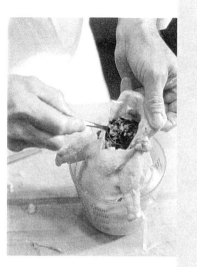

Set the chicken in a large measuring cup with the trimmed wings hooked over the rim, and spoon in the remainder of the herb mixture, pushing it down between the skin and the flesh.

When Is a Roast Chicken Done?

Though a roast chicken may look and smell done, you must check carefully. It is not only unappetizing to find pink, undercooked meat when you carve the chicken, it is unsafe, since bacteria can still be alive. If your chicken is not fully roasted, it must go back in the oven—better to have it cooked slightly more than slightly less.

Here are several ways to test if your chicken is done:

Pierce the breast with the tines of a carving fork and press to bring up juices. They should be clear yellow, without a trace of pink.

Pierce the skin under the thigh; the juices should be perfectly clear yellow. The legs should move quite easily up and down in the hip sockets when wiggled, and the thighs and drumsticks should feel tender to the touch.

The definitive test is to lift the chicken and pour the juice from the cavity. If you see any pinkness, the chicken is not done.

Jacques on Getting a Good Chicken

When I am shopping, I always try to get real organic, free-range chickens. I find that they have more flavor—a result, I believe, of more natural diet and growing conditions. The environment for mass-produced chickens, where the noise levels are horrible and the birds don't have any space, leads to stress that affects their growth. I can taste the difference in both the eggs and the meat from free-range chickens (more so in the eggs than in the meat). I also will often buy chickens from kosher butchers, since the selection and slaughtering of the birds tend to make them of better quality.

But even regular supermarket chickens in the United States are on the whole excellent buys for the price, and although people often say that chickens don't taste as good as they used to, I believe ordinary supermarket chickens are better today. Thanks to improvements from cross-breeding, the meat is more moist and tender than it has ever been. When I was a teenage apprentice, the chicken had to be constantly basted and rested upside down after roasting, in order to keep the breast moist, but today it is almost impossible to dry out the breast. I still turn the chicken over for resting—old habits don't change easily—but I hardly ever baste.

The famous chickens of Bresse, the region where I come from, have blue legs, white plumage, and a very thin skin. They can be excellent but very expensive.

I had an interesting experience a couple of years ago when I was visiting my friend Jean Claude in upstate New York. A farmer had given him a dozen free-range chickens, which we slaughtered and plucked and eviscerated, putting most of them away in the freezer. But when we cooked a few of them, the aroma was so distinctive I thought I was nine years old again—for me the taste was fantastic. However, when my friend's daughters tasted them, they found the flesh tough and the flavor too strong. So I am not so sure that most people would be happy if chickens were really the way they used to be.

A Natural Sauce from the Roasting Pan

The juices from any roast—poultry or meat—caramelize in the pan, leaving a residue of brown glaze with intense flavor. In the process called "deglazing," we melt these brown bits in hot liquid (wine, stock, and/or water), to create a quick sauce of concentrated natural essences. Make this pan sauce for either of our roast chickens, or the split roasted chicken on page 268.

Yield: About 1 cup

1 to 2 Tbs minced shallots
⅓ cup dry white French vermouth
  or dry white wine
⅔ cup or more chicken stock
Salt and freshly ground pepper
1 to 2 Tbs unsalted butter (optional)

Remove the chicken to rest; have ready a strainer set over a small saucepan. Tilt the roasting pan so the remaining fat and juices accumulate in one corner. Carefully spoon off most of the fat (reserve for vinaigrette or other uses).

Place the roasting pan on a stove burner over medium heat; add the shallots and stir for a moment, until sizzling. Pour in the wine or vermouth and the stock and heat rapidly to a simmer, scraping up all the glazed bits in the pan. Cook briefly until the glaze is melted. Strain into the saucepan, pressing the strained bits to release their juice. (If you like the bits, don't strain.)

Taste the sauce and adjust seasoning; you may add more wine or stock, and boil it down a bit to thicken. Whisk in the butter just before serving, if you wish, for a richer finish.

If you find it difficult to deglaze a large roasting pan over a burner, first scrape the defatted juices and as much of the glazed bits as you can into the saucepan. Pour a small amount of boiling water into the roasting pan and scrape to melt the remaining glaze. Add to the saucepan with the shallots, wine, and stock; bring to the boil and cook until thickened. Strain, and whisk in optional butter.

Carving a Roast Chicken

This simple carving method is suitable for either of our roast chickens:

Holding the fork in the breast, cut through the shoulder joint under the wing; continue to slice through the outer part of breast, and remove the piece of breast meat with wing attached. Repeat on the other side. Turn chicken and remove leg and outer breast piece, as on first side.

Remove the sternum, or center of the breast, by pulling it away from the carcass in one piece.

Remove any trussing strings and lay the roast chicken on its side. Holding your fork in the thick part of the drumstick, cut through the skin all around the thigh and leg. Lift the leg and pull away, holding down chicken with your knife. The thigh will break off at the hip joint. Cut free, and separate drumstick from thigh if you want.

The separated pieces

Jacques's Roast Chicken "Salad"

Not at all your usual chicken salad, this is a delicious way to serve nicely carved roast-chicken pieces on a bed of fresh lettuce leaves dressed with "roast-chicken vinaigrette." Add sliced fresh tomatoes when they are in season.

Yield: 4 servings

For the vinaigrette
> 2 Tbs red-wine vinegar
> 1 Tbs Dijon-style prepared mustard
> 1 tsp minced garlic
> ¼ tsp salt
> ¼ tsp freshly ground black pepper
> 1 to 2 Tbs warm chicken fat, from the
>   roasting pan
> 3 Tbs extra-virgin olive oil
>
> 6 to 8 cups Boston lettuce leaves,
>   trimmed, washed, and dried
>   (see photos on page 104)
> A roast chicken (either of our recipes),
>   carved into pieces
> Juices from the chicken-roasting pan

To prepare the dressing, whisk together the vinegar, mustard, minced garlic, salt, and pepper in a small bowl. Drizzle in a tablespoon of the chicken fat and the olive oil, whisking steadily, to make an emulsified vinaigrette. Taste and adjust the seasonings, and add more fat or some of the deglazed pan juices, for more chicken flavor.

Toss the lettuce with 3 or 4 tablespoons of the dressing to coat lightly, and distribute the leaves to cover a serving platter. Arrange the carved pieces of chicken on top of the lettuce and drizzle them with spoonfuls of pan sauce and vinaigrette. Serve with more pan sauce and vinaigrette on the side.

Jacques's Chicken Wing "Lollipops"

With a few twists, you can transform the outer sections of a chicken wing into a cleverly shaped "lollipop" to serve as an appetizer. I learned this technique from Danny Kaye, who was not only a great entertainer but an expert on Chinese cooking. Chinese chefs use these "lollipops" in stir-fries and soup, and Japanese cooks prepare them teriyaki-style.

They are also delicious Southern-fried. I dip them into milk, then roll them in cracker crumbs and deep-fry them. They make a great finger food, piled in a bowl made from Savoy cabbage leaves. Save the trimmed wing sections from your roaster and use packaged wings from the market as well.

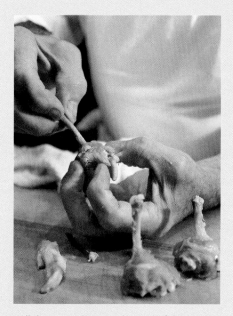

Pull the meat down to the end of the large bone, turning the skin inside out to form the "lollipop."

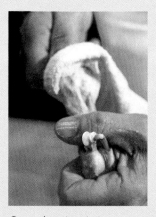

Grasp the wing tip in one hand (with a towel for a good grip) and the meaty middle section in your other. Pull apart to break the joint inside the skin. Pull the tip down, pressing with your thumb to expose the wing bones in the middle section.

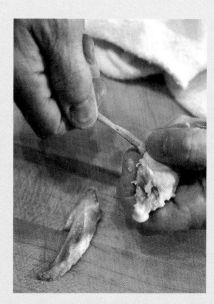

Cut off the wing tip; pull out the smaller of the two exposed bones.

Finished "lollipops"

Broiled and Split Roasted Chicken

Here's a method for cooking a large chicken—one that would take 2½ hours to roast conventionally—in little over an hour. You first "butterfly" the bird, splitting it open and nicking it carefully to expose the flesh to the oven's heat. To make sure that the chicken is cooked inside, I put it under the broiler first to partially cook the inside. For great flavor, color, and a crunchy skin, you may wish to give it a coating of the spice mix we suggest here. With a simple pan sauce—made just as we did in the roast chicken recipe—you'll have plenty of chicken to serve 8 to 10 people.

Jacques

In opening up the chicken, the small knife cuts in the shoulder and hip joints are important. These are places that always take a long time to cook thoroughly, and by exposing them to the heat you will shorten the roasting time. I like to chop off the ends of the drumsticks too, but this is only for aesthetic reasons. The skin and the drumstick meat shrink during roasting, and the leg will resemble a small ham shank.

You can be creative with the spices that you apply to the chicken. Experiment with other seeds, like fennel, cumin, or coriander, or other peppercorns. You will also find that you get a different effect if you apply the spices before the broiling—under the oven heat, the spiciness of cayenne will diminish, but other flavors will be more pronounced. Try it various ways and see which you like. This basic method will also work well with a smaller chicken.

Jacques's Split Roasted Chicken

Yield: 8 to 10 servings

A 5½-to-6-pound roasting
  chicken
1 Tbs butter, soft or melted

For the optional spice mix
1 tsp mustard seed
½ tsp caraway seed
1 tsp dried *herbes de Provence*
½ tsp black peppercorns
½ tsp paprika
¼ tsp cayenne
1 tsp salt

For the deglazing sauce
1 to 2 Tbs minced shallots
⅓ cup dry vermouth or dry white
  wine
1 cup chicken stock
1 Tbs or so unsalted butter
  (optional)

For serving
A large bunch of fresh watercress

Special equipment
A heavy knife; a large shallow-
  rimmed roasting pan, just large
  enough to hold the chicken and
  to fit under the broiler; a spice
  grinder or clean coffee grinder
  to grind the optional spice rub

Butterflying the chicken
Preheat the broiler.

Trim off the excess neck skin. Remove the fat from the cavity and cut out the wishbone (see photo on page 259).

With your knife or a cleaver, chop off the tips of the wings and the ends of the drumsticks.

Lift a wing, exposing the "armpit," and slice into the shoulder joint to open it slightly, but not through it. Repeat with the other wing.

To open the chicken, cut closely down one side of the backbone, starting at the side of the neck, cutting forcefully through the tail end. Cut down the other side to free the backbone (save it for stock with the other trimmings).

Spread open the chicken, skin side down, and nick the breastbone with the blade of the knife to split it.

A butterflied chicken

Then press firmly on both sides of the breast to flatten the chicken.

Lift the flap of skin that covers the leg and slice into the joint between the thigh and drumstick; open it slightly—just enough for the heat to get into the joint—but do not cut through it. Repeat with other leg joint.

Fold the wing tips under the shoulder, to hold them in place.

Broiling the butterflied chicken

Brush both sides of the chicken with the melted butter and arrange it skin side down in the pan. Place under the broiler, with the chicken about 6 inches from the heat, and broil for about 10 minutes, until the interior flesh is lightly browned. Remove the pan and set on work surface. Set the oven temperature at 400°F.

Coating with optional spices and roasting

Place all the spices and the salt in the grinder and process briefly to a coarse powder.

Sprinkle about a quarter of the spice mix over the broiled inside of the chicken, then turn it skin side up, flat in the pan. Sprinkle the rest of the spices over the skin, in a thick, even layer.

Place the pan in the center of the oven and roast for 1 to 1¼ hours, basting once or twice—quickly, so as not to lose oven heat—with the pan juices. Near the end of cooking time, check signs of doneness: the thigh should be tender, the juices from breast and leg joint should be clear, and the skin should be deeply colored and crisp. (See sidebar, page 261.) Roast longer if necessary.

Carving and serving

Remove the chicken to a platter and let rest for 10 to 15 minutes in a warm oven (180°F). Deglaze the pan, following the directions on page 263, using 1⅓ cups of liquid in all, to make a sauce for serving.

To carve, cut the butterflied chicken into 2 halves, straight down the middle of the breast. With parallel cuts, slice 2 thick slabs of breast meat (about ¾ inch thick) from the inside of each breast half. The remaining outside piece of breast on each side is served with wing attached.

Cut through the hip joint to separate 1 whole leg from the breast. Cut off the drumstick and split the thigh into 2 pieces. Repeat with the other leg. You should have 12 nice-sized pieces of chicken.

Arrange the pieces on a serving platter and garnish with bunches of watercress. Drizzle the pan sauce over all the pieces, and over the watercress as well. Serve, passing more sauce on the side.

Julia

I sauté my chicken until nicely browned all over, then drain out the fat, season the meat, and cover the pan, and in 20 minutes or so of slow steaming in its own juices, the chicken is ready to eat. When you have particularly fine fresh chicken and want nothing to interfere with its pure chicken flavor, you can do it plain, as in the master recipe. Or you can include onions, potatoes, mushrooms, and so forth.

While it is good to know how to cut up your own chicken, I often buy it cut up, because that way I can get all the dark meat I want. Looking at prices in the supermarket, you will see that chicken breasts are by far the most expensive per pound, and, according to me, they have the least flavor and the least satisfactory flesh quality. I choose chicken thighs for my sautés. They are easy to eat with their single bone, and to my mind the thigh has the best flavor and texture of all the chicken parts.

People who are afraid of fat shy away from thighs and dark chicken meat in general, because "they" (those nutritional naysayers) declare that dark meat has much more fat in it than light. However, trim off the several easily visible yellow fat globules nestling between the skin and flesh of the thigh, and note that much of the fat is rendered out and spooned off after the thigh is browned, and that more disappears when the

(continued on page 272)

Sautéed Chicken

Sautéing is one of the great basic ways to cook chicken, but—you'll not be surprised to discover—our methods vary in many respects. With both of the recipes here you'll wind up with nicely browned, tender chicken pieces, a good-tasting vegetable garnish, and an intense little sauce to coat them—all from the same pan—but you will follow different procedures to produce them. If you're a chicken lover, you could certainly do them both, perhaps the same week, and compare your notes with ours. You will learn a great deal and have 2 fine dinners along the way.

Dividing a whole chicken into pieces for sautéing is illustrated in the photos on pages 274 and 275. Jacques's technique requires only a few cuts with the knife to yield 8 neat pieces ready for the frying pan—2 large boneless breasts, 2 thighs, 2 drumsticks, and 2 wing pieces. It's a simple sequence that you can follow for all kinds of poultry: you will make the very same moves when dividing up a duck for Jacques's Skillet Duck with Parsnips and Shallots (page 301). If you choose, you can buy already cut-up pieces of chicken for these recipes, but you'll pay more, and won't have the bonus of a whole chicken carcass to make stock.

Julia's Simple Sauté of Chicken with Herbs

Yield: 6 servings

4 pounds fresh top-quality chicken parts,
all of one kind or a mixture of legs,
thighs, wings, breasts

3 Tbs or more unsalted butter and 1 of
vegetable oil, or oil only

¼ cup full-bodied dry white wine or dry
white French vermouth

1 cup chicken stock

Salt and freshly ground black pepper

Several cloves of unpeeled fresh garlic,
mashed (optional)

Herbs: *Either* several sprigs of fresh herbs
such as tarragon, thyme, or sage (plus
more sprigs for garnishing the finished
dish), *or* ¼ tsp fragrant dried tarragon,
thyme, or sage and sprigs of fresh parsley for garnish

2 Tbs minced shallots or scallions

1 Tbs or so unsalted butter to enrich the
sauce

Special equipment

A heavy 12-inch flameproof casserole or
sauté pan and cover, or an electric frying pan; tongs for turning the chicken

Preparing the chicken

Set the pieces of chicken on a tray and look them over
carefully, removing any visible gobs of fat, especially between
skin and flesh of thighs. Wash rapidly in hot water, and dry
thoroughly with paper towels, setting the chicken on a clean
tray as you do so. (To prevent bacterial contamination, remember to wash everything that has touched the raw chicken,
including the clean tray you have just used!)

Jacques

Deglazing is necessary to col-
lect the crystallized juices on the bottom
of the pan and bring that concentrated
flavor to a sauce. Yet in my Chicken
"Maison" I do not deglaze the sauté pan,
because the deglazing happens automatically during the covered cooking—
the brown "glaze" melts into the added
wine and the liquid that emerges from
the onions, mushrooms, and other vegetables. Everything combines to make a
sauce that is complete when I uncover
the pan at the end.

I remove the skin from the chicken
pieces because there is liquid in the
recipe. I only leave the skin on cut-up
chicken when the pieces are sautéed or
grilled to a crispy state. But when
cooked with moisture, the skin softens,
gets gooey, and curls up. There's no
appealing crispness, and the skin ren-
ders a lot of extra calories and fat. But in
this recipe, without the skin to add fat to
the pan, I don't have to skim the sauce
before serving.

Julia (continued from page 270)

juices of the sauté are degreased. Now how much more fat does the thigh have than the breast? Probably a minimal amount, but "they" never go into these culinary details.

Removing the chicken skin—that's fear of fat again. A large portion of fat is rendered out of the skin during cooking, and I'm against removal, because I don't like the look of a naked leg on my plate and, more important, the skin has good flavor. If you are a normal healthy person, you want all the flavor you can get.

In spite of the above, use any parts of the chicken you like for your sauté, because they all cook the same way.

From 3½ to 4 pounds of bone-in chicken should serve 6 nicely. But buy by eye. The chickens are usually fryers, weighing, whole, up to 3½ pounds. You'll want at least 2 thighs or drumsticks per person, for instance, or 1 whole breast. Have a number of extra pieces for big appetites, seconds, and tomorrow's lunch. It's always wise to have a little too much rather than too little.

Julia's Simple Sauté of Chicken with Herbs (continued)

Browning

This important step will take a good 20 minutes of careful cooking. Have a clean tray or platter ready. Set the pan or casserole over moderately high heat, swirl 2 tablespoons of the butter and the oil all around the inside of it, and when the butter foam starts to subside lay in as many pieces of chicken as will fit comfortably in 1 layer. Do not crowd them. Turn the chicken with your tongs every minute or so, letting all surfaces color a nice walnut brown. When 1 piece is ready, remove it to the clean tray and add another piece, until you have done them all.

Interlude

Pour out and discard all the browning fat, leaving the crusty browned bits in the pan. Pour the wine or vermouth into the pan and scrape into it these brown bits, adding a bit of the chicken stock if needed. Pour this liquid into the remaining stock and reserve for your sauce, later.

Do-ahead notes

The chicken may be cooked in advance to this point. Let cool uncovered, then cover and refrigerate if the wait is more than an hour.

Finishing the sauté (20 to 30 minutes)

Lightly season all of the chicken with salt and pepper (and a sprinkle of dried herbs, if you are using them). Set the pan over moderate heat, adding the remaining tablespoon or so of butter, and when melted return the dark meat (drumsticks and thighs) to the pan. Cover and cook slowly for 7 to 8 minutes. Then turn the dark meat over and add the white meat, which needs less cooking. Baste the chicken with accumulated pan juices, add the optional garlic, and if you are using fresh herbs, lay them on top. Cover and continue cooking at a low sizzle, turning the chicken and basting with pan juices several times, for 12 to 15 minutes more. Start testing when chicken juices begin appearing in the pan. The chicken is done when the meat is tender if pressed, and its juices run clear yellow when the meat is pierced deeply with the sharp prongs of a kitchen fork.

Holding the finished chicken for 20 to 30 minutes

If you are not quite ready to serve, place the pan over another of slowly simmering water, and set the cover slightly askew for air circulation. Too long a wait and the chicken will start to lose its juices.

Deglazing sauce

Remove the chicken to a hot platter, cover, and keep warm for the few minutes it will take to make the sauce. Spoon out and discard excess fat from the pan juices, as well as the fresh herbs, if you used them, and the pieces of crushed garlic. Set the pan over heat, stir in the shallots or scallions, and boil rapidly for a minute. Then pour in the reserved wine and stock and boil over high heat, stirring any coagulated meat juice into the liquid with a wooden spoon. When reduced to a light syrup, remove from heat, swish in the optional butter, and spoon over the chicken. Serve.

Variation: Chicken Sautéed with Potatoes, Lardons, and Mushrooms

Add a green vegetable or a salad to this dish and you have your whole main course. Follow the directions for the master recipe with these additions.

> A little more oil and/or butter as
> needed
> *Lardons* from a 5-ounce slab of
> bacon or salt pork (page 334)
> 1 pound mushrooms, cleaned and
> quartered
> 3 or 4 medium-size boiling pota-
> toes such as Yukon Golds,
> peeled and quartered
> Salt

Start browning the chicken as described in the master recipe. Meanwhile, heat a teaspoon of oil in a frying pan, 10 inches top diameter, and in it brown the *lardons* lightly. Remove with a slotted spoon and set aside, leaving their rendered fat in the pan. In it sauté the mushrooms, and set aside with the *lardons*. Drop the potatoes into a pan of lightly salted boiling water, bring again to the boil, and boil for 5 or 6 minutes, or until almost tender; drain, and reserve. Distribute *lardons,* mushrooms, and potatoes around and over the chicken as you start the final 20 minutes of cooking.

Place the chicken on its side and cut through the skin all around where the thigh is attached to the body.

Bend the leg at the knee in close to the body, then pull the knee out to crack the joint. Cut the tendon and pull the leg-thigh off. Repeat on the other side.

Pull the wing away from the body and cut through the joint. Repeat on the other side.

Jacques's Sautéed Chicken "Maison"

Yield: 4 servings

A 3½-pound chicken, divided according
  to recipe instructions
1 Tbs olive oil
1 Tbs butter
8 medium whole mushrooms (about 6
  ounces), washed just before using
8 large garlic cloves, peeled
1½ cups chopped onion, in 1-inch pieces
  (1 medium onion)
12 baby carrots, peeled (about 6 ounces)
¾ tsp salt
½ tsp freshly ground black pepper
1 cup fruity white wine (such as sauvignon blanc)
1 cup fresh or frozen baby peas
2 Tbs minced fresh chives

Special equipment

A large (12-inch) sauté pan or saucepan
  with a cover

Preparing the chicken

Cut up the chicken into pieces, following the method illustrated in the photos. Remove the wing tips.

Peel the skin from the breasts, thighs, and drumsticks (but leave the skin on the wings).

Sautéing the chicken

Heat the oil and butter in the pan. When hot, set in the chicken pieces in 1 layer and sauté over medium-high heat, turning them occasionally, until nicely browned on all sides, about 8 to 10 minutes.

Remove the 2 breast pieces to a plate and set aside. Add the mushrooms, garlic, and onion to the pan and cook for about 2 minutes, until slightly browned, stirring them.

Add the carrots, salt, and pepper, then pour in the wine and bring rapidly to a boil. Cover the pan, reduce the heat to low, and boil gently for 10 to 12 minutes. Return the breast pieces to the pan and cook, covered, 5 minutes more. Add the peas and cook for another 2 to 3 minutes.

Sprinkle the chives over the chicken and serve.

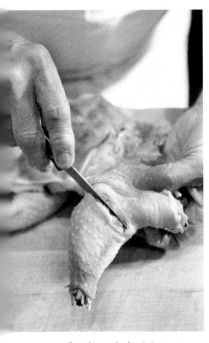

Cut through the joint to separate the leg and the thigh.

Slice along both sides of the breastbone and separate the two halves.

Lay the chicken on its side and cut through the upper shoulder joint. Holding down the carcass with your knife, grasp the breast and pull it. Repeat on the other side.

You now have 8 cut-up pieces: 2 breast pieces, 2 thighs, 2 drumsticks, 2 wings.

Jacques's Poached Chicken

"A chicken in every pot" may seem like a quaint metaphor for prosperity, but it certainly wouldn't be a bad thing if every stockpot were filled like this. Along with a plump chicken, we put in a neatly tied bundle of aromatic vegetables, a bouquet garni for more flavor, and a bunch of pearl onions and mushrooms. After simmering for just 20 minutes and steeping for 45, the chicken and vegetables are perfectly cooked, tender but still firm and flavorful. Arrayed on a bed of rice and moistened with broth, they make a very good home-style feast. The beauty of chicken is that it can be served with either white or red wine. Try a full-bodied Chardonnay or a light red, such as a Merlot, Beaujolais, or pinot noir.

The generous amounts we use here will likely leave you with enough chicken-and-vegetable leftovers to make the creamy Chicken Pot Pie or the soup, which follow. (And even when the meat and vegetables are gone, you'll still have broth and a pile of valuable bones to cook into a flavorful stock for future dishes; see sidebar, page 278.)

Yield: 4 servings

A 4-pound roasting chicken, giblets and fat removed

4 or 5 medium carrots (about ¾ pound) peeled, with ends trimmed

A whole celery heart (about ¾ pound), trimmed and sliced in half lengthwise

2 large leeks (about 1½ pounds), trimmed, cleaned, and sliced in half lengthwise (see page 54)

A bouquet garni with 4 sprigs fresh thyme, a large sprig of fresh tarragon (or 1 tsp dried tarragon), 8 peppercorns, 2 bay leaves, and 4 sprigs fresh parsley, tucked inside a leek leaf and tied with twine

¾ pound large pearl onions, peeled and trimmed (see page 196)

6 whole cloves

1 Tbs salt

1 cup white wine

10 cups lukewarm water

¾ pound small, whole mushrooms, rinsed if necessary just before cooking

For serving

2½ cups Plain Boiled Rice, fresh and hot (see page 169)

Fresh parsley sprigs

Special equipment

A large stockpot (at least 8 quarts) with a cover; a colander, strainer, or folding steaming basket small enough to fit entirely inside the stockpot; cotton kitchen twine; a large warm platter

Filling the stockpot and poaching

Rinse the chicken and place it in the stockpot.

Tie the carrots, celery heart, and leek halves together with twine into a tight bundle and put in the pot, along with the bouquet garni. Stud 2 of the pearl onions with the whole cloves, and toss all the onions into the pot. Add the salt, wine, and warm water. Set the colander (or steamer basket) on top of the chicken, upside down, to hold it and the vegetables down so they are covered with the liquid.

Heat rapidly to a boil, lower the heat to maintain a gentle boil, and cook for 20 minutes.

Remove the colander and add the mushrooms. Immediately raise the heat to bring the broth to a strong boil, cover the pot closely with the lid, and turn off the heat. Let sit for 45 minutes to an hour.

Carving the chicken and serving

When ready to serve, make a bed of cooked white rice on the serving platter. Lift the chicken out of the pot with a large strainer and place it, breast up, on a cutting board.

Cutting up the chicken is not hard, because the cooked pieces will separate easily from the carcass and the skin will peel off.

First, pull the leg-thigh sections from the carcass at the thigh joint, then separate the thighs from the drumsticks by cutting through at the joint. Slice off the wings and remove the tips. Peel the skin off the entire breast, lift off each breast half from the carcass in 1 piece, then cut neatly in 2. Save all the small bones and cartilage for further cooking in the broth. Discard the skin and the bouquet garni. Arrange all the chicken pieces on top of the rice.

Fish the vegetable bundle out of the broth. Cut the twine and arrange the carrots, celery, and leeks around the rim of the platter. Scoop out the onions and mushrooms and scatter around the chicken. Spoon a cup or so of broth over the chicken pieces and garnish the platter with sprigs of fresh parsley.

Serve portions of chicken, vegetables, and rice on dinner plates, with cups of broth at each place, and crocks of mustard, salt, and cornichons to be passed.

Jacques

The poaching method here for the chicken is simple and foolproof. Everything must be submerged in the cooking water—especially the chicken —with some kind of perforated implement, such as a sieve or colander or a folding steamer basket. Make sure that it is heavy enough to weight down the chicken, and small enough to fit inside the pot, even when it is tightly covered.

Chicken poached this way is much like *pot-au-feu*, the classic French dinner of boiled beef and vegetables. So I would serve it with the traditional accompaniments to *pot-au-feu*—crocks of coarse salt, cornichons (little French sour pickles), prepared Dijon mustard, and either fresh grated or prepared horseradish, and individual bowls of the broth and croutons or fresh French bread on the side. That is exactly the kind of big Sunday lunch we had during the winter when I was growing up.

A Simple Soup and a Savory Stock from Poached Chicken

To make a good soup from the leftovers of your poached-chicken dinner: Strain the broth and chill it overnight. When ready to serve, skim off the congealed fat from the surface and put the broth in a saucepan. Add any leftover chicken and vegetables, cut into bite-size chunks, as well as any leftover rice, and bring the soup to a boil. Its thickness will depend on the amount of leftovers you've added. Serve with croutons and grated Swiss cheese.

To make a flavorful stock from any remaining broth—you will have a quart, or even 2—put it in a large saucepan with all the reserved chicken bones and trimmings. Add water, if necessary, to cover the bones with liquid, heat to a boil, and boil gently, uncovered, for 1½ to 2 hours. Strain, chill, and skim off surface fat. Freeze in small containers. (Remember that this stock is salted, so season accordingly when you use it.)

Jacques's Chicken Pot Pie

Half of the Flaky Tart Dough on page 418 is just the right amount for covering the pot pie.

Yield: 4 servings

From the preceding recipe
2 cups or so poached chicken, removed from the bone, in ¾-inch chunks
4 cups or so poached vegetables (carrots, leeks, and celery in ½-inch pieces; mushrooms halved; pearl onions whole)

About ½ cup fresh or frozen baby green peas

For the velouté sauce
3 Tbs unsalted butter
4 Tbs flour
4 cups poaching broth, degreased
1 cup heavy cream
Salt and freshly ground pepper

9 ounces Flaky Tart Dough (½ batch) (page 418)
Flour for rolling the dough
1 egg

Special equipment
An 8-cup oval gratin or baking dish, preferably about 10 inches long and 3 inches deep; a rolling pin; a pastry brush; a cookie sheet

Making the velouté sauce and chicken filling

Preheat the oven to 400°F. Put the poaching liquid in a medium saucepan and boil rapidly to reduce by half (to 2 cups) to concentrate the flavor.

Meanwhile, mix the poached chicken and vegetable pieces together in the baking dish with the peas.

When the broth is reduced, melt the butter in a heavy 2-quart saucepan and whisk in the flour to make a thick paste. Cook over medium heat for a couple of minutes, whisking steadily, while the roux bubbles and foams; don't let it color.

Remove the roux from the heat and pour in the concentrated broth, whisking rapidly to blend well. Return to the heat, stir in the cream, and bring to a gentle boil. Cook for 2 to 3 minutes, stirring as the sauce thickens, until it coats a spoon. Taste and whisk in ¼ teaspoon pepper, or more, and a small amount of salt as needed—the concentrated broth will already have a good amount of salt. (If the sauce is too thick, thin with a bit of broth.)

Pour the sauce over the chicken and vegetables and fold in gently. It should just cover all the pieces, and come to ½ inch or so of the top of the dish. Taste a piece of creamed chicken and adjust seasoning. (If you like, you could now heat and serve this as "chicken à la king" without the pastry top.)

Rolling the pastry and finishing the pie

Set the tart dough on a floured work surface and dust the top with flour. If it is chilled and hard, bang it a few times with the rolling pin to soften. Roll out the dough and cut a shape (oval, round, or rectangular) approximately the size of your oven dish plus 1½ inches overlap all around—use the rolling pin as a convenient measuring stick. Flour both sides of the dough as you roll, and turn it over and rotate it occasionally to keep it even.

Crack the egg into a small bowl and beat well with a fork. Brush a thin layer of egg wash on the rim of the dish and all around the outside where the dough will rest, to help it adhere.

Roll the dough up around the pin, then unroll so it drapes over the baking dish, resting on the filling and extending evenly over the edges. Press the overlap against the egg-washed outside of the dish, sealing the pie. Brush the entire surface of the crust with egg wash, to glaze, and then, with a sharp paring knife, make shallow diagonal lines in the top of the pie, in a decorative pattern, without cutting all the way through the dough. Now poke the tip of the knife through to open three ¼-inch vent holes, spaced evenly in the middle of the crust. Place the dish on the cookie sheet and set in the oven.

Bake for 20 minutes and reduce the temperature to 375°F. Bake for another 15 to 20 minutes—or more, if the filling was cold—until the crust is golden and the filling is bubbling through the vents. Serve hot.

Overleaf: Chicken Pot Pie

Roast Turkey

It seems a shame to enjoy the traditional American turkey dinner only on one holiday. Turkey is available and reasonably priced any time of year—and with the special method here, you won't need a whole day off work just to roast it. Julia's technique separates the breast and leg-thighs before roasting, which cuts the oven time in half—you'll need less than two hours for an ample yet easy-to-handle twelve-pounder. And you won't lose the drama of serving a whole bird, since the golden, crisp-skinned pieces are rearranged into the plump, platter-filling natural shape that guests expect.

Quicker cooking is only one of the advantages here. Roasting the bird in pieces allows you to cook the dark leg meat separately from the whole breast (which in this case takes longer), so that each section is perfectly done. In addition, you can cut the bone out of the thighs and spoon a savory stuffing in its place, giving dark-meat lovers a neat medallion of thigh and stuffing together.

Another bonus is all the bones and scraps you will have for making a full-flavored turkey stock for your gravy. The Cornbread and Sage Stuffing (page 288) will give you all you need for both breast and legs, and Jacques's Cranberry Chutney (page 289) is an especially colorful version of this essential turkey accompaniment.

Elsewhere in the book are recipes for the other highlights of the turkey dinner table: Creamed Onions (page 196), buttered Brussels sprouts (page 187), and Mashed Potatoes, both white and sweet (pages 150 and 157). All can be made ahead and finished at feast time.

Bottles of both red and white wine and a pitcher of cider are also essential with a big turkey meal. Chardonnay, pinot noir, a simple Beaujolais, and Syrah are always good choices.

Opposite: Chicken Pot Pie

Jacques

I'd never done turkey this way until I did it with Julia, and it is a great idea. The legs are especially good this way. If you don't have a stuffing, you can flavor the boneless thighs with chopped mushrooms, or a sauté of shallots and herbs like the one I put in my roast chicken (page 258), or just use fresh herbs. Instead of skewering and trussing the thighs as Julia does, I wrap aluminum foil around them, to keep the flaps of meat closed around the stuffing. Be sure you don't wrap foil around the open end of the thigh, because you want the heat to really get in there. And remember to remove the foil halfway through the roasting, so the skin browns nicely.

In this recipe, we thicken the gravy with potato starch or arrowroot. (I prefer these to cornstarch, which tends to get gummy.) Unlike butter-and-flour pastes like roux or *beurre manié*, which must be cooked for a few minutes, the starch powder thickens instantly on contact with the hot gravy. You must mix it with liquid—here we use Julia's favorite, dry port—and then whisk a little bit at a time into the gravy. You can observe the thickening effect right away, and get the exact consistency that you want.

Julia

To make turkey this way, you could buy the pieces already separated—breast in one package and leg-thighs in another—but then you wouldn't have the backbone to make the stock for a great gravy. You would also miss the satisfaction of taking the bird apart yourself. It's more of a job to remove the backbone of a turkey than of a duck or a chicken, but you can't really go wrong. Don't worry if you leave a few ribs on the breast, or a bit of the spine attached to the legs—you can always trim them off. I just go at it with knife, cleaver, and mallet and do whatever it takes to get the pieces apart.

You certainly want to chop off the end of the drumsticks, so you can pull out the tendons after the legs have roasted—then the drumstick is a pleasure to carve. It would be even more convenient if the turkey producers would remove these tendons at the time the birds are slaughtered. I have never understood why they won't do it. They have a machine that mechanically pulls out the tendons, and it would make turkey meals much easier for us home cooks.

Julia's Deconstructed Turkey

Yield: Roast turkey and stuffing serving 12

The whole breast and the leg-thighs from a 12-pound turkey
Salt and freshly ground pepper
8 cups Cornbread and Sage Stuffing (page 288) or other stuffing
Fresh vegetable oil or clear rendered turkey fat
1 cup each diced onion, carrots, and celery, in ½-inch pieces

For serving
Giblet Gravy (page 286)

Special equipment
A meat cleaver, a mallet or hammer, and sharp knives for separating the turkey; 4-inch trussing skewers and cotton kitchen twine; 1 large, heavy-duty roasting pan that can hold both the breast and legs, or 2 smaller pans—1 with a wire rack; a bulb baster or brush for basting; a meat thermometer; a large serving platter

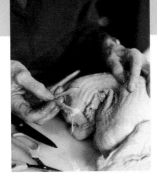

Preliminaries: Cleaning and cutting up the turkey

Arrange the rack on the lower level of the oven and preheat to 350°F.

Remove the giblets and neck from the turkey and set aside for turkey stock and Giblet Gravy (page 286). Pull any clods of fat from the cavity and discard, as well as extraneous plastic items, such as pop-up timers. Rinse the turkey in hot water and dry with paper towels.

As shown in the photos, remove the wishbone and the backbone. Cut off the leg-thigh sections and bone out the thighs. Trim the wings.

Preparing the turkey for roasting

Season the inside of the boneless thighs with salt and pepper and fill each with as much stuffing as it will hold easily—½ cup or so, as shown in photo (following page). Press the sides together to enclose the stuffing, and fasten with 3 or 4 skewers. Lace twine around the skewers to enclose the stuffing and knot. Rub the thighs all over with oil or clear turkey fat (which you will have if you've already made stock), sprinkle with salt and pepper, and arrange, skewered side up, either on the wire rack or around the breast when you have formed it later.

Smear the large roasting pan well with oil or fat. Mound the remaining stuffing in the pan, shaped to fit under the breast. Rub the breast with oil or fat, inside and out, season with salt, and place it on top of the stuffing. Set the turkey leg-thigh sections in the same pan, if you are doing it that way. Strew the diced vegetables around the turkey breast and place the pan (or both pans) in the oven.

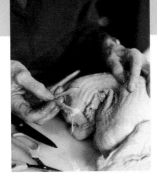

With knife, cut and loosen bone from flesh around wishbone and pull it out with your hand.

Remove the backbone.

After cutting off the leg-thigh section (see page 274 for photo), whack off the end of the drumstick bone.

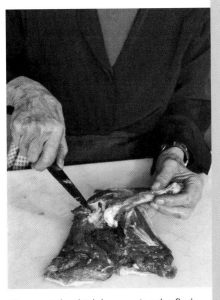

Bone out the thigh by scraping the flesh away from the bone.

Trim nubbins off wings.

Roasting the turkey

Roast leg-thighs and breast for about 30 minutes, then quickly baste with accumulated fat. Remove the pan for basting, if possible, so you don't lose heat from the oven. Roast for 30 minutes more and baste again. At this time, turn the leg-thighs over on the wire rack so the skewers are down and the outside skin will brown. (If they have been foil-wrapped, remove the foil and return the leg-thighs to the pan, skin side up, to brown.)

After skewering and tying the stuffing in place, set the leg-thigh pieces on a rack in a roasting pan.

After 1½ hours of total roasting time, baste the breast again and remove the leg-thighs from the oven to test for doneness. The thigh meat should register about 170°F on a meat thermometer, and you should be able to pull out the stiff tendons from the drumstick easily (see photo). Roast longer if necessary; if done, pull out as many of the leg tendons as you can, without tearing the meat or drumstick skin. (If the leg sections were in a separate pan, pour off the fat, deglaze any flavorful browned bits with a small amount of stock or wine, and add the pan juices to your gravy.)

Place the breast over the mound of stuffing.

Begin testing the breast for doneness after 1½ hours of roasting, sticking the thermometer into the thick meat near the shoulder joint. When the internal temperature reaches 160° to 165°F, the breast is done and should be removed from the oven.

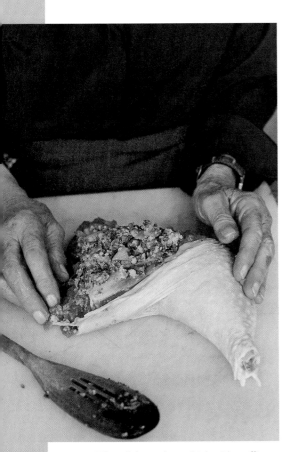

Fill each boned-out thigh with stuffing.

Reconstructing and serving the turkey

Before lifting, slide the spatula blades all around under the stuffing, to loosen any crusted bits, and use spatulas to transfer the entire mound of stuffing and the turkey breast to the serving platter, all at once. (With a very large roasting pan, you might shove a rimless cookie sheet or the removable bottom of a quiche pan under the stuffing and breast, then slide them onto the platter.)

With small pliers pull the tendons out of the drumstick.

Leave the roasted diced vegetables in the pan; deglaze it as described in the recipe for Giblet Gravy that follows. If not making gravy, you can deglaze the pan with stock or wine to make a simple sauce of pan juices, as is done for chicken on page 263.

Arrange the leg-thighs in their natural position alongside the breast and ladle some of the gravy over the reassembled turkey before bringing it to the table.

To carve the legs, slice the thighs crosswise into thick medallions with stuffing inside (see photo), then cut along the drumstick to remove slices of tendonless meat. To carve the breast, first cut horizontally several inches into the front, on one side—a bit above the shoulder joint. Then slice down the breast in the conventional fashion, to the first cut, for neat, even-sized slices. Spoon out stuffing from under the breast for each serving.

Tips on Turkey

Fresh or frozen? Either is fine, if it has been properly kept. It is important that a frozen turkey has remained solidly frozen—if it's been thawed a bit, and then frozen again, the breast meat will be shreddy. Always buy turkey from a reputable market.

To thaw a frozen turkey, make sure you defrost it *in the refrigerator, allowing three days or more.* Never thaw it at room temperature, or in hot water. The turkey will lose its natural juices, and you increase the risk of bacterial growth.

How big a bird? Count on 1 pound of turkey per person, if you want to have seconds and leftovers. If you don't want leftovers, ½ pound per person will do.

A small bird, 10 to 13 pounds, is easy to handle and will roast faster. You might want to buy two smaller turkeys for a large crowd.

How can you coordinate the cooking? Separate the turkey into pieces and bone out the thighs a day before roasting, and store them covered in the refrigerator. Then make turkey stock—you'll have all the bones and plenty of time to make and reduce it for Giblet Gravy (this page). Finish the gravy while the turkey is roasting.

Giblet Gravy

Yield: 3 to 4 cups

For the stock
- 2 to 3 Tbs vegetable oil or clear turkey fat
- The neck and all bones and meaty trimmings from a "deconstructed" turkey
- 1½ cups 1-inch chunks of peeled carrots
- 1½ cups roughly chopped onion
- 1 cup 1-inch chunks of celery
- Turkey giblets (heart, gizzard, and liver)
- 1 cup dry French vermouth, white wine, or water for deglazing
- 2 quarts chicken stock or water
- 2 imported bay leaves
- 6 sprigs fresh thyme, or ½ tsp dried thyme leaves
- Salt and freshly ground pepper

For the gravy
- 2 Tbs potato starch or arrowroot
- 2 Tbs dry (tawny) port or stock, plus more if needed
- Salt and freshly ground black pepper

Special equipment
- A large frying pan (12 inches top diameter) or sauté pan; a large saucepan or stockpot (at least 6-quart); a large strainer; a medium whisk

Making turkey stock

Set the frying pan over medium-high heat, swirl the oil or fat around in it, and toss in the turkey bones and trimmings, including the neck. (Don't crowd the pan; work in batches if necessary.) Brown the pieces well on all sides, turning them with tongs, then transfer to the large saucepan or stockpot. When there's room in the pan, add the chopped vegetables and sauté them rapidly, stirring and turning, until nicely colored on the edges. Transfer to the saucepan with a slotted spoon, leaving the rendered fat in the pan. Finally, sauté the giblets—the gizzard, heart, and liver—until brown; set aside.

Pour all the fat out of the frying pan, add the vermouth (or stock or water), and deglaze the pan over medium heat, stirring and scraping up all the crusted bits. Pour the juices into the stockpot and add stock or water to cover the bones by an inch or so. Bring to a simmer, then skim off fat and scum during the first ½ hour of cooking. Add the bay leaves and thyme, ¼ teaspoon or so of salt and grinds of pepper. Simmer the stock, partially covered, for another 1½ to 2 hours. During this time, set the liver aside and cook the heart for about 15 minutes and the gizzard for about 45 minutes in the simmering stock; remove them after cooking and set aside with the liver.

Strain the stock into a bowl or smaller saucepan—you should have about 6 cups. Discard all the bones now, but save the turkey neck for gravy. Let the stock settle so the fat rises to the top—or chill it overnight—then degrease.

Making the gravy

Pour the degreased stock into a saucepan and bring it to the boil. Cook down rapidly, by about half, until you have 3 cups of flavorful liquid. Meanwhile, pull the cooked meat off the turkey neck, cut off and discard the tough membrane from the gizzard, then dice all the neck and giblet meat, including the liver and heart, into very fine pieces. Stir into the saucepan of hot gravy liquid, and simmer together for a couple of minutes.

Whisk the starch and wine together in a small bowl to make a smooth paste. Remove the gravy pan from heat and whisk driblets of the gravy liquid into the starch mixture until you have added ½ cup, then whisk this back into the main body of the liquid. Finally, bring the liquid to the simmer, whisking slowly, and let it thicken into a gravy.

After the turkey has been removed from the roasting pan, tilt it and spoon off as much fat as possible. Set the pan on the

One or two ovens? Obviously two ovens would be ideal—one for the breast and the other for the leg-thighs. If you've but one, arrange the breast on a large roasting pan in such a way that the leg-thighs can go around it.

Stuffing You can make the cornbread-sage stuffing—and most other stuffings—a day or so ahead and refrigerate it. Do not stuff the turkey until you are ready to roast it, however, since moist stuffings inside raw turkey can increase the chance of spoilage.

stove over low to medium heat, pour in the thickened gravy, and stir and scrape up all the glazed vegetables and juices. Strain the gravy and vegetables back into the saucepan. Taste and adjust the seasoning, and reheat if necessary before serving.

Cornbread and Sage Stuffing

For this stuffing, you can make the cornbread from scratch (recipe follows) or buy unsweetened cornbread at the market.

Yield: About 8 cups

8 cups unsweetened cornbread in
  ½-inch cubes (about 1¼ pounds
  of cornbread)
3 Tbs canola oil
8 ounces pork-sausage meat
3 Tbs butter
1½ cups chopped onion in ¼-
  inch pieces
1 cup chopped celery in ¼-inch
  pieces
6 ounces mushrooms, coarsely
  chopped, about 2 cups
3 Tbs minced fresh sage or ½ Tbs
  dried sage
¾ tsp salt
½ tsp freshly ground black pepper
1 cup chicken stock

Put the cornbread cubes in a large mixing bowl.

Heat a 10-inch frying or sauté pan with a teaspoon or two of the canola oil. Crumble or chop the sausage meat into small pieces. Fry over medium heat until cooked but not brown. Remove the meat with a slotted spoon to a bowl.

Add the butter and the rest of the oil to any fat in the pan and set over medium-high heat. Add the chopped vegetables, the sage, salt, and pepper, and stir and toss together. Sauté rapidly until soft, about 8 minutes. Return the sausage pieces to the pan, pour in the chicken stock, and cook together for a minute or so.

Scrape the cooked seasonings over the cornbread. Toss together thoroughly, crumbling the bread cubes, until the stuffing is evenly moist and loose. Taste and adjust the seasonings. (The stuffing can be made a day ahead of cooking your turkey, but store it separately. Never stuff a turkey until you are ready to roast it.)

Homemade Cornbread for Turkey Stuffing

Yield: An 8- or 9-inch pan of corn-
bread (1¼ pounds), to make 8
cups of small chunks

Room-temperature butter for
  greasing the pan
1 cup flour
1 cup yellow cornmeal
1 Tbs baking powder
2 tsp sugar (optional)
1 tsp salt
2 eggs
1 cup milk
4 Tbs melted butter

Preheat the oven to 400°F. Butter an 8-inch square baking pan (or a round 9-inch pan).

Mix together all the dry ingredients in a bowl. In another bowl or a measuring cup, beat the eggs lightly, stir in the milk and melted butter, and pour all at once over the flour mixture. Stir together just until evenly moistened, then scrape the batter into the pan.

Bake for about 20 minutes, until the cornbread is golden and the top springs back when lightly pressed. Cool briefly in the pan and invert onto a cooling rack. Slice into serving pieces, or small chunks for stuffing.

Cranberry Chutney

This crimson condiment—tart and sweet, with a touch of heat—is delicious with all kinds of hot and cold meats, and particularly good on leftover turkey sandwiches. It will keep for several weeks in the refrigerator.

Yield: 2½ cups

1 large Granny Smith apple
1 lemon, medium-size
1 cup orange juice
3 cups fresh cranberries (one 12-ounce bag)
3 Tbs white-wine vinegar, plus more if needed
½ cup sugar
¼ tsp salt
⅛ tsp cayenne, plus more to taste

Halve and core the apple (peeled first, if you prefer) and dice it into small pieces, about 1½ cups. Pare 10 or so thin strips of peel from the lemon with a zester or paring knife, then trim off the ends and cut the lemon lengthwise into quarters. Cut each quarter into thin (⅛-inch) triangles.

Pour the orange juice and cranberries into a sturdy 2- or 3-quart saucepan and set over medium-high heat. Add the apple and lemon pieces, the strips of lemon peel, vinegar, and seasonings, and stir all together. Cover the pan and bring to the boil over high heat. Stir the ingredients, reduce the heat to medium, and cook covered for about 5 minutes, until all the cranberries have

burst. Uncover the pan, reduce the heat, and simmer for another 4 or 5 minutes, until the chutney is thick. Taste and stir in small amounts more vinegar, sugar, salt, or cayenne, as you like. Cool to room temperature before serving.

The chutney will keep in the refrigerator several weeks, or longer if you freeze it.

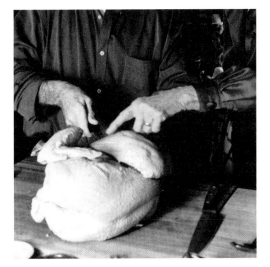

Jacques's Turkey Galantine

A galantine is a bird (or a meat or game animal, or fish) that has been completely boned and filled with a force-meat, then shaped into an attractive loaf or sausage, cooked, and cooled. When sliced, the galantine displays a handsome, variegated cross-section of skin, layers of meat, and savory stuffing.

A galantine can be made with chicken, duck, or other poultry using the same techniques, but the small turkey used here is easy to maneuver and to bone, yet large enough to make all the work worthwhile. You will easily get 15 to 20 slices, to serve warm as a ballottine, with a simple sauce of natural pan juices, or cold, as is traditional with galantines. All the steps for completely boning the turkey are illustrated here, and you can truss it following the photos for tying a veal roast on page 348.

Yield: 12 to 15 servings

A fresh 8-to-10-pound turkey, giblets and neck removed

For the stuffing
2 cups chopped onions
2 Tbs butter or vegetable oil
Giblets from the turkey (gizzard, liver, and heart)
2 pounds uncooked ground sausage meat
½ cup pistachio nuts
⅓ cup white wine
2 eggs
1 tsp dried thyme
½ tsp ground allspice
1 Tbs chopped garlic

2 Tbs chopped fresh parsley
2 cups fresh bread crumbs (about 4 slices home-style white bread)
Salt (amount will vary with sausage seasoning)
Freshly ground black pepper (amount will vary with sausage seasoning)

Salt and freshly ground black pepper
3 to 4 Tbs virgin olive oil or canola oil, for browning the galantine

For deglazing the roasting pan
½ cup white wine
1½ cups chicken stock (or turkey stock, if made)

For garnish
Watercress
Cherry tomatoes

Special equipment
A boning knife and a chef's knife; cotton kitchen twine; a large heavy-bottomed roasting pan (about 10 inches by 15 inches); a large serving platter; a bowl, a measuring cup or fat separator, and a fine sieve, for making pan gravy

Making the stuffing

Sauté the chopped onions in the butter or oil for about 5 minutes over medium heat, stirring occasionally, until soft and translucent. Let cool briefly.

Cut the tough white membrane from the turkey gizzard and any sinews from the liver, then chop the gizzard, liver, and heart into tiny pieces. In a large bowl, break up the sausage meat with your fingers, add the onions, the chopped giblets, and the remaining stuffing ingredients, and mix together well. To check the seasoning, fry up a spoonful of the stuffing until brown and cooked through and taste. Add more salt, freshly ground pepper, herbs, or spices if needed.

Set the stuffing aside, or refrigerate it, until you are ready to stuff the turkey.

Boning the turkey

Cut off the tail of the turkey and the 2 outer joints of each wing, and remove the wishbone, following the photos.

Cut through the skin of the turkey down the center of the back-bone.

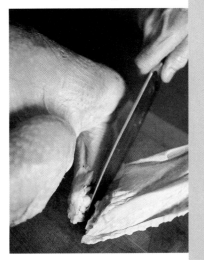

Cut off the outer joint of the wing.

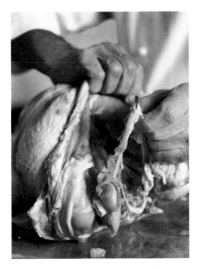

Pull back the flap and remove the wishbone.

Jacques

There's no great difficulty in any of the steps needed for boning a turkey. Many of the steps you've already practiced if you've prepared other recipes in this chapter. The 4 basic knife cuts needed for removing the carcass—severing the shoulder and thigh joints—are the same ones you make when separating a chicken for sautéing or for carving a roast chicken at the table.

Once the carcass is removed, it's a simple matter to take out the leg and wing bones, but you can leave either the wing and drumstick bones in place—or both—to give the galantine a more natural look. You must take out the thigh bones, though, so, if you want to leave the drumsticks in, slice through the knee joint, instead of scraping around it as shown in the photos. And when you are using a turkey, you should always chop off the ends of the drumsticks, even if you leave the rest of the leg bone inside. This exposes the tendons, and after roasting, you can remove them easily, so the meat can be carved.

It's convenient to make the forcemeat stuffing with store-bought sausage since it is already seasoned, but you can use other ground meats here, including ground turkey, pork, veal, or even beef. And you can vary the herbs and spices as you like. (Always check the seasoning by sautéing a little bit of the stuffing and tasting it before it goes in the turkey.)

With the turkey on its side, place the knife blade against the shoulder joint and slice through.

Pull the shoulder from the carcass and gradually peel the skin from the back of the turkey.

Holding the turkey at the back-bone, after cutting the flesh free from the bone, pull down the whole breast to free it from the carcass.

Jacques's Turkey Galantine (continued)

Put the turkey on its side, lift the skin near the shoulder joint, and locate the joint by wiggling the wing and feeling with your finger. Place the knife blade against the joint and slice through—wiggling the blade will make this easier (see photos). Turn the turkey on its other side and sever the other shoulder joint.

Hold the turkey near the neck with 1 hand, and with the other grasp 1 wing section. Pull the shoulder out from the carcass slowly, peeling the skin off the backbone, along the cut line, just far enough to reveal the meaty portion of the "oyster" on the backbone. Repeat the pulling and peeling on the other side of the turkey. Be careful not to tear the thin layer of skin on the back.

To remove the breast: Hold the turkey securely at the top of the backbone with 1 hand, and with your knife, cut around the top of the breastbone (the sternum) to free the breast flesh.

With your hand, pull down the whole breast, peeling it away from the carcass (see photo). The two meaty filets will remain on the carcass, on either side of the breastbone. You will remove those later.

To sever the leg joints: Hold one leg, with the knee bent, and cut under the "oyster" flesh. Grasp the knee and pull it away from the carcass, cracking and revealing the thigh joint.

Holding one leg with knee bent, cut under the "oyster" flesh.

Slice through the tendon in the thigh joint and pull the leg meat and skin from the carcass. Repeat with the other leg.

Pull the carcass free of the meat and skin. Spread the boned turkey on the work surface, skin side down, to remove the remaining leg and wing bones.

To remove both leg bones (thigh and drumstick bone), scrape the meat off the end of the thigh bone, so you can grasp it. With your

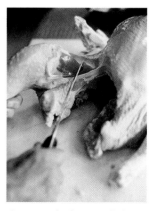

Grasping the knee, pull the leg-thigh away from the car-cass, and slice through the thigh joint.

The turkey with carcass removed

boning knife, continue to scrape down, clearing the meat off the bone and all around the knee joint—*don't cut through the knee joint.*

Scrape the meat off the drumstick bone.

With a heavy knife, chop off the tip of the drumstick on the outside. Then pull out the leg bones from the inside. Repeat with the other leg.

Scrape the meat from the inside end of one of the wing bones so you can grab it.

To remove the wing bones, scrape the meat from the inside end of 1 bone so you can grab it (just as you did the thigh bone), then scrape down to clean off all the meat. With a sharp yank, pull the wing bone free, drawing it in from the outside. This will pull the boneless wing skin inside out—push it back so you have a small pocket for stuffing. Repeat on the other side.

Return to the carcass. With your fingers and the knife, remove the meaty filets nestled along the breastbone. With your knife, slice away the white sinew that runs through each filet.

Lay these filets into the empty spaces you will see on the turkey skin.

Scrape the meat off the drumstick as far as you can.

Remove the meaty filets along the breastbone.

Chop off the tip end of the drumstick.

Lay the filets into the empty places on the turkey skin.

Stuffing and trussing the turkey

When the turkey is completely deboned, you are ready to stuff it. Preheat the oven to 425°F.

First, fill the boned legs and wings with some of the stuffing.

Sprinkle ½ teaspoon of salt and ¼ teaspoon of freshly ground black pepper all over the flesh of the boned-out turkey and spread the remaining stuffing in an even layer on top. Pull both long sides of the turkey up and fold them over the stuffing, overlapping them so the stuffing is completely enclosed. Roll the turkey over so the seam is down, and tuck the neck skin under. Press the sides to form a smooth, compact, evenly shaped cylinder. If there are any holes where the stuffing can ooze out, cover with patches of aluminum foil.

To truss the turkey: Using a length of twine several feet long, first tie the drumsticks together. Then form a half-stitch loop (following the photos for rolling and tying a veal roast on page 348) and put it around the galantine at the neck end. Slide the loop back toward the leg, then tighten it about 2 inches from the first knot. (It should be tight enough to hold the galantine in shape but must also allow the stuffing to expand slightly.)

Make a series of 6 or 7 half-hitches, circling the galantine every 2 inches (as shown in the veal photos). Roll the galantine over so the seam side is now up and draw the twine around each of the loops, tightening it as you go. Turn the galantine smooth side up again, and tie the twine at the drumsticks, completing the truss. Sprinkle ¼ teaspoon of salt and ⅛ teaspoon of pepper over the top and sides.

Browning and roasting the turkey

Place the roasting pan over medium to high heat, on the stovetop, with enough oil to film the bottom. When the oil is hot, lay the galantine in the pan and brown it to a light-golden color on all sides, rolling it over after 2 or 3 minutes on a side—browning it about 10 minutes in all. Lower the heat if the oil is too hot (and add more oil if the galantine is sticking).

With the galantine top side up in the roasting pan, place it in the hot oven. Roast for about 1¾ hours, basting 2 or 3 times with the pan juices. Check the temperature with a meat thermometer plunged into the stuffing at the thickest point. When it registers 160° to 165°F, remove roasting pan from the oven.

Transfer the turkey to the serving platter—you can pick it up by the trussing twine. Then cut the twine, pull it all off, and discard. Pull out the drumstick tendons, which will be exposed at the cut end of the leg. They should slide out easily, but take care not to tear the skin. Let the turkey rest for at least 20 minutes in a warm place on the stove (or in the turned-off oven, with the door ajar).

To make a pan gravy, pour off all the fat and uncrystallized juices from the pan into a bowl, measuring cup, or fat separator, and set aside to allow the fat to come to the top. Place the roasting pan over medium heat, and pour in the wine and the stock. Heat, stir, and scrape the crystallized juices until melted, then strain the liquid through the sieve into a bowl. Add the juices that accumulate around the turkey in the platter and the carefully defatted juices from the bowl or fat separator. Adjust the seasonings to taste. You can thicken the gravy if you want with potato starch dissolved in wine or port (as for Giblet Gravy, page 286).

Slicing and serving

To serve the galantine warm: Starting at the end of the breast, slice crosswise, straight down, into ½-inch slices, displaying a cross-section of turkey and stuffing. Work carefully, as the slices tend to fall apart when warm. You may find it helpful to move them with a broad spatula, or you can cut thicker slices, which are easier to handle, and divide them into half rounds for serving.

Arrange the slices overlapping on the platter or on individual plates, 1 slice per serving. Spoon some of the warm gravy over and around the slices—either in the platter or on the plates—and garnish with clusters of watercress and cherry tomatoes, cut in half.

To serve the galantine cold, slice in the same way—the meat and stuffing will now hold together better—and arrange on a platter or individual plates. Serve as you would pâté, garnished with cornichons, black olives, and lettuce, with prepared Dijon mustard and crusty bread on the side.

Julia

Don't be afraid of cutting up

a duck. Just go at it. You may make a few false moves, but nobody will really know—and in the end you can't go wrong. It's useful to fool around with raw poultry this way, since it teaches you where all the parts are. That in turn will make you a more able carver of cooked birds, so you'll do a better job at the table.

One of the good things about the duck recipe here is that you do the major preparations ahead of time. Set up the breasts and the legs in the morning, cover and refrigerate them while you make the stock and sauce, then finish everything up when you want to serve the meal. The preliminary roasting cooks the breasts to very rare. At that point, the breast meat needs only to be carved and to finish cooking in its sauce before serving—it's very important not to overcook it. The legs and thighs in their mustard-and-crumb coating are roasted separately.

Every part of a duck is full of flavor, and when you have made stock and cracklings, strained and saved the fat, and sautéed the giblets for our salad, you'll realize you have used every bit of your duck.

Duck

Duck, with its fine dark meat so full of flavor and its crisp skin, is certainly one of our favorites, and it always presents a challenge to the cook. You have the fat problem, and the breast-versus-leg problem. In our markets we get only the 5-to-5½-pound so-called "young roaster duckling," a beautiful bird indeed, but not so young that it can be roasted whole, in our opinion. Either the skin will be darkly crisp and delicious but the breast will be overdone and stringy, or the breast will be rare and rosy and just right and the legs will be inedibly tough.

In our two main recipes here, we solve the puzzle in pieces, by taking the duck apart. Julia's duck is cooked two ways. First it's roasted whole briefly, just enough to cook the breasts rosy rare and render some of the fat, then it's cut up and the remaining fat and all the skin are removed. Finally, the legs get a special bread-crumb coating and another brief roasting. In Jacques's method, the duck is divided first, and the pieces are fried in a skillet uncovered, rendering out all the fat and crisping the skin. Then they are cooked covered, surrounded with parsnips, shallots, and garlic—and the duck fat too—until all the duck and vegetable pieces are tender and flavorful. Then the fat is removed.

Separating the duck also provides several bonuses not available when you cook the duck whole. You will have a duck carcass and trimmings to make into stock and duck sauce (pages 300 and 301). The trimmed duck skin is cooked into crisp cracklings (see sidebar, page 303), to sprinkle over the meat, and you'll get lots of fine, clear duck fat to save and use in other dishes as well. Though Jacques's duck pieces are cooked skin-on, there will be plenty of trimmings for cracklings too. If you've never cut up a duck before, follow Julia's method as illustrated here, or refer to the photos on pages 274 and 275 to see Jacques's technique, which is the same for all poultry.

For both of these recipes, you want to buy a 5-to-5½-pound duck, large enough to serve 4. A fresh bird is always desirable, but most ducks we find now are frozen. Defrost your duck slowly in the refrigerator, allowing 2 or 3 days for it to thaw completely. Pull all the loose fat from the cavity of the duck, and be sure to look inside to find the giblets and the long neck. Use the neck in your stock, and the heart, gizzard, and liver in Jacques's Duck Giblets and Escarole Salad (page 304).

Accompany either of these main-course ducks with sautéed potatoes, or string beans. A pinot noir or a cabernet sauvignon would be a suitable wine to pour with either duck.

Julia's Two-Way Duck

Do the preliminary cooking, carving, and simmering of the duck sauce in the morning, or even on the day before, and you'll have plenty of time to give this dish the attention it needs.

Yield: 4 servings

For first roasting
    Vegetable oil
    1 duck, 5 to 5½ pounds, defrosted if
        frozen, giblets removed
For seasoning the breasts and crumbing the
   legs and wing pieces
    3 Tbs or so duck fat, from the roasting
        pan
    1 Tbs minced shallots
    1 cup fresh bread crumbs (see sidebar,
        page 212)
    ½ cup Dijon-style prepared mustard

Jacques

My technique for duck on page 301 is adapted from a method used for Southern-fried chicken. It starts with frying, but then the pan is covered and steam develops, which cooks the meat as it would be in a pressure cooker, so it becomes very tender.

With duck, most of the fat comes out during the first frying, and the skin, which is on the bottom of the pan, gets very crisp. At that point, the duck pieces are half submerged in fat, but you don't pour any out. Most people would want to get rid of the fat at that point, but in fact, if you continue to cook the duck in the fat, you will eventually be able to draw more fat out of the duck pieces.

You can see this if you take a piece of duck skin and put it on a wire rack in the oven (with a tray underneath). For a while it will render a lot of the fat, but at some point the juices and the sugars caramelize on the surface. This forms a kind of shield that prevents any more fat from coming out. But if that same piece of skin were cooked in fat the whole time, in the end you would get much more out of it. This is what is happening to the duck in the skillet.

When separating the duck, you are making the same cuts that I do with the chicken, as shown on pages 274 and 275. Feel for the joints with your fingers first, then just wiggle the blade of your knife into the exact articulation of the joint and cut through. To locate the

(continued on page 299)

For making the stock and sauce

The duck neck, carcass, and wings
2 Tbs duck fat
1 cup coarsely chopped onions
1 cup carrots, peeled and coarsely chopped
6 cups or so water
1 cup dry white French vermouth
A bouquet garni with 4 parsley sprigs, 2 thyme sprigs, 5 whole peppercorns, an imported bay leaf, tied in a 6-inch leek leaf
1 large fresh tomato, cored and coarsely chopped (about 1¼ cups)
1 large clove garlic, unpeeled
2 Tbs port, plus more if needed
1 tsp potato starch or arrowroot, plus more if needed
Salt and freshly ground black pepper
1 Tbs room-temperature butter

For heating and serving

1 cup or more finished sauce
Salt and freshly ground black pepper
2 Tbs Skin Cracklings (see sidebar, page 303)

Special equipment

For the duck: a shallow-rimmed roasting pan for initial roasting; a flameproof shallow-rimmed casserole for reheating the breast slices and serving all the pieces, or a smaller frying pan and a large warm serving platter; a small roasting pan for the legs; a pastry brush

For the stock and sauce: a sauté pan or wide saucepan for browning (12 inches in diameter); a large saucepan or stockpot (at least 6-quart); a large strainer; a medium whisk

Roasting the whole duck

Preheat the oven to 400°F.

Brush the bottom of the roasting pan lightly with oil and place the duck in it, breast up. Set in the oven and roast for 30 minutes. The duck will be only partly cooked—the breast should feel slightly resistant when pressed—and a good deal of fat will have melted from it.

Remove the duck to a carving board to cool slightly. Pour the fat from the roasting pan. Reserve about ½ cup of fat for use here, and store the rest.

Separating and skinning the duck

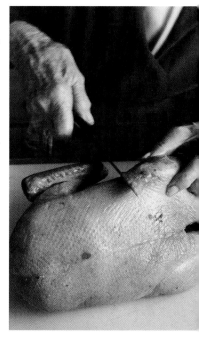

Lift the flap of neck skin, slice around the wishbone, and pry it out as was done for chicken on page 259. Cut through the skin all around one thigh of the duck, cut through the thigh joint, and remove the whole leg, including the "oyster" meat along the backbone. Repeat with the other leg. Separate the thighs from the drumsticks by cutting through the joint.

Cut through the shoulder joint to remove the wings.

Cut through the skin all around the thigh in order to get at the thigh joint, which you will cut through and then remove the whole leg-thigh section.

If you want, you can divide the wing sections and use the 2 large, meaty pieces for crumbing and roasting; otherwise, reserve for the duck stock.

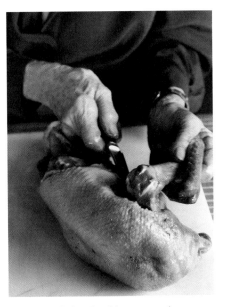

Cut through the shoulder joint and remove the wing.

Slice through the breast skin along the line of the breastbone and, with your fingers, peel the fatty skin from the meat, being careful not to tear off any shreds of meat. Slice along both sides of the breastbone with a long-bladed knife and remove each breast half in one solid piece. Trim any flaps of fat or skin from the 2 breast pieces.

Now peel all the skin and trim the fat from the thigh, drumstick, and large wing pieces, using your fingers and a paring knife as necessary. Be careful not to pull off any meat.

Finally, trim any bits of fat and skin from the carcass, gather all the duck fat and skin, and make cracklings (see sidebar, page 303). Reserve the entire carcass, the wing sections, and the wishbone to make stock and duck sauce, as described below.

Setting up the breasts, legs, and wing pieces for later cooking

Swirl a spoonful of melted duck fat in the flameproof casserole, and sprinkle the shallots in the bottom. Slice each of the breast halves at an angle into 4 neat slices and arrange them, slightly overlapping, over the shallots. Cover with plastic wrap and refrigerate until ready to reheat.

Slice along the side of the breastbone with a long-bladed knife and remove the breast half in one piece.

Jacques (continued from page 297)

shoulder joint, it is helpful to move the wing while you are feeling for the joint inside the breast.

You can also cut your duck in half lengthwise, straight through the breast and backbone, and then cut the legs from the breast pieces. It's simpler, and the pieces will still have all the bones when you eat them—preferably with your fingers.

You will have 6 pieces: 2 breast halves, 2 legs, and 2 thighs.

Slice each breast half at an angle into 4 neat slices.

Julia's Two-Way Duck (continued)

To prepare the legs, film the small roasting pan with duck fat. Drizzle another tablespoon or more of the fat over the bread crumbs and toss together in a shallow bowl, rubbing with your fingers, so the crumbs are evenly but loosely coated. With a pastry brush, paint a thin layer of mustard on the legs and thighs (and wing pieces, if you are using them), one at a time, and roll them in the crumbs to coat. Arrange them in the roasting pan, cover, and refrigerate until the final cooking.

Making the duck stock

Chop the duck neck and carcass into 2-inch pieces. Set the sauté pan over medium-high heat with the 2 tablespoons of duck fat. Toss in all the bones, including the wishbone and the smallest wing sections, and brown them well, stirring and turning, for 10 to 15 minutes. Add the chopped onions and carrots and sauté for about 5 minutes, stirring and tossing with the bones, until nicely colored on the edges. Transfer the bones and vegetables to the saucepan with a slotted spoon.

Pour out any remaining fat from the sauté pan. Then add 2 cups of the water and deglaze the pan, stirring and scraping up all the crusted bits. Pour the juices into the stockpot and add the vermouth, bouquet garni, chopped tomato, garlic clove, and the remaining water, to cover the bones by an inch or so. Bring the liquid to a simmer and cook uncovered for 1½ to 2 hours. Occasionally skim fat from the surface.

After painting the leg and thigh pieces with mustard, roll them in bread crumbs to coat on all sides.

Strain the stock into a bowl or smaller saucepan. Remove the bones from the strainer or colander so you can press the vegetable juices and a bit of vegetable puree into the stock. You should have about 4 cups. Let it settle for a few minutes (or chill it for a couple of hours), then skim as much fat from the surface as possible.

Making the sauce

Return the stock to the boil and cook it down rapidly, until you have only 1½ cups of strong, dark stock.

Stir 1 tablespoon of port into the stock. In a small cup, stir the teaspoon of potato starch with another tablespoon of port until dissolved. Remove the saucepan from the heat, and whisk in the starch slurry a bit at a time. Check the consistency and add more starch until the sauce is as thick as you like. (You can dissolve more starch in port, if needed.) Whisk in a good pinch of salt and several grinds of pepper. Taste and adjust the seasoning. Reheat the sauce just before serving, and swirl in the butter.

Final cooking and serving

About 45 minutes before you want to serve, arrange a rack in the upper third of the oven and preheat to 400°F.

Roast the leg and wing pieces for 25 minutes, until nicely browned and tender when pressed. Leave in the oven with the door open, or in a warm place on the stove, while you reheat the breast slices.

Shortly before serving, sprinkle about ⅛ teaspoon salt and several grindings of pepper over the breast slices, and spoon over about ½ cup of duck sauce. Set the casserole over low heat and gently warm until the slices are heated through and the juices are just bubbling.

Arrange the leg and wing pieces around the breast slices in the pan—or transfer all the meat to a warm serving platter—sprinkle a couple of tablespoons of cracklings over, and serve, with more sauce on the side.

Jacques's Skillet Duck with Parsnips and Shallots

Yield: 4 servings

1 duck, 5 to 5½ pounds, defrosted
  if frozen, giblets removed
¾ tsp salt
¼ tsp freshly ground black pepper
3 large parsnips (about 1½ pounds
  total), peeled, ends trimmed,
  sliced into 1½-inch pieces
2 cups large whole shallots, peeled
  (about 10 ounces unpeeled)
2 heads garlic, cloves (about 30)
  separated but unpeeled
2 sprigs fresh rosemary
2 bay leaves
Chopped fresh parsley, for garnish

Special equipment

A large sauté pan or heavy-
  bottomed saucepan (12-inch
  diameter or larger), non-stick
  preferred, with a tight-fitting
  cover; a large perforated spoon
  or skimmer; a large serving
  platter

Separating the duck

Cut off most of the fatty flap of neck skin and reserve. Insert a sharp knife into 1 breast near the shoulder joint and slice—in a semicircle—around the wishbone. Slide your finger in back of the wishbone and pry it out.

To remove the legs, lift the duck by one leg and cut through the skin all around the thigh, including the meaty piece along the backbone, called the "oyster." Grasp the leg at the knee and pull back the thigh, to

expose the joint. Cut through it and pull the leg off the carcass in 1 piece. Repeat to remove the other leg. Cut the drumsticks from the thigh pieces.

To remove the breast halves, slice along both sides of the breastbone. Lay the duck on its side, and cut through the upper shoulder joint. Hold the carcass down by the neck with one hand, grasp the shoulder section with the other, and pull off the entire breast half, in 1 piece. Repeat on the other side. Pull out the 2 slim meaty filets that remain on either side of the breastbone.

Chop off the wing tips. Cut around the wing on 1 breast piece to free it from the breastbone; separate the largest wing joint from the other 2. Repeat on the other side.

You should now have 12 pieces to put in the pan: 2 large breast pieces, 2 thighs, 2 drumsticks, 2 small breast filets, and 4 wing pieces.

Finally, trim any loose, fatty flaps of skin from the carcass, the breast, or the leg pieces and save for cracklings (see sidebar). Use the wishbone, wing tips, and carcass to make duck stock and sauce, as described in Julia's recipe (pages 300 and 301).

Frying the duck

Set the pan over moderate heat. Slice the reserved neck skin into 3 or 4 strips and put them in the pan to begin rendering fat. Season the duck pieces with ½ teaspoon of the salt and the ¼ teaspoon pepper. When there's enough fat to film the pan bottom, lay in all the pieces, skin side down (you can push aside the strips of neck skin, but leave them in the pan).

Raise the heat to medium-high, and cook skin side down and uncovered. The duck skin will shrink and color, and lots of fat will accumulate in the pan. Check the underside of the pieces once or twice to make sure they are not burning; lower the heat slightly if necessary. Fry until the skin on all the pieces is well browned and quite crisp; the whole process should take 20 to 25 minutes.

Turn the heat down to low. Leave the duck pieces on their skin—they should be half submerged in fat—and strew the parsnip pieces, shallots, and garlic cloves all around them in the pan. Add the rosemary and bay leaves, and sprinkle over ¼ tea-

Opposite: Skillet Duck with Parsnips and Shallots

Skin Cracklings and Duck Fat

You will have a pile of skin and fat trimmings with both our duck methods (a big one with Julia's and a smaller pile with Jacques's), and you can cook these up easily to get two useful products, skin cracklings and clear duck fat. The cracklings make a fine crunchy garnish for the cooked ducks and duck salad, and you can sprinkle them as well on scrambled eggs, salads, mashed potatoes, and other vegetables—unless they are consumed by snackers. The flavorful duck fat is great for sautéed potatoes, for basting chicken, and for *confits*, the classic way of cooking and storing goose, duck, and other meats.

To make cracklings, go over the skin pieces, discarding tough, thick parts, keeping those you can slice ⅜ inch wide. Arrange in a baking pan and roast in a 350°F oven for 35 to 45 minutes, until the cracklings are crisp and nicely browned. Or fry over moderate heat for 25 to 30 minutes, until the pieces are very crisp and the fat is clear.

With a slotted spoon, remove to drain on paper towels and season with pinches of salt, pepper, and allspice. Chop the strips into crunchy bits. Store covered in the refrigerator for several days. Store the fat in a jar or other sealed container in the refrigerator for several months. Duck cracklings go nicely with the Duck Giblets and Escarole Salad on the next page.

spoon of salt. Cover the pan, turn down the heat to low, and cook for 30 minutes. Check occasionally to make sure that the duck is gently steaming; adjust the heat as necessary.

When the duck and vegetables are tender—pierce with a sharp knife to check—turn off the heat. Immediately lift the duck and vegetable pieces from the pan with the spoon or skimmer, allowing the fat to drain, and arrange on the serving platter.

Pour off the clear duck fat from the pan—you will have 1½ cups or so—and save for other uses (see sidebar, page 303). Add 1 cup of water to the pan, bring to a boil, scraping with a wooden spatula to melt all the solidified juice, and pour over the duck. Scatter chopped parsley over and serve.

A Côtes du Rhône, Syrah, or Grenache-type wine would be good with this duck.

Jacques's Duck Giblets and Escarole Salad

To enjoy every bit of your duck, slice and sauté the giblets to top this simple green salad, add a spoonful of duck fat to the dressing, and sprinkle cracklings over all. Escarole or other assertive greens, like curly endive (frisée), cress, or mesclun, are a good match for the rich morsels of meat. Toss in some small, warm cooked potatoes and an extra handful of lettuce, and this will make a main course lunch for two.

Yield: 2 servings

For the dressing
2 tsp finely chopped shallots
1 Tbs Dijon-style prepared
    mustard
1 Tbs red-wine vinegar

¼ tsp salt
¼ tsp freshly ground black pepper
1 Tbs rendered duck fat, reserved
    from preceding recipes
3 Tbs extra-virgin olive oil

Giblets from a fresh duck (gizzard,
    heart, and liver)
2 tsp rendered duck fat
⅛ tsp salt
⅛ tsp freshly ground black pepper
4 cups (or more) escarole, curly
    endive, or other lettuce, cut into
    3-inch pieces, rinsed and dried
    well
1 Tbs Skin Cracklings (see sidebar,
    page 303)

To prepare the dressing, whisk together the shallots, mustard, vinegar, salt, and pepper in a small bowl. Drizzle in the spoonful of duck fat and the olive oil, whisking steadily, to make a nicely emulsified vinaigrette.

With a sharp paring knife, slice off the thick white membrane on one side of the gizzard. Cut the trimmed gizzard and the duck heart into thin slivers. Slice the liver into ¼-inch-thick strips.

Heat the 2 teaspoons of fat in a small frying pan over medium-high heat and add the gizzard and heart pieces only. Sauté for about 1½ minutes, tossing frequently in the fat, and season with the salt and pepper. Add the strips of liver, and sauté 1 minute more, tossing and stirring, until the liver is cooked through. Take the pan off the heat.

In a large bowl, toss the escarole pieces with 3 or 4 tablespoons of the vinaigrette, until evenly coated. Heap equal portions of the greens on 2 plates, and distribute half of the warm giblet pieces on top of each. Sprinkle cracklings over the salads and enjoy immediately.

Julia's Duck Leg Salad

Duck legs need special treatment, such as being crumbed and roasted, as we've seen, or stir-fried and sauced, as suggested here.

The duck meat

For 6 servings, peel the skin and any visible fat off the legs and thighs of 2 roaster ducklings. Bone them neatly, and pound the meat firmly between 2 layers of plastic wrap, doubling the meat in width. Slice it into lengthwise strips ¼ inch wide. Toss with a light sprinkling of salt, pepper, and allspice.

The dressing

Make a sweet-and-sour dressing by whisking together in a small bowl 1½ tablespoons each of minced shallots and fresh lemon juice with 1 tablespoon each of wine vinegar, Dijon mustard, and either hoisin sauce or minced chutney. Whisk in by droplets ½ cup of light olive oil, add droplets of dark sesame oil, and season to taste with salt and pepper.

Stir-frying

Just before serving, stir-fry the duck-meat strips in light olive oil for 2 to 3 minutes, until lightly browned but pink inside. Turn the meat into a bowl and toss with 3 tablespoons of the dressing.

Salad and serving

Toss your salad greens—curly endive or hearts of romaine cut into crosswise half-inch slices—in a bowl with the rest of the dressing and divide among 4 salad plates. Arrange the strips of duck meat attractively upon and around the greens. This would be an appropriate setting for a sprinkling of the duck cracklings on page 303.

To accompany the salad, you might include sliced freshly cooked beets, which go beautifully with duck and are quick to do in the pressure cooker as follows:

Beets in the Pressure Cooker

Fresh beets take hours to cook in the oven but only about 15 minutes in the pressure cooker, which does an excellent job.

Choose beets all of the same size, about 2 inches in diameter. Scrub them under the cold water tap with a stiff brush. Keep on the tails but cut off the tops, leaving a 1-inch stem. Cook under 15 pounds pressure for 15 minutes, release the steam, and check. They are done when a small knife pierces them through easily. Re-pressure cook 2 or 3 minutes longer if necessary.

Cool briefly in cold water, and slip off the skins while still warm. Remove the tails and stems.

To serve, cut them into slices and dress as follows. For 4 beets, purée a small clove of garlic with ¼ teaspoon of salt, then whip in 3 to 4 tablespoons of excellent olive oil. Toss in a bowl with the beet slices; correct seasoning. If serving them unaccompanied, you may wish to toss again with a handful of chopped fresh parsley.

MEATS

WHAT WITH ALL THE HEALTH ALERTS OF THE LAST COUPLE OF DECADES, SOME PEOPLE IN America are eating less meat these days. But meat is coming back into vogue, and we're giving it extensive coverage in this big chapter. We both love meat and we cook and eat it almost every day. Our portions may be smaller, which means that they should be all the more enjoyable. And the more you know about meat— particularly as the meat we are getting now has changed considerably—the better your stew, steak, roast, or simple sauté will be. It's not a matter of spending lots of money. When you know how to recognize quality in the meat you buy (whether beef, veal, pork, or lamb), and understand the characteristics of different meat cuts and the right methods to cook them, you can make fine dishes with modestly priced pieces. If you master some of the simple butchering and trimming techniques that Jacques demonstrates here, you can save even more (and will learn a tremendous amount about cooking too). And when you do splurge on an extravagant Chateaubriand, you can have confidence that you will be getting the flavor and natural tenderness that you have paid for, and the primal pleasure that only a great piece of meat can provide.

Julia on Steaks and Pan-Frying

For a meat eater like me, there's nothing so satisfying as a perfect steak: a beautiful piece of well-aged, prime beef prepared in the simplest manner—grilled or broiled, perhaps then roasted a bit if it's thick. I like it best with nothing more than salt and pepper, and a little plain or flavored butter or a small deglazing sauce.

But I am terribly concerned that such a wonderful piece of meat is getting more and more difficult to find, even in top restaurants. Too often I have been served a steak, beautifully prepared by a talented chef, only to find it has almost no flavor at all. As someone who eats beef several times a week, I have been forced to an unhappy conclusion: much of what is sold these days is just second-class beef.

One problem, I believe, is that people are so afraid of fat that they demand lean meat, thinking that leaner is better—and, so it seems, they have scared the meat producers. Prime grade—the finest beef, which gets much of its tenderness and taste from a generous marbling of fat—now accounts for only 2 percent of all the beef we produce. As a result, we are in danger of losing the irreplaceable flavor of well-marbled beef.

Then, too, beef is rarely aged as it used to be, either on the hoof or after slaughter. Older animals yield better meat, but most of what we get comes from young steers that are quickly brought to market size. And after beef is slaughtered, butchers say that there's just no room in their coolers to hang it for the weeks it takes to tenderize and develop flavor.

What this means for us meat lovers is that we must work harder to find the best. Get to know your butcher and ask him about the cuts and the quality of the meat you buy: where it comes from on the animal, how tender it is, and how well it has been aged. If you can find one, it's good to deal with an independent butcher who is always available to answer questions. In several of my local supermarket chains, I find the butchers happy to come forward and share their knowledge. And if they are not willing or able to answer my questions, or if there's no one there but a clerk, I change markets!

As for the fear of fat, I say just eat sensibly. If you stick to small helpings and no seconds, you can eat anything you want. There is a great deal of enjoyment to be had in a 4- or 5-ounce portion of well-marbled steak—the size of a pack of cards.

The pan-fried steaks that Jacques and I present in the following recipes are all quick to prepare, well suited for spur-of-the-moment occasions when you have just minutes to cook. All of them call for a small sauce made right in the sauté pan. When you deglaze the pan with a bit of liquid, you capture the essence of meat flavor. It's the bonus you get from pan-frying, something that is lost if you use a grill or a broiler. You won't have lots of sauce—just enough to coat the steak in an intimate way.

You can use different liquids—whatever stock you have on hand, or wine or water. Use as well herbs or other flavors that you like. And with a simple swirl of butter you can provide a natural thickening and a smooth finish to your sauce. These simple techniques are all-important lessons that I learned in France many years ago, and they still are to me the hallmark of really good home cooking.

Jacques on Steaks and Pan-Frying

If you're shopping for a good steak, it's more useful to have knowledge about meat than a lot of money. There are a number of lesser-known cuts of beef that you may find in the market, or order from your butcher, that are as tender and tasty as premium steaks from the rib, loin, and tenderloin—for a fraction of the price.

You may have to look a bit harder for some of these "butcher steaks" or "bistro steaks," but it is worth the effort. Using our recipes, you can prepare them in much the same way as you do a fancy strip steak or filet mignon. And you may find, as I do, that you actually prefer these inexpensive cuts for their full flavor and satisfying texture.

Butchers have always known about such juicy cuts as the hangar steak (or hanging tender), the oyster steak, the flank steak, and the skirt steak, and reserved them for their own use; hence "butcher steaks." Recently American chefs have discovered their taste and good value and have made them quite popular. Almost unknown in this country a few years ago, the hanging tender (so called because it is a single piece of meat that hangs inside the cavity below the tenderloin) is today as common in New York as in France, where *onglet* has long been a favorite. Skirt steak—the narrow, long diaphragm muscle—is much in demand for fajitas. Flank steak, a fibrous muscle from the lower side of the beef, is the best known of this group and is now nearly as expensive as a loin steak.

There are others even less familiar to us: the oyster steak—*araignée*, or "spider," in French, for the web-like appearance of the fiber—is similar to the tender "oyster" morsel found near the hip of a chicken. Of course, it is bigger in beef, about 10 ounces, and most likely has to be special-ordered. A favorite steak of mine is cut from the top blade muscle in the shoulder: easily found in any market, it is what we use in our recipe for country steak. Another tender muscle for steaks is the triangle or triangle tip, from the sirloin "butt" section.

Unfortunately, even if you know what you are looking for, you will be faced with considerable confusion in the names of meat cuts. Though the meat industry has attempted to set standard terminology, no one is obliged to use it. As a result, roasts and steaks are called by many names in different parts of the country—and markets and restaurants even in your own neighborhood may not identify cuts the same way.

This is true even of the most popular cuts: a boneless steak sliced from the top loin muscle—as we use for our *steak au poivre*—may be called a strip steak, New York strip steak, loin strip, sirloin strip, club steak, Delmonico steak, shell steak, or other names, and that is just in New York City.

The piece of beef shoulder that I cut up for our country steak is called the top blade in the East and the flatiron in the West; the little steaks you get from it may be called chicken steaks, top blade steaks, top-of-the-chuck steaks, blade steaks, butter steaks, and probably other names I haven't yet heard.

Don't be stymied by this confusion. If you know where the steak comes from on the animal, you can always tell the butcher the actual piece of meat you want, whatever the local name. And if that specific cut isn't available, or the price seems too high, another cut will be fine. Our recipes call for particular steaks, but you can substitute almost any of the others mentioned here. For instance, if your market has no top blade steak but you see a nice flank steak, don't hesitate to try it with the *persillade* topping from our country steak—or take an inexpensive top blade, crust it in peppercorns, and sauté it instead of a pricey loin cut in our *steak au poivre*. The results will be equally delicious.

Julia

A really thick cut from the boneless strip is one of my favorite steaks. But while *steak au poivre* is magnificent for those with a great appetite for pepper, it is not my favorite preparation. I think that, the better the piece of meat, the less you need to put on it.

I would simply "broil-roast" a well-marbled prime steak of this size (or even larger)—that is, I sear the whole piece in a pan, or under the broiler, very quickly, then roast it in a moderate oven for about 20 minutes. It's a good way to handle a thick cut because there's no risk of overcooking the outside until it is dry and tough, in order to get the meat inside to a perfect rare doneness. However, see Jacques's excellent "sauté–oven-rest" method for his version of Chateaubriand on page 322.

A word of caution: take care when flaming the cognac for the pan sauce. Jacques is an expert in what he calls "pyrotechnic" cooking, and pours the cognac right from the bottle. But it is safer to add a measured amount of cognac from a ladle, to be certain that the flames can't leap up into the bottle and perhaps explode. Of course, avert your face and stand back as you tilt the pan to ignite the alcohol.

Steak au Poivre

Steak au poivre is a classic preparation for sautéed steak, long associated with high-class—and high-price—restaurants. Here we use a top-notch loin strip steak, which has the intense beef flavor to match the spiciness of the cracked-peppercorn coating and is so naturally tender that a double-thick cut can be pan-fried in just a few minutes. But you could also use any tender steak that is suitable for pan-frying, including such inexpensive "butcher" cuts as the blade steak or hangar steak.

Traditionally, *steak au poivre* is made with just black peppercorns, but there are many other varieties available today that add different degrees of heat and spicy flavor. We use a mixture of black, green, and white peppercorns; Jamaican peppercorns, which are really allspice; and Szechuan peppercorns. You can make your own combination or buy one of the blends sold in specialty markets.

A sauté of mushrooms (see page 204) would be a fine accompaniment.

Yield: 2 steaks, each about 6–7 ounces,
serving 2 generously or 3

1 thick-cut well-marbled strip steak,
about 1 pound total weight, and 1½
inches thick
2 Tbs or so mixed whole peppercorns,
including black, white, green,
Szechuan, and Jamaican (whole allspice)
Salt
1 tsp vegetable oil
1 Tbs butter

For the pan sauce
2 Tbs minced shallots
2 Tbs cognac (or bourbon or red wine)
½ cup flavorful dark stock (page 41)
1 Tbs unsalted butter, at room temperature

For the garnish
Chopped parsley
Watercress

Trim the steak of all
the surrounding fat and
cartilage. Cut the meat
into 2 pieces and crush
the peppercorns, follow-
ing the photographs on
page 312.

Steak au poivre must be the
grandfather of all the spice "rubs" that
are so popular today. Here we vary the
classic approach only slightly—using
peppercorns with different nuances of
flavor—but there is nothing wrong with
trying different spices as a coating for the
steak. Be creative. See what you have in
your cupboard. You might use fennel, caraway, or cumin, or try some dried herbs,
such as thyme or *herbes de Provence*.

Remember that the flavor of the
spices you put on the steak will be altered
by sautéing, just as they are when you
roast spices. Some flavors will be intensified and others diminished: for instance, a
good deal of the heat of pepper, even
cayenne, is reduced by searing in a very
hot pan.

Our basic recipe calls for a thick
cut of the New York strip, which I then
divide into two round pieces, resem-
bling tournedos from the tenderloin. I
do this so that each single portion of
steak, about 6 to 8 ounces, will still be
thick and juicy. If I sliced a piece of this
weight off the strip, it would be too thin
for my taste. But you might prefer a thin
steak with a large, crusty surface area—
and you can prepare your pepper steak
that way as well.

Similarly, the pan sauce can be
varied with what you have on hand—
what I call *cuisine d'opportunité*. Good
stock is essential, but you could omit
the shallots; if you don't have cognac,
deglaze with red wine, or bourbon;
instead of butter, add a bit of cream to
the pan and reduce. Like any recipe, this
one allows for tremendous latitude in
variation and personal expression.

To crack the peppercorns, crush them with the back of a skillet.

Press cracked peppercorns into both sides of the meat.

Steak au Poivre (continued)

Sprinkle salt to taste on the top and bottom of the steaks; then press each side into the cracked peppercorns, encrusting the steaks lightly or heavily, as you prefer.

Heat the oil and the butter in a heavy sauté or frying pan over high heat. When the pan is quite hot, lay the peppered steaks in. Fry for about 1½ to 2 minutes, until the undersides are well seared. Turn the meat and cook the second side for about a minute. Press with a finger to test for the slight springiness that indicates rare. Cook to desired doneness and remove to a warm platter.

Making the pan sauce

Add the shallots to the pan and sauté briefly, stirring with a spoon to scrape up the drippings. Lean away from the stove (averting your face) and pour the cognac into the pan; tilt the edge of the pan slightly, over the burner flame, to ignite the alcohol. The cognac will flame up for a few seconds as the alcohol burns off; cook for a few moments more and then add the stock. Bring the liquid back to the boil, and cook about 1 minute to thicken the sauce, stirring occasionally.

Pour cognac into the pan, averting your face.

Taste and adjust seasoning. Finally, add the soft butter, swirling the pan until it melts and incorporates with the juices.

When blended, pour the sauce over the steaks. Sprinkle liberally with chopped parsley and garnish each plate with sprigs of parsley or watercress.

Opposite: Steak au Poivre

Julia

It is important to cook the steaks only briefly—this thin cut must remain rare—and to use a good stock as a base for the sauce. Veal stock or beef stock would be my choices, but any other flavorful dark stock will be fine (see page 41). In my steak Diane sauce, I mix the base with some Dijon mustard, which provides a natural thickening, or *liaison*.

I now use rib-eye steak—a boneless cut from the rib section of the beef. I used to use top loin, but since beef is so lean these days, I find top loin tough; the rib-eye is more tender and often has more marbling—hence more flavor. Look for rib steaks that have the largest amount of the tender "eye" muscle and less of the "rib cap," which you must trim off. Tell your butcher that you want steaks cut from the end of the rib that's near the loin, not the shoulder end. And don't be afraid to pound the meat firmly, since that tenderizes it.

Steak Diane

This is a fun—and delicious—way to make a steak. The meat is pounded thin, fried in a flash, and then bathed in a savory pan sauce that you create on the spot.

A very popular dish in fancy supper clubs during the 1930s and '40s, steak Diane was prepared with flair by the maître d'hôtel at tableside. You can do the same in the kitchen, but it's more dramatic in front of your guests, and since the cooking takes less than four minutes, it's a good choice for a small dinner party.

Serve with Pommes de Terre Savonnette (page 162).

Julia's Steak Diane

Yield: 2 large steaks, serving 4

2 rib-eye steaks, about 12 ounces each, with a large portion of "eye"
1 tsp or so fresh, tasteless vegetable oil (canola or other)
Drops of soy sauce
2 Tbs clarified butter (page 133)

For the deglazing sauce

½ to ⅔ cup flavorful stock, such as veal (page 40), beef (page 42), or Julia's Quick Dark Stock (page 41)
1 to 2 Tbs Dijon-type prepared mustard
1 to 2 Tbs clarified butter
2 Tbs finely chopped shallots or scallions
1 to 2 Tbs chopped parsley

Suggestions for sauce

Worcestershire sauce
Freshly squeezed lemon juice
Cognac, port, or Madeira
Fresh thyme or tarragon, chopped
Salt and freshly ground black pepper

Special equipment

A meat mallet or other heavy object with a flat surface (such as a small heavy skillet) for pounding the steaks; a large frying pan (at least 12 inches top diameter if you wish to sauté both steaks at once)

Preparing the steaks

Trim the steaks, removing all the fat, gristle, and any attached bits of meat that are not part of the "eye" or large central muscle. (You can save the meaty scraps and grind them for hamburger.)

Place a steak between 2 long pieces of plastic wrap or waxed paper on a solid work surface and pound to an even ¼-inch thinness. The meat will spread inside the plastic into an oval about 9 or 10 inches long. Remove the plastic wrap, dry the steaks with a paper towel, and rub each side of the meat with a little oil and drops of soy sauce. Set aside. Prepare the other steak.

Assemble all the sauce ingredients, including optional embellishments, for ready use at the stove. Stir together ½ cup of the stock or bouillon with 1 tablespoon of the prepared mustard, reserving a bit of stock. Have ready a warm platter for the cooked steaks.

Sautéing the steaks

Set the pan over high heat. When hot, add the 2 tablespoons of clarified butter, swirling to film the bottom of the pan. Lay the steaks in the hot pan and sauté for barely a minute. Turn and sauté the other side for 40 to 50 seconds, then remove to the platter. Don't overcook: the steaks should still be rare, lightly colored, and just slightly springy to the touch.

Making the sauce

With the pan still on high heat, add another spoonful or two of clarified butter and stir in the chopped shallots or scallions. Sauté for about ½ minute and pour in the stock and mustard. Mix the sauce vigorously, scraping up any browned bits on the bottom of the pan.

(continued on page 317)

Jacques

I never heard of steak Diane before I came to this country—like vichyssoise, this is a French preparation that is more famous in America than it is in France. But I agree with Julia that this kind of tableside dish is a nice way to vary your cooking: it is fast and gives guests a nice spectacle in the dining room. As with our Crêpes Suzette (page 410), I hope this dish makes a comeback!

However, for my taste, I would use a New York strip steak. The taste is just as good, and the rib-eye often has too much fat inside the cut, which must be removed.

I like to butterfly the steak, which thins the meat quickly, with less pounding. Slice the steak into two even layers, with the knife blade parallel to the work surface, but stop before you have cut all the way through. Then unfold as if you were opening a book, and you will have a steak that is already half as thick. Pound it just a bit more to get it to the desired thinness.

When pounding, we don't want just to crush the meat. It is important to pound it between pieces of plastic wrap; the plastic allows the meat to slide and get larger as it gets thinner. Or you can just sprinkle some water on the work surface, which is the traditional way to let the steak spread out without being crushed to a paste.

A Note About Tableside Cooking

Steak Diane is a dish to do at the table in front of your guests if at all possible. The main thing you will need is a big pan and an adequate heat source, preferably a chafing dish with a strong burner that uses liquid alcohol fuel. (Solid alcohol gel, like canned Sterno, will not provide enough heat.) You could also use a small, portable gas burner or an electric skillet, though they are less elegant.

Artfully arrange the ingredients—on a silver tray, perhaps—in small dishes, bowls, and pitchers. Assemble your guests in place as well. And to get things started efficiently, you can pre-heat your sauté pan in the kitchen and bring it to the chafer or portable burner when you are ready to start cooking.

Steak Diane (continued)

Now taste the sauce and flavor it to your liking, adding a bit more stock or mustard, a little of the chopped parsley, drops of Worcestershire, freshly squeezed lemon juice, cognac, chopped thyme or tarragon, and salt and freshly ground pepper.

Finally, return the steaks to the pan along with any meat juices. Bathe in the simmering sauce for just a few moments to heat through, turning them once or twice.

Remove the steaks to the warm serving platter again, spoon the remaining sauce over and sprinkle remaining chopped parsley generously on top. Slice each steak into 2 equal portions and serve immediately.

Do-ahead note

The steaks can be pounded and rubbed with oil and soy sauce hours ahead, and stored well wrapped in the refrigerator.

Julia on Testing Meat for Doneness

When sautéing steaks and hamburgers, experienced cooks press the meat to test its doneness. Here's what they are "feeling" for:

Uncooked meat has no resistance —it is mushy, and a finger press will leave an indentation.

When meat is very rare, it will still feel soft and squashy.

As it cooks to the rare stage, the juices begin to accumulate in the center and the meat will bounce back just a bit when pressed.

As meat cooks to medium, the tissue contracts, and it will resist more and more.

When it doesn't bounce at all, but remains firm to the touch, the meat is well done.

To get to know the "feel" of these different stages, press a finger against the fleshy muscle below your thumb. When your open hand is relaxed, the squashy feeling is that of raw or very rare meat. Clench your fingers: the tightening muscle will become springy, like rare meat. As you squeeze your fist, the flesh will get more resistant, just as meat feels when it is cooked to "well done."

Julia

I had never heard of this cut before Jacques demonstrated it, and it is a perfect example of what I like to call "secret steaks"—lovely small "steakable" cuts of meat that we too often overlook or don't know about. There's another muscle in the chuck which makes very nice small steaks, variously known as the mock tender, the blade tender, or the Scotch tender. It is easy to find in the supermarket, and would be delicious prepared the same way.

Country Steak (Top Blade)

Any pan-fried steak would be delightful finished "country-style," with a simple *persillade,* or garlic-and-parsley sauce. But here we introduce you to an unusual steak cut, from the top blade muscle of the chuck or beef shoulder, that is relatively inexpensive yet tender, juicy, and full of flavor.

The top blade—also known as the flatiron—is a long wedge-shaped muscle near the shoulder blade. In most markets, it is easy to find small boneless steaks cut crosswise from the top blade, under different names (see Jacques's comment on page 309). There is a wide, flat sinew that runs through the length of the muscle, which is visible as a line across the middle of these steaks.

What makes our preparation special, however, is Jacques's method of cutting the meat completely away from this sinew, so it is tender throughout to cut and eat. As you can see from the photos on pages 320 and 321, "splitting" the top blade this way is easy (and economical) to do yourself, but if you prefer, any good butcher should be able to do it for you. You can also use a conventionally cut blade steak, with the sinew still in the center, often called chicken steak. It will be smaller—and a bit more chewy—but still very good.

Serve this simple steak bistro-style, with excellent French fries, page 166.

Jacques's Top Blade Steak

Yield: 12 to 16 ounces of steak, serving
2 generously or 3

3 large cloves garlic, peeled
A large handful of fresh parsley leaves,
   washed, large stems removed
1 tsp canola oil
1 to 2 Tbs unsalted butter
2 large top blade steaks, split from the
   thin end of the flatiron (see pages
   320–321) (about ¾ to 1 pound total)
Salt and freshly ground black pepper
¼ cup water (or stock or wine) for
   deglazing

Prepare the *persillade:* mash the garlic cloves on the work surface and roughly chop; then lay the parsley on top of the garlic, and chop together until all is finely minced. You should have about 3 tablespoons.

Heat the oil and a tablespoon of the butter in a large, heavy sauté or frying pan over high heat for a minute or so. Season both sides of the steaks with salt and pepper. When the pan is quite hot, lay the steaks in. Fry for about 2 minutes over high heat and turn when the first side is well seared. Cook the second side for about 1½ minutes, then begin to test for doneness (see sidebar, page 317). Remove the steaks to a serving platter when rare, medium, or well done, as you like.

Making the pan sauce

If the pan is dry, add a couple of teaspoons of butter, swirl to melt, then toss in the *persillade* all at once, shaking the pan and stirring for about 30 seconds. Pour in the ¼ cup of water (or other liquid), and cook rapidly for ½ minute or so, tossing the pan and stirring to deglaze the pan juices. Remove from the heat and pour the sauce over the steaks.

Serve immediately, slicing the steaks across the grain.

Jacques

Though it is not usually done by butchers, some years ago I decided to remove the large central sinew from the "flatiron" before cutting it into steaks (see photos on next page). With the sinew removed, I find these as tender as steaks that cost three or four times as much.

Using this trimming method, you get two small steaks from the thin end of the top blade. The thick end could also be cut into a steak, but is best braised in red wine—a delicious pot roast for four.

About the pan sauce: In France we call this wonderful combination of parsley (*persil*) and garlic (*ail*) a *persillade*. For me it is the signature of home cooking. My mother used to use it on top of many things, on fish, tomatoes, zucchini, as well as steak, as we do here. If you like, you can deglaze the skillet with chicken stock, or red or white wine, but water is perfectly fine. Everything is simple here; that's why I like to call this a country steak.

Cutting a Country Steak from the Top Blade

To cut your own tender top blade steaks (and perhaps save a bit of money), order a whole top blade: trimmed by the butcher, it should weigh between 3½ and 4½ pounds.

2. Make a cut into the meat about 5 inches from the narrow (or far) end with a sharp, thin-bladed boning or carving knife, and, angling your knife blade, start slicing and scraping the meat away from the tough sinew layer in the middle of the muscle.

1. Trim both sides of the meat, removing any surface sinew ("silver skin") or fat.

3. Continue to cut through to the narrow end of the muscle, removing a steak about 1 inch thick and weighing 6 to 8 ounces. (Now you can see the thick, fibrous sinew.)

4. Turn the meat over and cut off a similar steak from the other side of the sinew. Trim any bits of ligament or fat from these pieces before cooking.

Jacques on Butter and Oil for Pan-Fried Steaks

When frying steaks and making a deglazing sauce, as with the country steak or the *steak au poivre*, I use regular unsalted butter, adding a little bit of neutral-flavored oil, like canola, to keep the butter from burning. The oil raises the temperature at which the milk solids in the butter will burn; when the fat from the meat melts and mixes in, this further prevents burning.

Clarified butter can be used, if you happen to have some on hand, as the milk solids have been removed completely and can't burn—but there's no need to go to the trouble of clarifying a small amount of butter just to make a quick steak.

When you remove the meat and start to prepare the pan sauce, make sure that there is enough fat in the pan for flavor—at least a couple of teaspoons. If the pan is dry, add more butter.

If you do not intend to make a pan sauce, you don't need butter at all. As I do with my hamburger and Chateaubriand, just rub them all over with a few drops of oil, which will keep them from sticking to the pan.

5. Cut the remaining piece of top blade crosswise, in approximately 1-inch thicknesses, for conventionally cut steaks, 6 ounces or so each. Or you can split the meat from the sinew as in step 2, yielding 2 large pieces, about a pound each.

Julia

In most books, the heart is the most tender and luxurious part of the tenderloin and technically it is known as the Chateaubriand. The butt end—Jacques calls it the head—is somewhat less tender, but here Jacques turns it into a large and impressive steak. If you divide the tenderloin yourself, you can cut a traditional Chateaubriand from the heart—it will be smaller—and prepare it the same way.

The tenderloin, a muscle running under the backbone, is tender because it is barely exercised. But I generally find more flavor in actively used muscles: to my taste the tenderloin is rather too mild, especially if it lacks sufficient marbling. Nevertheless, tenderloin steaks have great appeal, and their mild flavor matches well with a rich and highly flavored sauce like a béarnaise. And Chateaubriand always looks beautiful on a platter, surrounded by vegetables—well worth bringing to the table whole and slicing and serving with some ceremony for your guests.

Jacques's Chateaubriand

Chateaubriand is a large cut of the tenderloin, the most luxurious and expensive part of the beef. In this version, the thick end, or "head," of the tenderloin—or filet—is pounded to steak thickness, grilled briefly on the stovetop, then finished in a low oven. The result is a perfectly rare and tender piece of meat—you can think of it as either a steak or a roast—that can be the centerpiece of a special meal for four people.

Though once hard to find, tenderloins—or filets, as they are also called—are readily available now at most supermarkets, whole or cut into premium-priced steaks—large Chateaubriand, medium-sized tournedos, and small filets mignon. You can have the head of the tenderloin cut for this recipe or buy an entire filet and trim it yourself, as Jacques demonstrates in the photos on pages 324 and 325. It's a simple process, and economical as well, particularly when markets offer a special. Once trimmed, you can roast it whole (see sidebar, page 324) or divide it into steaks, just as you like them.

This recipe calls for searing and marking the Chateaubriand on a stovetop grill (or an outdoor grill), following the procedure called *quadrillage,* described on page 363. If you prefer, sauté the steak in a heavy frying pan until well browned, then just set the pan in the oven for the final cooking at low temperature.

The meat will relax and release its natural juices, which should be used to moisten the slices when you serve. You can also top the Chateaubriand with a flavored butter, such as the Beurre Maître d'Hôtel (page 230), or make a deglazing sauce in the frying pan (if you sautéed the meat).

For the most elegant and traditional presentation, serve your Chateaubriand on a large platter surrounded by a colorful array of *haricots verts,* sliced asparagus, and "turned" carrots and potatoes, steamed and sautéed in butter, as pictured here, or other sautéed vegetables (see pages 208–209). And for a special occasion, it is traditional, and well worth the effort, to serve Sauce Béarnaise (page 99) in a bowl on the side.

Yield: 1 large steak, serving 4

One 20-ounce piece tenderloin, cut
   from the large end (head)
¼ tsp salt
¼ tsp freshly ground pepper
1 tsp virgin olive oil or other vegetable
   oil

Special equipment

A ridged stovetop grill, or a heavy sauté
   pan; a sturdy kitchen towel, for holding
   the meat; a meat mallet or other flat
   heavy object (like a skillet) for pounding the meat; a small, shallow roasting
   pan; a warm serving platter

Forming the Chateaubriand

Preheat the oven to 250°F.

Stand the meat on its wider cut
end on a solid work surface. Fold the
kitchen towel once or twice, lengthwise, into a wide band and drape it
loosely around the upright meat like a
scarf. Gather the ends and twist to
form a tight collar that will hold the
meat in a round shape during pounding; grasp securely in one hand. With
the other hand, pound the top of the
meat with the mallet, until flattened
into an oval steak, about 2 inches
thick and 5 to 7 inches wide.

Grilling and oven rest

Set the grill over high heat and allow it to get quite hot.
Season the steak with salt and pepper on both the top and bottom and rub with the oil to coat all surfaces.

Grill the steak for a total of 10 to 12 minutes, depending
on thickness and how well done you like it. Follow these steps
and refer to the photos of pork chops on page 363:

Jacques

Julia and I disagree about
the precise definition of Chateaubriand.
To me, it is a large piece of the tenderloin—meant to serve several people—
cut crosswise, and cooked on the cut
side, like a steak. You can take the piece
from the head of the tenderloin, as I usually do, or from the heart (or *coeur de
filet*)—they are equally tender, in my
opinion. The advantage of using the
wide head is that you can get a large
piece—almost 1½ pounds—that will flatten easily into a steak that can serve 4
people. A piece of the heart of this
weight will be long and tubular, and
when you try to compress it to make a
steak, it will split or fold up like an accor-
dion. However, you can cut a smaller
piece from the heart, about a pound, and
prepare that as a Chateaubriand for 2.

An important part of the method
used here—one I use frequently with
thick pieces of meat and even fish—is a
period of rest and final cooking in a low
oven. When the meat is grilling or
sautéing, it shrivels on the outside, the
muscle tissue contracts, and the juices of
the meat—including the myoglobin,
which contains red pigment—is pushed
toward the center of the meat. If you cut
into the steak right after the sautéing,
you would find the outer parts gray and
hard, appearing overcooked, and the
center would look raw. However, resting
in the low oven allows the meat to relax
and the juices to flow back through the
whole piece. Then, when you slice the
steak, it will be an attractive pink color all
the way through.

Jacques's Whole Roast Tenderloin

A whole roast tenderloin is an easy and generous dish for a party. Because the meat is very lean—and you have trimmed it well, removing all the surface fat—it can be served warm, at room temperature, or cold, as convenient.

Tuck the thin tail of meat underneath the filet and tie it in place, so the roast is approximately of equal thickness its whole length. Season with salt and pepper and brown it well all over on top of the stove, in a couple of tablespoons of butter, or butter and oil, using a heavy roasting pan or large ovenproof sauté pan, preferably made of thick aluminum or copper—about 5 or 6 minutes in all. Set the pan in a 425°F oven for 20 to 25 minutes for a 3½-pound filet, or slightly longer for a larger one, for medium-rare. Rest it for at least 15 minutes, in a warm, draft-free place on the stove, or (if you have 2 ovens) a low oven, set to 180°F. Serve with just the natural juices, or make a sauce from the drippings with wine or stock.

Jacques's Chateaubriand (continued)

Lay the oval steak on the grill at an angle to the ridges and cook for 2½ to 3 minutes, until clearly marked. Turn it over, maintaining the same angle, and cook for 2½ to 3 minutes on the second side. Turn the meat over again and rotate it, so the visible grill marks—known as the *quadrillage*—are perpendicular to the ridges. Cook again for 2½ to 3 minutes, until a crisscross is clearly marked. Turn the steak over for the third time, maintaining the same angle, and grill for 2½ to 3 minutes, so that the second side has been on the grill exactly as long as the first side.

Finally, brown the steak on its thick outside edge—holding it with tongs or propping it against a potato as in the photos—shifting the meat so the entire edge is browned.

The meat should be barely springy to the touch, indicating that it is still rare inside. Transfer to the roasting pan and place in the warm oven for 15 minutes.

Remove the steak to the warm serving platter and surround it with sautéed vegetables if you like. Slice the Chateaubriand thinly on the bias, across the grain of the meat, and pour the accumulated pan juices over. Serve 2 or 3 slices per person.

Trimming and Cutting a Beef Tenderloin

A whole tenderloin is usually sold in a cryovac wrapping, with most of the surrounding fat already removed. It will weigh 6 to 7 pounds before trimming.

Remove the thin strip, called the "chain" (see photos). The good meat of the chain can be trimmed or scraped from its sinews and used in hamburger or other dishes. The sinew can be used in stock. Cut away all fat and sinew from the top and the bottom of the filet.

Remove the thick covering membrane, or "silver skin" (see photos), and reserve for stock.

The trimmed tenderloin weighs approximately 4 pounds. The thin, or "tail," end can be folded under and tied, for roasting the tenderloin whole.

Separate and cut away the thin strip, the "chain," that lies alongside the main tenderloin.

Divide into steaks: First slice off the entire head end of the filet (in the foreground of photo), about 5 inches wide, for use in the preceding recipe as Chateaubriand. The thick center, or heart, of the filet can be cut as shown for a smaller Chateaubriand—one piece about 5 inches wide—and the rest into tournedos or filet steaks, each about 2 inches thick and weighing 7 to 8 ounces.

As the tenderloin narrows, slice thinner filets mignon, each about 1 inch thick, weighing 3 to 4 ounces. Reserve the remaining tail of the filet for beef sauté dishes, like beef Stroganoff, and stir-fries.

Loosen a small section of silver skin with a knife, grasp it in your hand, and pull taut as you scrape off a long strip of membrane with your knife angled away from the meat.

Front to back: head end; center or heart; tournedos. To the left, a tournedo.

Jacques on Refrigerating and Freezing Meat

Pieces of the tenderloin, or other fresh cuts of meat, can be refrigerated, well wrapped, for 4 to 5 days.

To freeze, wrap the individual portions of meat first in plastic wrap, then in aluminum foil. In order to prevent bacterial growth, you must freeze them as fast as possible—put the wrapped meat on a relatively empty shelf, if you can, so that it has enough air to freeze fast.

Plan to remove meat from the freezer a day or two before you intend to cook it, and let it defrost gradually in the coldest part of your refrigerator. This will minimize the breakdown of muscle fibers and the loss of natural juices, and the meat will have good, moist texture.

In general, the rule for frozen storage is: *freeze food as fast as possible and defrost under refrigeration slowly.*

Standing Rib Roast of Beef

You seldom see a fine standing rib roast of beef served these days. And that's too bad, because it is so good. A whole 7-rib roast, trimmed, would serve about 16 people, and that would be for a gala occasion. A 4-rib roast would do for 8 to 10 people, and 3 ribs for a dinner party of 6 to 8; even a 2-rib roast is nice for a small dinner of 4 or 5. Ask your butcher for a trimmed roast, but don't let him trim off *all* of the protruding ribs, as they do now in supermarkets, or your roast won't stand high.

A roast-beef feast isn't complete without the traditional British accompaniment of Yorkshire pudding. It can be made the standard way, baked in a roasting pan, but it rises higher and has more crust if baked in individual Pyrex bowls (use either the medium or the small size, depending on how many you are serving). The puddings can bake while the roast is resting.

Yield: A 3-rib roast, serving 6 to 8

3-rib prime or choice roast of
  beef, trimmed, at room
  temperature
1 tsp salt
Freshly ground pepper
1 tsp *herbes de Provence* (see page
  363) or a combination of
  thyme, marjoram, oregano,
  and savory

For the mirepoix

3 medium-size carrots, peeled and
  roughly chopped
3 medium-size onions, peeled and
  roughly chopped
1 head garlic, unpeeled cloves separated
2 imported bay leaves, crumbled
2 or 3 sprigs fresh thyme or ½ tsp
  dried

For the *jus*

½ cup red wine
2 cups good beef stock, page 42
Salt and freshly ground pepper to
  taste

Special equipment

A roasting pan

Preheat the oven to 425°F.

Set the roast rib side down in the pan and rub the salt, several grindings of pepper, and the herbs into the meat. Put it in the oven.

After 15 minutes, reduce the heat to 325°F.

After another 15 minutes, remove the pan and rapidly strew the carrots, onions, and garlic (the mirepoix) and the herbs over and around the roast and return it to the oven.

Timing

A 3-rib roast will need a total of 1½ to 1¾ hours roasting time, but start checking 15 minutes before. When the thermometer reaches 105°F, continue to check every 10 minutes or so until desired temperature is reached. For the ends to be pinky-red rare and the rest very rare, roast to 120°F internal temperature. For medium-rare at the ends and still rare in the interior, roast to 125°F.

Remove from the oven, transfer to a platter, and keep warm. Let rest for at least 20 to 30 minutes to let the juices retreat into the meat while the Yorkshire pudding bakes and you prepare the *jus.*

To make the *jus,* skim the fat off the roasting pan, then set the pan over heat. Add the red wine and beef stock and stir, scraping up all the browned bits from the pan. Strain into a bowl, pressing the aromatic vegetables to extract all their flavor. Taste and add salt and pepper as needed. At the last, pour any accumulated juices from the resting roast into your finished *jus.*

When ready to serve, slice off a piece from the smaller end. Grab the roast and set it standing up on its flat cut side. Cut a little around the rib, then carve horizontally a few slices, carving from what was topside in the oven toward the ribs. Arrange some watercress on the platter and remove the Yorkshire puddings from their bowls (or, if you have baked them in a pan, cut them in pieces) and set them all around. Carve the remaining roast at the table.

Individual Yorkshire Puddings

5 large eggs
½ tsp salt
1 cup all-purpose flour
½ cup milk or more
Clear beef-fat drippings from the
    roast, or melted lard or veg-
    etable shortening

Special equipment

A food processor; six 10-ounce
    ovenproof bowls about
    4½ inches diameter (or eight
    6-ounce bowls) set on a baking
    sheet, or a baking pan 11 by
    7 inches

The batter

Blend the eggs, salt, flour, and milk in the food processor for 2 minutes. Now stop and test the consistency; it should be the thickness of medium cream. If it seems too thick, add dribbles of additional milk and blend again for 1 minute. Cover the container-bowl and refrigerate for at least 1 hour or overnight, allowing the flour particles to absorb the liquid.

Baking

Preheat the oven to 450°F. Paint the inside of the baking bowls liberally with fat, and set the bowls on their baking sheet in the upper-middle level of the oven for several minutes. Meanwhile, blend the batter another 1 minute, and when the bowls are sizzling hot, rapidly pour ⅓ cup of batter (or ¼ cup if you are using 6-ounce bowls) in each. Immediately return the bowls to the oven. Bake 15 minutes, until the puddings have puffed around the edges and almost out of the cups. They should be brown and crisp.

Serving

The sooner you can serve the puddings, the better. Slip them carefully out of their very hot bowls and arrange them around the roast beef or in a basket. They can keep in a warming oven, if necessary, for ½ hour or so.

Variation: Yorkshire Pudding Baked in a Pan

Pour the rested and well-whisked batter into a well-greased 11-by-7-inch baking pan, and bake about 20 minutes in a preheated 450°F oven, until puffed and brown. To serve, unmold and cut into serving pieces to place around the roast.

Julia

The pot roast and vegetables can be cooled and stored in the refrigerator. Reheat on top of the stove or in a low oven. It is particularly easy to slice the meat when cool, and reheat the slices quickly in the sauce. Or serve it cold *à la Parisienne*, page 124.

Pot Roast

Nearly five hours of cooking go into Jacques's generous pot roast, but very little of it is work time for the cook. It is the process of braising that produces remarkable tenderness and flavor in the large cut of beef bottom round used here. As the meat cooks slowly in the oven, the lean flesh becomes moist and tender, and exchanges flavors with the liquid and the aromatic vegetables and herbs that surround it.

Here, as with many of the other braised meat dishes in this chapter, you'll have most to do at the beginning. The roast is thoroughly browned on the stovetop; then wine, onions, tomatoes, thyme, and bay leaves are added. But aside from putting the big casserole into the oven (twice), the hard work is done. You also have the convenience of cooking all the vegetables for the meal right along with the meat. Open the pot after three or four hours, toss in turnip wedges, small white onions, and baby carrots, and return it to the oven. In an hour or so, they will be perfectly soft and shapely, and will have added even more flavor to the dish. Just before serving, set the pot on the stove and simmer some green peas, to add an extra touch of color to the feast when it is arrayed on your serving platter.

Jacques's Pot Roast

Yield: 10 servings

One 5-pound piece beef bottom round, from the "flat," trimmed of all fat

1½ tsp kosher salt (or 1 tsp regular salt), plus more if needed

1 tsp freshly ground black pepper, plus more if needed

2 to 3 Tbs canola or other vegetable oil

2 cups chopped onion, 1-inch pieces (about 8 ounces)

1 large tomato, cored and chopped into 1-inch pieces (about 1½ cups)

2 imported bay leaves

6 sprigs fresh thyme or 1 tsp dried thyme
   leaves
1½ cups white wine, plus more if needed
½ cup water
1½ to 2 pounds large white turnips,
   peeled, trimmed, and sliced into large
   wedges (10 to 12 pieces)
1 pound small white onions, about 20
   the size of Ping-Pong balls, blanched
   and peeled (page 196)
1 pound baby carrots
1½ to 2 cups green peas, fresh or frozen
Potato starch for thickening (optional)
1 Tbs chopped fresh parsley, for garnish

Special equipment

A heavy ovenproof casserole, 4- or 5-
   quart capacity, with a tight-fitting
   cover; a large, warm serving platter

Browning and braising the roast

Preheat the oven to 300°F.

Season the roast on all sides with 1 to 1½ teaspoons salt and 1 teaspoon black pepper. Set the casserole over high heat with 2 or 3 tablespoons of oil, just enough to film the bottom.

When the oil is hot, lay in the roast and sear for about 3 minutes, until the first side is well browned. Turn the meat onto another side and sear for several minutes, and continue turning and searing, over medium to high heat, until the entire piece is browned and the meat juices have crusted in the pan, about 15 minutes in all. If there is excess oil in the bottom of the pot, pour it out carefully and discard.

Arrange the onion and tomato pieces, the bay leaves, and the thyme sprigs around the meat and pour in the wine and water. Bring the liquid quickly to the boil, cover the casserole, and set it in the oven for 3 to 4 hours, until the meat is tender.

Adding the vegetables and final braising

Remove the casserole from the oven. Hold the lid ajar to keep the meat in the pot, and, if you want, pour the braising

Jacques

The piece of beef I prefer

for pot roast is cut from the "flat" muscle of the bottom round (part of the animal's hind leg). It is lean and solid and becomes very tender and moist during braising, but still holds its shape and slices easily. You can find this in any market, but may have to ask the butcher to cut the 5-pound piece I use here. I prefer it to the "eye round," a muscle that is attached to the flat, and often suggested for pot roast. It looks nice, but is more fibrous and will not be as tender.

The first step of browning the beef is most important, so be sure to give this plenty of time, about 15 minutes. You want the meat to get a deep-brown crust on all sides and the juices to crystallize in the bottom of the pan as well. The crust and glaze, where the natural sugars have caramelized, are full of flavor. You will see that during the braising all of this crusting will seem to disappear—it literally melts away into the liquid, bringing the flavors to the whole dish.

It's also necessary to use a good pot for pot roast, such as an enameled cast-iron Dutch oven or covered casserole. It must have a heavy bottom and good heat transfer, to form the best crust, and a tight-fitting lid that will lock in the moisture so the meat won't dry out.

It's fine to vary this recipe to suit your taste and what you have on hand.

(continued on page 331)

liquid though a strainer to remove the cooked vegetable pieces and herbs. Press the juices from the vegetables, then return the strained liquid to the pot.

Arrange the turnip wedges, onions, and baby carrots around the roast and season with ½ teaspoon salt. Bring the liquid to the boil, and put the casserole, covered, back in the 300°F oven for 1 to 1½ hours, until the roast is fork-tender and the vegetables are very soft but still holding their shape.

Finishing and serving the pot roast

Set the casserole on the stovetop, over low heat. Add the green peas to the pot, cover, and simmer for 2 to 3 minutes, just until the peas are tender. Lift out the meat and set it on the serving platter.

Taste the sauce and adjust the seasonings. It can be served as is, or, for a thicker consistency, stir together a tablespoon of potato starch with a teaspoon of white wine in a small dish. Stir the dissolved starch, a bit at a time, into the hot liquid. It will thicken immediately on contact with the hot liquid; stir in only as much as needed to reach the proper consistency.

Cut ¼-inch slices from the roast, enough for first servings, and lay them overlapping on the platter—set the rest of the roast on the platter too, if you have room. Spoon the vegetables all around the sliced meat and moisten all with the sauce. Sprinkle the chopped parsley over and bring the platter to the table.

Opposite: Pot Roast

You could use stock or just plain water for the braising liquid, or use canned chopped tomatoes instead of fresh. If you don't like turnips, you can add potatoes instead, or even use both. The flavorful braising liquid reduces slightly in the pot by the end of cooking, and will have a naturally pleasing viscosity for use as a sauce. If you like, though, you can easily thicken it just before serving, using potato starch as described in the recipe. I personally often add a split calf's or pig's foot to the pot at the beginning, as this adds flavor and a gelatinous texture to the juices, but it's fine without. The bits of meat I take from the foot are very nice to serve with the roast too.

Julia

The reason *boeuf bourgui-gnon* is so famous is that it has such good flavor, which depends in the first instance on a fine cut of meat, a good fruity wine, and dark stock. But even the minor ingredients are important. Browning the meat in pork fat, and adding the *lardons* to the stew, gives it an extra layer of taste. I prefer to make *lardons* from salt pork, with the thickest streaks of lean that you can find. Also, be sure to use real bay leaves, the imported *Laurus nobilis*, rather than California bay laurel, which has an oily taste.

People often complain that a beef stew takes so long to make, but, in fact, most of that is unsupervised cooking. You can do the active work in bits and pieces as your time allows and stagger the cooking over several days. With our *boeuf bourguignon*, you might brown the meat one day while you are making dinner and let it marinate in the cooking liquid, with the packet of herbs and aromatic vegetables. Simmer the stew the next day while you are eating dinner or playing tennis, then let it cool and store it in the refrigerator. Prepare your vegetables and finish the stew the next day or even the day after. Stretching the preparation over three or four days is not only convenient but will make a better-tasting dish, as the many elements have more time to exchange flavor.

Incidentally, you don't *have* to wrap the aromatic herbs and vegetables

(continued on page 334)

Boeuf Bourguignon

A classic *boeuf bourguignon* is essentially made in the same way as the other braised meats in this chapter—the preceding pot roast, and the veal roast *en cocotte,* and the stews. All follow the principle of slow, covered cooking in a small amount of liquid, with aromatic vegetables and herbs, to produce tender meat and a sauce full of flavor. Here, chunks of beef as well as *lardons* of salt pork are browned in pork fat, and then slowly braised in red wine—a good pinot noir is what makes it genuinely *bourguignon*—with the classic garnish of mushrooms and small onions added shortly before serving.

We both like to use beef from the chuck, or shoulder, for stewing. It has good flavor, will hold its shape during long cooking, and remains moist. It is a simple matter to cut up a boneless chuck roast yourself, as shown by Julia in the accompanying photos, following the natural seams. And once the meats have been browned, you can proceed with the recipe in stages to suit your schedule (see Julia's comment at left).

Serve the stew surrounded by buttered noodles or with Mashed Potatoes, page 150, or Pommes de Terre Mont d'Or, page 156. Crispy "Lion's Tooth" Croutons, page 337, are a classic garnish for sauced meats and stews.

Yield: 6 servings

5 ounces salt pork, in 1 chunk
2 Tbs vegetable oil, such as canola, plus
   more if needed
One 3½-to-4-pound boneless beef
   chuck roast or top blade
Salt and freshly ground pepper

For the herb-and-vegetable bouquet
1½ cups chopped onion, in ½-inch
   pieces
1½ cups peeled and chopped carrot, in
   ½-inch pieces

6 sprigs fresh thyme or ¼ tsp dried

3 imported bay leaves

A handful of parsley stems (about 10)

1 head garlic, cloves separated and
  crushed but not peeled

For the cooking liquid

1 large tomato, cored and chopped, or ¾
  cup canned Italian plum tomatoes,
  drained

1 bottle sturdy red wine, preferably a
  pinot noir

1 to 2 cups strong dark stock (page 42)

For the onion-and-mushroom garnish

18 small white onions, about 1¼ inch
  diameter, about 10 ounces

1½ Tbs butter

½ tsp sugar

Pinch salt

½ cup or more of the dark stock

10 ounces fresh mushrooms, about 1
  inch in diameter

For finishing the sauce

2 Tbs soft butter, or more as needed

2 Tbs flour, or more

Salt and freshly ground pepper

¼ cup or more red wine (same as you are
  serving at table)

For serving

Fresh parsley, finely chopped (¼ cup or
  so)

"Lion's Tooth" Croutons (page 337)
  (optional)

Jacques

Though the pot roast and the beef stew follow similar methods, it is important to select the right cut of beef for each preparation. The solid, lean piece of bottom round that I use for the pot roast, or a top round, would be too dry in this stew. The shoulder cuts that we recommend have more sinew and connective tissue and will stay moist. I particularly like to use the top blade—the muscle cut off the shoulder blade of beef, which we use in our country-steak recipe. For steaks, you want to get rid of the thick sinew in the middle of the muscle—which you can see in the photo on page 320—but for stews, you want to cut chunks in such a way that they contain all of this gelatinous material. It will melt and soften as the meat braises, and give a natural thickening and body to the sauce. The chuck roast is another good cut for stews, or use beef shank, another flavorful cut, which is lower down on the leg.

Since red wine is the hallmark of *boeuf bourguignon*, use a good red wine, fruity with a bit of acid, for the stewing. Drink an equally sturdy wine with your dinner, something that can really stand up to the beef, a good pinot noir or cabernet sauvignon. Just before serving, I like to pour a dash of the wine we will be drinking into the stew—the raw wine adds a different layer of winy taste. Incidentally, I don't bother to pierce small onions before braising them. I don't find it makes a significant difference.

Julia (continued from page 332)

in cheesecloth. Instead, just dump them into the pot before stewing, and, when the meat is done, strain the liquid, through a colander, into a saucepan. Remove the meat chunks, press the juices out of the vegetables, and discard vegetables. Then you can finish the liquid however you like, reducing it for a more concentrated flavor, or adding more stock, bouillon, wine, tomato paste, and seasonings. This is the method given for the veal stews later in this chapter, and is the one to follow when you want an especially fine sauce.

You will also find a different method for preparing small white onions and mushrooms in the recipe for Blanquette de Veau (page 351), which has this same traditional garniture. While Jacques's technique for cooking and glazing the onions and mushrooms together, as you will find in this stew, is convenient, you must be sure that you have cooked the onions sufficiently before you add the mushrooms to the pan. I prefer to cook them separately, so I can be certain that each is perfectly done, and then combine them in the stew for a final simmer.

Boeuf Bourguignon (continued)

Special equipment

A frying pan, 12 inches top diameter, for browning the meat; a large square of washed cheesecloth (about 18 inches) and kitchen twine; a heavy-duty oven-proof casserole, 4- or 5-quart capacity, with a tight-fitting cover; a wide, heavy-bottomed saucepan or sauté pan (about 10 inches) with a tight-fitting cover, for glazing the onions and mushrooms

Trimming and browning the meat

Preheat the oven to 300°F if you plan to stew the beef right away.

To make *lardons,* cut the salt pork into rectangular slices about ½ inch wide, then cut the slices into strips 1 inch long. Simmer them in a saucepan with a quart or so of water for about 10 minutes to remove the salt. Drain, rinse in cold water, and pat dry.

Heat 2 tablespoons of oil in the large frying pan over moderate heat and sauté the blanched *lardons* for about 5 minutes, stirring them around the pan as they render their fat, until lightly browned on all sides. Remove the *lardons* to the casserole with a slotted spoon, leaving all the fat in the frying pan. There should be enough to film the bottom; add more oil if necessary.

Meanwhile, trim the beef of all fat and gristle and cut into 2½-to-3-inch chunks (you should have about 18 to 20 pieces). If you have a chuck roast, slice the meat apart following the natural seams of the muscles, trim away fat, and cut into chunks (see photo). If

Getting ready to cut up the lardons and meat

using the top blade, trim the fat and silver skin (see photo, page 320, on removing silver skin) before cutting into chunks.

Stir and turn the lardons as they brown.

Dry the beef chunks on paper towels and sprinkle ½ teaspoon of salt and ¼ teaspoon or more of freshly ground pepper all over them. Heat the frying pan until the fat is very hot but not smoking, and set in a batch of chunks in a single layer, with a little space between them—if overcrowded they will steam rather than sear. Brown the pieces, turning them with tongs, until well crusted on all sides, about 5 minutes. Remove them as they are done to the casserole and add more chunks to the pan for browning. Adjust the heat to keep the fat hot, adding more oil as needed.

When the beef has all browned, drain and discard the fat. Pour a cup or so of the wine into the pan and bring to a simmer. Deglaze the browned bits in the pan bottom, scraping them up with a wooden spoon, then pour this liquid over the beef and *lardons*.

Preparing the herb-and-vegetable bouquet and stewing the meat

Brown the chunks of meat, turning them with tongs.

Pile the chopped onion and carrot, thyme sprigs, bay leaves, parsley stems, and garlic cloves in the middle of the cheesecloth. Fold up the corners of the cloth, enclosing the aromatics, and tie securely with kitchen twine to make a compact bundle. Push aside some of the beef chunks and nestle the bouquet in the middle of the casserole. Scatter the tomato pieces on top of the meat and pour in the remaining wine and enough stock (a cup or two) just to cover the meat chunks.

Bring the liquid to a simmer on the top of the stove, cover, and set into the preheated oven. Cook for about 2 hours, keeping the stew at a barely active simmer, until the beef is fork-tender but not falling apart. To be safe, test the meat every 15 minutes after 1½ hours of stewing—don't overcook.

When the meat is done, set the casserole on the stovetop. Remove the cheesecloth bouquet to a colander or strainer over a bowl and press out its juices. Pour the juices back into the stew and discard the bouquet. Proceed with the recipe immediately, or set the stew aside (see Julia's comment, page 332).

Fold up the sides of the cheesecloth to enclose the aromatics, then tie the ends together with string.

Drop the onions into a pan of boiling water for one minute, then remove them with a strainer or slotted spoon.

With the tip of your knife pierce a shallow cross in the root of the onion.

Boeuf Bourguignon (continued)

Preparing the onion-and-mushroom garnish

Blanch and peel the onions (following the photographs). Pierce a shallow cross in the root end of each to help prevent bursting. Trim and clean the mushrooms and cut them in halves or quarters if larger than 1 inch across.

Place the onions in one layer in a saucepan with the butter, the sugar, a pinch of salt, and ½ cup or more of stock or water, to come about one-third of the way up their sides. Bring

After shaving off the stem and root end, keeping enough of the root to hold the onion intact, slip off the skin.

to the boil, cover the pan with a tight-fitting lid, and cook for about 8 to 10 minutes, or until they are barely tender. Uncover and continue cooking until all the liquid evaporates and shake the pan so the onions are glazed all over in the butter and sugar.

Turn the mushrooms into the pan, fold and toss with the onions, and cook them together over moderate heat as the mushrooms release their liquid and begin to brown. When all the vegetables are glazed and colored, set aside. Deglaze the saucepan with a few spoonfuls of wine or stock and pour that into the stew.

Finishing the sauce

Return the stew to a gentle simmer for 10 minutes, then remove from heat. With a whisk, blend the 2 tablespoons of flour and 2 tablespoons of butter in a small bowl to make a thick paste, or *beurre manié*. Gradually whisk ½ cup or so of the stewing liquid into the paste to liquefy it. Blend this into the stew and bring it again to the simmer. Cook for a couple of minutes and check the sauce consistency. If you want it thicker, mix up more *beurre manié* and add it in the same manner, a tablespoon or so at a time.

Taste the sauce and adjust the seasonings.

The onions and mushrooms browned together in the pan

Serving the stew

When ready to serve, reheat the stew (if necessary), add the onions and mushrooms, stir in ¼ cup or so of red wine, and heat through. Taste and correct seasonings.

Serve the stew in large individual pasta bowls, with noodles or potatoes as suggested above. Top the beef chunks (about 3 per serving) with a portion of onions and mushrooms, plenty of sauce, and a sprinkle of chopped parsley. On each serving, you may wish to arrange a couple of the following pointed croutons.

"Lion's Tooth" Croutons for Boeuf Bourguignon

These crispy, parsley-dipped croutons are a colorful garnish for any stew.

> 6 slices home-style white bread
> 3 Tbs room-temperature unsalted butter
> 4 Tbs chopped fresh parsley

Preheat the oven to 400°F.

Slice each piece of bread on the diagonal into 2 triangular pieces. To shape each crouton, slice off the crust on one side of the triangle, then make a parallel slice, removing a corner of bread. Trim the remaining crust with three small cuts, as in the photo, to make a wedge.

Spread the butter with your fingers in the center of a cookie sheet. Press each wedge into the butter and rub gently to coat on one side, then turn it over, buttered side up. Arrange all the wedges on the buttered area of the sheet and place in the oven. Toast the croutons for 8 to 10 minutes, until nicely colored and crisp.

To serve, pile the fresh parsley in a small mound. Dip the point of the toasted wedge into the beef-stew sauce, then press the moistened end into the parsley to coat. Arrange 2 croutons on every serving plate or bowl of stew.

Julia

The safety of ground beef is a serious issue these days. For home cooking, it is important to have a butcher you trust, who you know is getting meat from proper sources, handling it correctly, and grinding it himself. That is one reason I prefer an independent butcher.

For mass marketing, I am in favor of irradiation as a method of guaranteeing the safety of our meat supply. It is an effective and well-studied method of food preserving and is regulated not to affect flavor. It has been tested for decades: I remember when we started our TV show in the 1960s, we visited a lab where they were studying irradiation. It could, I believe, prevent many unnecessary illnesses and save many thousands of lives.

I make my hamburgers thin—¼ inch—when I am doing a pan sauté, because I don't like a bulbous burger in a flat bun. I want my hamburger to fit flat in my bun, and I also like to season the meat before cooking it so that every bite is full of flavor. When you cook them right, in a really hot pan, you get a nicely browned outside and a rosy-red inside. It also cooks fast—about a minute on each side.

Hamburger

Here are two good ways to prepare that great American favorite, the hamburger. We make our burgers in slightly different shapes, using slightly different methods. Julia likes her hamburgers rare; Jacques, medium-rare—and we agree that a great hamburger spread must provide a big slate of extras from which to build your sandwich, possibly more than you can fit in one mouthful.

What beef is the best for hamburgers? Most supermarkets offer a wide selection of ground beef, with fat content varying from 10 percent to nearly 30 percent, and often labeled as ground beef, ground chuck, ground sirloin, ground round, and so forth. Not surprisingly, you'll find higher prices for the leaner meat with the fancier names—but the most expensive meat is not necessarily the best. Remember that fat is what gives flavor to meat: too little and the meat will be dry and you will lose much of the beefy taste. We both prefer a fat content of 20 percent. Julia buys chuck because she thinks it has better flavor.

Yield: 4 hamburgers

1 to 1¼ pounds fresh ground beef,
  preferably 15 to 20 percent fat
Salt and freshly ground pepper
1 Tbs vegetable oil, or butter
4 hamburger buns or Kaiser rolls
1 Tbs minced shallots or scallions (for
  Julia's thin burger)

An array of complements and condiments,
  including, but not limited to
    Thin red onion slices (*very* thin for Julia)
    Thin ripe tomato slices
    Iceberg lettuce leaves (*very* green leaves
      for Julia)
    Small whole pickles or pickle "stackers"
      or pickle relish
    Thin cheddar or Swiss cheese slices
    Bacon strips, cooked crisp
    Butter, at room temperature
    Ketchup
    Mayonnaise
    Dijon-type prepared mustard
    Salsa
    Potato chips

Jacques's Grilled Thick Burger

Set a stovetop grill (either a grill-pan or rimless griddle type) over high heat until quite hot.

Divide the meat into 4 portions. With cupped hands, form each portion into a loose round; then shape into a smooth disk, just under an inch thick and about 3½ inches in diameter. Rub each side of the patties with drops of the oil.

Lay the burgers on the hot grill and cook for about 3 minutes, until well marked, then turn and cook on the second side for the same amount of time. Test for doneness with a light finger press (see page 317). To make crisscross grill marks, follow the *quadrillage* method, turning and rotating the meat, as detailed on page 363.

Jacques

I was surprised to see how

Julia made her hamburger—mixing salt and pepper and sautéed onion into the raw meat—because that is the way we used to do it in France. But I have become Americanized in my taste for hamburger, and I don't put anything into the meat at all, not even salt, before I cook it.

This is most unusual for me, because I always season steaks and meat with salt and pepper just before cooking them. But with a burger I only sprinkle salt on after it comes off the grill. It has a completely distinct taste— the salt is only on the crust of the meat and the inside is unseasoned—and that's the way I like it best. I sometimes make a burger as Julia does, but it's different: the seasoned meat isn't red and tastes more like a meat loaf that's been fried. The beauty of burgers is that there are so many ways to do them.

It's important to have a certain amount of fat in the burger, not only for flavor, but for texture as well. If the meat is too lean, it will not hold together in the kind of loose patty that I make: it will crumble and fall apart. Shape the patty lightly with your hands—if it is too firm it won't be as juicy. And never press down on the meat with a spatula during cooking, which some cooks do when they are in a hurry. They think they are making it cook faster, but instead they're pressing out all the juices and all the flavor.

Julia: How I Build My Hamburger

I like everything on my hamburger, but I don't like it built so high you can't take a bite. Some things are best on the bottom (I put these on while my burger is cooking) and some are best on top.

I start by buttering a split and toasted bun; then lay on a leaf of

green iceberg lettuce and some very thin slices of red onion; then ketchup; and then a little pickle relish. Then I put on my burger, with a slice of cheese on top. On this go two slices of bacon and a couple of tomato slices. Finally, I put mayonnaise on the top half of the roll, cap the sandwich, and slice in half before gobbling.

Jacques's Grilled Thick Burger (continued)

While the burgers are cooking, you can cut the rolls in half and toast them directly on the grill for about a minute, then let your guests start building their sandwiches. When burgers are cooked to taste, remove them directly onto a roll bottom. Sprinkle with salt and pepper—or let your guests do it to taste—and top with more condiments.

Julia's Pan-Fried Thin Burger

Sauté the shallots in a small pan until soft in 1 teaspoon of butter or mild olive oil.

Divide the meat into 4 portions. One at a time, flatten each by chopping and spreading the meat with light strokes of your chef's knife. Sprinkle over each a big pinch of salt, 2 grinds of pepper, and ½ teaspoon of the sautéed shallots or scallions. Blend them into the meat, chopping and turning it as you shape the portions into 4½-to-5-inch round patties ¼ inch thick.

Toast the hamburger buns and distribute them to your guests. Suggest that they dress the bottom halves of their rolls as they wish while you cook the burgers. Cook two at a time in a 10-inch frying pan. Set the pan over high heat. Sprinkle the surface with a light dusting of salt. When the pan is hot but not smoking, pick up a patty with your pancake turner and lay it in the pan, rapidly adding the second burger. The meat will take just 15 to 20 seconds to brown on the bottom; lift gently to check. When browned, turn and brown the other side. If the heat seems too high, lower it slightly. As soon as the burgers test done (see sidebar, page 317), remove them to a warm platter, and as quickly as possible onto your guests' buns, for their final touches. Proceed to remaining burgers.

Jacques: How I Build My Hamburger

I start with a bulky Kaiser roll, split and browned on each side on the grill. While the burger is grilling, I make a layer of iceberg lettuce (yes, I like the crunchiness of iceberg); some tomato slices; slices of red onion; and a layer of sliced pickle—you must have some pickle.

When the burger comes off the grill, I salt it—I might put on black pepper if there's some handy, but not always—and lay it on the bottom of the sandwich, then top it with ketchup, another slice of onion, and then more iceberg lettuce. Finally, the top of my roll. I sometimes have to cut this in half just so I can grab a piece of it.

Julia

It's always good to learn new tricks. Freezing the cabbage head allows you to skip the laborious step of separating and blanching the leaves in boiling water, to make them pliable. And although in the past I have formed a stuffed whole head of cabbage in a bowl, or in cheesecloth, Jacques's foil method we tried here is easier and better.

I still like one of my old techniques. I take about half a dozen of the nicest-looking cabbage leaves from a very large head, or take some from another head, to cook separately. I blanch them in boiling water and refresh in icy water so they are soft but still bright green. When the braised whole cabbage is unwrapped it comes out a rather drab color, so I drape the colorful reserved leaves over the top. It's a nice touch, but even a dull-green cabbage looks appetizing when you cover it with tomato sauce before serving.

Stuffed Cabbage

It is always fun to stuff meat, and other good things, into vegetables. We feel we advanced the art of stuffing when working on this recipe, as we happened upon a very good method for wrapping and cooking a big cabbage filled with ground beef and rice. We used a piece of heavy-duty aluminum foil to mold the separated leaves into a replica of a whole head of cabbage that would hold it in shape over long cooking. But we cut the foil too short, so it didn't completely enclose the cabbage on the bottom. It turned out that this opening in the foil package provided a mutually beneficial exchange of juices and flavors.

You can use other techniques for stuffing a whole head of cabbage—it actually is a process of layering the leaves and the stuffing. Or follow Jacques's good trick for perfectly shaped small cabbage rolls (see sidebar, page 345). The large cabbage, an all-in-one meal for 6, takes some time to prepare, but good organization will make preparing the several components quick and easy. First, to soften the cabbage leaves, plan to freeze and defrost the cabbage head at least 2 days before assembling the dish, as detailed in the recipe. Cook the rice ahead of time, and chop up all the vegetables you need for the stuffing and sauce together. Then, with all the ingredients prepped and divided—chefs call this *mise-en-place*—make the stuffing, start the sauce, and reassemble the cabbage.

Jacques's Stuffed Cabbage

Yield: 6 to 8 servings

One 2½-to-3-pound head of Savoy or
green cabbage

For the stuffing
4 cups coarsely chopped center leaves
from the above cabbage
2 Tbs olive oil
1½ cups chopped onion
½ cup diced celery in ½-inch pieces
1 Tbs minced garlic
2 tsp salt, and more if necessary
½ tsp freshly ground pepper, and more if
necessary
1 tsp caraway seed
½ cup chicken stock
2½ cups plain cooked rice (see page 169)
1 pound ground beef, raw

For the sauce
2 Tbs olive oil
1½ cups chopped onion
1 cup diced celery in ½-inch pieces
1 cup diced carrot in ½-inch pieces
3 cups fresh *tomates concassées* (see page
243), or canned tomatoes, drained and
chopped
½ tsp salt
¼ tsp freshly ground black pepper
2 imported bay leaves
1 cup chicken stock
1 cup white wine

Jacques

The sautéed base for the
stuffing has to be heavily seasoned in
order to flavor both the ground meat
and rice that you mix into it, and the
cabbage leaves that enclose it. To
check that it is properly seasoned, you
can sauté some of the stuffing in a bit
of butter, and taste. I especially like the
flavor of caraway with cabbage, and
you can add more or less if you like.

You don't need to use meat at all
in the stuffing, though it adds a lot of
flavor; try mushrooms or other vegetables with the rice instead. Or use bul-
gur in place of the rice, or even leftover
pasta. This is a good dish for testing
out your creative improvisations.

Special equipment

A large sauté pan with cover, for the stuffing; a large heavy-bottomed casserole pan or deep ovenproof sauté pan (at least 10 inches in diameter and 4 inches deep) with a tight-fitting cover, for braising the whole cabbage; an 18-inch square sheet of heavy-duty aluminum foil

Preparing the cabbage leaves

At least 2 days before preparing the dish: to soften the cabbage leaves without blanching, cut the core out of the cabbage, and place the entire head in the freezer. Freeze for 24 hours or more, then defrost in the refrigerator for another 24 hours before using.

Cut a notch at the base of each cabbage leaf to remove the tough central rib.

When defrosted, peel the large outer leaves from the head, one by one. They should be soft and easy to remove. Cut a notch at the base of each leaf to remove the tough part of the central rib, then lay the leaves flat on paper towels and pat dry. Continue peeling until you have 18 to 20 large and medium-sized leaves. Don't peel the center of the cabbage—a tight cluster of small, pale leaves, about 4 or 5 inches in diameter—save it for the stuffing.

Alternate method of softening the leaves: Just before cooking, core the cabbage and separate 20 or more large leaves from the head, leaving the center whole. Bring a large pot of salted water to the boil and blanch the leaves for several minutes, until wilted. Drain them, cool under running water, then notch and dry them as above.

Preparing the stuffing

Preheat the oven to 375°F.

Chop the cabbage center into pieces approximately 1 inch square—you should have about 4 cups.

Heat the olive oil in the sauté pan, add the chopped onion and celery, and sauté over high heat for a couple minutes, tossing. Add the garlic and cabbage pieces and cook for another minute, stirring and tossing to mix. Season with the salt, pepper, and caraway seed. Pour in the stock, cover the pan, and bring to a boil. Cook steadily for 10 to 15 minutes, stirring occasionally, until most of the liquid has evaporated and the vegetables are soft. If there is still a lot of liquid in the pan, remove the cover and cook a bit longer. Turn the vegetables into a large mixing bowl and cool to lukewarm.

Dump the cooked rice and the ground beef on top of the vegetables and mix thoroughly with your hands, breaking up the clumps of meat. (To check the seasoning, you can fry up a spoonful of stuffing, then taste and adjust as needed.)

Preparing the sauce

Set the casserole over high heat, add the remaining olive oil, the chopped onion, diced celery, and diced carrot pieces, and sauté for 4 or 5 minutes to soften. Stir in the chopped tomatoes and the salt and pepper, and add the bay leaves. Cover and bring to a simmer, and set aside while you stuff the cabbage.

Re-forming and stuffing the cabbage

Lay the aluminum-foil square on the work surface. Select 5 of the largest wilted cabbage leaves and arrange them, overlapping. They should form a rough circle, 12 to 14 inches in diameter, with the notched base of each leaf on the outside of the circle, and the rounded tops of the leaves overlapping in the center.

Spread about a third of the stuffing in a circle on top of the leaves, leaving a 2- or 3-inch margin of leaves all around. Cover this stuffing completely with another layer of 4 or 5 leaves, slightly smaller than the first layer of leaves. Now spread another third of the stuffing in a circle and cover again with leaves. Repeat with a third layer of stuffing (using up all the stuffing, or reserving 1 cup to make small cabbage rolls; see sidebar). Finally, cover with a fourth layer of the smallest remaining leaves.

Spread another layer of stuffing on the leaves.

Now lift the corners and outside edges of the foil, bringing the large bottom layer of leaves up and around all the inner layers. Press on the foil to re-form and hold the round cabbage shape. The edges of the foil should leave a small opening on the top—soon to be the bottom—of the wrapped cabbage leaves.

Cooking and serving the stuffed cabbage

Pour the wine and the stock into the casserole with the sauce. Invert the foil-wrapped head and set it on top of the sauce, open side down, so the juices of the cabbage and the sauce will exchange flavors. Bring to a boil over high heat, cover, then set the casserole in the middle of the preheated 375°F oven. Bake for 2 hours.

Remove from the oven. Lift out the hot wrapped cabbage with a wide spatula or two skimmers or an inverted lid, and set it (open side still down) on a warm serving plate. To remove the foil easily, pierce it on the top and rip open, peeling off strips of foil and pulling them out from under the cabbage. Do this carefully, so as not to tear the tender outer leaves or disturb the beautifully re-formed cabbage shape.

Spoon a generous amount of chunky sauce over the top of the cabbage and garnish with sprigs of parsley. To serve, slice the cabbage in wedges, and spoon on more sauce.

Jacques's Stuffed Cabbage Rolls

Save some of the fixings from your stuffed whole cabbage to make a couple of small, plump cabbage rolls. They are a delicious cook's perquisite you can enjoy the next day. (You can, of course, make as many rolls as you wish, using ½ cup of stuffing and one leaf for each.)

To shape: Reserve 2 good-sized leaves from the softened cabbage, and 1 cup of the stuffing mix. Cut the thick ribs from the leaves and fit one into the bowl of a 6-ounce soup ladle. Press ½ cup of stuffing down into the ladle, then fold over the overhanging flaps of the leaf. Compress lightly, and invert to drop a perfectly shaped roll into your palm. Place it folded side down in a small gratin dish, and repeat to make the second roll.

To bake: Pour ¼ cup each of chicken stock and white wine and a tablespoon of olive oil over the rolls. Season with pinches of salt and pepper, cover the dish tightly with foil, and bake for a good hour in a 375°F oven. Moisten with the juices from the baking dish.

Julia

Veal in this country used to be decidedly inferior to European veal. But in recent decades our producers have learned to use special "Dutch-process" feeding formulas and now we have some of the best veal you can find anywhere. You will recognize real veal by its creamy-pink color, which indicates that the calf was raised only on milk or the milk by-product formulas. The so-called "naturally raised" or "free-range" calf is not veal at all; it is baby beef. Since it has been fed grass, its flesh ranges in color from deep pink to beef red, and the quality of its meat is nothing like that of real veal. It makes edible chops and scallops, but is grayish brown in a stew, and as a roast it is "mystery meat." I do not recommend it at all for any purpose except, perhaps, meatloaf.

Belgian endives are an interesting and delicious vegetable—members of the chicory family, they are grown covered with earth to keep them white. But they have a pronounced bitterness which I think is best handled by braising them separately from a roast. I like to put them in a casserole with a little water, a little lemon juice, and a lot of butter, and braise them slowly, covered, for 1½ to 2 hours. You can start them about the same time as the veal roast (on the top of the stove) and they will finish together.

I would prefer substituting large leeks for the endives with this veal roast; trim them to 5 or 6 inches in length, and cut in half lengthwise if very thick. Add them to the veal as the recipe specifies for endives—about 35 minutes before the end of braising.

Veal Roast en Cocotte

With carefully controlled diets and good husbandry methods on American farms, veal calves grow to market size quickly. Most of the veal you'll find in stores these days comes from animals that are only about 3 months old—the muscles have not had time to toughen, little fat has formed, and almost every cut is tender, lean, and delicately flavored.

This mild flavor makes veal particularly adaptable for stewing or braising, with different cooking liquids, seasonings, and vegetable garnishes. Chunks of veal are stewed in Julia's veal ragout and *blanquette de veau*, shanks are braised for *ossobuco*, and in this recipe a whole boneless veal roast is cooked *en cocotte* (which simply means "in a casserole").

As with our beef pot roast and most of the stews in this chapter—except, of course, the *blanquette*, which must stay *blanc*—the meat is first deeply browned, creating a flavorful crust on both the roast and the pan, which melts into the small amount of veal stock during covered cooking. But many other elements contribute to the distinctive taste of this braise: fresh savory, *herbes de Provence*, leeks, lemon zest, and, in Jacques's recipe, Belgian endives.

A veal shoulder roast, cut from the shoulder blade, is Jacques's first choice among many roasts you can use here. Ask for an "inside shoulder" or "top blade" (this cut is similar to the "top blade" from the beef chuck that we use for our country steaks, page 318). You might find it already rolled and tied in some meat markets, but you can do this yourself, using the method demonstrated by Jacques on page 348. If this cut is unavailable, use any other boneless shoulder roast, or a boneless roast from the leg, such as the sirloin, top round, or top knuckle.

Mellowing the endives: Endives usually have a slight bitterness that contrasts nicely with the other flavors, but at times the bitterness can dominate. If you want a tamer flavor, blanch the endives for this recipe briefly (about 4 minutes) in 2 quarts of lightly salted water, with a tablespoon of lemon juice, before adding them to the braising pot.

Jacques's Veal Roast en Cocotte

Yield: 8 servings

1 large leek, trimmed of tough green
    parts and washed (see page 54)
8 Belgian endives
One 4-pound boneless veal roast, from
    the shoulder or leg, tied (see photos,
    page 348)
1 tsp *herbes de Provence* (see page 363)
¾ tsp salt, plus more if needed
½ tsp freshly ground black pepper, plus
    more if needed
2 Tbs butter
1 Tbs virgin olive oil
3 large sprigs of fresh savory or 1 tsp
    dried savory
4 or 5 thin strips of lemon peel
2 cups veal or chicken stock
Chopped parsley, for garnish

Special equipment

A large (12-inch) heavy-bottomed sauté
    pan or flameproof casserole with tight-
    fitting cover; kitchen twine; a large
    deep serving platter

Preparing the vegetable garnish

Slice the leek lengthwise, then crosswise into 2-inch lengths, for about 2 cups of white and light-green pieces of leek.

Trim from the endives the discolored and tough parts of the root end; remove any loose or browning outer leaves, and cut each one in half lengthwise. If you prefer a less bitter flavor, blanch the endives as suggested on page 346.

Seasoning and browning the roast

If the roast has been tied by the butcher, season the outside with the *herbes de Provence*, ¾ teaspoon of salt, and ½ teaspoon of pepper. If you are going to roll and tie the roast yourself,

Jacques

As with most pieces of meat,

there are many different names for the veal shoulder roast I recommend here, which may lead to confusion at the meat counter. You might want to bring in this book and show the photos here to the butcher in order to get the cut you want!

In fact, the entire shoulder of veal is one of my favorite cuts of meat, both to cook, and to teach people about. I encourage you to buy a whole shoulder of veal, bone-in, and divide it up yourself. You will get meat to use in every kind of veal dish—roasts, stew, scallopini, ground veal, or pâté—and, of course, bones for veal stock.

Removing the blade bone from a shoulder of veal

In addition, working with the veal shoulder will demystify the process of butchering and teach you a lot about meat. It is easy to cut—you don't have to be an expert with a boning knife. And you don't need to worry that you will ruin the meat. This is not a delicate piece, like a saddle or loin—nothing can go wrong; however you cut the meat, you will be able to make something delicious with it.

A veal shoulder will weigh any-where from 12 to 20 pounds; it may have the shank bone in, or it may already be cut off; it may have more of the neck or

(continued on page 349)

Rolling and Tying a Roast

Tying a roast not only improves its aesthetic appearance, but will shape an irregular piece of meat, such as a veal shoulder roast, into a solid round for even cooking. This "half-hitch" trussing technique is also excellent for securing stuffed meat cuts or boneless poultry, such as a stuffed loin of lamb, or the Turkey Galantine on page 290.

1. This is a trimmed veal shoulder roast with the shoulder blade removed. Season the inside of the roast before tying it.

2. Fold the sides of the roast to enclose the seasonings and form an oblong roll. Turn the roast seam side down and tie a loop of twine around the end nearest you. Tighten and knot.

3. Make a half-hitch loop in the twine and fit it around the roast. Draw this loop toward you, until it is about 2 inches from the first loop, then pull it tight.

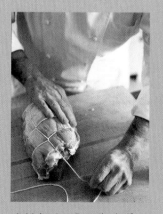

4. Make 4 or 5 similar half-hitch loops along the length of the roast. Hold the twine taut, then roll the roast over so the seam is up. Run the twine lengthwise along the seam side, drawing it over and around the crosswise loops as you did on the first side.

5. Turn the roast topside again and tie the end of the twine at the first knot, completing the truss.

Veal Roast en Cocotte (continued)

sprinkle half the herbs, salt, and pepper on the inside of the roast before tying, and the remaining portion on the outside, after tying.

Heat the butter and olive oil in the sauté pan or casserole over high heat. When sizzling, lay the top of the rolled roast in the pan and sear for 3 to 4 minutes, until nicely browned. Turn the meat onto another side and sear for several minutes, and continue turning and searing, over medium to high heat, until the entire piece is browned and the bottom of the pan is well crusted with crystallized juices, about 10 to 15 minutes in all.

Braising the roast and garnishes

Strew the leek pieces, the fresh or dried savory, and the strips of lemon peel around the roast and pour the stock over. Bring to a boil rapidly, cover the pan and adjust the heat to low, and cook for 35 minutes.

Arrange the endive halves, blanched or unblanched, in a single layer in the braising pan, surrounding the roast. (Or, if you are using a smaller casserole, lift the roast, fill the bottom with endives, and set the roast on top of them.) Bring the liquid back to the boil over high heat, then cover the pan, lower the heat to medium-low, and cook for another 35 minutes, until the endives are completely cooked through and soft.

Turn off the heat and let the veal rest in the hot covered pan for at least 20 minutes, allowing the meat to relax and become more juicy.

Serving the veal and endives

Remove the roast to a cutting board and cut away the trussing twine. With a flat strainer or a slotted spoon, lift out the endive halves and arrange them to form a neat ring just inside the rim of the serving platter. Slice the roast into thick (½-inch) slices—enough for a first serving for your guests—and set the remaining piece of the roll and the slices, neatly overlapped, in the center of the endives. Spoon the cooked pieces of leek over the meat; pour the pan juices over both the endives and the roast; and, finally, sprinkle chopped parsley over all.

Jacques (continued from page 347)

loin sections. Whatever the configuration, simply follow the bones with your boning knife to remove them.

Then separate the meat along the natural articulations and divisions of the muscles. You don't have to know exactly what each piece is: use your judgment to figure out a good use for the meat. If it is a large, solid, lean piece, like the cut from the shoulder blade, use it whole for a roast or a braise, as in this recipe. You could also slice off a couple of pieces to pound into scallopini. With meat that has more sinew and connective tissue—and is therefore tougher—cut it into chunks to use in Julia's veal ragout and *blanquette de veau*. And the fattier pieces you can grind up for pâté. Remember, whatever you do will work!

If you like to cook outdoors, you can easily grill the entire veal shoulder just as it comes from the market (only removing the shank if still attached). Grill it very slowly, over moderately hot coals, for almost 3 hours, turning frequently so it doesn't burn. Then let it rest, near the fire or in a low oven, for another hour. The meat is tender and juicy, enough for 15 people. I serve it with an herb butter—with herbs from my garden—as part of our feast for the Fourth of July.

Jacques's Veal Escalopes in Black-Butter Spinach

Thin slices of veal cut from the shoulder are called escalopes or scallopini. They should be sautéed very fast just before serving time, and they are particularly handy to make when you are pressed for time. They can be dressed with an infinite variety of garnishes.

Yield: 2 servings

4 veal escalopes, 3 to 3½ ounces each, cut ¼ inch thick, 4 inches in diameter
1 package fresh spinach (10 ounces), ribs removed, washed and drained
3 Tbs butter
Salt and freshly ground pepper to taste
Small dash of grated nutmeg
1 Tbs lemon juice
¼ cup chicken stock or water

Special equipment

A meat pounder; a large skillet

Pound the escalopes, if necessary, to the proper size. Refrigerate them until ready to cook.

Wash and drain the spinach.

At cooking time, melt 2 tablespoons of the butter in the skillet until the butter turns a dark-hazelnut color and starts smoking. Add the spinach (watch out for spattering) and mix with tongs in the hot butter for a few minutes, until the spinach is wilted and starts releasing water. Add salt and pepper to taste and grated nutmeg. Stir well and cook the spinach for a few more minutes, until all the juices have evaporated and the spinach is cooked. Arrange on 2 warm plates.

Melt the remaining tablespoon of butter in the skillet and heat until foaming, then add the 4 escalopes in 1 layer. Season with salt and pepper and cook on high heat for about 40 seconds on each side. Arrange two escalopes on top of the spinach on each plate and sprinkle lemon juice over them.

Pour the stock or water into the skillet and bring to a boil, stirring to melt any solidified juices from the pan. Pour this *jus* on top of the escalopes and serve immediately.

Julia's Blanquette de Veau

The beauty of this most famous of French veal stews lies entirely in its ingredients—real milk-fed veal of the palest-pink color combined with a fine cooking stock, the freshest mushrooms, the tenderest onions, and the loving hand of the cook.

Veal cuts for stewing: A recommended selection is neck and shank for meat and bones, breast for cartilage, and undercut of chuck (meaty strips on either side of the upper backbone) for solid chunks. You will need about four pounds of veal for six people, depending on bones and appetites.

Yield: 6 servings

For the veal
About 4 pounds milk-fed veal stew meat cut into 2-inch pieces (see notes on veal quality, page 346)
2 cups veal bones sawed into pieces (optional, but desirable for extra flavor)
2½ cups veal or chicken stock, or canned chicken broth
1 large onion stuck with 1 whole clove
1 large carrot, peeled and roughly chopped
1 medium celery stalk, washed and chopped
A medium herb bouquet: 4 parsley sprigs, ½ imported bay leaf, ½ tsp thyme tied in washed cheesecloth
Salt

For the onions
18 to 24 white onions about 1 inch in diameter
½ cup stock dipped from veal-cooking liquid
¼ tsp salt
1 Tbs butter

For the mushrooms
½ pound fresh mushrooms
¼ cup stock dipped from veal-cooking liquid
½ tsp salt
½ Tbs lemon juice
½ Tbs butter

For the sauce and final assembly
4 Tbs butter
5 Tbs flour
Salt and white pepper
Lemon juice

Optional classical enrichment
2 or 3 egg yolks
½ cup heavy cream

Special equipment
A heavy 4-quart stainless-steel pot or casserole for the stew; a 10-inch non-stick frying or sauté pan for the onions; a 3-quart stainless-steel saucepan for the mushrooms, then for drained cooking liquid; a heavy-bottomed 2½-quart stainless-steel saucepan for the sauce

Preparing the veal

Real veal exudes an enormous amount of scum, and it is best to blanch the meat as a first step. To do so, set the meat and bones in the pot, cover with cold water, and bring rapidly to the boil. Simmer for 2 to 3 minutes, until heavy scum has ceased to rise. Drain through a colander into the sink, wash out the kettle, and wash scum deposit off meat and bones. Return them to the pot, and add the chicken stock or broth, the vegetables, and the herb bouquet. Pour in enough cold water to cover ingredients by ½ inch. Bring to the simmer, skimming off additional scum for a few minutes. Salt very lightly. (While the veal is simmering, prepare the onions and mushrooms as described below.)

Simmer the stew slowly, partially covered, for about 1½ hours, or until the meat is tender when pierced with a fork—eat a bit to be sure. Salt lightly to taste, and let stand, uncovered, for ½ hour or more, allowing the veal to absorb additional flavor from its cooking liquid. Then drain through a colander set over a large saucepan. Taste the cooking liquid carefully, and skim fat off the surface. If it lacks strength, rapidly boil down the liquid—you should have 3 to 4 cups of delicious broth. Meanwhile, wash out the stewing kettle. Discard all loose bones and return the meat to the kettle.

Preparing the onions

Peel and pierce a cross in the root ends of the onions as described on page 196. Arrange in one layer in the pan; add the stock, salt, and butter. Cover and simmer very slowly for about 30 minutes, or until the onions are tender when pierced. Set aside until needed.

Preparing the mushrooms

Trim the mushrooms and brush clean. Leave whole if less than ¾ inch in diameter; halve or quarter if larger. Place in a saucepan with the stock, salt, lemon juice, and butter; toss to coat with the liquid. Cover and simmer for several minutes, until just tender. Add the mushrooms to the onions above.

Sauce and final assembly

Make a *sauce velouté* as follows: Melt the butter in the saucepan, stir in the flour with a wooden spoon, and cook slowly until flour and butter froth together for 2 minutes without coloring. Remove from heat, let cool for a moment, then vigorously whisk in a ladleful of hot veal-cooking liquid. Set over heat, stirring with wire whip and adding driblets of veal-cooking liquid to thin out the sauce; it should coat a spoon fairly heavily. Drain in the cooking liquids from the onions and the mushrooms. You will have about 3 cups of liquid in all. Simmer for 10 minutes, stirring occasionally, and skimming as necessary. Taste the sauce carefully for seasoning, adding salt, white pepper, and drops of lemon juice as you feel them needed. Add the onions and mushrooms to the veal kettle and pour the sauce over.

May be prepared a day in advance to this point. Film top of sauce with a spoonful or two of veal liquid, set aside uncovered until cool, then cover and refrigerate.

Finishing the *blanquette*

Shortly before serving, cover the veal and bring slowly to the simmer for 2 to 3 minutes, and taste again for seasoning. You may serve the stew now without further additions. Or continue as follows.

Optional classical enrichment

Blend the egg yolks and cream in a mixing bowl, then gradually beat in ½ cup of hot sauce to warm the egg yolks. Remove the stew from heat, and gradually fold in the egg-yolk enrichment. Set again over heat, folding the stew gently for several minutes as the yolks slowly thicken the sauce, but do not let it come to the simmer. Carefully correct seasoning again and serve.

Serving suggestions

Serve the *blanquette* on a warm platter, surrounded with steamed or boiled rice and decorated with parsley sprigs. No other vegetables are necessary, but you may wish buttered peas, asparagus tips, or braised cucumbers. Among wine choices are a mature red Bordeaux or cabernet, or a Médoc or Merlot, or a smooth full-bodied white such as a Graves or Chardonnay.

Braised Rice and Onion Soubise

Here is a savory accompaniment to veal dishes such as our Veal Roast en Cocotte (page 346), as well as to roast chicken and turkey. A *soubise* is made by slowly braising rice with lots of sliced onions. The onions are meltingly tender, while the rice grains softly retain their form. It is such a favorite of mine that I keep suggesting it in book after book, and here it is again. You can't but enjoy it, and it's easy to do.

For 4 to 6 people, very slowly cook 2 cups of minced onions in a covered heavy 2-quart saucepan with 2 tablespoons of light olive oil or butter until the onions are very soft and translucent but not browned—stir them up now and then. This will take about 20 minutes. Then pour in ¾ cup of raw plain long-grain white rice and blend thoroughly with the onions. Stir for several minutes over moderate heat until the rice grains turn from milky white to translucent then back again to milky white—this cooks the starch coating and helps to keep the rice grains from sticking together.

Stir in ¼ cup of dry white wine or dry white French vermouth, 1⅓ cups of light chicken stock or hot water, ¼ teaspoon of salt or to taste, and 1 imported bay leaf. Bring to the simmer, give one single thorough stir, then cover and let simmer rather slowly and undisturbed for 15 to 18 minutes, until the liquid has been absorbed and the rice is just tender. Uncover, fluff up briefly with a wooden fork, and correct seasoning.

The dish may be done in advance. Rewarm or keep warm, setting the loosely covered saucepan in another pan of simmering water. You may wish to enrich the rice before serving by fluffing in half a cup or so of sour cream and/or ⅓ cup of freshly grated Parmesan cheese.

Gremolata (Orange, Lemon, and Garlic Sprinkle for Veal Stews)

Sometimes spelled "gremolada," this zesty garlic-and-citrus addition is traditional with our *ossobucco* (page 354), and also goes nicely with the Veal Ragout on page 354.

Using a vegetable peeler, remove the zest (colored part of peel only) from one firm bright-skinned orange and 1 firm bright lemon. Cut the strips into matchstick-size julienne ¹⁄₁₆ inch wide. Blanch (boil) them slowly for 10 minutes in a quart of water, which removes their bitterness but not their flavor. Drain, and refresh in cold water.

Fold half into your simmering stew or ragout, and let the rest dry on paper towels. Line them up and cut crosswise into fine dice. Toss in a small bowl with a medium clove of garlic, finely minced, and a handful of chopped parsley. Cover and refrigerate. Sprinkle a bit over each portion as you serve.

Variation: Julia's Veal Ragout (Brown Veal Stew)

A ragout is an informal veal stew, much less exacting than the preceding *blanquette*. The meat is browned before being simmered in wine and meat stock with such aromatic vegetables as you wish—onions, carrots, tomatoes, and so forth. It is in fact a regular meat stew and could just as well be made with lamb, beef, or turkey as with veal—"A stew is a stew is a stew." Use the same cuts of meat, approximately 2-inch size, as for the preceding *blanquette,* plus other cuts from the shoulder, and cross-cuts from the legs—*ossobuco,* in other words.

For 6 people, set a 4-quart heavy casserole over moderately high heat and in it sauté 2 cups of mixed chopped onions, carrots, and celery with a tablespoon of vegetable oil. When nicely browned, set the vegetables aside and brown the meat plus any chopped veal bones you may have. Drain out and discard any accumulated fat. Add a cup of chopped fresh Italian plum tomatoes, a medium herb bouquet (page 351), a large clove of smashed garlic, ½ cup of dry white French vermouth, and enough chicken or beef stock barely to cover the ingredients. Bring to the simmer on top of the stove, taste, and salt very lightly, then cover and cook for about 1½ hours at a slow simmer, either on the stove or in a 350°F oven. Baste and turn the veal several times during its cooking.

When the meat is tender, pour the contents of the casserole through a colander set over a large saucepan. Rinse out the casserole and return the meat to it. Discard any bones. Press hard on the remaining ingredients to force their juices back into the cooking liquid. Skim off and discard surface fat. If necessary, rapidly boil down the liquid to concentrate its flavor, correct seasoning, and pour over the meat.

Ahead of time. May be cooked a day or two in advance.

Serving. Bring to the simmer and cook for several minutes, folding meat and sauce together until well warmed through. Correct seasoning again, and serve.

Serving suggestions. Serve on a bed of rice or noodles, or with polenta or roast or sautéed potatoes. Provençal Tomatoes (page 210) would go nicely, and/or fresh peas, page 206. As to wine, I would choose a country red like Beaujolais or zinfandel, or a Côtes du Rhône.

Variation: Ragoût de Veau aux Carottes (Brown Veal Stew with Carrots)

Veal and carrots braised together are a happy combination, and much appreciated in France. Rather than the aromatic vegetables suggested above, use only a cup of sliced onions, browned as described (or the small glazed onions on page 196, 3 per serving, finished off in the ragout). Add ready-to-cook small whole carrots—3 or 4 apiece—after the ragout has cooked ½ hour.

Variation: Blanquette of Veal with Carrots

You might adapt the same system for the preceding *blanquette,* using the onions but substituting carrots for mushrooms. It is an attractive presentation, especially when the carrots are young, shapely, and nicely hand-peeled.

Variation: Ossobuco (Braised Veal Hind Shanks)

The hind shank of veal, the back leg from knee to ankle, contains the bone with the marrow, the right and the desirable cut for this increasingly popular dish. If you use the foreshank, which is larger and bonier but has no marrow, you cannot call it *ossobuco,* simply because you are not using an *ossobuco*. Since hind shanks are sometimes hard to find and they freeze nicely, pick them up whenever you see any and save them in your freezer until you have enough for a party. One per person is ample, and you'll probably have a few leftovers. You can, of course, use foreshanks, but then you'd call them simply "braised veal shanks."

Every Italian cookbook has its author's very own, very special personal recipe for *ossobuco* (sometimes spelled as 2 words). It will be, essentially, the same type of brown veal stew as our brown ragout above, and you will be perfectly in order using that. But the classic dish has its unique finale, its Gremolata, described on page 353.

Some markets sell ready-cut shank pieces 1½ to 2 inches thick; count on 2 or 3 per person. Or ask your butcher to cut them for you. For 6 people, you will want 5 to 6 veal hind shanks sawed into about 18 crosswise pieces 1½ inches thick. Season with salt and pepper and dredge in flour, shaking off excess. (The flour is an automatic sauce thickener, and is always useful when you want more sauce and less "boiling down of braising juices," as in the preceding recipes.)

Brown and braise the shank pieces for about 1½ hours, as directed for the ragout. As soon as the veal is simmering, prepare the Gremolata, unless you wish to do so in advance.

When the veal is done, finish as described in the ragout recipe, leaving the shank pieces in the washed-out casserole and the sauce in a saucepan. After it has settled for a moment, skim fat off its surface; the sauce should be lightly and nicely thickened. Boil down rapidly if necessary to concentrate flavor, correct seasoning, and pour over the meat.

May be prepared a day or two in advance.

Just before serving, bring to the simmer for several minutes, basting, until hot through. Correct seasoning again. Arrange either on a warm platter or on individual dinner plates. Be sure each serving has a couple of marrow bones clearly in view, and furnish each guest with a little spoon to dig it out. Strew the Gremolata over all, and serve. The white beans on page 170 would go nicely here, or the endives on page 346, plus the carrots and turnips on page 198.

Variation: Braised Lamb Shanks

Braised lamb shanks—the hind and forelegs—have become a popular restaurant item. The hind-leg shank is the smaller and tenderer, and 2 per person give a generous serving. One meaty foreshank, sawed into crosswise pieces 2 inches thick, serves 1. Brown and braise lamb shanks as for the veal in the preceding ragout.

Julia

It is just as easy to roast a large boneless pork loin as a small one, and then you will have plenty of slices for wonderful sandwiches or a nice meat salad. For a different taste, you can coat the loin roast with the special spice rub that I put on my pork chops (see sidebar, page 360). Rub the spices into the meat several hours or the night before roasting so they have a chance to penetrate the meat. Then you can roast it just as Jacques does here, with apples. Golden Delicious are definitely the ones to use in this dish. The flavor is always good and the wedges hold their shape, giving you an attractive garnish that makes a nice sauce as well.

Long boneless pork-loin roasts (4 pounds, or about a foot in length) can be folded and tied so they are double thick. In that form they are roasted more slowly (350°F) for a couple of hours. If your market doesn't prepare roasts that way, you can ask them to do it, or tie it up yourself, using Jacques's technique, shown on page 348.

Roast Pork Loin

Here is an easy roast for a family dinner, out of the oven in an hour, with a golden, saucy apple garnish. The boneless pork loin is a solid, slender piece of meat, taken from one of the most tender parts of the pig—the "center cut" of the top loin muscle. It cooks quickly and evenly, and carves effortlessly into neat oval slices.

You can find loin roasts in every market, already trimmed, with no boning or tying necessary. Many supermarkets, in fact, buy entire pork loins already boned, and simply divide them into sizes convenient for their customers. If you don't see a 4-pound roast (serving 8), as we call for, ask the butcher to cut one—or a smaller or larger roast if you want. With minor adjustments in the seasoning, you can use this recipe for a delicious roast of any size. Since the thickness of the loin is about the same—a heavier roast is just cut longer—the cooking time will still be only an hour or so. In any case, you want to use a meat thermometer. Today's pork is so lean that a loin can become dry if roasted to an internal temperature higher than 150°F or so (the temperature will rise while the meat rests).

Our method here keeps the meat moist—it is first browned on the stove, then roasted on a bed of apple wedges, which soften and release their juices. With a flameproof gratin dish or casserole, you can sear and roast (and even serve) the loin all in one dish. You can also make a colorful presentation by surrounding the roast on a large platter with both the golden apple wedges and our Braised Red Cabbage (page 197).

Yield: 8 servings

One 4-pound boneless pork loin, well
    trimmed of all fat, "silver skin," and
    sinew
1¼ tsp salt
½ tsp freshly ground black pepper
2 tsp *herbes de Provence* (see page 363)

2 Tbs butter

1 Tbs vegetable oil

5 large Golden Delicious apples, peel on,
  each cored and cut into wedges (about
  7 cups)

¼ tsp sugar

Special equipment

A large flameproof, shallow baking dish
  or heavy metal roasting pan (about 14
  inches long and 10 inches wide); an
  instant-read meat thermometer

Preheat the oven to 375°F.

Sprinkle 1 teaspoon of salt, ¼ teaspoon of pepper and the *herbes de Provence* all over the pork, and rub in the seasonings so they adhere. Set the baking dish over high heat with the butter and oil. When it is sizzling, lay in the roast and brown it over medium-high heat, turning it until nicely colored on all sides, about 6 to 8 minutes.

Remove from the heat, lift the roast out of the baking dish, and set it on a plate or cutting board. Spread the apple slices in one layer in the dish and sprinkle the sugar and ¼ teaspoon each of salt and pepper over them. Replace the roast on the bed of apples.

Set the dish in the oven and roast for about 1 hour, basting occasionally with the juices in the dish. After 50 minutes, start checking the internal temperature with a meat thermometer inserted into the thickest part of the loin. Roast to a temperature of 150°F, remove the meat from the oven, and let rest for about 10 minutes.

Slice the pork crosswise into thin slices, and serve on top of the apples, right in the baking dish if you like. Or remove the roast to a cutting board, scoop the apples onto a large serving platter, and spread them to form a ring around the edge of the platter. Arrange pork slices and the remaining roast in the center, and serve.

Jacques

The boneless loin of pork corresponds to the loin muscle that in beef is called the strip, or New York strip, which we cut for Steak au Poivre (page 310). If you look at a cross-section of the pork loin you can see that it resembles a strip steak, and, in fact, you can cut it into steaks of whatever thickness you like. Grill or pan-fry these in the same way as we do pork chops or beef steaks. If you buy a large loin roast—or if you get an entire side of pork loin to bone out yourself, as I recommend (see sidebar, page 358)—you can always cut a few steaks (or "boneless chops," as they call them in the store) and still have a nice piece for roasting.

All pork used to be cooked to 180°F and any pinkness was considered dangerous. But that's no longer necessary: the parasite that causes trichinosis is very rare today and in any case is killed at a temperature of 140°F. Further, at a temperature near 180°F a very lean pork loin or tenderloin would be quite dry. I make sure to trim away all fat and sinew—which need longer cooking—and remove the roast from the oven when it reaches a temperature of 150°F. The meat will continue to cook inside as it rests. At 155° or 160°F it is perfectly safe and the slices will be moist and tender, with a slight rosy color.

Jacques on Dividing Up a Whole Pork Loin at Home

All the pork used in our recipes here—the boneless roast, chops, and tenderloin—comes from the whole pork loin. This is a long piece that runs from the shoulder to the hip of the pig (one on each side of the body), and contains the most tender and popular cuts of pork. The whole loin, which usually weighs 15 to 20 pounds, is equivalent to the rib roast, loin, and filet sections of the beef.

If you are interested in learning about meat—and love pork, as I do—I recommend that you order a whole loin from a good butcher, and cut it up yourself at home. As with the veal shoulder I discuss on page 348, dividing the pork loin takes no special skill. It is easy to identify the pieces, easy to separate them with a sharp knife and a sturdy cleaver, and you really can't make any serious mistakes. If you have left a bit of meat on some of the bones, you can cook them up with barbecue sauce and enjoy them as spareribs.

The greatest advantage of doing this yourself is that you can use every bit of the whole loin for cooking. Here's what I do at home: I divide the meat first, into boneless loin roast and steaks, bone-in rib roast and chops, a sirloin roast, a shoulder-blade roast, the whole tenderloin, and meaty bones for spareribs. Whatever I'm not cooking that day I freeze. Then I get all my bones together for a big soup, with beans, perhaps flavored with chili. Then I get all my meat trimmings together, and grind them for sausage, and save all the fat trimmings for pâté. When I'm done, nothing has been thrown away.

Sautéed Pork Filet or Tenderloin

The pork tenderloin, or filet, is much smaller than the beef tenderloin, but it is a similarly prized cut, tender, very lean, and versatile. You can roast it whole or cut it into chunks or medallions for a quick sauté, as we do here. As with the pan-fried beef steaks in this chapter, you will get a good crust in the pan, which adds flavor to a nice sauce of port and prunes. This makes an attractive and easy supper dish for 4, surrounded with a ring of plain rice pilaf (page 168), small orzo (pasta in the shape of rice), or quick-cooking couscous.

Pork tenderloins are now conveniently sold in cryovac packages of 2, about 1½ to 2 pounds total weight. The filets are already trimmed, but for this dish you will want to remove all remaining bits of fat, gristle, and silver skin.

Jacques's Sautéed Pork Tenderloin with Port and Prunes

Yield: 4 servings

6 ounces pitted prunes (20 to 24 small prunes)
½ cup port
2 small pork tenderloins, completely trimmed (about 20 to 24 ounces)
½ tsp salt, plus more if needed
¼ tsp freshly ground black pepper, plus more if needed
2 to 3 Tbs pure vegetable oil
2 Tbs minced shallots
3 Tbs red-wine vinegar
⅔ cups flavorful brown stock (page 42)
1 Tbs black-currant jam
1 Tbs ketchup
Fresh parsley or basil (whole sprigs, or chopped), for garnish

Special equipment

A 10- or 12-inch heavy-bottomed frying pan or sauté pan (regular surface); an ovenproof serving platter or baking dish

Preliminaries and sautéing the meat

A couple of hours (or longer) before cooking, pour 2 cups boiling water over the prunes and macerate for 30 minutes. Drain the water and add the port to the prunes, and let macerate until ready to use.

Preheat the oven to 200°F.

Slice each tenderloin on the diagonal—changing the angle of the knife with each cut—into 6 equal-sized chunks, 2 inches or so at their thickest part (about 2 ounces each). Season the chunks with the salt and pepper.

Set the pan with the oil over high heat and swirl to film the bottom. When hot, set in the chunks with plenty of room around them (in batches if necessary). Sear the chunks for about 5 minutes, over medium-high heat, turning them until they are well browned on all sides and the pan bottom is crusted. Remove the meat to the platter and place in the oven to relax and finish cooking.

Making the sauce

With the pan over medium heat, add the shallots and sauté for about 30 seconds, stirring with a wooden spoon. Pour in the red-wine vinegar—keep your face averted as the acetic acid evaporates—and stir and scrape the pan bottom to deglaze the crust. Pour in the stock, stirring, and then the port and prunes. Bring the sauce to a gentle boil and let it reduce for about 5 minutes, until slightly thickened.

Stir in the spoonfuls of black-currant jam and ketchup, mixing well to melt the jam. Remove the meat from the oven and pour the accumulated meat juices into the sauce. Stir and simmer for another minute or so—tasting the sauce and adjusting the seasonings—until viscous and shiny.

Spoon out the prunes and arrange them among the chunks of pork, then pour the sauce over all. Garnish with the fresh herbs, and serve.

Jacques

The pork filet, when it is completely trimmed, is an extremely low-fat meat—the same as chicken breast—yet it is tender and very flavorful. I like to form pieces of filet into little pork steaks, each about 4 or 6 ounces, by butterflying and pounding them to ½-inch thickness. For grilling, I pound them into "paillards" that are only ¼ inch thick, which can be grilled in a matter of moments.

The black-currant jam is really a "secret ingredient" in this sauce. (If unavailable, replace with a blackberry or plum jam.) It adds a touch of nice flavor, but, even more important, it gives good viscosity to the sauce, thickening it slightly and creating a nice sheen. Make sure you use a sturdy, heavy-bottomed frying pan with a regular, *not* non-stick, surface that can develop a good crust in the pan for deglazing. If you use a non-stick pan, the glaze will stick only to the meat, and there will be nothing left in the pan to make a sauce.

Julia

The spice blend that I rub on
my pork chops (see sidebar, page 356) is
a flavoring technique that you can adapt
as you like. Mix up your own blend of
favorite spices, or just use one or two
that you have in your cabinet, perhaps
allspice, sage, or thyme, along with
white pepper. Whichever spices you use,
rub them into the meat well before
cooking, so the flavors can really sink in.

Lean pork can dry out easily, so
slow cooking in the pan is terribly important here, especially with thick chops.
Use moderate heat only to brown the
chop, then give it a good 8 to 10 minutes
of gentle simmering in the sauce. For the
sauce in this recipe, I throw in a sprig of
fresh savory during the simmering, and
stir in black-currant jam or chutney at the
end for a touch of sweetness, but as with
the spice marinade, you can use what
you like and have on hand. I strongly recommend the final swirl of butter, though,
as nothing gives a sauce such a satisfying
taste and velvety texture.

Pork Chops

The center of the pork loin, which gives us the convenient
boneless roast in the preceding recipe, also yields the finest pork
chops. Instead of trimming the long top loin muscle away from
the bones, the butcher gets chops by cutting through the loin,
backbone and all. If the cut is nearer the hip of the pig, they are
"loin chops," which resemble a porterhouse steak, with a small
portion of tenderloin muscle. If the cut is toward the shoulder
end, and includes a rib bone, you get "rib chops."

Either loin or rib chops will be delicious prepared by the
two methods we give here—rubbed with herbs or spices, then
sautéed or grilled. But they must be "center cut" with a large
eye of solid, pale-pink meat, and quite thick—between $1\frac{1}{4}$ and
$1\frac{1}{2}$ inches. A rib chop is a particularly tempting sight for a meat
lover, when its long, curving bone is neatly trimmed into a
manche, or handle, as Jacques demonstrates in the photos on
page 363.

Thick chops need careful cooking to ensure that the lean
meat does not become dry or tough. After browning, Julia's
sautéed chop simmers in its sauce for a few minutes, while
Jacques's grilled chop is set in a low oven (or under a bowl on
the grill) to finish cooking and let the natural juices flow
through the meat.

Julia's Sautéed Pork Chops

Yield: 2 chops, serving 2

2 center-cut pork rib or loin chops, each
   about 10 ounces, $1\frac{1}{4}$ to $1\frac{1}{2}$ inches
   thick
1 Tbs or more fresh vegetable oil
$\frac{1}{4}$ tsp salt
$\frac{1}{2}$ tsp or more Julia's Special Spice Blend
   (see sidebar, page 362)
$\frac{1}{4}$ cup dry white French vermouth
$\frac{1}{2}$ cup flavorful brown stock (page 42)

A sprig of fresh savory, or thyme, or a big
  pinch of dried herbs
1 tsp chutney
1 Tbs soft butter

Special equipment
A heavy frying pan large enough for
  both chops, with a cover

At least ½ hour in advance of cooking, trim rib chops as shown in the photos on page 363; trim loin chops of excess fat and sinew. To season the chops, rub each side with drops of vegetable oil to coat lightly, sprinkle with salt, and rub in some of the spice blend, using about ½ teaspoon in all. Cover the chops and refrigerate until ready to cook. Set the frying pan over moderately high heat and film the bottom with oil. Meanwhile, rapidly dry the chops on paper towels, and when the pan is very hot lay in the chops. Sauté to brown each lightly on both sides—3 to 4 minutes per side.

Pour the vermouth and stock into the pan, add the herbs, cover the pan, and adjust heat to maintain a slow simmer. Cook slowly 4 to 5 minutes, turn, and cook 4 to 5 minutes on the other side. They are done when you cut close to the bone with a little knife and the meat is still faintly pink. (I do not like rare pork, since, to me, it has not developed its optimum flavor.)

Sauce and serving
Remove the chops to a side dish while you rapidly boil down the pan juices until syrupy. Stir in the chutney and simmer a moment, then return the chops to the pan. Basting with the sauce as you simmer to rewarm the chops, taste and correct seasoning. Remove the pan from heat, and arrange a chop on each warm dinner plate, leaving the sauce in the pan. Reheat the sauce to the simmer, remove from heat, and, swirling the pan by its handle, drop in the butter, swirling to incorporate it completely. Pour over the chops and serve immediately.

Jacques

A ridged stovetop grill is a handy kitchen implement for anyone who loves to grill but lives in an apartment or is stuck inside in wintertime. You can find such grills in different sizes and shapes, both pans and flat griddle types. If you are using the kind that covers two burners, be aware of cool spots in the middle, where the food will not cook as fast or might stick. Always get the thickest, heaviest kind of grill, made of cast iron or other material that really retains heat and will mark the food nicely.

In the photos on page 363, I demonstrate a procedure called *quadrillage*, which I use to give pork chops, steaks (like my Chateaubriand in this chapter), or other grilled foods a beautiful crisscross marking. But this series of turns also ensures that the meat cooks evenly on both sides. If your chop stays on one side only while you mark the cross, the meat will contract too much and toughen on that side, while the myoglobin, or internal juices, will be forced to the other side. The over-crusted meat will not be able to relax and become tender.

But turning the chop at regular intervals makes the contraction of the meat on the two sides exactly the same, and the myoglobin goes to the center. Then, when set in a low oven, the meat decontracts evenly and becomes uniformly tender, and the juices can permeate the whole chop.

Julia's Special Spice Blend

The following blend of ground spices is good as a dry marinade for pork chops and roast pork, duck, and goose, and as a sausage seasoning. You can make it in any quantity, using the recommended proportions—if using a tablespoon measure, you will have ½ cup of mix. Use ¼ to ½ teaspoon of the blend for every pound of meat. Rub it on chops at least ½ hour before cooking and on roasts several hours before.

Spices to add in equal amounts (1 teaspoon or 1 tablespoon each): ground bay leaf (imported), clove, mace, nutmeg, paprika, thyme.

Spices to add in half amounts (½ teaspoon or ½ tablespoon each): allspice, cinnamon, savory.

Add in a double amount (2 teaspoons or 2 tablespoons): freshly ground white pepper.

Mix well in a bowl and store in a screwtop glass jar.

Jacques's Grilled Pork Chops

Yield: 2 chops, serving 2

2 center-cut pork rib or loin chops, each about 10 ounces, 1¼ to 1½ inches thick
½ tsp salt
½ tsp freshly ground black pepper
1½ tsp chopped fresh rosemary leaves
1½ tsp corn or canola oil
Fresh rosemary sprigs, for garnish

Special equipment

A ridged stovetop grill (flat grill or grill pan); one half of a large potato, cut crosswise; a baking dish or ovenproof platter for resting the chops, or a metal bowl to cover chops on the grill

With a knife, trim off the sinew along the curving rib.

Preheat the oven to 180°F.

Trim rib chops as shown in the photos; trim loin chops of excess fat and sinew. Sprinkle both sides of the chops with the salt, pepper, and chopped rosemary, and pat the seasonings so they adhere to the meat. Pour the oil into a plate and dip in the chops on all sides to coat lightly with oil.

Set the grill over high heat and allow it to get quite hot. To give the chops crisscross marks, follow the procedure shown in the photos.

Cut around the rib bone about an inch from the end and scrape off all fat, meat, and sinew to make a neat *manche*, or handle.

Lay the chops on the grill at an angle to the ridges and cook for 2 minutes, until clearly marked. Then turn them over, keeping the same angle, so the now visible marks align with the ridges. Cook for 2 minutes on this side.

Hack off the protruding bone at the other end.

Turn the chops over again and now rotate them as well, so the visible grill marks are perpendicular to the ridges. Cook for 2 minutes, until a criss-cross is clear.

Turn the chops over for the third time, keeping them at the same angle. Cook for 2 minutes, so that the second side of the chops has been on the grill exactly as long as the first side.

Finally, stand the chops on their thick outside edges, balanced against the potato half or other prop. Brown for about 2 minutes, shifting the chop as needed so the entire edge is browned.

Remove the chops to a platter and place in the oven for about 10 minutes, to allow them to decontract. (Alternatively, turn off the heat and cover the chops with a bowl on the grill.) Garnish with a sprig of rosemary and serve.

Jacques's Herbes de Provence

The fragrant blend of dried herbs known as *herbes de Provence* is used widely in cooking in southern France. It adds a nice flavor to various meat and vegetable recipes in this book, including the pork loin on page 356. You can buy commercially packaged *herbes de Provence* in both supermarkets and specialty-food stores, but you can also make your own blend from individual dried herbs, or, as I do, with fresh herbs from my garden.

The essential herbs for the mix are thyme, savory, marjoram, and oregano, which are blended in equal proportions. Optional herbs are sage, rosemary, lavender flowers, and fennel seeds, which should be added in half the amount of the required herbs.

You can dry fresh herbs quickly by spreading the leaves on baking sheets (keeping the varieties separate) and putting them into a 180°F oven for about 30 minutes. Crumble the large leaves slightly and measure them before mixing together. Seal in airtight plastic bags to preserve freshness.

The microwave also does a good job drying fresh herbs. Spread the leaves out, cover them loosely with paper towels, and microwave full-speed for about a minute. Grab the herbs by their branches and rub the dried leaves off. Store as above. I keep the branches to use when grilling fish or barbecuing.

Julia

Rather than waiting for the meat to cure, you can mix and cook up homemade sausage the same day, or the next, giving the pork just a few hours or overnight to absorb the flavors of your seasonings. In this case, you must reduce the amount of salt—start with 1 to 1½ teaspoons of salt and several grinds of pepper for the amount of meat here. I also recommend about ¾ teaspoon of my spice blend (page 362). If you do it this way, it is most important to sauté a spoonful of the sausage mixture, until it is cooked through, then taste it and adjust the seasonings as needed.

Homemade Sausage

There is nothing like a large savory sausage, served warm on a bed of potato or lentil salad. It will be especially satisfying, though, when you've made the sausage yourself, from scratch.

If you have never made sausage before, or if you have struggled with casings and stuffers, you will be delighted with Jacques's simple method of hand-shaping in plastic wrap. It takes just minutes to form a large, firm, and perfectly shaped sausage, without any special equipment. After several days of curing in the refrigerator, it will have the well-developed flavor of *saucisson* from a good *charcuterie,* but at a fraction of the price.

You want to use relatively lean, coarsely ground pork for this recipe, with a fat content of about 20 to 25 percent. A Boston butt or other pork shoulder cut is ideal for sausage. It is easy and economical to buy a small shoulder roast, cut the meat into chunks, and grind it yourself, with a meat grinder or grinding attachment to an electric mixer. If you prefer, buy very fresh ground pork from the market. As with beef, many markets specify the fat content of ground pork on the package—or you can ask the butcher to grind the amount of pork shoulder that you want.

Plan to season and form the sausage at least three days, or up to a week, before serving, to give it time to develop flavor. The salt and pepper amounts in the recipe allow it to cure safely and should be followed as given, but the other seasonings can be varied as you like. Add herbs, such as thyme or rosemary, substitute pistachio or walnuts (or omit the nuts completely), or mix in some of Julia's Special Spice Blend (page 362). See Jacques's Sausage in Brioche (page 26) for an elegant variation using white wine, pine nuts, and black truffle. Once it is cured, you can poach any sausage mixture as detailed here, bake it in brioche dough, or stuff it into casings to form links (see sidebar, page 366). If you like, you can also cure the mixture in a bowl and just form it into patties to fry or grill.

Yield: 6 servings

1½ pounds coarsely ground pork, about
    20 percent fat (from the Boston butt or
    shoulder)
2½ tsp salt
½ tsp sugar
¾ tsp freshly ground black pepper
3 Tbs coarsely chopped pecan pieces
3 Tbs red wine (very good quality)
½ tsp garlic (1 small clove)
⅛ tsp potassium nitrate (saltpeter)
    (optional)

Special equipment
A piece of plastic wrap and a piece of
    aluminum foil, both about 18 inches
    long; a large saucepan (14 inches
    diameter or more)

Mixing and forming the sausage several days ahead

Lay the plastic wrap, long side in front of you, on the work surface. Put the pork and all the seasoning ingredients (including the saltpeter, if using) in a large bowl and mix together well with your hands.

Press the meat together into a rough log shape and place it on the plastic wrap. Fold the wrap over and form a thin, even sausage, about 12 inches long and 2 inches in diameter—press firmly to eliminate any air pockets in the meat. Now roll the sausage back and forth under the wrap so it is perfectly smooth and cylindrical.

The sausage should be centered on the near edge of

Gently squeeze the meat out to form a 12-inch roll.

Jacques

Curing the sausage over several days or a week gives it particularly good flavor. The sugar in the recipe balances the harshness of the salt, which is necessary for curing. The small amount of potassium nitrate, or saltpeter, is used to preserve an appetizing red color in the meat, but it is entirely optional. You can usually purchase saltpeter at a drugstore.

This type of large sausage, called *saucisson à cuire* ("sausage to cook") in France, when packed into a casing can also be hung up in a cool place to cure and air-dry for many weeks. Then it becomes the very hard type of salami called *saucisson sec* (dry sausage), which can be eaten without cooking.

Homemade Sausage in Casings

The sausage mixture in this recipe, and the variation with truffles found on page 26, can also be stuffed into casings, to make link sausages of whatever size you like. There are various devices for stuffing sausage at home, including the hand-powered plunger style, and attachments to electric mixers. Follow the manufacturer's directions for whatever type you are using.

The thickness of sausage is determined by the type of natural casings (made from animal intestines) that you use. Lamb casings are the smallest, generally stuffed for breakfast links; hog casings form larger Italian-style sausages and bratwursts; and beef "middle" casing would make a large 1½-to-2-inch *saucisson*, about the size we form here.

All casings are packed in salt and must be thoroughly soaked in cold water to rinse and soften, and then the insides must be flushed with tap water before filling. Ask a local butcher who makes sausage to sell you a short length of casing (2 or 3 feet) to stuff this amount of meat. Otherwise, casings are sold for commercial use in enormous lengths, which will keep indefinitely in the freezer or refrigerator, in the salt packing.

Homemade Sausage (continued)

the plastic with several inches of wrap on either side; roll it up tightly in the plastic wrap, then twist or fold the wrap on the ends and tuck these flaps under. Place the sausage on the aluminum foil, and roll it up and seal it the same way. Set the sausage in the refrigerator to cure for at least 3 days, or up to a week.

Cooking and serving the sausage

Fill the large saucepan with enough water to cover the sausage (you can set the foil-wrapped log in the water to check) and heat to 180° to 190°F—there should be small, slowly rising bubbles on the bottom of the pan. Place the wrapped sausage in the water and weight it with a plate or pot cover to keep it submerged (don't cover the pan). Cook for 40 minutes, carefully maintaining the water at the bare simmer. Turn off the heat and let the sausage remain in the water until ready to serve.

To serve, unwrap the warm sausage and slice crosswise into rounds, ½ inch thick or thicker. Arrange the slices overlapping on a platter, or on top of Lentil Salad (page 128) or Jacques's French Potato Salad (page 123). Wine choices for this include Beaujolais, zinfandel, or the very good red that you put into the sausage mixture.

Opposite: Homemade Sausage with Warm Potato Salad

Julia

Lately I've been roasting and eating some pretty tough legs of lamb. Obviously American lamb today is not what it used to be. Not too long ago, a leg of American lamb was aged, meaning that a mature whole leg weighing over 8 pounds was hung in a cold, dry aging room (34° to 40°F) for several weeks. During the aging process, natural enzymes go to work developing flavor and, at the same time, tenderizing the meat. Meanwhile, the leg loses some 2 percent of its weight. Multiply 2 percent by several hundred pounds and it is clear why processors are happy to eliminate this step, which costs money and takes up time and space. Hermetically sealed plastic "aging" has its disadvantages, our markets haven't room for old-style hanging, customers don't complain, and as a result we have tough meat. See additional discussion on page 372.

Leg of Lamb

Roast leg of lamb is always a fine main course for a family gathering or other festive occasion. It's also one of the easiest and most versatile large cuts of meat to prepare, and here are two recipes that illustrate the variety of cuts, cooking methods, and seasonings you can use.

To suit customer demand and convenience, legs of lamb in the market are cut into various small sizes and shapes, but we prefer the two largest cuts. Jacques's recipe is for a whole leg—the traditional *gigot* for a Sunday family dinner in France. It includes the meaty sirloin end, as well as the whole pelvic bone, which you can remove yourself (and use for stock), as shown in the photos on page 375. Julia's recipe is for the "short" leg, which has the sirloin and most of the hip bone already removed but still looks like the traditional leg—with lots of meat and a protruding shank bone—that looks handsome on a serving platter.

Both of these cuts are available at any market, and either would be delicious with the many traditional lamb accompaniments in this book, including Stuffed Tomatoes Provençal (page 210), Pommes de Terre Dauphinoise or Boulangère (pages 160 and 161), or the Eggplant and Zucchini Gratin (page 200). For a home-style meal, set the lamb right on top of a big platter of Jacques's Ragout of White Beans (page 171). A red Bordeaux or a fine cabernet is classically served with roast lamb, but a pinot noir would also be a good choice.

Jacques's Roast Leg of Lamb

Yield: 8 to 10 servings

1 whole untrimmed leg of lamb, weighing about 6 pounds with shank and
 pelvic bone (trimmed of pelvic bone
 and most fat, about 4¾ pounds)
4 garlic cloves, peeled
Salt
2 Tbs fresh rosemary leaves, stripped off
 the stem
Freshly ground black pepper
1½ cups lamb stock (see sidebar, page
 371), chicken stock, or white wine, or
 a mixture of wine and stock

Special equipment

A shallow-rimmed roasting pan, large
 enough to hold the whole leg

Trimming and seasoning the roast

Prepare the lamb leg, as shown in the photos on page 375, removing the hipbone, trimming all fat, and scraping ("Frenching") the shank bone.

For the herb seasoning, chop the garlic cloves coarsely. Pour a teaspoon of salt on top of the garlic and mash to a paste with the flat of the knife, then chop together with the rosemary leaves until they are finely minced.

Thrust the tip of a sharp, thin-bladed knife into the thick top of the leg, about 1 inch deep. Push about ½ teaspoon of the seasoning paste into the slit with your finger. Make a dozen or more such incisions in the meaty parts of the leg, both top and underside, and fill with the seasoning. Rub any remaining paste over the boneless sirloin end of the leg.

The leg can now be roasted, or refrigerated for several hours or overnight, to allow the seasoning to permeate the meat.

Jacques

A whole untrimmed leg of spring lamb (domestic lamb is the best) usually weighs anywhere from 6 to 8 pounds. You can choose the size appropriate for your party, and prepare it as explained in the recipe.

The most important step in preparing lamb, however, is removing the fat. The assertive taste that some people find objectionable in lamb is always in the fat, and when it is mostly trimmed away before roasting, they are surprised at how mild it tastes. For the same reason, it is important to pour off as much of the fat in the roasting pan as possible before you make your sauce and, if you are making lamb stock, to defat it well. If you freeze lamb, remove the fat beforehand, as it will grow rancid.

When the leg is well trimmed of fat, you can also roast the lamb at a higher temperature, as I do here, and even a large leg will roast to rare in about an hour or a bit more. I like to turn the leg once while it's in the oven, and then there's no need for basting. If you prefer, you can baste the roast once or twice with the pan juices, instead of turning it. I remove the lamb when it is still quite rare—at an internal temperature of 125° to 130°F—but you can roast it to a higher temperature if you like. In any case, allow the meat to rest for at least 20 minutes before carving.

(continued on page 371)

Jacques on Doneness

I like many cuts of meat rare, but there is an obsession about "not overcooking" these days that is ridiculous. I go to restaurants and get rare sausage, rare fish, rare chicken, and rare—really raw—vegetables. I want to tell them, "Please don't undercook the food!"

This fashion has made people feel that if they serve or even like something that is well cooked it somehow reflects on their IQ. I was at a dinner where we had to specify how we wanted rack of lamb prepared. After I ordered mine medium-rare, the woman who was sitting next to me apologized profusely for ordering her rack of lamb well done. "I'm sorry," she said to me, "but would you mind terribly if I take my lamb well done? I don't want to offend you."

Why would I be offended? If you prefer something well cooked, by all means follow your taste. You are not on a lower social scale if you want your steak medium or well done. You are the one who is going to eat it, so have it exactly the way you like.

Jacques's Roast Leg of Lamb (continued)

Roasting and resting

Preheat the oven to 400°F; arrange a rack in lower third of oven.

Just before roasting, sprinkle ¾ teaspoon salt and ½ teaspoon of freshly ground black pepper over both sides of the leg. Set it on the roasting pan topside up.

Roast the leg for about 30 minutes, then turn the roast over, grasping it by the shank bone (with a thick towel or pot holder to protect your hands). Continue roasting for another 30 minutes or so—1 to 1¼ hours total, depending on the size of the leg—until the internal temperature of the meat is about 125° to 130°F when measured at the thickest part.

Remove the leg to a carving board or platter and rest—topside up—for 20 minutes, allowing the meat to relax and reabsorb the natural juices.

Meanwhile, deglaze the roasting pan to make a simple sauce. Tilt the pan and pour off as much of the fat as possible. Place it over medium heat, pour in the stock and/or wine, and bring to a simmer, stirring and scraping up the browned glaze in the bottom of the pan. Strain the sauce into a bowl and add any juices released by the resting meat.

Carving and serving the roast

Carve the roast as shown in the photo on page 374. Slice into the top of the roast and cut toward the shank, holding the knife blade at a flat angle. Remove the first slice and start the next cut a bit farther away from the shank, again slicing through the top and toward the shank. Continue slicing off the top of the roast, arranging the slices on the serving platter. Drizzle the pan juices over before serving.

To serve with Ragout of White Beans (page 171), turn the beans into the center of the serving platter and set the leg right on top. As you carve, lay the slices on the beans alongside the roast, then drizzle the pan sauce over the meat and beans, flavoring both, and serve together.

Julia's Slow-Roasted Leg of Lamb

To get the best effect and flavor here, plan to prepare the lamb for roasting several hours or the day before cooking it, and leave room for it in the refrigerator. An herbal mustard-and-garlic coating not only gives the meat a subtle flavor, but means that the roast needs no basting. For an even more robust flavor, you may want to start by inserting the garlic stuffing directed in Jacques's recipe (page 369). Then spread on the mustard, and refrigerate until you are ready to roast.

Timing. Actual oven time for a ready-to-roast 5-pound bone-in leg is about 2 hours at 325°F, plus a good 20 minutes of rest before carving, which allows its juices to retreat back into the flesh. Sometimes you'll get a slender rather than a chunky leg. In this case it will take less time to roast—1½ rather than 2 hours. Therefore, checking temperatures is important.

Yield: 8 to 10 servings

One 5-pound ready-to-roast "short" leg
of lamb, as described on page 372
Jacques's herb seasoning (page 369)
(optional)
½ cup herbal mustard-and-garlic coating
(page 373) (optional)

Special equipment

A roasting rack, V-shaped preferred; a
pastry brush or narrow spatula to
spread the mustard; a jelly-roll pan
about 11 by 17 inches and ½ inch
deep; a closed container such as a large
plastic bag or an old-fashioned covered
roaster to hold the lamb in its rack in
the refrigerator; an instant-read meat
thermometer; an accurate oven thermometer would be useful

Jacques (continued from page 369)

The chopped-garlic-and-rosemary seasoning I use here is a variation of the traditional technique of studding the roast with garlic slivers and whole rosemary leaves. But you could use other herbs as well, such as oregano, thyme, savory, or sage. And sometimes I just take a whole head of unpeeled garlic and cut it in half or break it apart, and throw it unpeeled into the pan with the lamb. Then I have wonderful roast garlic to squeeze out and enjoy with the meat.

Jacques's Quick Lamb Stock with One Bone

With the pelvic bone that you remove from the whole leg, or the piece of bone that remains in a "short" leg, you can easily make a small quantity of lamb stock to use for a pan sauce.

Cut the bone with a cleaver, if you have one, into 2 or 3 pieces; otherwise, leave it whole. Put the pieces or whole bone in a saucepan with 1 medium peeled onion, 1 bay leaf, and 4 cups of water. Bring to a steady simmer and cook for 1½ hours. The stock will reduce as it cooks, but add water if necessary to keep the bones covered at all times. Strain the stock and skim off as much fat as possible (if you have time, chill the stock and remove the congealed fat completely). In a small saucepan, reduce the defatted stock over high heat until only 1½ cups remains. Use to deglaze the roasting pan as in the recipe.

Julia on Roasting Legs of Lamb

Toughness. Toughness has to do with the age of the animal, which is indicated by its weight—a whole bone-in leg of American lamb weighs 8 pounds and over when it is mature. Gordon Hamersley, chef-owner of his own bistro here in Boston, speculates that, because butchers can charge much more for the rack (the lamb-chop section) than for the leg, producers are going in for large, mature lamb with larger and meatier racks. Larger and meatier racks means older lamb, and tougher legs, unless they get special treatment.

The solution. Restaurateurs and chefs can, of course, make their own arrangements with butchers and processors. The solution for us home cooks, unless we have cultivated special sources, is to buy smaller and younger lamb—a leg weighing 6 to 7¼ pounds—if we can find one. It will not have the flavor of mature aged lamb, but it will be tender enough when allowed at least a 5-day rest after slaughter, and you won't have the strong-smelling fat problem. You will probably have to order it in advance, and your butcher can advise you here. Get to know him, and make him your friend.

Slow roasting and timing. When meat is tender to begin with, you can afford to roast in a hot oven. When you are not sure, a lower temperature can give a tenderizing effect, and I use 325°F throughout. Our 5-pound ready-to-roast leg of lamb takes about 2 hours at 325°F to reach an instant-meat-thermometer reading of 140°F, or 24 minutes per pound—count on 23 to 25 minutes per pound as a general rule.

How can you tell tough from tender? Ask your friend the butcher to cut a sliver of the raw meat off the large sirloin end and chew raw. You'll know at once.

New Zealand and Icelandic lamb. The leg, which comes oven-ready, often boned and frozen, is smaller and younger than American lamb. Treat it like a slow-roasted "short leg" (described below), or like Jacques's 400° roast; it will do well in high heat, because you have a young and tender beast.

The "short" or "three-quarter" leg, also described as "lamb leg, sirloin off." Meat expert Merle Ellis advises home cooks to buy the "short leg." In this case, the sirloin is removed. A part of the tailbone and a small end of the hipbone are usually still in the meat, but are easily cut out in much the same way as Jacques does the whole bone. After eliminating these impediments to carving, slice excess fat off the exterior as shown by Jacques on page 375. Finally, tie the large end of the meat together with a loop or so of cotton twine. You want the lower part of the shank removed at the "break" joint, and 2½ inches of meat scraped up the end of the shank, giving you a good handhold for carving. You now have a neat leg-shaped roast that fits into any standard roasting pan. My last 7½-pound whole leg weighed around 5 pounds prepared like this.

Some markets automatically open the stifle joint at the knee and bend the shank back, giving you no handhold for carving. Discourage this practice.

Number of servings. A 7-pound whole leg, minus sirloin as described above, will weigh about 5 pounds, and serve 8 to 10.

The boneless sirloin, removed when the leg was shortened, I treat exactly like a steak. I trim and butterfly it, and cook it on my stovetop grill or the barbecue. It's a good cut of meat and serves 2 people very nicely.

Preliminaries

After inserting the herb seasoning if you are using it, lift up the leg of lamb by its shank-end handhold. Smear the surface of the meat generously with mustard coating, reserving the remains. Set the leg, its fattest side up, in the roasting rack. Cover and refrigerate.

Roasting

About 4 hours before you plan to serve, remove the roast from the refrigerator and set it, in its rack, on the baking pan. Preheat the oven to 325°F. Smear on any remaining mustard coating. Then, 3½ hours before serving time, slide the oven rack onto the lower-third level and set the roast in the oven.

Timing and when it is done

Start testing after 1½ hours, and note that once the interior meat temperature has reached 110°F the temperature rises rapidly. When the thermometer reaches 140°F, the meat will be a nice pinky red, or medium-rare. Immediately remove the roast from the oven, and let rest 20 minutes before carving and serving.

Carving and serving

Follow Jacques's directions on page 370.

Julia's Simple Sauce for Roast Lamb

You will not have many juices in the pan, but it is nice to have 2 cups or so of stock at hand so that you can make a simple sauce. Here is an informal method.

For best flavor, you'll want ideally a big handful of lamb bones and scraps of lamb which your butcher may have on hand—ask that they be sawed into 1½-inch pieces. Brown them in a heavy saucepan in a little vegetable oil along with a small chopped carrot, and a medium chopped onion and celery stalk. Pour in a cup of chicken stock or broth and enough water to cover the ingredients by 1 inch. Add a small chopped plum tomato, a large unpeeled clove of smashed garlic, and an herb bouquet made of several parsley branches folded around an imported bay leaf and a sprig of rosemary. If you are without lamb bones, simmer the vegetables in all-chicken stock, and add any leftover meat scraps, brown stock, or gravy you think appropriate—never throw out such little treasures, since this is just the kind of occasion when you need them.

Bring to the simmer, skim off fat and scum for a few minutes, then salt very lightly. Simmer, partially covered, skimming occasionally, for 2 hours, adding a little more liquid if needed. Strain, pressing juices out of vegetables, and skim off surface fat.

To store, let cool, cover, then refrigerate or freeze.

Use this stock to make a simple pan sauce following the method on page 263.

Julia's Mustard Coating for Roast Lamb

I like to paint my roast of lamb several hours ahead with an herbal mustard-and-garlic coating, which gives flavor and a special plus—the roast needs no basting.

Yield: About ½ cup, enough for an oven-ready 5-pound short leg

⅓ cup Dijon-style prepared mustard
1 Tbs soy sauce
2 or 3 large cloves fresh garlic, puréed
½ tsp pulverized rosemary
2 to 3 Tbs olive or vegetable oil

Whisk the mustard in a small bowl with the soy, garlic, and rosemary. By droplets, whisk in the oil to make a thick paste.

Jacques on Preparing
a Whole Leg of Lamb

As you can see in the photos here, you need only remove the pelvic bone from the leg before roasting. But you can also remove the two long bones in the leg, the femur and tibia (or shank bone), in the same way. Don't worry if you leave a bit of meat on the bones—it will just add flavor to your stock. And when your leg is completely boneless, you can roll and tie it up for an oven roast, or spread it out as a butterflied leg and grill it, which I love to do in summer.

ove the pelvic bone.

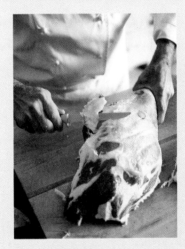

Trim off excess fat.

Cut around the shank bone about 5 inches from the end, then scrape away the meat from the bone.

Make incisions in the meat for the herb and garlic mixture.

With a meat saw or hacksaw, cut off the very end of the shank bone.

posite: Roast Leg of Lamb

DESSERTS

WHEN IT COMES TO DESSERTS, HOME COOKS WOULD DO WELL TO TAKE A LESSON FROM the pros. We don't mean undertaking fantastic architectural constructions and exotic flavorings, but following the fundamentally simple principle that pastry chefs do: take a few conventional components—a base such as pastry or cake; a cream or fruit filling; a sweet sauce; a colorful garnish, perhaps—and play around with them.

In restaurants, the building blocks of desserts are in constant production, always at the ready for artful assembly. At home, it's not necessary to have all the components on hand—most can be quickly made when you need them—but you want to keep the process of creative construction in mind. Then you can take the elements of the desserts we offer in this chapter—whether crêpes or cream puffs, poached fruit or custards, or any of the sauces—and put them together any way you like.

You can, of course, replicate these desserts exactly as we made them when we cooked together on television, and as written here in the recipes. It's a good way to start—the results will be unfailingly good, and along the way you will learn important techniques for handling dough, cooking custards, and poaching fruit. But then we hope you will make these components into desserts of your own design. Although we have written down everything we did (as well as some further observations), we often just started with a tableful of ingredients—and then we played around.

Julia

When making custards with egg yolks, like our crème anglaise, crème brûlée, and pots de crème, you must mix the yolks properly with the sugar—to prepare them for what's to come. I don't dump in the sugar all at once. That can "burn" the yolks, making them grainy. I add it gradually, whisking all the time, so the sugar melts and dissolves. As you keep beating them, the yolks will clearly change color from a frank yellow to a pale yellow, and thicken enough to form a "ribbon." This phrase, common in baking, means that when you lift the whisk and let some of the beaten yolks fall back into the pan the thick mixture stays briefly on the surface, gathering on itself like a folded ribbon, before it melts away.

When custard is cooked slowly on top of the stove, as in our crème anglaise, you must have the courage to heat it to the point where it "coats a spoon," just before the yolks scramble. It's not enough that the spoon has a film of custard on it—it must be thick enough so that a trail will remain when you draw your finger across the back of the spoon. This signals that the sauce is done.

Custard Desserts

Custards are among the most satisfying desserts. They require only the eggs and milk in your refrigerator, the sugar in your cupboard, and a few minutes to mix them together. But for all its essential simplicity, a perfectly textured custard, like a well-roasted chicken, is a dish that any cook can be proud to serve.

The five recipes here exemplify the various forms and flavors of custards. Three of them are baked desserts: The crème caramel is a large golden round, just firm enough to stand unmolded on a dessert platter, bathed in glistening caramel sauce. Crème brûlée is a softer, egg-yolk custard baked in individual ramekins, then crusted with a brittle sheet of glazed brown sugar. The same rich base, when mixed with bitter chocolate, becomes chocolate pots de crème, small cups of dark, intensely flavored, and creamy custard.

The fourth recipe in this section is crème anglaise, a simple custard sauce that is cooked on top of the stove. While not a dessert, it is the essential dessert sauce, the classic accompaniment for Ice Cream Profiteroles (page 394), cream-filled Choux à la Crème (page 394), or Poached Pears (page 397). The final recipe is for a sabayon, a light foamy custard, to be served with fruit.

Eggs are the fundamental ingredients in all custards, the source of the silky, smooth consistency—whether firm, soft, or thickly flowing. As with the various savory dishes presented in our chapter on "Eggs," successful custards require the cook's understanding and attention. We specify milk, heavy cream, and half-and-half in the different recipes, but you can combine these or substitute one for another to suit your taste, your diet, and what you have on hand. There's considerable latitude as well in the use of flavoring agents. Where we steep vanilla beans and orange zest in milk or cream, or stir in rum or bitter chocolate, use your own favorite liqueurs, extracts, fruit, or nut flavors. And you can always adjust the sugar amounts in the custard mix, to balance other flavors and to best satisfy your own sweet tooth.

Jacques's Crème Caramel

Crème caramel—or flan, as it is widely called—is understandably one of the most popular desserts in the world. Baked in a dish coated with a thin layer of hard caramelized sugar, when it is unmolded, the custard is dripping with the dark, sweet caramel liquid. Here we make the caramel coating for the mold and a thick caramel sauce at the same time. (The process of cooking sugar syrup and caramel is further detailed on page 382).

Our custard base gets a distinctive flavor from vanilla beans, which are first steeped in the hot milk and half-and-half or cream, then split open to reveal their seeds. Vanilla beans are easy to find in many markets, and you can re-use them. For even more flavor, we also add vanilla extract, or flavor the custard with almond extract, rum, or other liqueurs. You can make caramel custard in individual ramekins, coating each small mold with caramel, or in one big mold, as we do here.

If you have been served flan in a restaurant, you might wonder why the caramel that coats the custard is so much thicker than the liquid that comes out of your baking dish at home. The chef has probably poured off that liquid and used a thick caramel sauce that has been separately made. You can do the same: with the caramel sauce you make in this recipe. For added flavor, stir a spoonful or two of cognac into the caramel sauce when it is completely cool.

Of all the sugar syrups, caramel is the easiest to make, because there is no problem of crystallization. Once the sugar starts to caramelize, well over 300°F, it is so hot that any crystals melt. For this recipe, you can just set the pan over high heat and let it cook until the sugar starts to color, then you can swirl and shake the pan without worry.

Jacques

A perfect custard depends on properly using and controlling the properties of egg yolks and whites. In the egg-yolk custards, the lecithin acts as an emulsifier, and will thicken the milk or cream if heated slowly. For a custard cream if the temperature gets above 180°F, you will have crème brûlée rather than a smooth sauce.

In our crème caramel, though, we need the egg whites to coagulate and hold the custard together, so it can be unmolded. The problem here is that if the whites cook rapidly in the heat of the oven they will expand and form air bubbles—and then the side of the custard will look like a sponge, rather than remaining solid and smooth. That's why you must use a water bath to slow down the cooking of all our baked custards. Some people mistakenly think the water is supposed to be boiling, but that would cause the whites to cook too fast. Pour lukewarm water into the water bath to start, and check it to make sure that it is never simmering. If it looks as though it is about to boil, throw in a couple of ice cubes, to cool it down right away.

Yield: A 4-to-5-cup mold, serving 8

For the caramel coating and sauce

1 cup sugar

3 Tbs water

2 Tbs or so cognac, rum, or other liqueur (optional)

For the custard

2 cups milk

1 cup half-and-half

2 vanilla beans

5 large eggs

1 egg yolk

⅓ cup sugar

1 tsp vanilla extract

Special equipment

A heavy, deep 4-cup saucepan for cooking the caramel; a 4-to-5-cup soufflé mold, with 3-to-4-inch sides; a wire whisk; a sieve; 2 mixing bowls or 1 bowl and a large (4-cup) measuring cup; a baking pan with 2-inch sides for the water bath; a round serving plate

Making the caramel and caramel sauce

Put the sugar in the saucepan and stir in about 3 tablespoons of water, just enough to moisten all the grains. Set over high heat and, without stirring or shaking the pan, allow the sugar to melt into syrup and cook at a rapid boil.

After several minutes (usually 6 to 8), the syrup will start to color. You can tell when

Large, thick bubbles indicate that it is close to caramelization.

When the syrup is a dark-caramel color, pour ¼ cup of it into the mold.

it is approaching the caramel stage by the appearance of the bubbles—see photo. Have the soufflé mold ready, as well as ⅓ cup or so of cold water.

Swirl the syrup so it colors evenly and watch it carefully—as soon as it is a dark-caramel color, pour about ¼ cup of syrup into the soufflé mold, leaving about ½ cup of syrup in the saucepan, *off* the heat. Tilt the mold so that the syrup runs over the whole bottom—but not the sides—forming an even coating of caramel, about ⅛ inch thick.

To make the sauce, holding the pan at arm's length and averting your face, pour 4 or 5 tablespoons of the cold water, a bit at a time, into the caramel in the saucepan. Put the saucepan back over high heat, bring to a boil, and cook for about ½ minute, stirring well to dissolve all the caramel. Pour the sauce into a heatproof bowl or cup and allow it to cool and thicken. (Stir in cognac or other liqueur when cool, if you like.)

Tilt the mold so that the syrup runs all over the bottom.

Making the custard

Preheat the oven to 350°F.

Pour the milk and half-and-half into a medium saucepan, add the vanilla beans, and heat to the boil. Remove from the heat, cover the pan, and let the beans steep for 5 minutes. Meanwhile, blend the eggs, the egg yolk, and the sugar in a mixing bowl, stirring with a whisk until the sugar dissolves—do not whip the eggs and create foam or bubbles.

Remove the vanilla beans from the hot milk, and gradually pour the milk into the eggs, stirring (but not beating) with the whisk, to blend well without producing foam. Set the sieve over a second bowl or a large measuring cup, and pour the custard through, to remove any coagulated bits of eggs.

Dry the vanilla beans and slit them in half lengthwise. With the tip of a paring knife, scrape up the tiny black seeds from inside the beans and stir them into the custard, then stir in the vanilla extract. Pour the custard into the mold—the caramel in the bottom should be cool and hard—scraping in all the vanilla seeds. Spoon off any foam or bubbles from the surface of the custard.

Baking the custard

Place the mold in the empty baking dish and set in the oven. Fill the dish with lukewarm water—not hot—to a depth of 2 inches, or at least halfway up the mold.

Bake the custard for 50 minutes or so. Check the water bath occasionally to make sure that it is never boiling—add ice cubes to cool it if necessary.

When done, the top of the custard should be set and slightly colored, but will still tremble when the mold is gently shaken. To test, pierce the custard with a sharp knife midway between the center and the edge—the blade should come out clean. Cook longer if the blade has wet custard on it. (Do *not* stick the blade down farther than the center of the custard, lest you pierce the bottom, which can cause it to split apart when unmolded.)

Carefully remove the water bath from the oven and lift out the mold. Let the custard cool for at least 4 hours before serving. Store covered in the refrigerator.

Unmolding and serving

To unmold, insert the blade of a long sharp knife straight down between the custard and the inside of the mold. Holding the knife still in one hand, with its sharp edge tight against the mold, with your other hand, rotate the mold on the work surface, so the knife cleanly separates the custard from the mold all around (see photo).

Run a long knife around the edge of the custard to loosen it from the mold.

Place the serving platter on top of the mold, hold tight, and invert the two quickly, setting the platter on the table. Lift the mold straight up—the custard and thin caramel liquid should slide out onto the platter. If the custard seems stuck, slide the tip of a small knife in between the edge of the custard and the mold, allowing a little bit of air to break the vacuum—the custard will now drop out of the mold.

You can serve the custard as is, or replace the thin liquid from the mold with the thickened caramel sauce. Tilt the platter slightly and pour off the liquid (don't let the custard slide off). Spread half of the thick sauce over the top of the custard, letting a bit drip down the sides. Spoon portions of custard and sauce onto individual dessert plates or bowls, and serve, with more sauce on the side.

Lift the mold straight up so that the custard and caramel liquid slip off onto the serving plate.

Do-ahead notes

The custard can be served room temperature within an hour or so, but it will unmold best if allowed to cool for at least 4 hours. When cool, store covered in the refrigerator; serve within a day or two.

Spread the thickened caramel sauce over the top of the custard.

Julia on Sugar Syrups and Caramel

Anyone who wants to master cakes and pastries must become familiar with sugar syrups and caramel. Sugar syrup moistens cake layers before they are iced, sugar syrup poaches pears and peaches, sugar syrup is whipped into egg whites to make meringues, and caramel is sugar syrup that is boiled down until the liquid has all but evaporated and the sugar is beginning to brown.

I think you should learn the classic techniques for making sugar syrups and caramel. I always use them. But try Jacques's method, too, for the caramel and see if it works for you.

Simple Syrup: You start out with a simple syrup, which is, officially, ⅓ cup of sugar heated in 1 cup of liquid until the sugar dissolves. This is the standard degree of sweetness for poaching fruits, for moistening cake layers, and so forth. The proportions can vary a little from cook to cook—Jacques uses less sugar, for instance—but it is useful to have a standard, and you need no special utensils to produce it.

Caramel: However, when you are going into the serious business of boiling sugar and especially of making caramel, since caramel hardens almost at once, have your mold or molds ready at hand. Or, if you're making caramel sauce, have a second saucepan nearby.

The saucepan. Number one, choose a moderately heavy 6-to-8-cup saucepan 2½ to 3 inches deep with a tight-fitting lid.

Proportions. Use the correct proportions, which are the same as for simple syrup: ⅓ cup of granulated sugar per 1 cup of water—or other liquid, such as wine, fruit juice, etc.

Dissolve the sugar. Before the real boiling begins, be sure that the sugar has completely dissolved—as you are bringing it to the boil, swirl the pan by its handle, then look closely to be sure there are no undissolved crystals in the water. When you are sure there are none, bring to the complete boil.

Never stir. Swirl the pan only, since stirring could cause the syrup to crystallize.

Cover tightly. Steam collects on the underside of the cover and washes down the sides of the pan to prevent crystals from forming.

Continue boiling for several minutes with the cover in place, peeking now and then to see how the syrup is bubbling. When the bubbles are large and thick, you are not far from caramelization. Remove the cover, and continue swirling slowly as the syrup gradually begins to turn a caramel color. As soon as it is the shade you wish, pour it into your mold and follow directions, or pour it into your other saucepan and set over very low heat, just warm enough to keep it liquid.

Caramel Syrup: When you want extra syrup to serve with your caramel custard, pour out what you need for completing your dessert and let the remaining syrup cool in the pan for several minutes. Then, standing well away, pour ½ cup of water into the pan. It will probably bubble up, and the caramel will have congealed. Let it boil slowly to dissolve the caramel, and you have a lightly thickened caramel syrup.

Caramel Sauce: Make the caramel syrup, above, and when it has cooled briefly, pour in 1 cup of heavy cream. Simmer, stirring, until the caramel has dissolved. Season with a pinch of salt and ½ teaspoon or so of pure vanilla extract.

Crème Brûlée

The pleasure of this deliciously rich dessert lies in its contrast of textures, the soft and creamy custard hidden under a brittle sheet of caramelized brown sugar. The custard is baked and served in small ramekins—shallow ceramic soufflé-type molds, round or oval, with a ½-cup capacity. You don't *have* to crust them, since the cooked and chilled custards can be served simply as pots de crème.

The custards will still be soft when the ramekins come out of the oven. Give them plenty of time to chill and set before glazing.

You can melt and caramelize the sugar with a handheld blowtorch or under a broiler. With either method, watch the sugar carefully, since lovely dark caramel can turn to burnt ash in an instant. It is best to practice with 1 or 2 custards the first time you glaze crème brûlée, to gauge the effect of your blowtorch or broiler. Here we use light-brown sugar, which gives a very nice flavor to the crust, but you could glaze granulated sugar instead. Don't try to melt "brownulated sugar," though—it won't work.

Yield: Eight 4-ounce ramekins

> 3 cups heavy cream
> 1 vanilla bean, or 2 tsp vanilla extract
> Grated zest of a large orange
> 6 large egg yolks
> ½ cup granulated sugar
>
> ½ cup light-brown sugar, or more if needed

Special equipment

Eight 4-ounce ramekins (small soufflé molds); a wire whisk; a sieve; a mixing bowl and a large (4-cup) measuring cup; a baking pan with 2-inch sides, large enough to hold all the ramekins; a propane blowtorch (optional)

Making the custards

Preheat the oven to 350°F.

Pour the cream into a 6-cup saucepan, stir in the vanilla bean or vanilla extract and the orange zest, and bring to the simmer. Remove from heat, cover the pan, and let steep for 5 minutes.

Whisk the egg yolks and sugar in the mixing bowl for several minutes until the yolks are thick, pale yellow, and form a fat, slowly dissolving ribbon when dropped from the whisk back into the bowl.

Remove the vanilla bean from the hot cream (save it—you can use it again). So as not to scramble the egg yolks, stir by dribbles half a cup of the hot cream into the yolks, stirring (not beating—you do not want to form bubbles). Adding it in a slow stream, stir in the rest of the cream. Set the sieve over the quart measure and strain the custard mixture through it to eliminate any coagulated bits of egg and the orange rind. Skim off any bubbles from the surface of the custard.

Arrange the ramekins in the baking pan and pour or ladle ½ cup of custard into each, leaving ¼ inch at the top for the glaze. Set the baking pan in the oven and pour in enough hot water to come halfway up the ramekins.

Bake the custards for 30 to 35 minutes, until the tops are set but the custard in the center is still quite soft to the touch. Carefully remove the baking pan from the oven, and lift the ramekins from the hot water. Let them cool briefly, then chill thoroughly in the refrigerator, at least 4 hours. Either serve them as pots de crème, or glaze them as follows.

Forming the brown-sugar crust

Loosen the brown sugar if packed and break up any lumps with your fingers. Sprinkle a tablespoon or so over each custard and smooth it gently with the back of a spoon, forming an even layer of sugar that completely covers the surface.

To make the crust with a blowtorch:

Ignite the torch and direct the flame downward over a ramekin, always keeping the tip of the flame about 8 inches above the sugar. Move the torch around constantly, shifting the focus of the heat as the sugar melts. Heat each custard gradually—for 10 seconds or longer, depending on the power of the torch—until lightly caramelized all over. If one section of sugar is darkening too fast, move the flame to another area, or start heating another ramekin. When all the custards have been crusted, give them a few moments to harden, then serve.

To make the crust under a broiler:

Set the ramekins on a heatproof tray or baking dish (1 or 2 at a time if you are not sure how quickly your broiler will crust them). Turn on the broiler and place the ramekins underneath, so the surface of the sugar is about 5 inches below the heat. Leave the door open so you can watch as the sugar melts and starts to caramelize. Turn the ramekins around if one side gets too brown, so that the glaze is consistent all around. Remove the custards as soon as the sugar has turned to a smooth sheet of brown glaze. If it has blackened in spots, set the remaining custards lower or reduce the glazing time. If the ramekins have been heated by the broiler, chill them briefly before serving.

Chocolate Pots de Crème

The term "pot de crème" refers both to a soft baked custard and to the small ceramic pots, often with lids, that they are baked in. If you don't have authentic "petits pots de crème," which only hold ⅓ cup or so, use 4-ounce ramekins without a cover.

The custard for this recipe uses the same egg-yolk-and-cream base as for crème brûlée, but here it is poured steaming hot over bitter chocolate and stirred until smooth. You can use vanilla and orange zest, as in the crème brûlée, or add other flavors, like coffee. The custard will be quite soft when it comes out of the oven after only 20 minutes or so, but it will set to a luscious creamy consistency in the refrigerator. Enjoy it well chilled.

Yield: Six 4-ounce ramekins, or 8 petits pots de crème

4 ounces unsweetened chocolate, chopped into small pieces
2 cups heavy cream
1 tsp grated orange zest (optional)
4 large egg yolks
⅓ cup sugar
1½ tsp vanilla extract

Special equipment

Six 4-ounce ramekins (small soufflé molds) or 8 petits pots de crème; a wire whisk; a sieve; a bowl and a large (4-cup) measuring cup, or 2 mixing bowls; a baking pan large enough to serve as a water bath for all the ramekins

Preheat the oven to 350°F. Put the chopped chocolate in the large measuring cup or one of the mixing bowls and set the sieve on top. Pour the cream into a medium saucepan and bring to the simmer, then remove from the heat. If using orange zest, stir it into the cream before heating and steep 5 minutes covered, off the heat.

Meanwhile, whisk the yolks in the empty bowl, adding the sugar gradually. Continue whisking for a minute or more, until the yolks are pale yellow and thick and form a ribbon when dropped from the whisk.

By driblets, pour the hot cream into the yolks, stirring (not beating) with the whisk, until evenly blended. Immediately pour this custard through the sieve over the chocolate pieces, removing any coagulated bits of eggs, and stir gently with a large spoon to melt the chocolate and blend it into the custard. Stir in the vanilla extract. Skim off surface bubbles.

Arrange the ramekins or petits pots de crème in the baking pan, fill each with ½ cup of custard (less for the petits pots), and spoon off any foam or bubbles on the surface. Cover the cups if you have small lids for them. Set the baking pan in the oven and pour in hot water to come halfway up the ramekins.

Bake the custards for about 25 minutes, or until the tops are just set (if baked uncovered). The custard will still be quite soft. Carefully remove the baking pan from the oven and lift the ramekins from the hot water. Let them cool briefly, then chill thoroughly in the refrigerator, at least 4 hours, before serving.

Julia's Crème Anglaise

This is the basic custard sauce that you want to have in your repertoire, to transform any plain pastry or poached or fresh fruit into a special dessert. Crème anglaise is an essential component of such classics as floating island, and the foundation of many other dessert preparations—when frozen, it becomes ice cream; if you add gelatin and fold in whipped cream, it becomes Bavarian cream. If flour is added before cooking, you have pastry cream, and then if you fold in beaten egg whites you have a dessert soufflé.

This recipe calls for milk and vanilla and dark rum, but, as with all custards, you can change it to your taste—using half-and-half or cream, or other flavoring agents. The stovetop cooking of custard, which this recipe uses, is an important method to master, and you will want to read the general discussion of custards in the preceding pages.

Yield: About 2 cups

> 6 egg yolks
> ⅔ cup sugar
> 1½ cups hot milk
> 1 Tbs butter
> 1 Tbs vanilla extract
> 2 Tbs dark rum (or cognac or
>   other liqueur)

Special equipment
> A heavy-bottomed 2-quart
>   saucepan; a wire whisk; a flat
>   wooden spatula or wooden
>   spoon; a 5- or 6-cup mixing
>   bowl set in a larger bowl of ice
>   cubes and water; a fine-meshed
>   sieve

Start by whisking the egg yolks in the saucepan, then begin whisking in the sugar gradually, pouring it over the yolks in a thin stream. Continue beating steadily for a minute or two after all the sugar has been incorporated, until the yolks are thick and pale yellow and form a ribbon when dropped from the whisk.

By dribbles, pour in the hot milk, stirring with the whisk rather than beating to minimize foaming. Be sure to scrape the yolks from the sides and bottom of the pan and stir until thoroughly blended.

Set the pan over moderate heat. Using the wooden spoon in place of the whisk, stir continuously for several minutes, clearing the sides and bottom of the pan to prevent any bits of egg from coagulating. As the sauce heats—do not let it boil—and nears the thickening point, the foam in the pan will begin to subside, and faint whiffs of steam will appear. Remove from heat and test: when it coats the spoon well, a trail will remain when you draw your finger across it, and the sauce is done.

Immediately remove the pan from heat and pour the sauce through the sieve into the bowl set in the ice bath. The sieve will catch any coagulated bits, and the ice bath will stop the cooking. Stir in the tablespoon of butter until it melts, further cooling the sauce, and then the vanilla extract and the rum.

The sauce can now be served warm, or let it chill further in the ice bath. Store in a covered container in the refrigerator, where it will keep for 2 days.

Sabayon with Strawberries

Here is another rich and versatile custard sauce. As with crème anglaise, the silky texture of a sabayon comes from the careful cooking of egg yolks, sugar, and liquid. But instead of stirring the yolks slowly with milk or cream—and trying to avoid bubbles—here you energetically whisk the yolks with wine, over simmering water, creating a light and foamy sauce that has more than doubled in volume. The distinctive flavor and pale color of sabayon comes from Marsala, the fortified red wine traditionally used in zabaglione, the Italian version of the sauce, but you could use white wine, vermouth, sherry, rum, or bourbon instead.

Fresh strawberries, lightly sugared to release their juices, are topped with warm or cold sabayon in dessert glasses. You may also fold whipped cream into the sauce, pour it over the strawberries in a gratin dish, and glaze the topping quickly under the broiler. Don't limit yourself to strawberries, though—almost any fresh or poached fruit (such as the pears on page 397) could be used here. And sabayon is a fine accompaniment to custards and cakes too—try it with Susie's Gâteau of Crêpes (page 408).

Jacques

In a restaurant, a sabayon (or zabaglione if it's an Italian restaurant) would probably be made to order, with an egg yolk and wine whipped together and cooked in just a couple of minutes. But with a larger amount, as we give here, it is easier to do it ahead of time and chill it. You will see that the sauce gets even thicker when chilled. You can then fold in whipped cream, which makes it still richer and smoother, and store the sauce in the refrigerator until you need it. The cream is necessary if you want to glaze the sabayon, but it is a delicious addition even if you are not glazing.

You also want to cut up the strawberries ahead of time and let them macerate with sugar, to get soft and juicy. Here we toss them with lemon juice, but either Marsala or a little bit of vinegar— particularly a good balsamic vinegar—is also delicious on strawberries. To clean strawberries, just put them in a bowl of cold water and lift them out to rinse. Don't hold them under running water— and don't cut the stems or hull them before cleaning, or the water will get in the berry and make it mushy.

Notes on crème anglaise: Incidentally, when I make a crème anglaise, I mix the sugar with the egg yolks in one stroke, stir for 30 seconds, and then add the boiling milk all at once rather than gradually. The hot milk re-cooks the mixture, and I then take the pan immediately from the heat.

Julia

The trick with a sabayon is to heat the sauce close to 180°F, so it thickens beautifully without letting the yolks scramble. When it is fully cooked, driblets of sauce from the whisk will form a soft, melting ribbon on the surface. If you are careful, you can whisk it, until thick, directly over very low heat in a stainless-steel saucepan.

However, don't let sabayon sit around while it is warm—an egg-based dish like this is too susceptible to bacterial growth. Either serve it right away, or chill it as described in the recipe. For more body and lightness, you can whip up an egg white or two and fold it in. And though the flavor of a sabayon is fine when made with just Marsala, I prefer a half-and-half mixture of dry white French vermouth and either Marsala, sherry, or rum.

Sabayon with Strawberries

Yield: 6 to 8 servings

1 to 1½ pounds fresh ripe strawberries
(3 pints)
1 Tbs sugar, plus more to taste
2 tsp freshly squeezed lemon juice, plus
more to taste

For the sabayon
6 egg yolks
1 cup sweet Marsala wine or port, sherry,
or Madeira
⅓ cup sugar, plus more to taste
Drops of freshly squeezed lemon juice
(optional)

For the whipped cream (for the glazed variation)
½ cup heavy cream
1 tsp sugar

Special equipment
A large stainless-steel or copper bowl,
plus a larger bowl for holding
(optional); a large saucepan of simmering water; a balloon whisk; dessert gob-
lets or large martini glasses, or a
medium gratin or baking dish (4-cup
volume) or individual gratin dishes (for
glazed sabayon)

Preparing the strawberries

About an hour before serving the dessert, rinse the strawberries (stems on) and drain them on paper towels. Slice off the stems and halve or quarter the strawberries lengthwise, depending on size, into a bowl. Sprinkle over the sugar and the lemon juice; fold gently together to blend well. Taste a strawberry, add more sugar or lemon juice if needed, and set aside to macerate.

Whipping the sabayon

If you want to serve the sabayon warm, make it at the last minute. If you want to glaze the sabayon under the broiler, or make it ahead of time to serve chilled, have ready a large bowl (larger than the one in which you whip the sauce) partly filled with ice cubes.

Whisk to blend the yolks, Marsala, and sugar in the stainless-steel bowl. Rest the bowl in the saucepan over hot water. Whisk constantly for 4 to 5 minutes or more to cook the sauce, until it has the consistency of lightly whipped cream. Clear the bottom of the bowl constantly with the whisk so that the eggs do not scramble, and adjust the heat as needed. Taste the sauce—the sabayon should never get so hot that you can't stick your very clean finger in it—and whisk in drops of lemon juice or more sugar if you want. When thick, foamy, and tripled in volume, remove from the heat. It can be served hot as is, tepid, or cool.

Serving

Spoon a portion of strawberries—½ cup or more—into each goblet or glass, and top with ⅓ to ½ cup of warm or cool sabayon. Or put the sauce in the glass first, then the strawberries.

Variation: Strawberries Glazed with Sabayon

Cool the sabayon to room temperature. Whip the cream and sugar until soft peaks form, and fold the cream into the sabayon with a rubber spatula.

Turn on the broiler. Spread the strawberries in the baking dish in one layer (or in individual dishes). Spoon the sauce over the berries so they are completely covered and set the dish under the broiler, 5 to 6 inches from the heat. With the door open—so you can watch carefully—broil for a minute or two, turning the dish as needed to glaze evenly, until the top of the sabayon is nicely browned and slightly crusted. Serve right away.

Julia

It's a shame that people aren't making *pâte à choux* much anymore. Perhaps they don't know how, or think it takes too long—it's certainly not the kind of quick, quick cooking that people like these days. But, in fact, it is quite simple, and gives you plenty of pastry that you can keep frozen and fill whenever you need a dessert.

Don't be afraid to use a pastry bag either. If you've never done it, just make up a batch of dough and practice with the bag—it's fun, and the pastry will be delicious whatever shape you make. Remember, nobody is born knowing how to use a pastry bag properly.

Pâte à Choux

Pâte à choux, or cream-puff dough, is one of the essential elements of the pastry maker's art, and something that the home cook can easily master. The eggy pastelike dough can be shaped into many forms that are guaranteed to inflate in the oven. When cooled, the pastry has a deep color and crisp texture and, most useful of all, a hollow interior, ready to be filled with all manner of sweet creams.

Here we bake two sizes of puffs: small profiteroles, to hold little scoops of ice cream, and larger *choux* ("cabbages" in French, which these resemble in shape). The big ones are filled with softly whipped cream, crème Chantilly, to make *choux à la crème,* such as you'd get in a Paris bistro. Served with crème anglaise or chocolate sauce, either puff always makes a popular dessert.

To form the puffs, use a pastry bag—the photos on page 393 will help guide your hand. But you can also use a spoon to fill the puffs. A batch of this *pâte à choux* will provide enough puffs, small or large, for 10 or more generous servings. If you don't use all of them immediately, store the cooked *choux* in the freezer. You can thaw and crisp them quickly in the oven whenever you need them.

You can also use the same dough to make other classic pastries, like éclairs stuffed with pastry cream, St. Honoré cake, or Paris-Brest cake. And if you omit the sugar from the dough, and add a bit more salt, profiteroles can be stuffed with all sorts of savory fillings to make attractive appetizers.

Yield: About 40 small profiteroles, or 20
larger *choux*, serving 10 to 12

1 cup milk
4 Tbs butter (½ stick)
⅛ tsp salt
1 tsp sugar
1 cup flour (unsifted, weighing 5 to 5½
    ounces)
5 large eggs

Special equipment

A 2½- or 3-quart saucepan; a food
    processor; a large baking or cookie
    sheet (12 by 18 inches) or 2 smaller
    sheets; parchment paper or a silicon
    sheet liner; a pastry brush; a pastry bag
    (14-inch or larger) with a ½-inch plain
    tip and a ¼-inch star tip

Making the *pâte à choux*

Preheat the oven to 375°F and arrange oven racks to
accommodate 2 cookie sheets if necessary.

Put the milk, butter, salt, and sugar in the saucepan and
set over high heat. Stir as the butter melts and bring the liquid
to a boil. Immediately remove the pan from heat, dump in the
flour all at once, and stir rapidly with a sturdy wooden spoon,
until all the flour is moistened and the paste comes together.

Set the pan over medium heat and continue to stir vigorously. The dough will leave the sides of the pan and gather into
a soft lump. Continue stirring the dough in the pan to dry it
slightly, for a minute or so, until a whitish, cakey skin forms on
the bottom of the saucepan.

Remove from the heat and scrape the lump of dough into
the bowl of the food processor. Allow it to cool for about 5
minutes, so the eggs do not cook when added. Meanwhile,
break 4 of the eggs into a measuring cup or bowl and crack the
fifth egg into a separate small bowl (do not beat the eggs).

Jacques

The food processor makes it
easy to mix *choux* paste quickly. But
you can do it by hand as well, stirring
in one egg at a time. At first the ball of
dough will slide around in the egg;
then, all of a sudden, it will tighten and
absorb the egg—and that's when you
add the next one.

It is important to leave the puffs in
the shut-off oven with the door partially
open after baking them, which allows
the interior moisture to evaporate and
helps the puff to hold its shape. If you
take them out of the oven right away,
they can collapse. Some recipes
instruct you to poke or slice open the
puffs to dry them, or to remove the soft
dough inside before filling. I do neither:
I like my puffs to be somewhat soft,
holding their shape, rather than dry and
crumbly like old bread. And the soft
dough inside is fully cooked and delicious, so I generally don't take it out—
but if I do, I eat it!

Pulse the dough in the food processor a few times to break up the lump. Then, with the machine running, tip the pitcher or bowl of eggs over the feed tube, allowing only 1 egg to slide into the work bowl. Process for 5 or 6 seconds as the dough absorbs the egg, then 1 at a time slide in each of the remaining 3 eggs, processing for a few moments after each addition. It will take about 30 seconds to incorporate all the eggs.

Stop the machine and check that the dough has a soft paste consistency. If it is still too stiff, lightly beat the fifth egg, add a teaspoon or two of it to the dough, and process briefly. (Save this egg, whether you have used any of it or not, for the egg wash.)

Piping the profiteroles or *choux*

Line the cookie sheet, or 2 sheets if small, with parchment paper or a reusable silicon liner.

Following the instructions and photos on page 393, fit a plain tip into the pastry bag, and fill with the *choux* paste. If you don't have a pastry bag, you can make one by cutting a hole in the bottom of a sturdy plastic bag. Pipe small profiteroles, using about a tablespoon of dough for each, or larger *choux,* using 2 to 3 tablespoons. Alternatively, push mounds of dough onto the sheet from a spoon. Leave at least 1½ inches between each puff, using both baking sheets if necessary.

For the egg wash, spill off about half the white from the reserved egg, so there's an equal amount of yolk and white, and beat well with a fork. (The whites make the puffs shiny and the yolks give them a deep color.) Using the pastry brush, lightly paint the top of each puff with the egg wash, gently smoothing down the point of dough left by the piping bag.

Baking the puffs

Place the sheet (or both) in the oven and bake for about 25 minutes for smaller profiteroles or 35 to 40 minutes for *choux,* until the puffs are a deep golden brown all over.

When the puffs appear done, turn off the heat and prop the oven door open about 2 inches. Allow the puffs to dry out in the oven for 30 minutes or so before removing. Cool them completely before using or storing.

Do-ahead note

When cool, baked puffs can be stored for a couple of days in a closed plastic container or a covered cookie tin, or frozen for several weeks in airtight containers or freezer bags.

Pastry Bag Techniques

Filling the pastry bag

Fold the top of the bag down several inches and, to prevent any paste from coming out of the tip, tuck about an inch of the bag into the wide end of the tip.

Set the bag into a tall container, like a measuring cup or blender jar, with the collar of the bag hanging over the top, and fill with *pâte à choux.*

Fold and twist the top of the bag, pushing the dough down into the tip. (If you have plugged the bag as suggested, open it now by pulling on the tip and extending the bag.) Keep one hand on the twisted top of the bag to squeeze out dough and the other hand near the tip.

Piping *pâte-à-choux* puffs

Profiteroles: Use a plain tip with a ½-inch round opening. Hold the tip close to the baking sheet, and without moving it, squeeze out 1 tablespoon or so of dough in a small mound. As shown in photo, stop squeezing and lift up the tip quickly, right over the mound—don't pull away from it—leaving a small point of dough, or tail, sticking up in the center.

Choux: With a round tip in the bag, pipe *choux* as for profiteroles, but squeeze out 2 or 3 tablespoons of dough in a mound, depending on the size of the puff you want to make. You can also use a star tip with a ¼- or ½-inch opening, as shown in the photos. Form the puff by swirling the bag and tip in a small spiral pattern as you squeeze out the dough.

Using a pastry brush, lightly paint the puffs with egg wash.

Ice Cream Profiteroles

Yield: 4 servings

12 to 16 small profiteroles (see preceding recipe)
2 Tbs raspberry jam
½ pint vanilla or other ice cream
1 cup Crème Anglaise (page 386) or Chocolate Sauce (page 399)
Fresh strawberries, raspberries, or blackberries, for garnishing

With a sharp serrated knife, slice off the top third of each small puff to use as a cap. (You may leave the soft dough inside the puff, or remove it before filling.)

Spread a dab of raspberry jam—about ¼ teaspoon—in the bottom of each profiterole. Using a spoon, a melon baller, or a small ice-cream scoop, form neat balls of ice cream and drop them into the bottoms. Cap with the top of the puff.

Spread ¼ cup or more of chilled crème anglaise or chocolate sauce on each dessert plate and arrange 3 or 4 filled profiteroles in the pool of sauce. Garnish with fresh berries.

Do-ahead note

Puffs can be filled with ice cream and kept in the freezer for a couple of hours before serving.

Choux à la Crème

8 to 12 *choux* puffs (see preceding recipe)
1 to 2 cups Crème Anglaise (page 386) or Chocolate Sauce (page 399)
About ¼ cup raspberry jam
1½ cups heavy cream
1 to 2 Tbs sugar
½ tsp vanilla extract
1 Tbs cognac, rum, Grand Marnier, or other liqueur
Powdered sugar
Fresh strawberries, raspberries, or blackberries, for garnishing

Slice open the *choux* as for profiteroles. Spread ¼ cup or more of chilled crème anglaise or chocolate sauce on each dessert plate. Drop 1 teaspoon of raspberry jam for each puff in the pool of sauce, as a sticky base for the puffs. Set a puff bottom on each spot of jam and press in place.

Whip the cream with the sugar, vanilla, and liqueur to form soft peaks (as for Crème Chantilly, page 403). Fit the pastry bag with the star tip, fill it with the whipped cream, and squeeze into each puff bottom (see photo). Cap with the *choux* tops and dust them with powdered sugar shaken through a small sieve. Garnish with berries, or with a single large strawberry sliced at the top and fanned open (see photo).

Fit your pastry bag with the star tip, fill with whipped cream, and squeeze a generous swirling mound into each puff.

Opposite: Choux à la Crème

Julia

Poaching pears in white-wine syrup is a classic method that you can use with many other fruits, including apples, peaches, nectarines, and bananas. This formula for the syrup—1½ cups of sugar per quart of liquid, or 6 tablespoons of sugar for every cup—can be easily multiplied if you are poaching a larger amount of fruit or if you just need a little more syrup to make sure everything is covered. Don't discard the syrup when you've finished the pears. You can bottle it, store it in the refrigerator or freezer, and use it as a poaching liquid again and again.

Pears and Chocolate Sauce

Poaching fruit is a good trick to have in your bag of dessert techniques. With a half hour or so of simmering in a flavorful liquid, you can transform an ordinary supermarket pear or other fruit, such as a peach or an apricot, into a first-class dessert at any time of year.

Pears are especially good for poaching. The fruit's natural flavors blend well with many cooking liquids—here we use a sugar syrup with white wine, lemon, and vanilla, but you can use red wine, other spirits and beverages, and various sweeteners and flavoring agents to poach them.

Serve your pears plain or fancy, as we show you here. They're good either lukewarm, after they have cooled in the liquid for an hour or so, or chilled, if you've made them a day ahead. You can simply moisten them with syrup right from the pot, or reduce the syrup into a thick, fruity sauce, with a touch of cognac. You also can make the simple but excellent chocolate sauce given here, to pool in the plate, or to coat the whole pear with a round of pound cake soaking up all the juices.

The other dessert sauces in this chapter—Crème Anglaise (page 386) or Sabayon (page 387)—are delicious with pears, and a mound of Crème Chantilly (page 403) or good ice cream or sorbet would be other choices. Whatever sauce—or combination of sauces—you serve, you'll want to give your pears the decorative touches demonstrated by Jacques in the photos—a charming "hat" formed by the peel, and a flared, fluted spiral bottom.

Poached Pears

Yield: 6 pears

2¼ cups sugar

1½ cups dry white wine, such as Orvieto
    or Muscadet

4½ cups water

2 lemons, for peel and juice

2 tsp vanilla

6 large, firm, ripe pears, such as Bosc or
    Bartlett (about 8 ounces each)

For serving

Chocolate Sauce (recipe follows)
    (optional)

Slices of pound cake, homemade or
    store-bought (optional)

Mint sprigs

Special equipment

A large saucepan or stockpot, about 6
    quarts, with a cover; a smaller pot lid
    or plate that fits just inside the pot

Preparing the poaching syrup and the pears

Pour the sugar, wine, and water into the pot and stir well. With a sharp vegetable peeler, shave 10 or 12 strips of peel from the lemons (yellow zest only). Cut the lemons in half and squeeze out the juice—through your impeccably clean fingers or a strainer to catch the pits—and add the peel, juice, and vanilla to the pot. Bring to a boil, cook for about 2 minutes to dissolve the sugar, and turn off the heat.

Meanwhile, prepare the pears:

Slice the bottom of each pear flat, so it can stand upright.

With a vegetable peeler, peel the pear from the stem end to the bottom, leaving a decorative pattern of skin at the top.

Jacques

You can poach almost any kind of pear, but each will have a different cooking time, depending on the degree of ripeness and the variety. We suggest Bosc pears first in the recipe, but you can use softer varieties, from Anjou to that queen of all pears, Passe-Crassane, as long as you cook them only to the point where they can be pierced with a knife. A firm Bosc pear might take an hour of poaching, but a ripe Bartlett might take only a few minutes, so you must test frequently.

To keep the pears from discoloring, they have to be covered with liquid at all times. Don't use more liquid than necessary; select a pan in which all the pears fit tightly, preferably in one layer.

I prefer a less sweet syrup than Julia's, which is the one given in the recipe. Instead of the 6 tablespoons of sugar for every cup of liquid that she suggests, I would add only 4 tablespoons for every cup—or 1 cup per quart. And use a dry, acidic wine—like an Orvieto or a Muscadet—to balance the sweetness. I poach pears in many different liquids, with various sweeteners—sometimes whole, as here, and sometimes in slices. I like to poach them in red wine, grenadine (pomegranate-flavored syrup), tea with mint, even espresso with brown sugar. In all of these, the pears take on both the flavors and the beautiful colors of the poaching medium.

Peel the pears, leaving the stems and a small amount of skin near the top, for decoration—see photo on preceding page (this decorative peeling is optional). Start peeling about ¼ inch below the stem, with the middle of the peeler blade, to form the arched top of each strip. Then trim off all the peel between the strips, leaving only a thin,

Scoop out the inside of the pear with a knife or melon baller, removing the entire core and all the seeds.

tapering line of peel, about an inch long, between the arches.

With a melon baller or a knife, scoop out the inside of the pear through the flat bottom, removing the entire core and seeds, as shown in photo. You will have to scoop 3 or 4 times to get out all the seeds.

Cooking and cooling the pears

Set the pears in the hot syrup, which must cover them completely—add more syrup, if necessary. Lay a double

After setting the pears in the hot poaching liquid, weight them down with a plate to keep them submerged.

thickness of paper towels over the pears, then weight them down with the small lid or plate, to keep them submerged and prevent discoloring.

Return the syrup to the boil and cover the pot. Reduce the heat to maintain a gentle boil and poach for about 30 minutes, just until the pear can be pierced through with the tip of a sharp knife. Remember, the

poaching time for pears will *always* vary, and you must test them frequently for doneness.

Remove the cooked pears from the heat and let them cool in the syrup for at least 3 hours or overnight, leaving the towels, the weight, and the pot cover in place.

Serving the pears

You can serve the poached pears as they are, moistened with their syrup, or in any of these variations:

To make a sauce from the syrup: Bring 3 cups of the cooking syrup to the boil in a deep saucepan and cook rapidly, uncovered, until reduced to 1 cup. Cool to warm, then stir in a tablespoon of cognac or Grand Marnier. Use warm, or allow to cool.

Stand a pear—fluted or not, as you wish—in a bowl or dessert goblet, garnish with the poached strips of lemon zest, and pour over it the thickened syrup. Make a tiny slit near the pear stem and insert a sprig of mint, as shown in photo.

To make a composed dessert with pound cake and chocolate sauce: Cut ½-inch slices of cake and

To "flute" a pear: Slice through the side of the pear with diagonal cuts at ½-inch intervals all around. Press down gently on the top to separate and display the fluted slices.

A fluted pear with thickened syrup, garnished with lemon zest and a sprig of mint

remove a 3- or 4-inch disk from the center of each slice with a round pastry cutter or a paring knife. Pour a pool of chocolate sauce onto a dessert plate, set a cake round in the middle, and stand a pear on the cake, as shown in photo.

Or dip the pear into a small bowl full of chocolate sauce to coat it, let the excess drip off, then stand it on the cake, as shown in photo.

Of course, you can serve your pears with *both* chocolate sauce and syrup.

A poached pear standing on a disk of pound cake with chocolate sauce surrounding it

Chocolate Sauce

Yield: About 2 cups

    1 cup half-and-half or cream
    6 ounces best-quality bittersweet
       chocolate, chopped into small
       pieces
    ¼ cup strong espresso (or ¼ cup
       strong black coffee mixed with
       1 tsp instant espresso powder)
    Vanilla extract, rum, cognac, or
       bourbon (optional flavorings)

In a small saucepan, heat the half-and-half or cream to a bare simmer. Whisk the chocolate pieces and the espresso or coffee into the hot cream, until completely smooth. Add 1 teaspoon vanilla extract or 1 tablespoon rum, cognac, or bourbon. Cool before using. Store covered in the refrigerator.

A poached pear that has been dipped in chocolate sauce and set on a disk of pound cake

Julia

This is the best chocolate *roulade* I have ever had, it really is. Sometimes I find that sponge-roll cakes can be dry, but this one has a moistness that is lovely. Using the *ganache* as a soufflé base is a marvelous idea.

Jacques's Chocolate Roulade

A *ganache* is a combination of cream and fine bittersweet chocolate from which *chocolatiers* and pastry chefs make truffles and glaze cakes. Here the rich mixture is combined with egg whites to make a flourless batter which is baked into a tender, thin sheet cake. It is then spread with softly whipped cream—crème Chantilly—and rolled up jelly-roll-style, into a delectable *roulade*.

Rich though it may sound, a slice of *roulade* is light, moist, and full of chocolate flavor. This is also a large dessert you can literally whip up by hand in about 10 minutes—and the sheet cake takes less than a quarter of an hour in the oven.

The *roulade* needs no garnish other than a dusting of cocoa powder, but would be delicious served with our crème anglaise or chocolate sauce, or just an extra dollop of crème Chantilly.

Yield: A 15-inch cake roll, serving 10 to 12

For the soufflé
    1 cup heavy cream
    8 ounces bittersweet chocolate, in small pieces
    7 egg whites, at room temperature
    2 Tbs granulated sugar

For the crème-Chantilly filling
    1 cup heavy cream, well chilled
    1½ Tbs granulated sugar
    ½ tsp vanilla extract
    1 Tbs cognac

    1 Tbs butter for the pan and parchment
    1 Tbs or so unsweetened cocoa powder

For garnish
Powdered sugar
Cocoa powder
Strawberries

Special equipment
An 11-by-17-inch jelly-roll pan or 13-by-18-inch rimmed baking pan (a "half sheet"); baking parchment; a fine-meshed sieve; a large oval or rectangular serving platter (at least 15 inches long)

Getting ready
Preheat the oven to 350°F. Line the baking sheet with buttered parchment paper. (For Jacques's method, see sidebar on page 402.)

Making the *ganache* and batter
Heat the cream to the simmer in a medium saucepan (1½ quarts). Add the chocolate pieces all at once, lower the heat, and stir briskly with a small wire whisk to melt the chocolate thoroughly. As soon as the *ganache* is completely smooth and a uniform dark color, remove the saucepan from the heat and let cool for a few minutes.

Fold the lightened *ganache* and the egg whites together gently.

Whip the egg whites and the 2 tablespoons of sugar either by hand or in an electric mixer (see pages 94 and 95) until they have formed stiff peaks with a glossy sheen—don't let them become dry or grainy-looking.

Scoop about one-fourth of the beaten whites into the saucepan of *ganache* and stir briefly with a wire whisk to blend. Pour the lightened *ganache* back onto the remaining egg whites in the mixing bowl and fold them together gently with a rubber spatula (see photo). Work quickly, breaking up any lumps of egg

Jacques

This versatile batter of *ganache* and egg whites is really a soufflé batter, and you can make several different desserts from it. You could bake it in one large or a number of small molds, and serve it warm as a classic chocolate soufflé. Or you could let it cool and unmold it—it will deflate, of course—and serve it as a rich, dense flourless chocolate cake. Or you can make this wonderful *roulade*. I often make a number of these at holiday time, and use them as the base for the Yule-log cake, *bûche de Noël.*

Lining a Baking Sheet

Here is a fast and neat method to line the baking sheet with parchment paper.

Cut a piece of parchment that covers the bottom and sides of the pan completely, with the edges of the paper rising slightly higher than the rim of the pan.

Butter half of the parchment generously with about one tablespoon of soft butter. Fold the sheet in half and press so that the entire inside of the paper is completely buttered.

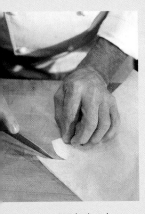

With the sheet still folded, cut a one-inch diagonal slit (pointing toward the center of the sheet) through the two outside corners (not the folded corners).

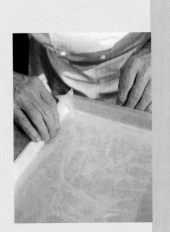

Unfold the sheet and press it, buttered side down, into the pan. Tuck the slit corners of the paper over each other to make a neat pleat in each corner of the pan.

Jacques's Chocolate Roulade (continued)

white until the *ganache* is thoroughly incorporated.

Pour the batter into the prepared pan and spread it in an even layer with a rubber spatula (see photo).

Baking the soufflé sheet

Place the pan on the middle rack of the preheated oven to bake for 10 to 12 minutes. When done, the cake should be nicely set and puffy. Remove the pan from the oven to a wire cooling rack, and allow the cake to cool, still in the pan, to room temperature.

Pour the batter into the paper-lined pan in an even layer, and with a rubber spatula spread it against the rims and into the corners of the pan.

Filling and forming the *roulade*

Lifting up the near edge of the parchment, roll the cake away from you over the whipped cream.

Whip the cream with the sugar, vanilla, and cognac to make the crème-Chantilly filling (see sidebar on next page).

Lift the parchment to remove the cake from the pan, which should be cool, and set it on a flat work surface, with a long side facing you. Using a fine-meshed sieve, lightly dust the top with cocoa powder, then spread all of the whipped cream over the cake evenly, covering the entire surface.

Continue until you complete the roll, leaving the cake on the far edge of the parchment. Use the loose parchment to wrap the roll before refrigerating.

Lift up the near edge of the cake and parchment, fold it away from you about 2 or 3 inches over the whipped cream, and begin to peel the paper off the cake (see photos). Roll the cake another few inches, pressing against the parchment to make a tight spiral, and then gently peeling it off as the cake layer rolls away from you. Complete the roll, keeping it just on the far edge of the parchment sheet. Cover the roll by tucking the loose parchment around and underneath so that the cylinder is well wrapped and can be moved easily. The *roulade* can now be refrigerated in the paper for 3 or 4 hours or transferred immediately to a platter for serving.

Serving the cake

When ready to serve, transfer the *roulade* to the serving platter. Remove the parchment paper, gently rolling the cake into the center of the platter, with the seam on the bottom. (If the roll has slumped or twisted, lay a piece of plastic wrap over the top and sides and reshape with your hands.)

With a sharp knife, trim both ends of the roll with neat crosswise or diagonal cuts and discard (meaning, eat them yourself). Dust the top of the *roulade* with powdered sugar and cocoa, and garnish with strawberries.

To serve, cut the roll into 1-inch-thick slices and lay them flat on dessert plates. Top with additional crème Chantilly if you like.

Crème Chantilly

Crème Chantilly is a quickly made and versatile dessert component, the softly whipped cream that fills this *roulade* and our *choux à la crème*, and accompanies our apple tart.

If you are making a small amount of crème Chantilly, do it by hand. You need a flexible wire whisk, and the heavy cream and the mixing bowl should both be well chilled. (Julia always sets the mixing bowl into a larger bowl containing ice cubes and water, making sure no water splashes into the cream.)

Beat the cream by whipping the whisk in a back-and-forth motion. Do not whip in a large circular motion, as with egg whites, as this can lead to overbeating and turn the cream to butter. Add sugar and flavorings (such as vanilla, cognac, rum, Grand Marnier, or other liqueurs) as you begin to beat. Whip only until the cream thickens into soft peaks that hold their shape.

Crêpes

A thin, lacy crêpe, warm from the pan, is a delicacy all by itself, with just a sprinkling of sugar, perhaps, or a spoonful of jam. But, like cream puffs, crêpes are a versatile foundation for countless desserts. You can spread or fill the pancakes with almost anything sweet, from a scoop of ice cream to fresh or poached fruit to a delicate soufflé batter. And then you can roll, fold, or stack them; cover them with sauce; or bake or flambé them. With crêpe batter in the refrigerator—or, more convenient, a package of finished crêpes in the freezer—you have a sure starting point for dessert improvisation.

Making the crêpes themselves is one of the stovetop-cooking skills that every home cook should master—a challenge at first, but always fun, whether you are a beginner or an expert. It is very much like omelet making, involving a series of quick moves with the pan. The more you make crêpes, the faster your moves will be and the more consistent your results. With crêpes, of course, you have more chances to practice, as a batch of batter will give you many opportunities to perfect your technique, and you can toss out your "mistakes"—or eat them.

Crêpe baking, like omelet making, is much easier in the era of non-stick pans. We recommend the same non-stick frying pan with 10-inch top diameter for crêpes that we use for our omelets in the chapter on "Eggs." The flat bottom—the only part of the pan that is coated with batter—is 7 inches across, a good size for dessert crêpes. You can also use specialized, shallow-sided crêpe pans, which come in various dimensions, from 4 inches to 10 inches, some with non-stick surfaces. Traditional steel crêpe pans need seasoning and frequent use to be effective. (And it is a good idea, even when using a non-stick pan, to brush on melted butter occasionally, if your crêpes start to stick.)

The following recipe for crêpe batter should give you 12 to 15 crêpes of the 7-inch size (more or less if you use pans of a different dimension). This is a sufficient number to make the 2 desserts in this section, classic Crêpes Suzette, in our slightly different versions (pages 410 and 412), and Susie's Gâteau of Crêpes (page 408).

Opposite: Chocolate Roulade

Jacques

The speed at which you spread the batter in the pan determines how thick your crêpe is going to be. The secret to a thin crêpe is to swirl the batter all around the bottom very fast. The batter starts to set as soon as it hits the hot surface, and if you spread it slowly, you end up with a thick crêpe. The kind that's called *crêpe dentelle*, for its lace-like edges, is made with a very thin batter, as thin as light cream.

It helps to pour the batter on one side of the pan bottom, never in the center. This way it spreads more rapidly as you tilt the pan. And even when the batter has started to set and has almost stopped flowing, you must shake the pan so the remaining batter keeps moving to cover the pan even more.

In contrast to Julia, I often add only 2 tablespoons of batter at first. I find it is better to put in less than too much. If you don't have quite enough batter to cover the bottom, you can always add a bit more in the bare spots.

One of the best ways to serve crêpes is right from the pan, with the simplest toppings. When I was a kid, we would eat them out of the hot pan with our fingers as my mother made them. We'd put a little butter and sugar on one, then jam on the next one, and maybe a bit of grated chocolate on another. When my daughter Claudine was little, I would do the same for her when she came home from school. Crêpes never taste better.

Julia

When I am making crêpes, I find it is easier to add a bit more batter to the pan, about ¼ cup, swirl to coat the bottom, and pour out the excess. You can always wipe or break off the little tail of batter that forms where you poured. When they are cooked on both sides, I like to lay the crêpes out on wire racks to cool before I stack them up.

The first side of the crêpe that you cook should get nicely browned before you turn or flip it over. You can lift an edge with a spatula to check that it is ready to turn. This pretty side is the "public" side, the one that you want to show in all your desserts like crêpes Suzette. The second cooked side will not get more than a few brown spots. When you stack your crêpes for storing or filling, be sure that all the public and non-public sides are facing the same way.

Jacques uses his crêpe batter right away, but I always let the batter rest in the refrigerator for at least an hour, or even overnight, before frying the crêpes. My theory is that the flour particles absorb the liquid and that gives you a more tender crêpe. If you are making batter in the blender, you can just put the blender jar in the fridge, then give the batter a whirl again before cooking the crêpes.

Crêpes (continued)

The batter takes just a few seconds to make in the blender or food processor—and barely a minute if you do it by hand—so you can multiply the recipe or make several batches if you want more crêpes. In the beginning, you may be a bit wasteful, using 4 tablespoons for each crêpe, before you get the hang of coating the pan with half that amount. And remember too that the first 1 or 2 crêpes may stick or fall apart, because, as Jacques says, "the pan must get in the mood."

Dessert Crêpes

Yield: Twelve to fifteen 7-inch crêpes

1 cup all-purpose flour
2 large eggs
1 egg yolk
¾ cup milk
⅓ cup melted butter
2 Tbs sugar
A large pinch of salt
¾ cup water

2 or more Tbs melted butter for brushing the pan

Special equipment

A blender, or a mixing bowl and wire whisk, for the batter; a non-stick frying pan with a 7-inch bottom or other crêpe pan; a 2-ounce ladle or other ¼-cup measure for pouring batter; a pastry brush; a plate or wire rack for the cooked crêpes

Mixing the batter

If using a blender, put the flour in the jar, then add the egg and egg yolks, milk, melted butter, sugar, and salt. Blend for 5 or 10 seconds to make a thick, lump-free batter. Add the water and blend until smooth. Refrigerate the batter for at least an hour.

To make the batter by hand, whisk the flour, the egg and egg yolks, milk, melted butter, sugar, and salt together, to make a very thick, smooth batter, then whisk in the water. Refrigerate the batter for at least an hour.

Cooking the crêpes

Whisk the batter well. Set the pan over moderate heat for a minute or two. When hot, brush the bottom with a very thin coat of butter. Ladle up 3 or 4 tablespoons of batter (or use a measuring cup) and pour onto one side of the bottom of the pan.

Immediately tilt and rotate the pan to spread the batter all over the pan bottom as quickly as possible. Shake the pan to keep the last bit of batter flowing. If the batter doesn't cover the entire bottom, drizzle a few more drops of batter onto the bare spots and tilt to spread it in a thin, even layer.

Cook over medium to high heat for about 45 seconds to 1 minute, until the edges are cooked and the bottom is lightly browned. The first cooked side—the side that is always presented—should be distinctly colored, with dark streaks and swirls. If it is still pale after 45 seconds, raise the heat slightly and cook a little longer; if too brown, lower heat. To loosen the crêpe, bang the bottom of the pan on the stove—or smack the side of it with your hand, padded by a towel or pot holder. Then toss the pan to flip it over, or lift one edge of the crêpe with a fork or spatula, then pick it up with your fingers and turn it over rapidly.

Cook the crêpe on its second side about 30 to 45 seconds—it does not need as much color—and slide it onto a plate or a wire rack to cool, first side up. Wipe the pan clean of any crumbs or cooked bits of batter, return it to the heat, brush with butter, and repeat the process, until the batter is all used up. Stack the crêpes on top of each other as they come out of the pan, or cool first on the racks if you wish. (If you have a non-stick pan, you may not need to coat it with butter each time—but brush again whenever the crêpes begin to stick.)

Do-ahead notes

After the crêpes are cool, stack them (if you've spread them on racks) and wrap them in plastic wrap. Store in the refrigerator for a couple of days, or keep frozen for several weeks.

Julia

Following Susie's handsome family crêpe gâteau, we come to another and even more famous classic, crêpes Suzette, a dish I really love. I have made and taught it many times and always think, "Oh, that old saw, crêpes Suzette." But every time I eat it I realize this is the way to go.

Using the food processor to make the butter is certainly a help. In the old days, when I was in Paris studying *"la cuisine,"* we had to rub and rub the sugar lumps over the orange until they absorbed the oil, a terribly time-consuming process.

I recommend doing the saucing and flambéing at the table if you can; if not, follow Jacques's excellent oven system. You need a strong heat source, such as the Sterno burner shown on page 411. Remember that it takes a while for the sauce in the pan to thicken before it's ready for the crêpes, and you have to think of wonderful stories to tell your guests.

Susie's Gâteau of Crêpes

This is a simple dessert made by covering open crêpes with layers of raspberry jam and ground pecans, then stacking them to form a cake, to be cut and served in wedges. We were shown this by Susie Heller, the culinary producer of our TV show, who learned it from her mother and grandmother. It's a traditional Hungarian dessert, known as *palacsinta*, usually served warm, Susie tells us, but we found it quite delicious at room temperature, with a drizzle of Chocolate Sauce (page 399). A late-harvest Johannisberg Riesling would be a fine wine to serve with this.

The *gâteau* can have as many layers as you like. With raspberry, crêpes, and chocolate to enjoy, the more the better, we say—so you might want to make a double batch of batter to provide 20 or more crêpes for stacking. Moreover, you can create many other desserts in this fashion, varying the nuts and jam, or putting sliced fruit in the layers.

Yield: A cake serving 8 or more

2 cups pecan halves (8 ounces)
4 Tbs sugar
15 to 20 Dessert Crêpes (page 406), 7
   inches across, at room temperature
1¼ cups raspberry jam, stirred to soften
Chocolate Sauce (page 399)

Put the pecans and sugar in the work bowl of a food processor. Pulse in short bursts, for 5 or 6 seconds total, to grind the nuts into a coarse powder—don't overprocess.

Lay one crêpe on a round serving plate. Spoon a tablespoon of raspberry jam on top, and spread it—using the bottom of the spoon—over the whole crêpe in a thin coat. Sprinkle about 1½ tablespoons of ground nuts all over the jam.

Cover the first crêpe with a second, and top it in the same way with jam and nuts. Repeat the layering with all your crêpes, stacking them to form a round cake with even sides. Reserve the prettiest crêpe for the top of the *gâteau*—and don't put anything on it.

Serve the *gâteau* the same day you have assembled it, warm or at room temperature. (Heat it in a 300°F oven for 10 minutes, or longer if chilled.) Slice in wedges, and drizzle chocolate sauce over each serving, if you like. Leftovers will be soft but still delicious; store in the refrigerator.

Jacques

The method I use for my crêpes Suzette on page 412 is a good one when you want to serve a number of guests at the same time. If you have more than 6, you can set up 2 platters of folded crêpes, and broil the second one while everyone is enjoying a first helping.

If you prepare the platter (or platters) ahead of time, and the crêpes are cold, you can heat them in a very hot oven—about 450°F for 10 minutes or more—rather than broiling them. This will heat and caramelize them on both sides, not just the top. The platter will be very hot, of course, which is an advantage, since you need it sufficiently hot or the alcohol won't evaporate on contact.

I sometimes make crêpes Suzette in a pan at the table, but I don't fit them in the way Julia does. I like to leave the folded crêpes in one layer, rather than overlapping them on the side of the pan, so they can caramelize a bit on the bottom, and then turn them over to brown briefly on the second side, before adding the liqueurs. But unless you have a very large pan and a strong burner, you can only do a few crêpes at a time, and must caramelize and flambé them in batches.

The orange butter we make here would be almost impossible to prepare without a food processor. It is always difficult to incorporate liquid into butter, and here the machine emulsifies almost an equal amount of liquid into the butter, which is fantastic. And by the way, this orange butter is also delicious to use as a buttercream filling for layer cakes.

Crêpes Suzette

The creature named Suzette may or may not have been the mistress of the Prince of Wales, as we have heard, but whoever she was, she long ago inspired a magnificent dessert that is still one of our favorites.

In the classic method, crêpes Suzette are prepared at tableside with drama and literal "flare." The host rubs lumps of sugar over an orange to impregnate them with the essential citrus oils, and then, in a large flambé pan set over a burner, he makes a sauce with the sugar, a great deal of butter, and the orange juice. When it thickens and begins to caramelize, he bathes the crêpes, folded neatly into triangles, in the sauce and cooks them briefly. Finally, he pours cognac and Grand Marnier all around, ignites, and spoons the flaming sauce over the crêpes.

Our two slightly more modern methods preserve the beauty, the richness, and most of the drama of the dish. For both of our recipes, an orange-flavored butter, made in the food processor, is the base for the sauce. Julia's method then follows the traditional steps of folding, heating, and flaming the crêpes in the pan. You can do it at the table if you have a portable burner, and you can easily prepare eight of our basic crêpes at once— serving four—if you have a large pan like the traditional copper one shown in the photo, or something similar. (If you have a smaller pan, or want to serve more guests, you can prepare the crêpes in batches.)

Jacques's broiler method allows you to prepare twelve crêpes at a time. They are spread with the soft butter, folded, and arranged on a large serving platter before heating—well ahead of time, if you choose—and then caramelized in a couple of minutes under the broiler.

The flambé is a moment that no one will want to miss. With our methods, the liqueurs can be ignited in the kitchen and the pan or platter carried to the table all aflame, or you can bring them unlit to the table for all of the pyrotechnics.

The flambé provides not only excitement but additional caramelization and coloring of the crêpes as you pour the flaming sauce over them. The liqueurs must be ignited as soon as they are added, though, since the alcohol vapors dissipate in a few seconds, leaving nothing to burn. You want to have all the ingredients and utensils ready for this step, including thick towels or pot holders to protect your hands. And you must be *absolutely* certain that nothing except the dining-room ceiling is directly over the pan when you pour in the spirits—especially not your face—because the flames can shoot several feet into the air.

A late-harvest riesling is a good choice of wine to serve with either version of this legendary dessert.

Julia's Crêpes Suzette

When you decide to do your crêpes for a party at the table, plan to give it a bit of fun and drama. And it is certainly a good idea to try out making your crêpes Suzette ahead of time, even several times, in front of a critical yet friendly audience. I find it useful to have all the elements attractively dished on a tray—the sugar in a nice bowl with a spoon, the ready crêpes on an attractive salver with serving spoon and fork, etc. The cognac and Grand Marnier are in their original bottles, and practice how much you pour to make about ¼ cup—a little more is always better than a little less here! By the way, never pour the liqueur bottle into a flaming platter, since the flames can leap into the bottle, which can explode into your face and even put out your eyes!

Yield: 4 servings

> 1 recipe Orange Butter (page 412)
> 8 Dessert Crêpes (page 406)
> Sugar to sprinkle
> About ¼ cup cognac
> About ¼ cup Grand Marnier

Special equipment

> A shallow chafing dish or attractive skillet, 12 to 14 inches top diameter; a strong heat source; a long-handled serving fork and spoon; a ladle for pouring on the liqueur; matches just in case; warm dessert plates

Heating the butter and the crêpes

Set the skillet over moderate heat and scrape in all the orange butter. Heat for 4 to 5 minutes—longer if necessary—as the butter melts, boils and bubbles, and begins to thicken into a syrup. Have your utensils at hand and crêpes ready for dipping.

Lower the heat so the sauce is bubbling slowly and lay the first crêpe into the pan, "best" side up, to moisten for an instant. Turn it over quickly with the fork and spoon; fold it in half and again into fourths. Move the wedge-shaped crêpe to the side of the pan and lay in the next.

Working quickly and steadily, bathe and fold the remaining crêpes and arrange them around the edge of the pan, overlapping as necessary, to leave an open space for moistening the last crêpe in the sauce. Sprinkle a little sugar over them.

Flaming the crêpes

Pour the cognac into the ladle and over the crêpes; rapidly do the same with the Grand Marnier. Spoon it dramatically once or twice over the crêpes, then tilt the pan quickly but ever so gently into the flames to ignite all the contents. With high flourish, spoon the flaming sauce over the crêpes until the flames have subsided to a flicker, and start serving 2 crêpes per person and the still flickering sauce onto the warm plates.

Jacques's Crêpes Suzette

Yield: 4 to 6 servings

> 1 recipe Orange Butter (recipe
> follows), at room temperature
> 12 Dessert Crêpes (page 406)
> 2 Tbs sugar

To flambé
> ¼ cup cognac
> ¼ cup Grand Marnier or other
> orange liqueur

Special equipment
> A large stainless-steel or other
> broiler-proof serving platter,
> about 17 by 10 inches; a large
> spoon; matches (optional); warm
> dessert plates

Assembling the platter of crêpes

Smear the platter generously with 2 or 3 table-spoons of the orange butter.

Spread 1 tablespoon of the butter over the inside of a crêpe (the second or less browned side). Fold the crêpe in half and then again into fourths and lay it at one end of the platter. Butter and fold all the remaining crêpes and arrange them, slightly overlapping, to nearly fill the platter. Leave an empty spot at the end of the platter to gather and spoon up the sauce. (The platter can be assembled ahead of time and refrigerated.)

Broiling and flaming the crêpes

Shortly before serving, arrange a rack in the middle of the oven and turn on the broiler. Sprinkle the crêpes with the 2 tablespoons of sugar and set the platter under the broiler. Check after a minute or so, and turn the platter if necessary so the crêpes brown evenly. Broil about 2 to 3 minutes, until the tops of the crêpes have caramelized (but not burnt) and the butter is sizzling in the platter. Remove the platter to the stovetop burner, set on medium to low, using towels or large pot holders to protect your hands.

Avert your face before flaming. I pour the cognac and Grand Marnier directly from the bottle—Julia is more cautious and insists on putting the alcohol in a ladle or pitcher first—and pour them all over the crêpes. Let the spirits heat for only a second, then ignite, by tilting the platter slightly over the stove burner or with lit match held near the edge of the platter.

Immediately bring the platter to the table (hands well protected). Tip it so the flaming liquid gathers at the empty end, scoop up the liquid with the large spoon, and pour it back over the crêpes. It will continue to flame and brown the crêpes for a few moments.

When the flames have subsided, arrange 2 or 3 crêpes on each plate, coat with some of the sauce, and serve.

Orange Butter

Yield: 1¼ cups

> Zest of 1 large orange, removed
> with a vegetable peeler or zest-
> ing tool
> ¼ cup sugar
> 1½ sticks butter, cut into chunks
> ⅓ cup freshly squeezed orange
> juice

Put the orange zest and sugar in the work bowl of a food processor or blender and process until the peel is finely chopped. Add the butter and the orange juice and process to blend thoroughly, stopping the machine and scraping the sides of the bowl as necessary.

The orange butter should be light, fluffy, and a uniform orange color. (The butter can be stored, well sealed, in the refrigerator for a couple of days, or frozen.)

Other Crêpe Batters from Julia

Rather than thin classic crêpes you may on occasion want them slightly thicker, particularly if you are to serve them simply with butter and sugar or syrup, or if you are planning stuffed crêpes. Here are two versions, one a yeast batter and the other a lightly puffed batter with beaten egg whites.

Yeast Batter Crêpes

Two hours before you plan to cook the crêpes prepare the batter on page 406. Warm ¼ cup of the milk to tepid (about 90°F). Sprinkle on 1 package of active dry yeast, and let dissolve for about 5 minutes. Add this to the container and finish the batter. Cover and let sit at room temperature until bubbly, about 2 hours. Cook the crêpes almost at once to prevent overfermentation.

Souffléed Crêpes

Just before you plan to cook the crêpes, when your batter has rested and is ready, beat 3 egg whites to stiff shining peaks and fold one half into the batter, then the other half. Cook the crêpes at once.

Crêpes Stuffed and Baked with Orange-Almond Cream

Serve these just as they are, freshly baked, or you may flame them at the table. To do so, pour ⅓ cup each of cognac and orange liqueur into a pretty small pan and heat over a candle warmer when the time comes. Have matches at the ready.

For 6 people lay 12 cooked yeast or souffléed crêpes, underside up, on your work surface. Beat 1½ cups of pulverized almonds and ¼ teaspoon almond extract into the Orange Butter on page 412, and spread 2 or 3 tablespoons over each crêpe (freeze any remaining filling). Roll up the crêpes and arrange them smooth side up in a handsome well-buttered baking dish. (May be prepared in advance; cover with plastic wrap and refrigerate.)

Preheat the oven to 375°F. Twenty minutes before serving, sprinkle a good half teaspoon of sugar over each rolled crêpe and slide the dish onto a rack in the upper third of the oven. Bake for 15 minutes, or until the sugar coating is beginning to caramelize.

Bring in the hot baking dish and, if you want the crêpes flambéed, pour the warmed liqueur over and around them. Averting your face, ignite the crêpes with a match, tilt the dish, and spoon the flaming liqueur over the crêpes until the flames subside. Serve.

Julia

You can use different varieties of apples in this tart, but I think you are always safe with a Golden Delicious. Some apples, like Granny Smiths if they're old, may puff up and come apart, but a Golden will always hold its shape.

I am astonished that some people are so afraid of sugar, as they are of fat, that they will serve or bake cut-up fruit without adding even a bit. But tossing fruit with sugar—like the apples here, or the strawberries for our sabayon—brings out the natural juices, making the dish much more delicious. And there are hardly any calories in the small amount of sugar in each serving. Similarly, the bits of butter that dot this tart will hardly affect anyone—only 2 tablespoons divided among 12 servings. Leave out the butter if you feel you must, but the tart is certainly better with it.

Free-Form Apple Tart or Galette

A quickly made country-style apple tart like this is as easy as pie—easier, in fact. You don't need to fuss with pans, fancy dough crimps, or lattices, or arrange the fruit slices as with other apple tarts. Just pile your chunked-up apples on the rolled-out sheet of dough and fold up the edges. The casually pleated pastry crust comes out of the oven golden and crisp, and does a fine job of holding in the soft and juicy fruit filling. Each tart has a unique, rough beauty, made more sumptuous with a coating of apricot glaze.

The Flaky Tart Dough here takes a few moments to make in the food processor. It's a fine version of classic *pâte brisée*, the versatile short dough that is used in both dessert and savory pastries—the same dough that is used to top Jacques's Chicken Pot Pie (page 278) as well. One batch of dough is enough for this large tart or two pot pies. You can multiply the formula easily, and since the dough freezes well, you can make a couple of batches and have some on hand for a tart, or a pot pie, whenever you want.

The assembled tart takes a good hour in the oven, but cools rather quickly, so you can even bake it during dinner, if you want to take a short break before dessert. It is delicious warm or at room temperature, with a bit of softly whipped Crème Chantilly (page 403) and a dessert wine, such as a late-harvest riesling or a sauternes.

Apple Tart/Galette

Yield: About 12 servings

Julia's glaze

    1 cup apricot jam, best-quality

    2 Tbs sugar

    1 to 2 Tbs Grand Marnier

Jacques's glaze

    1 cup apricot jam, best-quality

    2 Tbs Calvados or cognac

    2¼ pounds Golden Delicious or other apples, such as Granny Smith, Rome Beauty, or McIntosh (5 or 6 medium apples)

    ½ cup dried currants

    ½ cup ½-inch pieces of dried apricot

    1 tsp cinnamon

    ¼ cup sugar, plus more for sprinkling on the dough

    Flaky Tart Dough (recipe follows)

    Flour for rolling the dough

    2 Tbs butter

For serving

    A cup of cream, for Crème Chantilly (page 403) (optional)

    Sprigs of mint (optional)

Special equipment

    A small (1-quart) saucepan and a wire sieve (optional) for the glaze; a rolling pin; a large, rimless cookie sheet, 17 by 14 inches preferable; a pastry brush; a wooden cutting board

Jacques

I like the rough country quality of this tart, which we would call a *galette* in France. Sometimes I don't even peel the apples—though I think Julia would never do it that way. And while she strains her apricot glaze, I don't bother—I like the pieces of fruit in the jam, even if they make little lumps on top of the tart. On the other hand, you can make this more elegant if you wish. Instead of cutting the apples into pieces, just peel and cut them in half, then slice very thin, crosswise. Place the apple halves on the dough and slide them like a deck of cards, so the slices are neatly overlapping.

In the fall and winter, I often use apple varieties that grow in nearby orchards, like Macoun, McIntosh, Stayman, and Rome Beauty. They are softer, I find, and each gives a different taste to the tart. But Golden Delicious are always a reliable choice, too.

You have to bake the tart on a rimless sheet so you can slide it onto a serving platter. But for the photos you see here, we had to bake the tart on an inverted ordinary sheet pan, because we forgot a rimless one. If you don't have a rimless sheet but have a good-sized jelly-roll or sheet pan, turn it over and use the bottom.

Julia on Tart Dough

Years ago, I used to make piecrust doughs by hand, rubbing the flour and fat together between my fingertips, a laborious and time-consuming process. But after seeing how easy it is in the food processor, I have never gone back.

Jacques and I do things differently, though, even with the machine method. I prefer to use the plastic blade, which is gentler, and when I'm using all-purpose flour I always add a little vegetable shortening since that tenderizes the flour. After I have processed it, I still like to do a final step by hand, called *fraisage*. You push the dough out with the heel of your hand, smearing a bit at a time across the work surface—this ensures the even blending of butter and flour and makes for a smooth, tender dough that is particularly suitable for tart shells and tartlets. Then I give the dough a chilled rest, so the gluten relaxes, and that makes it easy to roll out.

Apple Tart/Galette (continued)

Preheat the oven to 400°F.

Making Julia's glaze

Put the jam in the saucepan and set over low heat to melt. Sieve the jam into a bowl, then scrape it back into the saucepan. Reserve the strained bits of apricot for the apple filling.

Stir the sugar into the warm jam, heat to a boil, and cook rapidly for a couple minutes to thicken. Scoop up a bit of hot glaze with a teaspoon and let it fall back into the pan; when the last drops fall very slowly, and almost form threads, the glaze is done. Remove from the heat and let cool for a few minutes, then stir in the Grand Marnier.

Making Jacques's glaze

Put the strained or unstrained jam in a bowl with the Calvados or cognac and stir gently with a spoon until mixed.

Preparing the apples

Peel and core the apples (see page 421). Slice them in half (stem end to blossom end) and cut into ½-inch pieces. Toss the pieces in a mixing bowl with the currants, dried apricot pieces, cinnamon, ¼ cup of sugar, and the bits from the apricot jam, if strained.

Rolling the dough

Set the disk of dough on a floured work surface and dust the top with flour. If it is chilled and hard, bang the rolling pin against it several times, to soften and get it moving (see photo). Roll the dough into a large oval, occasionally turning it over and rotating it on the work surface, and keeping both sides well floured. Continue to roll out until the dough is about ⅜ inch thick and the oval is about 18 inches long and 15 inches wide. Patch any cracks or uneven edges with dough trimmed from the long end.

If the dough is cold and hard, bang the rolling pin down on it at intervals to get it moving.

To transfer the dough, roll it up around the pin (starting at a narrow end) and unfurl it, centered, on the baking sheet (see photo)—it doesn't matter if it extends an inch or two over the edges.

Unfurl the dough that you have rolled up on your rolling pin, centering the dough on your baking sheet with the edges hanging over. Note that the baking sheet here is an upside-down jelly-roll pan, which is fine to use; you don't want a baking pan with sides.

Forming and baking the tart

Brush the center of the dough with a thin layer of warm glaze, leaving a 2-inch margin unglazed all around. Spill the apple mixture on top of the glazed area and spread them in a thick, even layer over the pastry, to within 2 inches of the edge. Lift the edge of the pastry all around and press it over the apples, making pleats in the dough (see photo). Dot the top of the fruit with the 2 tablespoons of butter and sprinkle sugar on the pastry border to give it more color.

Place the tart in the oven and bake for an hour, until the dough is nicely browned and the apple chunks are soft.

Fold in the edge of the pastry all around and press it over the apples, making pleats to create a neat, tight, rounded border.

Glazing and serving the tart

You may glaze and serve the tart while warm or let it cool to room temperature. Shake the baking sheet slightly just after removing it from the oven to prevent the tart from becoming glued by caramelized fruit juices. When it has cooled, slide the tart onto a wooden cutting board for slicing.

Warm the glaze and thin it with a bit of liqueur, such as Calvados, cognac, or Grand Marnier, if needed, until just pourable. Spoon ⅓ cup or so all over the apple chunks, then spread and smooth the glaze with a pastry brush. Brush a thin coat on the pastry border as well, if you like.

Jacques on Tart Dough

I make this dough very quickly. I use the metal blade of the processor—and only butter, no vegetable shortening—and process it very briefly so that there are still bits of butter clearly visible. I never *fraise*, or knead, the dough in the classic manner, because that would eliminate these small butter lumps. I want to keep them: when you roll them out, they form thin layers that give the flakiness of a puff pastry. Also with my method, the dough has been handled for only a few seconds and there's been no development of gluten, so I think it is fine to roll out the dough right away—no need to rest it in the refrigerator.

This dough is excellent for all kinds of savory dishes. In addition to pot pies, you could wrap and bake our homemade sausage or pâté in this dough.

Cut the tart into wedges. Reassemble them on a serving platter and present on the cutting board, surrounded with grape or maple leaves. Or serve wedges on dessert plates.

If you like, whip a cup of chilled cream—with ½ teaspoon of sugar and a bit of Grand Marnier—to the consistency of Crème Chantilly (see page 403). Spoon a small mound of cream alongside each piece of tart and garnish with a sprig of mint.

Flaky Tart Dough

Yield: Dough for 1 large tart

2 cups all-purpose flour (about 10 ounces)

7 ounces unsalted butter (1¾ sticks), chilled and cut into ½-inch pieces

1 Tbs vegetable shortening, chilled

Scant ½ tsp salt

Scant ½ tsp sugar

⅓ cup ice-cold water, plus more if needed

Special equipment

A food processor fitted with a steel or plastic blade; plastic wrap

Place the flour, butter pieces, shortening, salt, and sugar in the work bowl of the food processor. Blend in short, second-long bursts, pulsing the machine 8 or 9 times. Uncover and check the consistency—the dough should be crumbly, with the butter broken up into small but still visible pieces, about ¼ inch or so. If there are larger chunks of butter, pulse a few times more.

Add all but a tablespoon of the water through the feed tube of the machine, and immediately pulse 3 or 4 times, no more than 5 seconds in all. Feel the dough and press some of it in your hand to see whether it clumps together and is evenly moist. If it does not adhere, add another spoonful of water and pulse only for another second or two—don't overmix so the dough clumps together in the center.

Spread out a large sheet of plastic wrap and turn the loose dough onto it. Lift up the sides of the plastic, gathering the dough together, then fold the wrap over and press the dough into a single compact mass. If some dry bits don't adhere, sprinkle those with drops of water and press together.

The dough can be used right away if necessary, but will benefit from refrigerated rest for an hour or two. Wrap tightly in the plastic wrap, pressing it into a flat disk shape, and enclose in a plastic bag. Refrigerate until needed. Dough that will not be used within a day or two should be stored in the freezer, where it will keep for several weeks.

Opposite: Apple Tart

Julia

I'll always remember the first apple charlotte I baked on an early TV program. In those old black-and-white days we did no editing, and mistakes stayed where they were. No fixing! On this occasion, the whole 27½ minutes of the show were taken up by this one recipe. When the dessert, all browned and beautiful and fragrant, finally came out of the oven, I was delighted. I set it up on the counter and ran my small sharp knife around the inside of the mold to loosen the dessert. Then I turned it upside down on a serving platter, grabbed the mold by its ear pieces, and lifted it proudly off the dessert. Perfect. We all admired it sitting there, upstanding and handsome. Suddenly I noticed a little split at one side of the top, and as we all watched the split widened and the whole side of the charlotte collapsed inward. What to do? Nothing. With tears in my voice I started serving, saying that I didn't like the apple filling to be too stiff. It tasted fine, of course.

That was my consolation, but also my lesson. Be sure that the apple filling has body enough to stand up. If you use the wrong apples, bolster the filling with cake crumbs or bread crumbs.

Apple Charlotte

The apple charlotte is a classic French dessert of beautifully flavored apples either puréed or in small pieces formed in a special cylindrical dish, a charlotte mold, lined with butter-soaked strips of brioche. Charlotte molds of tinned metal come in a number of sizes, from 3 cups or less to 12 cups; you can find them in any French hardware store, and in most of our gourmet shops here. They are characterized by the little metal ears attached ½ inch from the rim on either side, which are useful handholds when you want to lift the mold off onto a serving plate. Besides the apple charlotte there is also the charlotte russe, a rich Bavarian cream molded in liqueur-dipped ladyfingers.

Yield: 1 charlotte, serving 8 to 10

4 pounds Golden Delicious (or other firm) apples
½ cup plus 2 Tbs clarified butter
½ cup brown sugar
Dash of cinnamon
Grated peel of 1 lemon
⅓ cup apricot jam
2 tsp vanilla extract
3 Tbs dark Jamaican rum
13 slices firm, home-style sandwich bread, crusts cut off
½ cup apricot glaze, either Julia's or Jacques's (page 415)
Crème Anglaise (page 386)

Special equipment
A large sauté pan; a large frying pan; a 6-cup charlotte mold or similar baking dish 5 to 6 inches deep; parchment paper

Preparing the apples

With a paring knife cut out the cores of the apples, top and bottom. Try to shape the stem ends into neat cones with the stems attached and save several of these for decoration. Now peel each apple, starting with your paring knife at one of the trimmed ends and going around removing the peel as you rotate the apple slightly against the knife. When all are peeled, halve the apples and cut out the center cores with your knife or a spoon. Slice, then chop the apples into small pieces, less than ½ inch.

Melt 2 tablespoons of the butter in the large sauté pan and toss the apples in it. Cook over medium heat, shaking the pan frequently and tossing the apple pieces so they don't stick and can cook evenly. After a few minutes, add the brown sugar and lemon peel and continue to cook, tossing frequently, until the apples have released all their water and are beginning to caramelize. Add the dash of cinnamon and stir in the apricot jam, vanilla, and rum. Sauté a minute or two more, until the apples have absorbed the liquid and are tender and glazed.

Preparing the charlotte mold

Preheat the oven to 425°F.

Line up 4 slices of the trimmed bread on the counter to create a large square, set the charlotte mold on top, and with a serrated knife cut all the way around the bottom to make a circle of bread that will fit exactly into the bottom of your charlotte mold. Reserve, along with the trimmings.

Using a cookie cutter or a glass about 2 inches in diameter, cut out a circle from another slice of bread. Reserve with trimmings.

Melt 3 tablespoons of the clarified butter in a large frying pan and gently brown the pieces that form the circle for the bottom of the mold, the small circle you have cut (which will be used to decorate the top), and all the trimmings. When they are a light golden brown on one side, turn and brown the other. Turn off the heat.

Cut out a circle of parchment paper the size of the bottom of the charlotte mold, following the directions on page 242. Butter the bottom of the mold and fit the paper in. Now arrange on top of the paper the sautéed pieces of bread that you cut for the bottom of the mold.

Cut the remaining slices of bread in half lengthwise. One by one dip the slices into the clarified butter and arrange them upright all around the inside of the mold, slightly overlapping, so that you make a secure wall. Spoon a layer of the sautéed apples into the dish, then cover with a few pieces of reserved sautéed bread trimmings, another layer of apples, and a few more bread scraps, until the dish is full and humping up ¾ inch in the center. Cut off any protruding bread strips and press them along with the few remaining butter-dipped strips to cover the top.

Baking the charlotte

Set the mold in the middle of the oven, with a baking pan on the rack below to catch any buttery juices, and bake in the preheated oven for 30 minutes. Two or three times during the baking, press down with a spatula on the top of the pudding to compress it. If you find that the top crust is getting too brown, cover the mold loosely with foil. The charlotte is done when you slip a knife between the bread strips and the dish and see that the bread has browned nicely.

Unmolding and decorating

Let the charlotte rest at least 1 hour. Set a serving plate on top of the mold and reverse the two. The charlotte should slip out easily, but if it sticks, run a knife around the edge and try again.

Paint the apricot glaze over the top and sides of the charlotte, center the reserved toast circle on top, and glaze it also. Decorate the dish with the little cones of apple-stem trimmings you have saved. Serve with crème anglaise.

Index

A Note on the Type

The text of this book was set in Bembo, a facsimile of a typeface cut by Francesco Griffo for Aldus Manutius, the celebrated Venetian printer, in 1495. The face was named for Pietro Cardinal Bembo, the author of the small treatise entitled *De Aetna* in which it first appeared. Through the research of Stanley Morison, it is now generally acknowledged that all old-style type designs up to the time of William Caslon can be traced to the Bembo cut. The present-day version of Bembo was introduced by the Monotype Corporation of London in 1929. Sturdy, well balanced, and finely proportioned, Bembo is a face of rare beauty and great legibility in all of its sizes.

The sans serif typeface is Avenir, designed by Adrian Frutiger and released by Linotype-Hell AG in 1988. The design is based on two earlier sans serif typefaces, Erbar and Futura. Avenir is unusual in that it has weights (Light and Book, for example) that are similar but designed for different purposes, allowing optimal results under varied printing conditions.

Composition and color separations by North Market Street Graphics, Lancaster, Pennsylvania

Printed and bound by R. R. Donnelley & Sons, Willard, Ohio

Designed by Carole Goodman